Industrial Marketing Communications

Industrial Marketing Communications

Business-to-Business Advertising, Promotion and PR

Norman A Hart

KOGAN PAGE

First published as *Business to Business Advertising* in 1971, 1978, 1983
Published as *Practical Advertising and Publicity* by McGraw-Hill in 1988
This edition published by Kogan Page in 1993

Kogan Page Limited
120 Pentonville Road
London N1 9JN

© Norman Hart, 1971, 1978, 1983, 1988, 1993

British Library Cataloguing in Publication Data

A CIP record for this book is available from the British Library.

ISBN 0 7494 0861 8

Typeset by DP Photosetting, Aylesbury, Bucks
Printed and bound in Great Britain by Biddles Ltd, Guildford and King's Lynn

To M.D.H.

ACKNOWLEDGEMENTS

The author would like to thank John Armitage and David Neaves of Primary Contact Limited for their very considerable assistance in producing the research which appears as an Appendix to this book.

CONTENTS

FOREWORD

John Samuel FCAM, FIPA
Director of the Association of Business Advertising Agencies

In the last ten years, industrial marketing has been finally accepted as vital to national and individual company interests, where markets lie in the commercial or business area.

If the acknowledgement is finally there, performance is not universally good and recent audits show that companies attacking these markets are still not satisfied with the quality of their promotional planning and execution, nor with the skills of their people and the interest of their agencies. Improvement is slow and the need for the use of the highest skills and talent not yet wholly accepted. Promotion in all its forms is still seen in too many boardrooms as an *alternative* to profit and not a *cause* of it and investment in it treated with suspicion and prejudice.

The need is to raise standards 'on the job' and each marketing director has a unique problem in training and inspiring his present team. This new book is an effective starting point and should be mandatory reading for everyone concerned with industrial or business marketing.

For senior management, it gives an opportunity to understand the real nature of the task and of the contribution communications can make. It makes clear that this is an area of company investment that can be managed and controlled as effectively as any other. It removes the jargon and myth of which senior management (often from the more precise disciplines of accountancy or engineering) are rightly so suspicious but equally challenges them to understand more fully the workings of communications so that their judgement of proposals in this area will be more discerning and less subjective.

For middle managers—particularly those already expert in one aspect of the marketing mix (sales, PR, research)—the book yields an unprejudiced picture of the totality, making clear the overriding need for calm assessment of *all* media; for unbiased choice of the most effective mix; and, above all, for the full-blooded integration of the total program.

For the younger or less experienced, the book is a marvellous accelerator of their understanding of the total communications picture while they work, inevitably, in only one narrow area of it.

The book IS *practical* but don't be misled. After careful reading you will find that you have learned a great deal; will be readier to accept and demand better planning of communications; can argue your corner more coherently and assess more dispassionately the validity of the recommendations of your colleagues or agency.

PREFACE

The marketing concept is now well accepted by most companies in Britain and Europe even though they continue to lag behind the United States. Indeed, from the commercial area, the idea of 'customer orientation' has spilled over into institutions, government services, charities, social activities and even political parties.

Acceptance of marketing, however, has always been faster among consumer goods companies than in those concerned with industrial/business products and services. Every single function in consumer marketing has developed to a high degree of sophistication: research, product development, advertising, sales promotion, selling, distribution, planning and budgeting—all have become specialist activities with an increasing emphasis on productivity and effectiveness.

Business-to-business marketing has developed at a much slower rate and with some companies is still little more than the old selling function repackaged under a new name. And little wonder since in contrast with consumer marketing there are few opportunities to learn about business marketing: few courses and seminars, few textbooks, few periodicals and no institution or association dealing with the special needs and interests of executives in this particular sector. Similarly, in the academic world, the introduction of marketing to many business studies continues to concentrate on consumers and mass media, which is after all where public visibility is high and where massive million-pound budgets are commonplace.

When it comes to business-to-business marketing communications this is perhaps the most neglected area of all, a situation which existed when this book was first published under the title *Industrial Advertising and Publicity*. Since that time it has become the accepted work on the subject, both in the United Kingdom and elsewhere. Over a number of editions and reprints it has gathered together such meagre data as has emerged, relying heavily on American research, and it is now presented as a completely updated text, devoted simply to getting the best value for money out of budgets which are almost universally low compared with their consumer counterparts.

Industrial Marketing Communications has been written with a belief that in putting together a promotional campaign there is a need to consider every channel of communication in order to arrive at a media mix which will target with accuracy the precise audience that has to be reached in order to secure action. The book is intended for those managers and executives who have a responsibility for planning and undertaking business-to-business marketing communications, i.e. advertising, public relations, sales promotion and all the related activities. Students will also find it of value: indeed it has been a recommended text from the outset for those studying for the CAM Diploma and the Diploma of Marketing.

Part 1

STRATEGIC PLANNING

1.

PROLOGUE

Terminology in business-to-business marketing is particularly susceptible to ambiguity and confusion. For this reason, it is necessary at the outset to give some definitions to ensure a complete understanding of the terms used. Evidence of this need is to be found in the United States where 'publicity' is commonly understood to refer to 'free editorials', whereas in the United Kingdom the term is used in an all-embracing sense of publicizing anything for any purpose. It thus includes activities which contribute to selling and may be known as sales promotion, and those which set out to provide information to any of a number of publics and is therefore related more to public relations.

The terms 'publicity' and 'sales promotion' are both subsumed by 'marketing communications' under which heading are included all the various 'channels of persuasion' such as advertising, direct mail, exhibitions and so on. It is not, however, 'the medium' which qualifies an activity as *marketing communications* or *public relations*, but rather 'the purpose for which the medium is employed'.

Public relations is dealt with separately and briefly since its objectives are far broader than simply the promotion of sales, though it must be emphasized that almost without exception the channels of persuasion used for marketing purposes are applicable in some form to public relations.

A good deal of confusion exists about the meaning of advertising; whether this applies only to press and television, or whether direct mail, for instance, is included in the term. For the sake of clarity it will be used only when it relates to press and television; moreover it will be qualified, e.g. press advertising.

There is even more confusion on the meaning of marketing. For many people, particularly in the industrial sector, it is taken to be synonymous with selling. For others it means getting a product to market, or simply distribution. Since both these interpretations are incomplete, and since this book is based upon publicity within the marketing concept, it is essential to agree at the outset on the meaning of the term when it is used here.

Adam Smith was close to the mark when he wrote, in 1776, 'consumption is the sole end purpose of all production; and the interest of the producer ought to be attended to, only so far as it may be necessary for promoting that of the consumer'.

A more recent explanation has been by L. W. Rodger[1] who states that

> marketing has come to be increasingly concerned not merely with the problem of how to dispose profitably of what is produced but also with the much more basic problem of what to produce that will be saleable and profitable, in other words, with nothing less than the profitable matching of a company's total resources, including manufacturing technique, to market opportunities.

The Chartered Institute of Marketing goes further by defining marketing as 'the management process responsible for identifying, anticipating and satisfying customer requirements profitably'.

Marketing starts then in the market-place, with the identification of the customer's needs and wants. It then moves on to determining a means of satisfying that want, and of promoting, selling and supplying a 'satisfaction'. The principal marketing functions might be defined as marketing information and research, product planning, pricing, advertising and promotion, sales and distribution.

It is sometimes argued that while the marketing concept is vital in relation to consumer goods, the situation is so different in the industrial sector that the same concept cannot be usefully employed. It is true that many managements have achieved great success in the past by intuition and brilliant guesswork, and it can also be argued that many areas of industrial or business marketing are quite different and sometimes a good deal more difficult than their equivalents in the consumer field, but a convincing argument against this is given again in *Marketing in a Competitive Economy*.[2]

> The differences between industrial and consumer goods and their respective markets in no way invalidates the applicability of the marketing concept to industrial goods. Indeed because of the high value of unit sales and unit purchases of many industrial goods, and because of the longer manufacturing cycle and high cost of building and maintaining stocks associated with a wide range of such goods, the importance of the marketing concept may be even greater than consumer goods to the extent that the consequences of being wrong—through bad business and sales forecasting, faulty product planning, inadequate or inaccurate information, failure to identify, contact and follow up sales prospects with well conceived sales promotional activity—can be a great deal more costly.

The differences between industrial, or business, and consumer marketing are not in their concept, nor indeed in their value or relevance. Rather they are to be found in the techniques to be employed, the nature and complexity of the purchasing decision-making, and the size of the budgets available for achieving the objectives. This latter factor if anything makes the task a great deal more difficult, especially in view of the continuing lack of data on which to make valid judgements.

References

1. L. W. Rodger, *Marketing in a Competitive Economy* (Associated Business Programmes, London, 1974), Preface.
2. *Ibid.* p. 65.

2.

STRATEGIES

It is vital to the efficiency of the operation that all marketing communications activities be conducted within the broad framework of a marketing plan. Moreover, such planning must be comprehensive and written down in a master document which relates all the functions to one another for maximum effect. This key document, the marketing plan, sets out to define:

1. *Strategic and corporate objectives*   Where does the business wish to be in 5/10 years? Industry sectors, profit, turnover, locations, financial base, employees.
2. *External factors* – PEEST   Political, Economic, Environmental, Sociological, Technological.
3. *Internal factors* – *SWOT*   Strengths, Weaknesses, Opportunities, Threats.
4. *Marketing objectives*   Market share, market/product segmentation, product portfolio
5. *Sales objectives*   Sales targets/forecasts, territory/products, staff motivation.
6. *Communications objectives*   Company/product awareness, perception/positioning, sales leads, re-assurance, information.
7. *The market*   Size, location, trends, decision makers, international opportunities.
8. *The market need*   Customer requirements, buying motives, changes in demand.
9. *Product portfolio*   Specifications, benefits, profitability, life cycle.
10. *Competition*   Market shares, product specifications, prices, promotions and expenditure, company images, nature and magnitude of selling activities, strengths and weaknesses.
11. *Price*   Pricing strategy in relation to competition, special incentives and discounts.
12. *Distribution channels*   Retailers, wholesalers, agents, delivery times.
13. *Service*   Pre-sales, sales, and post-sales service.
14. *Research and evaluation*   Pre and post measurement of markets, awareness, attitudes, copy, advertisements, concepts, sales leads, orders.

15. *Budget and programme*   All expense budget items, all income, projected profit, cash flow.
16. *Human resources*   Training, recruitment, motivation.
17. *Selling platform*   Unique selling propositions (USP), outline of features to be stressed in all selling activities.
18. *Production plan*   Build up of output, flexibility and relation to sales targets.
19. *Profit objectives*   Both short- and long-term.

Before coming to the promotional strategy in detail there is a sequence of events that must necessarily occur if a product or service is to be launched within the framework of a marketing operation.

Development of a marketing operation

MARKET ORIENTATION

The changes that have led to the acceptance of marketing as a management function can be traced as far back as the Second World War when factories changing over from war work were oriented to and around their production capability. The plant and equipment existed: the management problem was how to fill it. This was production orientation and while there were shortages and a lack of sophisticated consumer demand, it was adequate.

With the re-emergence of branded products, and as supply began to overtake demand, managements were faced with an excess of products and the need to find markets for them. This then was a position of sales, or product, orientation. In the first instance the management universe revolved about a production nucleus; in the second case, selling and sales were the centre of the operation. Finally, and following the lead of consumer marketing, the industrial nucleus has changed to the market-place—to the buyer and his needs and wants.

It should not be assumed too readily that the marketing concept has become accepted fully or even widely. A study by the author of what practising marketing managers considered should comprise a marketing plan showed that the majority of respondents associated this primarily with market research and advertising. This is shown clearly in Figure 2.1.

MARKET RESEARCH

A marketing operation starts then with an examination of markets and the needs which exist or can be demonstrably created. Clearly many needs can be discarded as outside the scope of an organization's activities, but certain opportunities will be identified which can be translated into products or services that appear to meet basic criteria on manufacturing suitability,

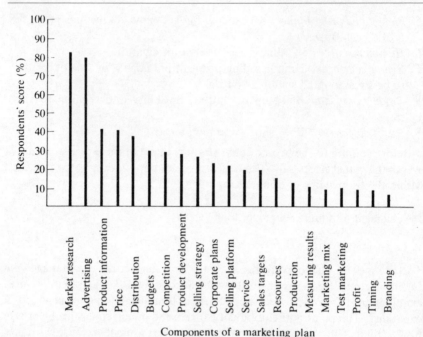

Components of a marketing plan

Figure 2.1   Contents of a marketing plan

capital investment, management capability, profit margin and growth potential.

PRODUCT DESIGN

The identification of a potential product is a vital part of marketing development. This involves the services of research and development, design engineering, production and buying departments, all of which coupled with a viability study contribute to the evolution of a prototype. In the case of a service it is more likely that a 'concept' is looked at.

If at this stage the project appears to be sound and profitable, there follows a period in which the product is tested on the market to determine whether it provides the necessary benefits to satisfy the market needs. This may be termed compatibility evolution in which all the elements are subject to minor changes, product performance, appearance, price, shape, market segmentation ... until there is a match between product and market needs and enough profit to justify the investment.

TEST MARKETING

The proving of the product in the market-place, based upon a prototype or pilot batch, after the policy decision to continue the project, brings the operation to the stage where a full marketing strategy is written.

It is more than likely that such a strategy will call for further sounding out of the market before the final stage of decision is reached. This is the point of no return for management and the last opportunity to assess the chances of success or failure.

The product must now be test marketed, that is to say given a full scale launching but in a restricted area. This is sometimes more difficult with an industrial product or service than with a consumer product or service, but nevertheless it is possible. Marketing can be restricted to a specified region only, or to a relatively small overseas market. Alternatively, the product can be promoted and exploited exclusively in one industry or market segment. All these activities will provide feedback of essential information which will lessen the risk of failure.

DECISION

In the light of the assembled data, coupled with the best experience and judgement which can be brought to bear, the point of decision is reached.

The launch of a product within the framework of a marketing operation resembles a military exercise in which many armaments are brought to bear upon a target according to a carefully produced strategic plan. Furthermore, all the logistics of the operation are provided for, objectives are set, and contingency plans made for unforeseen events: in particular the reaction of the enemy forces.

The marketing strategy is such a plan and it outlines in detail the method of launching a product and the means for feedback and research in order to provide intelligence on how the campaign is progressing. Having set sales targets and campaign objectives against which to compare performance, it is vital to provide for flexibility in the organization so that rapid changes can be made in order to intensify or reduce the campaign as this becomes necessary.

ROUTINE MARKETING

Much of this chapter has dwelt on the marketing of a new product but clearly each of the disciplines involved can be applied to an existing product and its future development. Indeed each of the functions described above is essentially of a continuous nature.

The marketing mix

Just as in the recipe for a dish, the ingredients must be specified in quantity and quality, and the ways of mixing them together and cooking them made clear, so in marketing, the mixture must be blended to achieve maximum effect. The marketing mix has been defined as the 'planned mixture of the elements of marketing in a marketing plan. The aim is to combine them in such a way as to achieve the greatest effect at minimum cost'.[1]

A more academic approach to the marketing mix postulates that it comprises what is known as the 4 Ps and S:

1. Product
2. Price
3. Promotion
4. Place

The S stands for service. The balance of ingredients then is made under 4 or 5 heads and depends largely upon the nature of the product and the markets it serves. For instance with petrol, price and place may be the key factors to success. With a new scientific instrument it is the product that counts. For a computer it may be both pre- and post-sales service which secure the sale.

In this book the mix will be considered as it relates to marketing communications in which each component has a communications element. The 'product', for instance, in addition to ultimately providing satisfaction to the customer, also sends out pre-sales messages which contribute to the development of the overall perception upon which a purchasing decision will be made. Its size, shape, colour, weight, presentation and packaging may signal high or low quality, reliability or ruggedness. The 'price' of a product can also have a communications element. In many instances where performance is difficult to evaluate, the price is taken as a measure of quality—the lower the price, the lower the quality. The 'promotion' element of the marketing mix is obviously where the main thrust of marketing communications is to be found. As to 'place', with industrial and business products this usually relates to a combination of distribution outlets and delivery time and is less important as a message source than in consumer marketing where the outlet may be a key factor in the purchasing decision. For instance, who could ever doubt the reliability of a product which Harrods decided to put on display? Finally 'service', pre-sales, sales, and post-sales, sends out a continuous stream of messages which enhance a product, or undermine it. In other words, first-class service can only help to build up a perception of a first-class product.

THE DECISION MAKING UNIT

It is useful to consider the various people within an organisation who might be called upon to contribute to a purchasing decision. These can be categorised under the following six headings:

1. *Specifier* This is simply the initiator or the person who first identifies the

need for a purchase. It might for example be a design engineer who specifies that a certain component is required for a piece of equipment which has been newly designed. There may even be a number of people who have had a hand in the design, and this might lead to some debate as to which component, or type of component, precisely is required. A specifier might be persuaded to stipulate a catalogue number, thus in effect identifying who the supplier should be.

2. *Influencer* There will be all manner of people within an organisation, especially the bigger ones, who have no purchasing function, but know someone who has. A regional factory manager for instance may have no authority to purchase his own raw materials, but he will more than likely have a point of view as to where the best material comes from. So for that matter might the operatives. Similarly a secretary might not have the purchasing authority for a new word processor, but she won't be slow in keeping her boss informed of her preferences.

3. *Authoriser* In almost all corporate purchases there will be someone within the system who has the authority to say yes or no. This is very often the chief executive, even for the most trivial of purchases. Added to this may be the functional head, say the marketing director, and then perhaps the finance director. In fact many of the major purchasing decisions are considered by the whole board.

4. *Purchaser* Someone has to place the order; probably an executive in the purchasing department, and sometimes also the purchasing manager.

5. *Gatekeeper* It is worth considering any possible barriers to communications reaching a target audience. A salesperson calling on a prospect might be impeded by a receptionist, or indeed a gatekeeper. Similarly with a letter, or a telephone call where a secretary might frustrate the connection.

6. *User* There might be one user, or there might be a hundred. For sure they will have a point of view, and this could just be the factor which decides in favour of one supplier as against another.

The point about being so precise in identifying target audiences, as also with segmenting the market, is that purchasing motivations will vary from one person to another according to each individual's interests. That being so, there is not just one selling message to be delivered but several depending on the audience being addressed. Not only must the message be fitted to the target audience, the media also must be similarly selected so as to get maximum impact.

A further factor in selecting the optimum audience is what has been called the 'buy class'. If for instance the purchase is a repeat of what has been a routine supply for some time and there is no change in the product, and say no change in the supplier, then the whole decision making unit is hardly likely to be involved. Given a situation in which a supplier has failed in some way and is required to be replaced then the procedure is likely to become more involved with perhaps a few more people having a hand in the selection of a new supplier, ie the DMU will become larger. This is referred to the 'modified buy' as opposed to the 'straight rebuy'. Come now to a 'new buy' and the size of the DMU increases yet further, and the higher the value of the purchase, the more people are likely to be involved.

CHANNELS OF PERSUASION

From the definition of the market, distinct groups of prospects will emerge whom it is desired to influence. To achieve this object, a number of methods of communication are available, such as personal selling, exhibitions and advertising. These are channels of persuasion, and the extent to which any of them is used must depend on the nature of the market and how far each communication channel fits in.

It is useful to consider each typical prospect in a given segment of a market and then to examine each channel of persuasion to determine if it is relevant. An 'impact diagram' (Fig. 2.2) can be developed in which the promotional mix can be demonstrated simply and visually. From this can be developed the timing, intensity and interrelationship of each individual item (see Chapter 3, Fig. 3.3).

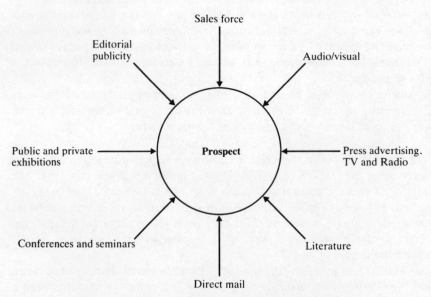

Figure 2.2 'Impact diagram'—channels of persuasion

The appropriation as between one channel and another is changing rapidly as the cost of personal selling increases at a faster rate than any of the non-face-to-face media. Hard evidence for this comes from the United States where selling costs have risen by over 200 per cent in 10 years. This compares with the consumer price index increase of under 150 per cent over the same period. Looking at each of the non face-to-face media, costs have increased more in line with the price index.

In the United Kingdom the average cost per 'industrial' sales call is well over £150 and rising. The outcome of this fact must lead to a completely new approach to what may be termed the media mix. For instance, in comparison with a salesperson who can influence say three or four persons a day, a publication can reach thousands or indeed millions of people in the same time. The message in an advertisement must necessarily be shorter and the percentage of readers upon whom the message will have any impact may be of a low order but the impact can be increased by various devices such as the number of appearances, size of space and so on. To be effective, a salesperson must first find the prospect and then secure an interview. With an advertisement this is not necessary: prospects need only be defined in general terms and a publication by virtue of its blanket circulation will ensure a large coverage of a potential market. The cost of delivering a particular message is also relevant since for a salesperson it may amount to a factor of 100 compared with an advertisement.

Since the nature of relative media costs is vital, not only in examining press advertising, but in the chapters which follow, it is worth considering in a little more detail.

Recent research in the United States has shown that the cost per sales call is rising at a rate approximately double the rate of that of advertising space. Figure 2.3 shows the trend.

In order to make a comparison with press advertising, another piece of American research has been taken,[3] and here a sales call costs around 500 times that of an 'advertising contact'.

While the above data relates to the American market, it should not be difficult for any advertiser to produce his own figures in relation to his own company. These can be examined using the same criteria as in Chapter 3.

Setting targets

It is now time to examine in more detail the way in which the various promotional elements fit into the marketing plan.

It cannot be over-emphasized that in progressing towards more efficient and effective management, it is necessary to set objectives and to quantify them: to identify targets that are attainable and can be measured. Only in this

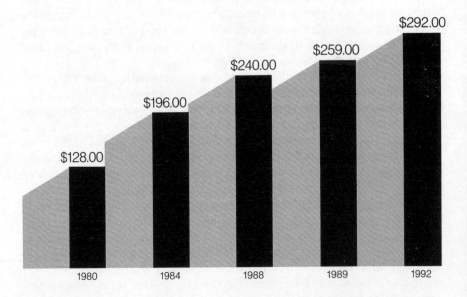

COST OF A PERSONAL SALES CALL

$292.00

$259.00

$240.00

$196.00

$128.00

1980   1984   1988   1989   1992

Figure 2.3 Increase in cost of industrial sales calls (*Source:* Cahners Research Report)[2]

way can exact courses of action be planned and progress compared with objectives.

The marketing strategy, in addition to outlining the plan of action, must set targets for each component part of it to achieve. There must be sales targets, production targets and profit targets. Such targets do not only deal with the short term, but cover as many years ahead as the nature of the business requires, sometimes up to five years, and, for capital-intensive industries, even longer.

Targets and forecasts differ in their nature and their purpose. A forecast can be considered to be an estimate for the future, assuming a number of constants and given an adequate amount of historical data from which to make an extrapolation. It is based upon the assumption that the past pattern of development is likely to continue in the future, subject to the influence of current events and possible future occurrences. A target, on the other hand, is a positive statement of intent backed up by whatever plan of action is judged to be necessary to achieve it. It may or may not have its basis in historical data or other guidelines.

To be effective a marketing strategy must include a quantitative and qualitative statement of objectives to be achieved by promotion. It is not enough for a campaign only to provide 'a general background of support for the selling operation'.

As will be seen later, such campaign objectives may or may not include a direct relationship with sales targets. It is most important to discriminate between 'communications goals' and 'sales' since the former can well be achieved, and the latter not, due to other factors such as price, service or product performance.

An authoritative statement on advertising objectives comes from *Managing Advertising Effectively*.[4]

● If advertising is to be effective and handled with the maximum efficiency it is necessary to know what it is intended to achieve. Hence the need for advertising objectives.

● Advertising objectives need to be expressed in clear, precise, appropriate, attainable and written terms.

● Advertising objectives must be distinguished from marketing objectives, but must be compatible with both these and the overall company goals.

● The process of setting precise advertising objectives is an invaluable management discipline which focuses thinking on the service or product.

● Objectives ensure that management are aware of the assumptions being made and consequently know the degrees of risk involved.

● Precise objectives assist in determining advertising budgets.

● Setting objectives aids the appraisal of advertising plans and control of ongoing situations by top management.

● Written objectives help the advertising and research agencies to prepare and evaluate relevant plans for advertising practice.

● Setting advertising objectives permits meaningful measurement.

The particular goals of a campaign will vary from time to time and company to company. A piece of research on this in the United States[5] identified six major goals of advertising programmes, and these are shown in Figure 2.4 below.

Marketing communications strategy

A prerequisite of a promotional strategy and a plan of action is a detailed set of targets upon which the success of the marketing operation depends just as much as the capability of the factory to produce the goods.

If sales leads are required, a marketing plan must state how many; if product awareness is to be built up, this must be represented as the percentage of the potential market it is required to influence.

For example, a new branded range of electric switches is to be launched. It can be defined in advance whether they should become known as quality switches with built-in reliability, or whether as very cheap and easy to

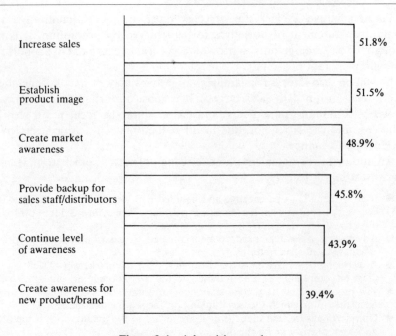

Figure 2.4   Advertising goals

replace. Given the market share which it is required to achieve, a figure can
be set for the number of buyers who must recall the brand name and be able
to associate the product with the company name after a given period of time.

A further example might be the requirement in a large potential market,
say for internal telephones, to identify the proportion of potential buyers
who have an active interest at that particular moment; in other words to
build up a live sales-call list. This may demand a campaign which will bring
in large numbers of enquiries: the number can be quantified in advance.
Given an existing conversion rate and knowing the sales objectives, the
quantity of enquiries can be calculated. A further calculation as a double
check will be the number of calls per salesperson, multiplied by the number
of salespersons, minus the number of calls on existing accounts, which will
equal the number of new sales leads.

If such targets are calculated for, say, a year, then split up into weekly
figures based upon the build-up of the campaign and perhaps seasonal
factors, it is possible within a very short time to determine whether the
promotional mix is right and whether the campaign is producing the desired
results.

Just as in the marketing plan there needs to be an optimum mix of the 4 Ps
and S, so in marketing communications the media mix must be carefully

formulated to ensure optimum performance. The appropriateness of each medium must be assessed methodically in relation to such factors as the potential market—its size, nature and location; the degree of competition and thus demand; the nature and availability of the media themselves.

The strength of each medium, therefore, must be considered and then each element brought to bear on the target in relation to the campaign as a whole. It is only at this stage that the cost of achieving the results can reasonably be considered. Matching costs to desired results is commonly known as the 'task method' of budgeting (see Chapter 3).

Running parallel with the selection of media and budgeting will be the interpretation of the selling message in terms that fit the various media to be employed. The two inevitably interact. A complex message may not be suited to posters or even sometimes to press advertising. Alternatively such a message may require large space advertisements to cover all the points adequately: or a series of small advertisements taking one point at a time may be more suitable. The number and form of direct mail shots will be influenced by the sales message and vice versa.

Finally an essential feature in any properly planned campaign is a predetermined scheme for measuring results and feeding them back quickly for corrective action (see Fig. 2.5.)

Given the setting of written and specific goals the planning of a campaign can be summarized as involving six basic elements:[6]

1. Identifying the audience to be reached.
2. Determining and creating the specific advertising messages to be directed at this audience.
3. Selecting the most effective and most economical media to reach this audience.
4. Scheduling the chosen media to provide the best timing, frequency and impact.
5. Determining the advertising budget.
6. Measuring advertising results.

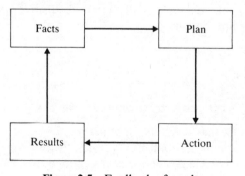

Figure 2.5   Feedback of results

Creative strategy

It is not the intention of this book to examine the creative aspects of industrial publicity in any detail since this is a specialized subject worthy of a book in its own right, but it would be wrong in this chapter on strategies to ignore the essential planning element which can be applied to the creative function.

It is in fact rare to come across the application of a disciplined approach to creativity. One agency has developed what is known as the 4D approach which, while devised largely in consumer terms, has equal relevance to business-to-business advertising. 4D is an abbreviation for four dimensions, which break down as follows:

FIRST DIMENSION

Pinpoint the single selling idea—the particular consumer need that the brand satisfies

1. Understand the consumer needs and attitudes in relevant product fields.
2. Appreciate what competitive brands are offering in each field and all that our particular brand can offer.
3. Select and define what our brand will offer and to whom.

SECOND DIMENSION

Create the most effective and appealing expression of the idea

1. Recognize the real problems of gaining consumer attention and what is already competing for it.
2. Make sure the selling message is clear, distinctive, believable and convincing in consumer terms.
3. Create in all material an equally clear, distinctive total identity and underline the brand name.

THIRD DIMENSION

Find the most efficient media to communicate the idea

1. Select the media that reach the right people.
2. Choose the media best capable of carrying the message.
3. Use the media with the greatest impact, economically; with understanding of competitive strategies.

FOURTH DIMENSION

Eliminate uncertainty as far as possible before and after the advertising appears

1. See whether research can help, and understand just what is to be measured.
2. Be creative and forward-looking in the use of research.
3. Present results clearly, to help decision-making.

A methodical approach such as this does not set out to replace creativity, but merely to channel the creative process through each stage of development in a minimum of time and with maximum effect.

Checklist

1. Has a marketing strategy been prepared?
2. Does the marketing strategy set specific goals to be achieved by marketing communications?
3. In formulating a promotional strategy, has consideration been given to
   - (a) Identifying the potential market?
   - (b) The selling platform and the advertising message?
   - (c) The most effective media?
   - (d) Timing in relation to other sales activities?
   - (e) The budget to achieve the objective?
   - (f) Feedback, and measurement of results?
4. Has the usefulness of each of the following media been evaluated in order to arrive at an optimum media mix?
   - (a) Press advertising
   - (b) Direct mail
   - (c) Exhibitions
   - (d) Literature
   - (e) Audio-visual
   - (f) Photography
   - (g) Editorial publicity
   - (h) Conferences and seminars
   - (i) Sales aids
   - (j) Posters and display
   - (k) Point of sale and packaging
   - (l) Gifts and novelties
   - (m) Television and radio
   - (n) Brand name
   - (o) Special events

5. Has the marketing communication strategy been developed in conjunction with the advertising agency?
6. Is marketing/sales management fully aware of its contents and purposes?
7. Has the cost per sales call been calculated together with the average number of calls required to secure the first order?

References

1. N. A. Hart and J. Stapleton, *The Marketing Dictionary* (Heinemann, London, 1992).
2. Cahners Research Report No. 542.1H.
3. *US Steel/Harnisachteger Study* (American Business Press).
4. D. R. Corkindale and S. H. Kennedy, *Managing Advertising Effectively* (MBC Ltd, 1975).
5. Cahners Advertising Report No. 101.1.
6. Lintas Ltd.

3.

PLANNING AND BUDGETING

The need for a marketing strategy, encompassing all the elements of marketing and their interrelationships, was emphasized at the beginning of the book. From this overall strategy stems a plan of action for marketing communications which uses and integrates the channels of persuasion which are applicable.

After assessing the advantages and limitations of each medium, and the extent to which it can be used, a quantified media mix emerges. Expenditure figures can be put against each of the media on the basis that the total deployment of these forces will result in the objective being achieved. Thus the budget is compiled. In practice it is not simple, and the difficulties likely to be encountered will be examined in some detail later.

Planning

One aspect of marketing communications that needs to be touched on now is the time-scale. There is clearly an interrelationship between the start of a campaign and the receipt of the first order. Hence production planning must be related to sales planning and in turn it will be evident that sales will influence the timing of raw materials purchasing, tooling, finance, labour, up to the end of the whole business operation.

The chart, Figure 3.1, shows how certain key functions may relate to each other on a time and quantity basis. Here an investment of £500 000 is shown at a certain point in time. This is intended to represent a piece of capital equipment for the production of a new product. Soon after the initial investment, a publicity campaign begins—way before the equipment becomes operational. Start-up of production is shown to coincide with the first order being received. This planning is essential if adequate funds are to be available at each stage of development. Moreover it follows that having laid down such a plan it is necessary to build in accurate feedback in order to identify deviations as soon as they occur so that corrective action can be taken.

The time-scale of some industrial developments can be of a very long-term nature. Obviously it takes time to build a factory and to install new plant,

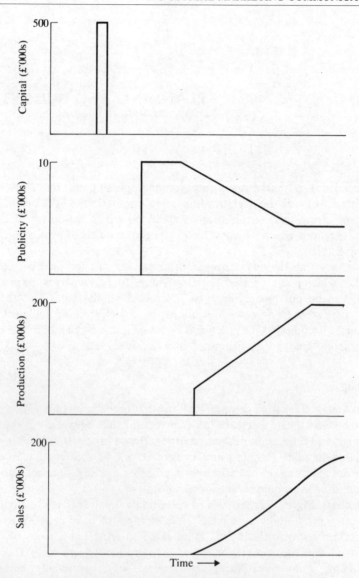

Figure 3.1 Timing of publicity in relation to capital, production and sales

often a year or two. It is equally important to remember that it can take fully as long to build up a demand for a product. The idea of beginning a campaign two years before the product becomes generally available may be rare for some managements but for certain products and services, this is the length of time involved. This is not only true of a new product launch. For existing products there is a good deal of evidence that the sales of today are largely the results of efforts made months or years before and this is a significant factor in determining the promotional budget.

The detailed scheduling of media on a time-scale is the next stage in planning. A typical plan is shown in Figure 3.2. It begins with a press conference and is followed by the campaign launch which reinforces the editorial publicity, with trade press advertising and an intensive direct mail operation backed by advertising in the national press. The sales force is held back in this plan in order to achieve sales leads which will enable it to operate more efficiently and with greater impact.

Trade press advertising, personal selling and editorial publicity are shown to be continuous with periodical sales review meetings. A second intensive phase is centred around a trade exhibition when direct mail and national press are re-introduced.

Campaign evaluation research is timed for the end of the first year, though there will be continuous feedback of results weekly or monthly against targets in respect of enquiries, quotations, visits and orders throughout the year.

Administratively all the activities will follow a budget broken down into monthly expenditure with strict control exercised. Thus the work which has gone into the preparation of the marketing strategy begins to manifest itself in a co-ordinated drive to achieve preset targets with maximum effect and at minimum cost.

Before reaching the stage of implementation, the final part of the plan has to be determined and agreed. This is the budget.

Budgeting

The basis upon which a marketing communication budget is established must clearly be the 'objective' in view or the 'task' to be done. This has been summed up well by the Institute of Practitioners in Advertising:

> Advertising expenditure must be related to the marketing objectives which the company aims to achieve. Therefore the company should start by forming a realistic marketing plan. Such a plan needs to be based on the knowledge of the overall size of the market, the company's share of the market, the economic trend of industry in general, and the trend of the company's own particular market. It should be shaped to take account of the weak as well as the strong points of the product and its probable life cycle, and the same competitive products. It should pin-point who buys the product and why, and the several influences on the buying decision that may exist at various levels from the factory floor to the board room.[1]

In view of the good sense contained in this statement, it is surprising to find that on the evidence of some researchers and in the experience of many experts, the 'task method' of budgeting is often not used in industrial

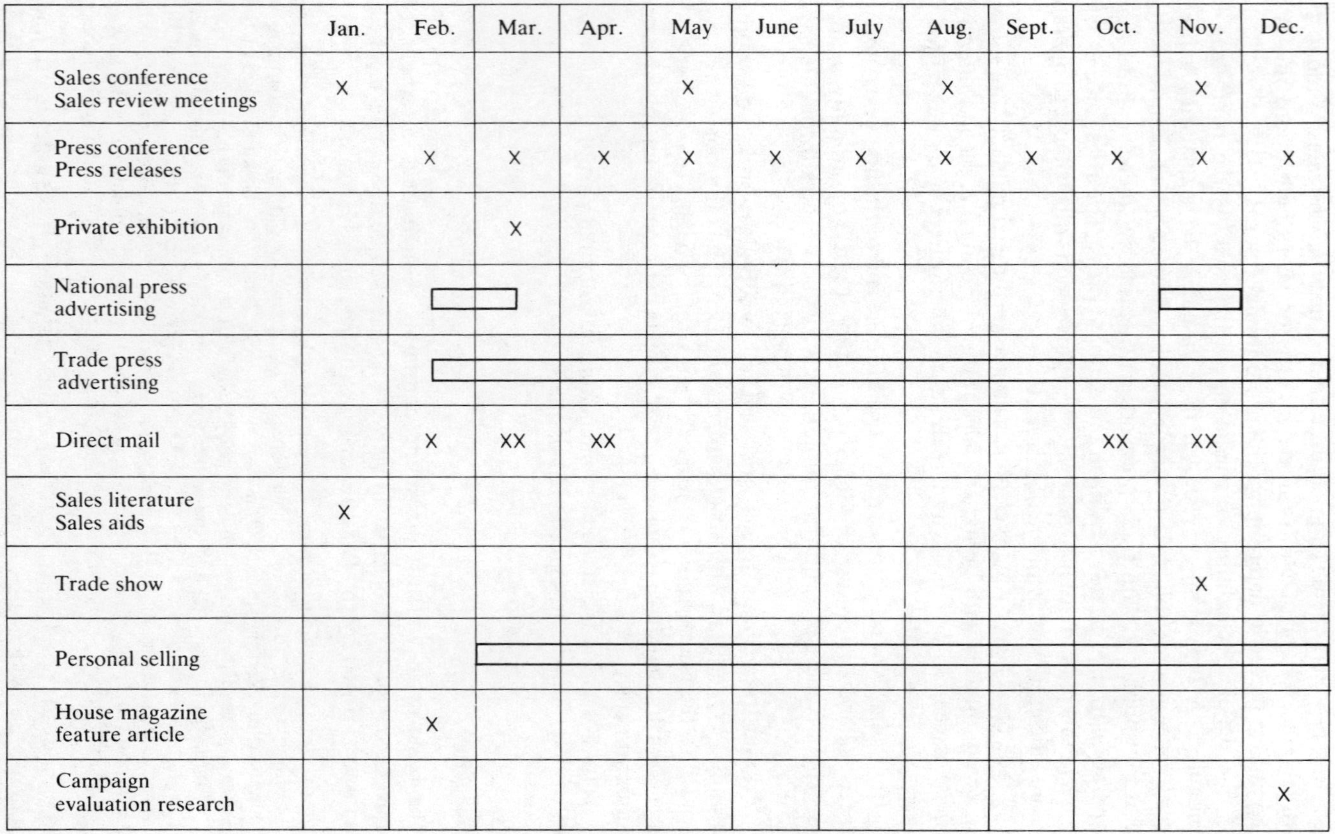

	Jan.	Feb.	Mar.	Apr.	May	June	July	Aug.	Sept.	Oct.	Nov.	Dec.
Sales conference Sales review meetings	X				X			X			X	X
Press conference Press releases		X	X	X	X	X	X	X	X	X	X	X
Private exhibition			X									
National press advertising		▭	▭								▭	
Trade press advertising		▭	▭	▭	▭	▭	▭	▭	▭	▭	▭	▭
Direct mail		X	XX	XX						XX	XX	
Sales literature Sales aids	X											
Trade show		X										
Personal selling			▭	▭	▭	▭	▭	▭	▭	▭	▭	▭
House magazine feature article												
Campaign evaluation research												X

Figure 3.2 Detailed scheduling of promotional media

marketing. The same IPA publication makes a statement which seems too far-fetched to be believable were it not supported by many similar views— 'Think of a number. Halve it. Then decide what your advertising has to do. This is not the exaggeration that it may seem of some companies' way of deciding how much to allocate for industrial advertising.'

Another authority, Harry Henry, has written,

> Since British industry is currently spending upwards of £1,800 millions a year on advertising, it might be expected that the companies and organisations responsible for such expenditure would take reasonably seriously the problem of deciding just what ought to be the size of their advertising budgets. Whether or not this is invariably the case, examination of the variety of methods used for the purpose, and the wide divergence often found between what an advertiser thinks he is doing and what he actually does in practice, indicates that this is an area of managerial activity replete with confusion.[2]

An enlightening piece of research work on this subject is to be found in McGraw-Hill's *Special Report on Buying and Selling Techniques used in the British Engineering Industry*. This analysed[3] the various methods of arriving at a promotional budget (see Table 3.1).

Table 3.1   Basis of advertising budgets (1)

		Percentage of respondents
(a)	Percentage of last year's sales turnover	7
(b)	Percentage of this year's expected turnover	17
(c)	Percentage of last year's actual and this year's estimate	4
(d)	A fixed target without specific reference to sales	39
(e)	No known basis	29
(f)	Other formulae	4

A later piece of research conducted by the author provided data which is given in Table 3.2. This brought to light the fact that many industrial companies are now using techniques which approximate to the task method.

Table 3.2   Basis of advertising budgets (2)

	Percentage
% sales turnover	4% (17)
Cost related to objective	68% (53)
Arbitrary sum	14% (30)
Other	14% (NA)

Note: See Appendix

Since the data in Table 3.2 was derived from the larger industrial advertisers, it is probably not typical, but it can certainly be regarded as indicative of a more rational approach to the matter.

It is perhaps useful to examine briefly each of the bases upon which a budget is arrived at.

PERCENTAGE OF LAST YEAR'S TURNOVER

This has the advantage of being simple to arrive at and indeed may be valid in circumstances in which a market is static both in terms of total demand and competitive activity. It makes no provision for a company to use promotional expenditure to improve its position, neither does it take into account any change in products, economic conditions, customer requirements or competition. It must therefore be regarded as a hazardous method of determining the level of promotion.

PERCENTAGE OF THIS OR NEXT YEAR'S ANTICIPATED SALES

At least this has the merit of being related to future events and at the same time being easy to calculate, but it does not face up to the reality of the marketing situation. If the demand for products has suddenly increased, a promotional budget based upon a fixed percentage of forecast sales may be higher than necessary, and indeed may result in orders being received which cannot be satisfied by the production capacity. Conversely if market demand enters a period of decline a higher percentage expenditure may be required to produce the required sales targets. Furthermore, to use next year's sales as a basis ignores the fact that for some capital goods, the gestation period for promotional activities is more than one year.

In any case to use a percentage of anything presupposes that one can obtain from some source the optimum percentage level for efficient expenditure. That this is not so is evidenced by the wide range of percentage expenditures in different industries. An example quoted in the appendix to the IPA publication mentioned above shows the range of expenditure in the United States (see Table 3.3).

FIXED FIGURE UNRELATED TO SALES

The kindest observation that can be made on this method of fixing the budget is that it may be supposed that over a period of years it has been found by trial and error that a given expenditure results in a level of sales and profit which is regarded as satisfactory. This method, however, can hardly claim to have any place in modern marketing, or, indeed, in modern business management.

Table 3.3 Advertising as a percentage of sales

Industry	% of industrial sales expended for industrial advertising	
	High	Low
Paper	4.0	0.2
Printing and publishing	1.65	0.1
Chemicals	9.3	0.003
Rubber and plastic products	8.0	0.1
Primary metal industries	3.0	0.0004
Fabricated metal products	16.2	0.003
Machinery	18.5	0.001

N.B. Even where specific product groups are examined, wide differences occur.

COMPETITIVE ADVERTISING

Some companies are known to base their publicity on what their competitors are doing. While this has the advantage of at least countering competitive activity, it assumes that it is possible to measure competitors' expenditure with some degree of accuracy: it also assumes that the competitors know what they are doing and have arrived at their budgets on a sound basis. Both assumptions are unlikely.

THE 'TASK METHOD'

This involves defining the objective, or the task to be done, then determining the best media mix to achieve it. From this a budget can be drawn up which will represent the best estimate of the optimum promotional expenditure. (See Fig. 3.3.)

In a comprehensive review of budgeting methods Harry Henry[4] lists ten other possible lines of approach:

Intuitive, or rule of thumb This is someone's subjective assessment of 'what should do the job', and is an amalgam of hunch and experience (experience being what has been done before, not necessarily having regard to its outcome). It is very dependent upon the person making the decision: should he be replaced, a different view may be taken.

The affordable method This method, spending 'as much as can be afforded' (which means what is left over after all other cost and profit requirements have been met) is not one which many firms claim to follow. But the attitude towards advertising which this approach reflects does in practice often emerge as a constraint on a good many other methods of budget determination, including those which on the face of it are rather more logical.

Figure 3.3   'Task method' of budgeting

Residue after last year's profits   Often regarded as being a ploughing-back of profit, or as re-investment in the future, this approach concentrates on the source of funds rather than on the purpose to which those funds are devoted.

Percentage of gross margin   This keeps advertising expenditure in proportion to turnover and profits, but begs the question of what advertising is for, or how its cost-efficiency may be improved.

Fixed expenditure per unit of sales   Although expressed in different terms— 'so much per case for advertising'—and born of standard costing procedures, this method is not all that different in its effect, in the short term, from the percentage of sales method.

Cost per capita   In this approach, which is used mainly by industrial advertisers, the advertiser calculates the advertising cost per head for his present customers and, when he wishes to gain more, increases his expenditure pro rata.

Matching advertising to brand share   This is an apparently sophisticated approach, based in fact on rather simplistic analysis. It is essentially a development of matching competitive advertising.

The marginal return approach   The cost of an extra unit of advertising activity is compared with the increased profit which is expected in consequence. A standard technique in direct response advertising, it becomes very complicated when there are other factors in the marketing mix, and has to be used in conjunction with marketing models.

Marketing models   These are designed to describe the relationship between sales or profit and the main elements in the marketing mix—including advertising—and from these relationships it is theoretically possible to determine the optimum advertising budget. The technical problems involved in gathering and interpreting the necessary data are, however, formidable.

Media weight tests   The theory behind this approach is that if, in a test situation, a given weight of advertising expenditure produces a particular level of sales, the level of advertising in the total market which will produce a required level of sales can be deduced. For a variety of reasons, the theory rarely works in this way.

Cost of advertising

As has been indicated, the cost of advertising in relation to the overall marketing expense and to turnover varies considerably, and particularly between one industry category and another.

In drawing up budgets, it is important to make provision for every element of expenditure and to relate it as far as possible to each product group or profit centre.

A good example of the various items which might be included in a typical publicity budget is given below

1. Advertising programme:
   - (a) Space costs
   - (b) Production
   - (c) Service fee
   - (d) Agency commission
   - (e) Pulls for internal circulation
   - (f) Research
2. Other media:
   - (a) Direct mail
   - (b) Exhibitions and trade shows
   - (c) Postage
   - (d) Sales literature
   - (e) Customer publications
   - (f) Films and AV
   - (g) Photography
3. Public relations
4. Department's expenses:
   - (a) Salaries (plus extras)
   - (b) Travel and entertainment expenses
   - (c) Office equipment and supplies
   - (d) Telephone and cable costs

(e) Rent, light and heat for department
(f) Subscription to associations, news services, magazines
(g) Press cutting services

To allocate each of these items to profit centres may be difficult and will certainly involve a degree of estimating, but the procedure is necessary if a true level of profit is to be calculated. Perhaps the biggest obstacle is attitude of mind which tends to allocate publicity expenditure as part of the general overhead rather than an intrinsic part of the cost of 'production and distribution'. A cost accountant, however, will find that the breakdown of publicity costs is no more involved or inaccurate than the breakdown of works supervision or even of machine time and expense on the shop floor.

ANALYSIS OF MEDIA EXPENDITURE

The allocation of expenditure to the various media varies a good deal as between consumer and industrial publicity (see Fig. 3.4).

The results in Table 3.4 based on the author's own research show press advertising at the head of the list, with sales literature featuring predominantly. On the whole, the breakdown between principal media groups has

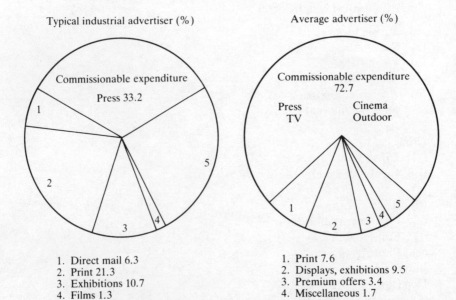

Typical industrial advertiser (%)   Average advertiser (%)

1. Direct mail 6.3
2. Print 21.3
3. Exhibitions 10.7
4. Films 1.3
5. Clients administration and
   agency service fee 27.2

1. Print 7.6
2. Displays, exhibitions 9.5
3. Premium offers 3.4
4. Miscellaneous 1.7
5. Clients administration 5.1

Figure 3.4 Comparison between industrial and consumer appropriations (*Source: IPA Forum 19, Institute of Practitioners in Advertising, London*)

Table 3.4 Analysis of media expenditure

	Percentage
Press advertising	33% (40)
Sales literature	28% (27)
Exhibitions	13% (15)
Direct mail	14% (9)
Public relations	13% (9)

Note: See Appendix

Table 3.5 Expenditure on business-to-business media[5]

	Percentage
Business press	34.5
Brochures, catalogues	14.4
Exhibitions	14.1
Direct mail	8.1
PR	6.0
Directories	5.5
Regional newspapers	2.9
National newspapers	2.8
Videos/AV	2.8
Premiums	2.1
Point of sale	1.5
Posters	1.4
TV	1.2
Sponsorship	1.0
Radio	0.5
Others	1.2
(Base 807 advertisers)	100.0

shown very little change over time. Further confirmation is given in a study by MIL Research which is reproduced in Table 3.5.

The promotional mix will of course vary considerably from one company to another and the above data are simply averages for industry as a whole.

Financial appraisal

The failure of the task method of budgeting to gain the widest usage in business can be explained in two ways. Firstly it involves a great deal more work, and a considerable measure of expertise. Given that this is available, the second reason may be the belief that, having arrived at a budget by 'scientific' means, it is now sacrosanct and regardless of any other considerations cannot be changed. It must be emphasized that the only element of science in the task method of budgeting is its methodology. The essential 'mixture' is still a matter of judgement, and can be accurate or inaccurate.

Most important of all is that a budget, arrived at in this way, must now be subjected to appraisal in terms of its relationship to the total sales expense, and in particular to the projected turnover and profit. It is more than likely that adjustments will have to be made, not only to the publicity budget, but to the sales expense and turnover before a profit margin is arrived at which is satisfactory in business terms.

An advertising campaign may be expanded or cut back providing the implications are known, and it is not done blindly. As with any investment, the returns are seldom linear, and it may be found that a reduction in advertising expenditure, say, of 40 per cent will result in a reduction in effectiveness of only 15 per cent or a reduction in sales turnover of only 2 per cent. A planned initial approach to the budget enables revisions to be made from a sound base which is likely to produce results closer to target than a blind guess.

Finally it is interesting to note how the budget breakdown compares with that in the United States (see Table 3.6).

Table 3.6 Media expenditure, United States ((*Source*: McGraw-Hill Research Report 8009.4)

	Percentage
Press advertising	36
Sales literature	24
Exhibitions	20
Direct mail	8
PR	5
Other	7

Checklist

1. In timing a promotional campaign, is there a clear understanding throughout the company on the length of time between starting publicity and seeing results in terms of sales?
2. Is a master schedule produced, as a routine for each campaign, to show the relationship between all the various media and including sales force activities?
3. Is budgeting for promotion based upon the 'task method'? If not, is top management aware of the shortcomings of other methods?
4. Is the advertising agency committed to 'task method' budgeting, rather than accepting a sum of money and recommending the best way of spending it?
5. Has any attempt been made (a) to monitor competitors' expenditures: (b)

to obtain inter-firm comparisons—in particular the proportion of promotional expenditure in the marketing expense budget, and as a percentage of sales?

6. Has a strict system of budgetary control been established?
7. Is this broken down into shorter control periods than a year?
8. Has provision been made for each item of expenditure to be set against product groups, as in Table 3.7 (on p. 34)?

References

1. *How to Budget for Industrial Advertising* (Institute of Practitioners in Advertising).
2. H. Henry, Deciding how much to spend on Advertising, Cranfield Broadsheet No. 2.
3. *Special Report on Buying and Selling Techniques used in the British Engineering Industry* (McGraw-Hill) p. 3.
4. H. Henry, *op. cit.*, pp. 3 and 4.
5. *How British Business Advertises* (British Business Press, London, 1986).

Table 3.7 Budget outline

	Product 1	*Product 2*	*Product 3*	*Total*
Marketing services				
salaries				
overheads				
expenses				
Advertising agency				
PR consultancy				
Press advertising				
space				
production				
Direct mail				
database				
production				
distribution				
Exhibitions				
space				
design				
standfitting				
transport				
staff				
miscellaneous				
Literature				
creative				
production				
distribution				
Photography				
Video and AV				
production				
distribution				
Research				
Editorial publicity				
Posters				
Point of sale				
Packaging				
Conferences and seminars				
Sales aids and manuals				
Gifts and Christmas cards				
Miscellaneous (enumerate)				
Contingency				
Total				
Sales forecast				
% Promotion to sales				
Other marketing expense				
Total marketing expense				
% Marketing expense to forecast sales				

Part 2

ELEMENTS OF MARKETING COMMUNICATIONS

4.

PRESS ADVERTISING

Press advertising relates to any form of advertisement which appears in a publication and is paid for. It is viewed primarily from the point of view of selling a product or service, though clearly it can have other aims such as building goodwill, establishing confidence in an organization, or recruiting personnel.

Purpose

The purpose of press advertising, as of any other channel of persuasion, is primarily to communicate a selling message to a potential customer.

The starting point is what is known as a 'target group audience' (T.G.A.) or a defined market or public, i.e. a number of people whom it is wished to influence. A proportion of this public will be exposed to the advertising pages of various publications and, depending upon the impact of an advertisement, a proportion of these will take note of a message.

Press advertising in the industrial sector has come in for a good deal of criticism on the grounds of its ineffectiveness, relative to the money spent on it. Much of this has arisen from the inadequacy and inaccuracy of media selection and the incompetence of some advertisement design and copywriting. Often the failure, however, is traceable to different reasons, namely that the purpose of advertising has not been defined in advance or, if it has, it has been lost sight of.

For example, there is the sales manager's view when he or she sees some hundreds of thousands of pounds being spent on press advertising, and relates this to the number of additional salespeople that could put on the road for such an expenditure. If, however, the purposes of these two channels of persuasion have been pre-defined, the one to provide active sales leads, the other to clinch the sale, they become mutually dependent and not competing alternatives.

The position of press advertising within the broad communications framework must be established at the outset, and its strengths and weaknesses analysed. The following criteria examine press advertising in relation to other media.

1. *Market size*   The total size of a market segment and all of the people that go to comprise it must be the starting point of media choice. With a market size of 10 units there is clearly not much room for more than personal contact supported by whatever back-up might be required. Move to 100 units and the situation hardly changes. At 1000 the personal contact must become selective, and here one can add direct mail, specialized press, editorial publicity, literature, maybe sponsored video and AV, local demonstrations and perhaps telephone selling. At 10 000 personal selling falls away and press advertising and most other non-personal media take over. Exhibitions have a particular merit here, combining unit economy with the benefits of face-to-face contact. Direct mail sometimes starts to become difficult to handle. Editorial back-up is of course well worth full exploitation. At 100 000 one starts to move into mass media with television, radio, national newspapers and posters replacing or heavily supplementing the other media already listed. The following grid can be used to evaluate the whole range of media in relation to the size of the audience.

AUDIENCE SIZE GRID

	100	1,000	10,000	100,000	1 M
Personal contact					
Letters/DM					
Telephone					
Demonstration					
Seminars					
Conference					
Private exhibition					
Public exhibition					
Literature					
A.V.					
Editorial publicity					
Press advertising					
Radio advertising					
TV advertising					
Poster advertising					
Sponsorship					

2. *Intrinsic impact*   The extent to which an advertising message is transmitted, received, stored and able to be recalled with accuracy is vital. Each

medium has its own intrinsic impact potential. Clearly a medium which facilitates two-way communication is top of the list, and so personal selling, exhibitions, demonstrations, telephone selling are all worthy of a high rating. Direct mail, properly conceived, can expect to perform well here, as can editorial publicity, sponsored videos and literature. All the research evidence we have on page traffic and Starch measurements would indicate that press advertising performs least well in achieving impact.

3. *Message*   What is the nature of the selling message? Is it simple or is it a reminder? Is it complex, technical or innovative? In the former case, press advertising, point-of-sale, posters and radio will do well. For a complicated messge, however, the need is for demonstrations, seminars, feature articles, literature, videos, and the sales force.

4. *Coverage and penetration*   This is the breadth and depth of a medium's capability. In breadth the question is what proportion of the target audience (i.e. people within a market segment) is covered by readership as opposed to circulation? In other words, will they have an 'opportunity to see' (O.T.S.)? In direct mail the answer could be 100 per cent, with a national newspaper perhaps 60 per cent but with great wastage. Commonly one is looking for an in-depth coverage of around 80 per cent. Turning to penetration, certain media are known by long-standing practice to penetrate decision-making units even where the actual names of the people involved cannot be identified: a major trade fair, for instance, or a weekly trade magazine that has to be seen by anyone who is anyone in order to keep up to date.

5. *Negative characteristics*   Some people resent some advertising and it is as well to check out in advance of using a particular media group whether your intention could be counter-productive. Most people in the United Kingdom dislike selling messages on the telephone or at the front door or on the street corner. They also dislike loose inserts, direct mail that is too intensive or repetitive, and for many, radio and television commercials are intrusive. On the whole, however, press advertising does not suffer from 'intrusion'.

6. *Positive characteristics*   We are looking for an added plus which comes over and above the basic medium itself. Examples are with an ad in a very prestigious publication where to be seen in good company lends an extra credibility to an advertising proposition. Similarly a strong editorial base helps. With an exhibition stand a comfortable lounge can be a welcome oasis after the formal business has been completed. An in-house exhibition or seminar may draw together people with common interests who have not met for some time and who welcome the chance of informal discussion almost as much as the event itself.

7. *Cost*   There are two costs—and also the price—to be considered. The

first cost is the total capital investment involved and whether this is compatible with the cash-flow position, and also the other major capital expenditures in marketing activities. Then the cost per contact must be evaluated, ranging as it does from the latest estimated call cost for an industrial salesperson of over £100 to just a few pence for press advertising. Media planning decisions are often made on the outcome of aggressive media buying, and this is where price comes in. All rate cards have their price, and 10 per cent or more off quoted rates can be a lot of money.

8. *Speed*   Under pressure, television, radio, newspapers and direct mail can all be transmitting messages within 24 hours or less, and to very large audiences simultaneously. The sales force can respond even more quickly, but at a rate of just a few people a day. At the other extreme it may be two years before an appropriate trade fair takes place. Thus, if the time for activating consumer/customer behaviour is a critical factor then choice of media must be influenced by this.

9. *Complexity and convenience*   Nothing could be simpler than taking half a million appropriation and allocating half of it to a single commercial network on television, and the other half to full pages in national newspapers. Such a media strategy may even be right. As against this can be compared the complexity of a multi-market multi-shot direct mail campaign, coupled with regional presentations tied in with local PR, back-up sales visits, regional press, supporting literature and posters with a culminating business gift. Media choice just might be influenced by ease of use (idleness), coupled with such other non-professional factors as good or bad agency commission. Is there any possible justification for some media paying commission and others not? Media choice within an agency must therefore have some regard to the amount of effort required to service each medium (a cost) in relation to the income and aggravation it is likely to receive. Specialized trade press and small spaces may be very effective but they can be complicated to handle and with only 10 per cent media commission are expensive for an agency to handle.

10. *Feedback*   Examine any advertising medium and you will find that the greater majority of advertisements invite no explicit response in the way of a direct feedback, and thus they receive very little. Hence press advertising, and television, are essentially single-channel communication systems. Since impact is greater where a dialogue can be established, there must be an intrinsic advantage in all the face-to-face media, and even with direct mail and editorial publicity where there are some instances of feedback. It is worth noting that many of the popular sales promotion techniques draw heavily on the customers' participation.

11. *Creative scope*   Should a medium be chosen for its creative scope? Increasingly this is regarded as a major factor but within the rather strict

limits of availability of colour or movement. What is meant here is the opportunity for some quite novel or extraordinary approach to be made entirely as a result of the medium being used. In press relations the creative opportunities to set up an extremely newsworthy event are limitless, and needless to say this would be done in such a way as to involve the product or company inextricably. With direct mail there is complete freedom on material, size, shape, colour, smell, timing, audience and frequency. Exhibitions also have an almost infinite variety of creative opportunities. Where the product itself is mundane, the choice of media where creativity can be exploited fully is especially relevant. Clearly creative opportunities are somewhat restricted in press advertising.

12. *Data availability*   There is a somewhat naive idea in industrial advertising that since the amounts of money to be spent are relatively small the need for information about what one is buying is not therefore very great. This is a quite extraordinary and quite illogical situation since the advertising task may well be of the greatest importance to the company; the fact that the cost of achieving it may not be astronomical does not mean that the media-buying operation should be incompetent.

With any media that overlap into consumer marketing a good deal of information is likely to be available, but otherwise it is hard to find. The technical press is rarely able to provide reliable readership data and exhibitions are way behind the press. Some advertisers set up their own sources of audience information and it may be that in respect of 'data' media choice should be biased towards those channels from which the most reliable facts can be obtained.

13. *Subjective factors*   So far, the factors being discussed on media choice have been largely objective and quantitative. In practice of course there are many other sources of influence, apparently trivial, but perhaps of far greater significance in the media-buying decision than many people either realize or are prepared to admit. Why else do advertisers opt for a particular medium? Here are a few reasons:

(a)   Good service from the publisher or media house.
(b)   Good salesmanship—hard selling—pleasant personality.
(c)   The buyer's ego trip—he likes his products to be seen in a particular medium.
(d)   Good lunches, Christmas presents, and all forms of what might kindly be termed 'grace and favour'.
(e)   Because the managing director says so.
(f)   Competitors use it.
(g)   The title of a publication, also its format; with exhibitions, location is a factor.

(h) Inertia—we've always done it this way.
(i) Personal prejudice and ignorance.
(j) The good reputation of a medium; with publications, the quality of their editorial.
(k) Hunch.
(l) The agency gets a better service or higher commission.

While the above criteria do not in any way lead to scientific media planning, their evaluation in relation to press advertising and all the other media can lead to a systematic ranking of each of the channels of communication. Figure 4.1 provides a simple grid leading to an effective media mix.

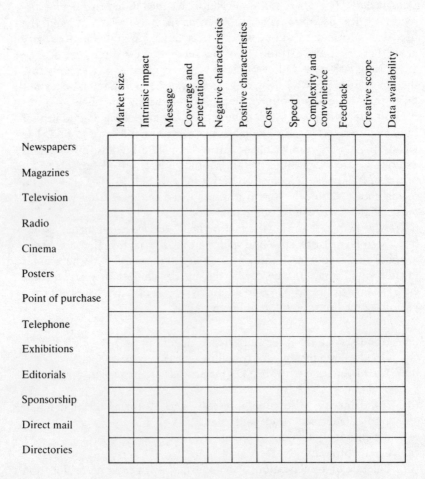

Figure 4.1   Criteria for media choice

Effectiveness

A very early survey of sources of information, *How British Industry Buys,*[1] indicated that advertisements in the trade press had a relatively small part to play in providing information which influenced the purchase of industrial products. The highest category was 'operating management' of whom 32 per cent cited press advertising as one of the two most important channels of communication. Perhaps the most important category, board members, scored only 14 per cent.

There is good evidence in this survey that respondents are not always willing to admit even to themselves what are the outside factors they allow to influence them in reaching purchasing decisions. Sales engineers' visits for instance were rated at 66 per cent by board members, yet elsewhere in the survey only 18 per cent of board members ever saw a sales engineer! Since the first figure is an expression of opinion and the latter one of fact, 18 per cent is more likely to be the accurate figure. If not from sales engineers, where did board members obtain the information upon which to make decisions? Advertising may well in fact deserve a higher rating than these respondents were prepared to admit.

In the United States a good deal of work has been done to relate on a very broad basis the effectiveness of press advertising to sales.

A survey published by McGraw-Hill[2] showed that in 893 industrial companies, when the ratio of advertising to selling expense, i.e. advertising plus direct selling costs (salespeople's salaries, commission, travel and entertainment), is higher, the ratio of selling expense to sales turnover is lower. On average it was found that 'high advertisers' (where advertising accounted for more than 20 per cent of selling expense) had a 21 per cent lower overall selling cost than 'low advertisers'. The trend was found to be consistent regardless of the volume of sales and of product groups. In the former case, 'high' advertisers in each of four sales size groups had average selling expense 16 to 30 per cent lower than the 'low' advertisers.

For the machinery group (all special industrial machinery such as machine tools and construction machinery, motors, instruments and controls, transport and communications equipment) the sales expense ratio was 25 per cent lower on average among 'high' advertisers than among 'low' advertisers.

For the materials group (raw materials and ingredients such as steel, industrial chemicals, rubber and plastics, structural products) the difference was 27 per cent. For the equipment supplies group (maintenance and operating supplies such as furniture, paper products, lubricants, tyres, valves, machine tool accessories, paint, lighting fixtures, electronic components) the difference was 15 per cent.

It can be argued of course that these data are of a general nature and will hide wide variances. The conclusions, however, are important enough for industrial advertisers to take steps to obtain information relating to their own particular business, maybe through their trade association using inter-firm comparisons.

There are wide differences in the amount of investment in industrial advertising even among firms in the same industry. This is only to be expected but it is unfortunate that the reasons for such differences are often subjective or illogical. They are sometimes based on a philosophy of 'I don't believe in advertising', a comment which has as much rational justification as not believing in raw materials. Or perhaps the sales manager thinks he knows exactly who his customers are, calls upon them at frequent intervals and therefore does not need advertising—a proposition which can almost always be disproved on methodical investigation. Too often sales staff and managers completely underrate the importance of the corroborative function of industrial advertising. Because they may not be able to point to sales or worthwhile prospects obtained by advertising they assume that their advertising is not effective. In fact however a company's generalized reputation is most important; and although advertising is only one factor in building up this reputation it is a vital one. This is discussed further in Chapter 14.

The industrial and business press

Publications can be broken down into six main groups:

1. National dailies
2. Provincial dailies
3. Sunday newspapers
4. Local newspapers (weeklies)
5. General interest and class magazines
6. Trade and technical publications

The primary concern of industrial or business advertisers is in the very many trade and technical publications. These journals are diverse and complex. They encompass a comprehensive range of activities, vary greatly in size, scope, authority and in the method of circulation. In recent years there has been a good deal of rationalization in the industry which has led to a large proportion of the total publications being produced by a relatively small number of publishers. Many changes have taken place, some of which have been to the benefit of the advertiser, for example the availability of research services. Fundamentally journals have tended to move away from an editorial basis where a brilliant editor published material about a particular subject in which he was an expert, to a marketing basis where the whole concept of a publication is to provide information and a service to meet the needs of a particular market or specialized group of people. This matter is dealt with in greater detail in Chapter 16 on publishing.

The advertising schedule

The starting point once again must be a written definition of the people it is desired to influence. For example it is not uncommon in the development of a campaign to aim at four groups—the people who specify a product, often the engineers, designers or technologists; the people who have contacts with the suppliers and place the order, usually the purchasing officers; the user; and most important the authorizers, often the board of directors. To these can be added two further categories—'influencers' in the making of decisions and 'gatekeepers' e.g. a secretary or a receptionist/telephone operator. It is essential to establish at the outset which of these or other groups, it is required to reach. Moreover it is necessary to take the analysis further to include factors such as geographical location, age, sex and so on.

The selection of the most effective publications is vital, for even a poor advertisement in the right journal has some chance of success, whereas a first-rate advertisement in a quite inappropriate publication is absolutely useless. It follows then that time and effort invested in the methodical selection and final evaluation of media is a very worthwhile investment. In practice the data available from publishers is usually grossly inadequate, often misleading and sometimes blatantly inaccurate. Media research is a growing activity in industrial advertising and is dealt with at length in Chapter 13.

Given a potential market, there will be a number, often a large number, of journals whose circulation will cover part or all of it. Circulation, however, is not the real criterion since it is only readership and, in particular, effective readership, that counts. One journal may have a high 'pass on' factor in relation to its circulation, but are the recipients also effective buyers? Furthermore it is not enough for a magazine to appear on a desk, it must be read in order to be effective.

The total circulation or readership of a journal is usually of no great significance in itself. If for example the brief is to reach 1000 chemical engineers in the food industry it will probably be of little value that a journal also reaches 10 000 chemical engineers in plastics, petroleum and other trades in which food has no application. In assessing media and in making comparisons the aim must be to isolate the readership that is directly relevant to the marketing objectives.

Quite often it will be found that there will be numerous publications all having good coverage of the market. The question is whether to concentrate on a limited few, or whether to spread into all publications to secure the widest audience. This judgement must be made in the light of knowledge of readership duplication and also the impact which a campaign is required to achieve. It is generally true in press advertising that after the first two or three publications in a specialized field, any additions will add only a few per cent more to the coverage (reach) of a market (see Chapter 13).

COST-EFFECTIVENESS

The cost per thousand total circulation basis, so popular with publishers and agency media departments, is quite inadequate for effective media assessment. Equally unrealistic as a rule is cost per order originating from a given journal, since the number of traceable contracts is usually of such a low order as to be statistically unreliable.

Cost per reader within the defined market segment is probably the most effective basis of assessing a publication, though in some instances cost per enquiry can be an even better guide. This latter factor necessarily depends on whether enquiries are what an advertisement is designed to achieve. A study of packaging media for instance showed the cost per thousand circulation to vary little between one publication and another. When the required readership for a particular type of pack was examined, the cost per reader varied from £1.5 per thousand to £20 per thousand. Moreover, after the top two publications had been added together, further additions made no significant difference to the number of readers reached. In this instance it was found possible to reduce the number of publications from eight to two, increase the concentration and level of advertising, and thus impact, while reducing expenditure.

CIRCULATION AND ADVERTISING RATES

When the overall economics of publishing are considered it is generally found that advertising rates are reasonably geared to production costs. Within any specialized sector it is usual to find the forces of competition have caused the cost per thousand copies of one journal to be much the same as another. Indeed so far as the absolute level of cost per page is concerned it may be argued that the rates in general tend to be too low to enable a publisher to provide a good enough all-round service to maximize the marketing efficiency of his publication.

The important differences between rates begin to emerge only when readership 'segmentation' is considered and here the advertiser is at a great disadvantage. Accurate and authentic data on total circulations are beginning to emerge, but circulation breakdowns are usually no more than a publisher's statement and the bitter fact is that these must be treated with reserve. Until circulation breakdowns are subject to independent audit as in the USA it is unwise to pay any serious regard to them since the basis on which they are compiled is unknown and they cannot be subject to comparative study. Nevertheless the work done in the UK by the Audit Bureau of Circulation in developing and promoting Media Data Forms represents a very important advance in providing a quantitative basis for media selection.

Given the difficulty of determining cost/readership effectiveness, there are still opportunities for significant savings on the basis of rates alone. For instance in determining how many publications to place on a schedule in relation to how many insertions in each, graduated scales of charges are worth examining since quantity reductions in page rates can effect major economies. Long-term contracts can enable further savings to be made, and notwithstanding the existence of published rate cards, many publishers are prepared to negotiate prices in order to increase their share of business.

A growing trend among publishers is to offer discount rates based on the total business placed in certain groups of publications. Another variation is to consider financial concessions related to the time of year.

An alternative to looking for special rate reductions is to look for special services from a publisher. There are many facilities which can be placed at the disposal of an advertiser which will help to make his campaign more effective. Progressive publishers are recognizing this and are prepared to co-operate, for instance in split runs, inserts, and joint research. One questionable service is the occasional offer of editorial preference in consideration of the placing of advertising. If a journal is willing to do business on this basis it can only mean that it is prepared to forfeit its editorial independence in order to make short-term gains at the expense of the reader and therefore the advertiser.

An interesting term in the publishing business is the 'numbers game'. It is a reflection on the gullibility of some advertisers that the journal most likely to be chosen as number one on a schedule is that having the greatest total circulation. Before the introduction of free-circulation journals, this might have been a valid criterion in a homogeneous market, but where it represents, as is now sometimes the case, simply an expression of the print order, its claims are quite misleading.

Over the past decade a large number of publications have appeared, almost always given away, with circulation methods which are sometimes not controlled with any degree of effectiveness. Such journals have had circulations inflated by a factor first of two, then three and then four—each publisher going one better in quoting a higher number. Rates for such journals expressed in relation to circulation totals have seemed reasonable, but any company librarian will quote example after example of the inflow of duplicate copies of such journals which serve to benefit the printer, papermaker and publisher, but not the advertiser.

In numerous readership surveys there is ample evidence of magazines quoting massive circulation figures but receiving extraordinarily low readership ratings. The moral, as always, is let the buyer beware, and verify all facts by independent audit.

While page rates in relation to circulation may be fairly standard, this is by no means so of special positions, rates and concessions. The advertising value of such positions may be questionable, but all the same, there is a good deal of scope for skilled media buying.

Wide variations between one publisher and another will be found in respect of facing matter, covers, additional colours, bound-in and loose inserts, and bleed pages. The combination of these factors can entirely change the economics of an advertising schedule and this points the need for a very close liaison between media buyers and the creative staff of agencies in order to achieve the maximum cost-effectiveness. Some journals for example make no charge for bleed whereas others have a high premium: cover positions in particular are susceptible to variations quite unrelated to their advertising value which in itself is questionable.

Skilful media planning and buying is therefore a high priority though many advertising agencies greatly underrate it for technical advertising. This is often because with the complexity of the task the client's 'intimate' knowledge of the trade is allowed to predominate without a critical examination.

Media selection

Intra-media comparisons in the trade and technical press are particularly difficult with the relevant facts often unknown and sometimes misleading. Although this makes the task more difficult, it does not provide a reason for ignoring it. Some of the principal criteria in selecting media are:

1. Total circulation
2. Total readership
3. Segmented circulation
4. Segmented readership
5. Standard rates in relation to 1, 2, 3 and 4
6. Reductions and premiums in relation to special circumstances
7. Credibility of publisher's data
8. Editorial excellence
9. Journal's reputation
10. Format, paper, printing
11. Method of circulation
12. Frequency
13. Special services from publisher
14. Readership duplication

In the limit, of course, given adequate research, and feedback of information, the sole criterion is the extent to which a publication serves as a means of achieving the written specific advertising objectives in terms of the market to be influenced. This hinges largely on the extent to which an advertiser has access to reliable research data. Chapters 12 and 13 deal with this in some detail.

It is necessary at this stage to touch briefly on other criteria which are often employed but which in general are less helpful in assessing media.

Probably the biggest single misleading factor in media selection is the use of reader reply cards. This is a service introduced largely by 'controlled circulation' journals as a means of securing a maximum of enquiries. Viewed in this light alone, and provided the specific campaign objective is to secure the maximum of enquiries without qualification, then these cards can be said to provide a useful service. However, from an examination of advertisements in the technical press the conclusion must be reached that the principal purpose of many advertisements is not to secure enquiries, since so few offer an incentive, either specific or implied, to make an enquiry. If this is so, reader reply response is not specially valuable.

It is the quality of enquiries which is of prime importance in most cases of a campaign to obtain sales leads. Here reader reply cards will be found to need scrutiny in two respects: firstly there tends to be a higher proportion of enquiries from people lower down the scale of purchasing influence; secondly the very ease with which one can make an enquiry using a reader reply card makes such an enquiry less serious, and more casual than would otherwise be the case. Evidence of this is to take at random returned cards in a publisher's office and examine the number of ticks per card, sometimes so many as to be ludicrous. It is not unknown for a card to be received on which every number has been ticked, including all the spare ones against which no advertisement or editorial item has appeared. While it is important to be cautious, the plain fact is that reply cards on balance provide a valuable service to advertisers and to publishers, but more to the point it is a service which is applauded by the readers as can be seen in Figure 4.2.

Reader reply cards in respect of editorial items are also used as an argument for the advertising effectiveness of a journal. This may be valid in some instances, but it is open to considerable doubt. Consider the timing of an editorial on a new product. The first journal in a specialized field to publish a new product item will tend to mop up the enquiries of those having immediate interest. Subsequent appearance in a competitor journal may pull significantly less because of the later timing. Furthermore a brief notice editorially about a new product giving only a few of the necessary facts will tend to pull more enquiries than an editorial which gives a full and detailed description. Indeed the journal which is so interested in a product as to give a full-scale article on the subject can be fairly sure of pulling virtually no enquiries at all. This interesting fact should be considered in relation to

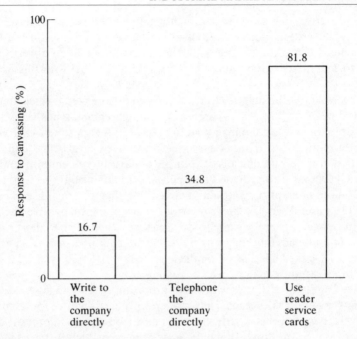

Figure 4.2   Use of reader service cards (*Source:* Cahners Research Report No. 240.1)

copywriting for an enquiry-getting advertisement.

The number of advertisements carried by a journal is by and large evidence neither for nor against its value as an advertising medium. The argument that many advertisements mean less exposure of one's own advertisement, or conversely that few advertisements mean greater exposure and therefore greater effectiveness, is unsupported by evidence. Likewise the inclusion of competitors' advertisements in a publication is only indicative of its value in advertising terms if an advertiser is confident that his own assessment of media is inferior to that of his competitors!

The list of irrational reasons for selecting media is long. It includes personal views influenced by the salesmanship of the media representative, the views of company employees assessing editorial content from an entirely different viewpoint than the customer, the opinion of the sales force or any other department.

There is in fact no substitute for objective media readership analysis and since this requires an investment in terms of formal research, whether desk or field, it is unlikely that an advertising budget which does not set aside a significant sum of money to evaluate its advertising will secure maximum value for its total advertising investment. It can be argued that in industrial advertising, a research budget of say 10 per cent total publicity expenditure is the minimum required to explore methods for maximum efficacy.

Impact in press advertising

The first requirement of an advertisement is to have the power to stop the reader—to secure attention. From that point on there occurs a series of mental processes which determine the degree of impact achieved. Factors such as advertisement size, novelty, position, frequency and subject matter will affect the impact on a person's mind. It is all too easy for advertisers who are very conscious of their own advertisements to suppose that their impact is likely to be of a much higher order than is actually the fact. From the research work carried out in the United States and to some degree in the United Kingdom there is evidence that advertisements in the trade and technical press are noticed, on average, by only a relatively small percentage of readers and that real impact is achieved with perhaps as few as 2 or 3 per cent. In some studies described in Chapter 13 on research there are indeed instances of advertisements consistently scoring zero in their readership rating. It is essential therefore to examine continuously methods of obtaining maximum effectiveness, and here the following criteria have some bearing.

CREATIVE EXPRESSION

There can be little doubt that all other factors being equal, the creative expression of the sales message—the customer benefit—is paramount. Equally this factor is the most difficult to evaluate and quantify. As an example of this a new range of fluid power equipment was produced for which six selling features were identified. These were thought to be equally important in terms of satisfying buyers' needs, but applying the 'single selling idea' a series of six advertisements was designed, each featuring one sales point. The advertisements were couponed and designed specifically to pull enquiries. The result was that one advertisement pulled far more enquiries than any other and from this the conclusion was drawn that this selling feature must be the most important to buyers. A new campaign was designed centring on this one feature, but the result was a disastrous failure. The simple fact was that the successful advertisement had achieved its success due to its creative excellence in attracting attention, not to the selling feature.

The advertiser therefore must look to the copywriter and visualizer for those touches of inspiration which cannot be defined and yet are so decisive in the success of a campaign. There may be little an advertiser can do to stimulate such inspiration, but at least a serious effort can be made to establish a good rapport with the creative team, and to provide a full and adequate brief.

Many attempts have been made to effect some measurement of 'creative expression', particularly as perceived by readers of advertisements, namely, buyers. One of the most extensive was by G. McAleer of Florida Technological University. This examined four industry groups to determine the extent to which specific advertising propositions were regarded as valid by advertisers on the one hand and purchasers on the other. The market segments selected for study were consulting engineers, electrical contractors, architects and building contractors. A list of 48 advertising appeals was drawn up in a questionnaire and mailed to both parties in the four groupings. Respondents were asked to use a numerical scaling between + 5 and − 5 to indicate the extent to which they felt that each proposition had validity to them personally in their professional capacity.

Clearly if both parties showed a similar score (as indicated by comparing arithmetic averages) then there would be a good understanding by advertisers of the needs of their customers. Alternatively, if the ratings for a particular proposition were significantly different then there was good reason to suppose that advertisers were not as aware as they should be of the motivating factors relating to their customers. Table 4.1 is an extract from a very comprehensive listing of items, some of which have similar ratings between the two groups, and others differences which are significant.

The conclusion of the survey was 'that advertisers to each of the market segments studied did not correctly perceive the influence of advertising appeals upon the market concerned'. Such a conclusion does not imply that all companies are operating with such a lack of understanding of their customers nor indeed that in other countries the data has a direct validity. It does, however, lead one to give consideration to carrying out a review of selling propositions to check their correct relevance.

Table 4.1 Creative expression as perceived by advertisers and buyers

Advertising appeal	Advertiser (av. mean)	Customer (av. mean)
Ease of installation	2.05	1.87
Low maintenance cost	2.30	2.61
Physical features	2.88	2.40
Reliability of the seller	2.35	2.34
Ability to keep delivery promises	1.67	2.32
Newness of product	0.63	− 0.43
It is widely specified	2.53	− 0.53
Testimonial by a supplier of the product	1.96	− 1.08
Easy to repair	0.40	2.65
Announcement of new installation	1.51	− 0.24
Automatic operation	− 1.00	2.52
Increasing output	− 0.48	2.76

PRE-TESTING ADVERTISEMENTS

The wider implications of advertising research will be considered later in Chapters 12 and 13. At this stage, however, serious consideration should be given to testing the 'creative proposition' to ensure that what may appear to be highly compelling and lucidly persuasive copy really is just that.

It is commonplace in consumer campaigns to pre-test advertisements, and experience has shown that there is a good correlation between such research findings and actual performance. With industrial advertising there is a widespread point of view that pre-testing is unnecessary, too complicated, and anyway costs too much. Such an argument is fallacious in that the task of an advertisement is to communicate a selling message to a potential market irrespective of cost, and if that message is not adequately received then a vital part of the marketing communications process is missing, perhaps with a disastrous effect on sales.

SIZE

The size of an advertisement must clearly influence the impact it produces. Research in this field gives some evidence, however, that this is not a linear relationship, and thus large and particularly multi-page advertisements need to be justified by other considerations. Factors which properly enter into the selection of large spaces are the nature of the sales message, the pictorial content required, prestige, and the nature of the publication and the advertisements it carries. There is no doubt that for some products and services a quarter page can be as effective as a whole page.

The importance of bleed has often been neglected. The additional cost is minimal whereas the additional area available is substantially greater. There is some indication from field research work that bleed advertisements score disproportionately higher than non-bleed, perhaps because they are so rare. Another option to consider is the use of a loose insert. Some will hold that with more than, say, one insert the readers become antagonized to the extent that they either ignore the advertising message or even build up resentment to the advertiser. Again looking to American research data, there is some evidence as in Figure 4.3 that advertising readership increases significantly by the use of inserts.

POSITION

A great deal of inconclusive and misleading research has been conducted on the importance of the position of an advertisement in a publication. In newspapers there is probably scope for being particularly selective in the positioning of an advertisement. In the trade and technical press there is little evidence to justify paying the premiums demanded for special positions even

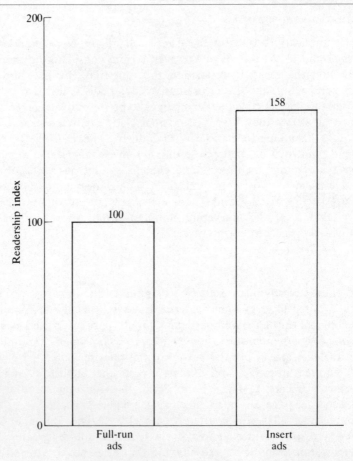

Figure 4.3   The influence of inserts (*Source:* Cahners Research Report No. 117.1)

where a journal is carrying a hundred or more pages of advertising. The same doubts should also be raised about cover positions which, while undoubtedly having a high prestige connotation, may turn out to have a very low page traffic rating, particularly front covers where so often a circulation slip is attached by the librarian before a journal is circulated in a company.

FREQUENCY AND DUPLICATION

Once again there has been research in the United States which seems to indicate that if the first appearance of an advertisement is seen by, say, 10 per cent of readers, the second appearance will also be seen by 10 per cent but of substantially different readers.

This is probably an area in which a great deal more research should be carried out, particularly to establish how often an advertisement should be changed. There is a general consensus that three appearances is a good minimum and that up to six can be justified. This is borne out by advertisements which set out to get enquiries and therefore enable a response rate to be traced.

Frequency and duplication must often, at this stage in advertising knowledge, depend upon experience and intelligent guesswork having regard to the market share aimed for, the speed with which the message needs to be

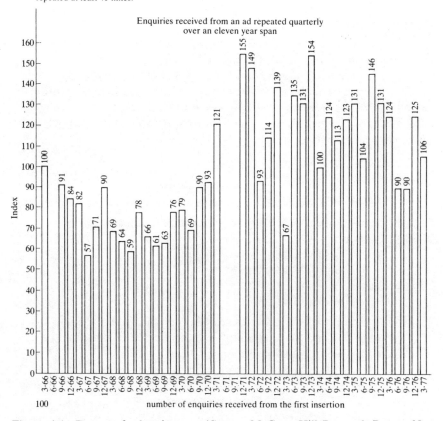

**Ad repeated 41 times
and still working**

The Ludlow Corporation has demonstrated, by counting enquiries,
and by running the same ad over eleven years in
Engineering News-Record that an ad can be successfully
repeated at least 41 times.

Figure 4.4 Repeat of advertisement (*Source:* McGraw-Hill Research Report No. 3043.2)

delivered, activities in other media, the frequency with which orders are placed, reminder advertising and the overall impact which it is desired to achieve. Some hard evidence is provided by an example[3] from the States of an advertisement which was repeated 41 times over a period of eleven years and produced an apparently ever-increasing number of enquiries as shown in Figure 4.4.

COLOUR

The effect on impact of colour depends very much upon the circumstances and as a general rule is not nearly so important as creative expression and product illustration. In a magazine full of colour advertisements a black-and-white design can obtain a very high score. In a publication with no colour at all, a multicoloured advertisement will clearly have an advantage.

Limitations and advantages

The limitation of press advertising is that, due to the excessive number of publications and the lack of precision in defining readerships, there is a strong risk of wasting large sums of money without ever realizing it.

The advantage is that extensive coverage, even saturation, of a market can be obtained with a minimum of effort—often influencing purchasing units which cannot be reached easily in any other way; which are often indeed not even known to exist.

Checklist

1. Has the potential audience for an advertisement been defined in terms of
    (a) Size (numbers of DMUs and their purchasing powers)?
    (b) Location?
    (c) Market segments?
    (d) Individual's job categories?
    (e) Special characteristics?
    (f) Purchasing motivation?
2. Have the proposed media been selected (a) on the basis of the information from item one and (b) in relation to authenticated readership data?
3. Has readership duplication been considered?
4. Does a particular advertisement or series (a) have a tangible objective, (b) can this be measured, (c) does it fit in with the overall marketing strategy?
5. Has a full and written brief been prepared?
6. Does the brief include
    (a) Advertisement size?

    (b) Frequency?

    (c) Position?

    (d) Number of colours?

    (e) Essential illustrations?

    (f) Action required?

    (g) A means of media identification?

    (h) Provision for measuring effectiveness?

7. Has the number, frequency and timing of advertisements been scheduled in relation to other parts of the marketing mix?

References

1. Hugh Buckner, *How British Industry Buys*, (Hutchinson, London, 1967), tables 8 and 9.
2. McGraw-Hill, *How Advertising Affects the Cost of Selling*.
3. McGraw-Hill Research Report No. 3043.2.

5.

DIRECT MAIL

Direct mail means the use of the postal services to carry a persuasive message, in any form, to a prospect. The mailing piece can be as simple as a sales letter, or a postcard. Alternatively it can be as sophisticated as a major catalogue, a complex gimmick or an expensive sample. For practical purposes, items which are distributed door to door by a commercial organization will be included under the term direct mail.

Referring back to the basic impact diagram in Chapter 2 (Fig. 2.2), direct mail is one of the major channels of persuasion available to a company for reaching a prospect and achieving maximum impact. Its importance in the marketing mix will clearly vary, depending on the nature of the product and market, from being of paramount significance (e.g. drug promotions to doctors) to being almost useless (e.g. promotion of nuclear power plants to a government agency).

Special advantages

Direct mail enables the user to aim a message at a precisely defined prospect, and to place the mailing piece in front of that prospect at the exact time required, and, indeed, as soon and as often as is wished. Moreover a mailing piece has an advantage over a press advertisement or editorial item in that for a moment at least it occupies a solus position, gains greater attention and therefore greater impact. There is no absolute restriction on size, number of words, colour, illustrations or quality of reproduction. Hence there is a good opportunity to put across an argument in full. A further benefit is that since it can be addressed directly and personally it can be so designed as to produce a response, and where this is a particular objective a very high rate of replies can be obtained.

Direct mail is a versatile tool which can be varied widely in magnitude, direction and frequency; can be brought into use virtually overnight and, sometimes most important of all, can be an extremely cheap method of communication.

Disadvantages

The advantage of direct mail, that it aims at a precise target, is also one of its limitations. In Chapter 2, dealing with strategy, the importance of defining the market in detail was stressed as was the large number of purchasing influences likely to be involved in the placement of an order. For direct mail to be fully effective it is essential to be able to define precisely the audience to be influenced. This means broad market categories, companies within these categories, plants within the companies and people within the plants.

Definition of target audiences cannot be overstressed. Just as with press advertising, it is pointless to develop a first-class proposition if it is placed in front of a non-prospect.

A further limiting factor in practice is the lack of experience which promotion people in general have of direct mail, coupled with the fact that it is complex, difficult to set up, easy to go wrong, and perhaps not yet developed to the state of relative sophistication found in other media. While this generalization cannot be applied, say, to the promotion of pharmaceuticals or to certain specific products, for instance *Reader's Digest*, it is nevertheless true of most industrial operations. Here, however, is the opportunity to gain the edge on competition. There can be little doubt that in trade and technical campaigns, direct mail is going to play an increasingly important role.

Databases

Establishment of an effective database is the prerequisite of a mailing campaign, and upon it will rest the success or failure of a promotion.

The marketing strategy will have defined the markets, their sizes and locations, their relative importance, and the key people to influence. The promotion strategy will have defined the role of direct mail and which of the various targets it is to be used to attack and with what intensity. Most important it will also have defined exactly and quantitatively the objectives of the direct mail operation.

It will be useful to identify the principal sources of databases, but while doing so it is important to stress that there are usually available in any campaign a wide range of special sources which a creative mind can explore. Careful thought and consultation can be most rewarding here.

SALESPEOPLE'S CALL LISTS

Where a direct mail campaign is required to support a field selling drive it is vital to incorporate the salespeople's call lists. Indeed with some product groups in which the market is compact and easy to define, the call list may be all that is required. If so, however, it is still necessary to have a foolproof system of feedback from the sales force covering changes immediately they occur, and to achieve this the full co-operation and sympathy both of sales managers and sales representatives is required.

The limitation of such a list is that salespeople, however good, cannot always unearth all prospective companies, far less determine accurately which individuals in an organization influence purchasing decisions. Even if such people can be identified, a salesperson may not be able to make contact with them and accordingly they may not be on the call list.

ENQUIRIES

From the publicity activities in which a company engages come a variety of enquiries. These are usually obtained at considerable cost and are a major source of contacts for a mailing campaign. They often serve to supplement the sales call list by identifying within a prospect company individuals who, while not strictly 'purchasers', are very much 'influencers'.

It is not uncommon to include the need for enquiries as a means of list building as one of the objectives of a campaign. An example in press advertising is to include a specific offer of a brochure or a sample; similarly at exhibitions to record meticulously all callers on a stand whether they have some immediate requirement or not.

CUSTOMERS

The nature of a campaign may not require that existing customers shall be included but in other circumstances they must head the list as a top priority. Once again, it is not just the person that signs the order who must be reached, but all the other individuals who contribute to the purchasing decision.

DIRECTORIES

These are particularly useful when entering a new market where a body of knowledge and a range of contacts do not already exist. There may be severe limitations since all directories are well out of date before they are published, many of them are not comprehensive, and some of them are substantially inaccurate. An example of how easy it is to waste money here is with the use of what is probably the best-known business directory to promote a particular training programme to marketing directors and the like. In one of the lists supplied 53 per cent of the names and addresses had an error in them, ranging from a wrong spelling to a person who had left the company five years previously.

Where names of executives are included, this can be of great value: where they are not, a good deal of research is probably going to be necessary to personalize the list in order to make it effective.

EXHIBITIONS

A list of exhibitors is an excellent supplementary source of prospects within a given market. This can very usefully and easily be extended by setting up a survey in which visits are made to each stand and representatives questioned as to who in a certain company is likely to be interested in a particular product. The degree of co-operation that can be achieved, particularly at a slack time, can be very high, almost total.

A new opportunity which is being created by certain exhibition organizers is to invite each visitor to identify himself by filling out an enquiry card. This builds a bank of purchasing influences which is likely to be more extensive than any other method, but a fairly disciplined scrutiny of job category is necessary here.

HOUSE MAGAZINES

From the point of view of direct mail a benefit of external house magazines is that over a period of time they build up a circulation list which often includes many people behind the purchasing scenes whom a company wishes to influence. Additions to the circulation of a house magazine should automatically be considered for addition to the promotional mailing list.

PUBLISHERS

An increasing number of publishers are exploiting their circulation lists by hiring them to advertisers and others for direct mail. As with all lists it is important to be cautious about their value and, as far as trade and technical journals are concerned, the circulation lists are not always as extensive and accurate as is sometimes thought. Many are often directed to libraries, academics, students—indeed to all manner of non-commercial people.

TRADE ASSOCIATIONS AND INSTITUTIONS

Such bodies often publish, or will provide, a comprehensive list of members.

NEW APPOINTMENTS AND NEWS

A large number of publications carry news items of new appointments which clearly identify prospects for a mailing list.

DIRECT MAIL AGENCIES

There are a number of commercial organizations which provide an extensive service for direct mail users. The service usually offers some hundreds of specialized lists which are in effect available for hire; the mechanics of addressing, enclosing, franking and posting the mailing pieces; a creative design studio; also sometimes a research unit to help in list building if one is not already in existence.

There is little doubt that with the right degree of co-operation and understanding, a direct mail house is very useful: indeed sometimes almost essential. It is necessary, however, for a client to realize that with many campaigns in hand at any one moment it is not possible for a direct mail company to give the kind of attention to minute detail that the client would himself, and it is therefore important to give a most thorough briefing with written confirmation in order to avoid misunderstandings.

Finally it should be realized that with very few exceptions a mailing house has access to only the same sources of lists as anyone else. Given time a company can usually produce a better list itself. What it probably cannot do is process it more efficiently.

COMPUTER SERVICES AND LIST BROKERS

With the widespread availability of computers and word-processing machines the use of direct mail is becoming more widespread. This is because the development and maintenance of in-house mailing lists has become much more simple, as has the reproduction of personalized letters. Coding and fast retrieval is now available to companies with only the most elementary equipment.

Computers have also become part of the standard equipment for direct mail houses which have become more sophisticated in the storage of and access to, their mailing lists. Some outside services have specialized to the extent that they handle only mailing lists. Such list brokers in practice are in the business of simply selling labels.

UNUSUAL SOURCES

For each product group and each market there may well be a variety of unusual sources of lists. Announcements of births and marriages for instance, or graduations at university. Co-operation with complementary trades can provide a source such as the names of people buying turfs as a sales lead to a company selling lawn-mowers. Other useful sources might be shareholders, rating lists, return guarantee cards and records of companies.

Campaign planning

Having defined the market and identified the names and addresses of people who will influence the purchasing decision, it is now necessary to consider the form which the campaign should take. A number of factors need to be examined in order to formulate the most effective campaign mix. The number of shots is going to depend on how complex the sales message is and also the percentage return which is set as a target. If 3 per cent is required (a common but highly misleading norm) then one shot may be adequate. Two shots would possibly bring 6 per cent, or maybe 5 per cent, since the law of diminishing returns clearly applies, particularly on a short time base. If there are six major selling features, and these are not well known, it will be necessary perhaps to send out six shots.

The same general guidelines as used in a press advertising campaign clearly apply but with the additional opportunities of attention, space and colour. In the end it is experience which determines the final plan. This is not the subjective experience of whim or fancy, but rather the building up of a set of data relating to the reaction of prospects to a given mailing technique. One of the interesting characteristics of a direct mail operation is the opportunity to carry out test mailings to small samples of a given list. In this way the likely reaction of the entire list can be determined before becoming committed to the total campaign or indeed the total expenditure.

A direct mail shot can vary from a cheaply duplicated circular to a personally signed letter, to an impressive colour brochure, to a bottle of whisky, to a quarter-sectioned hydraulic cylinder weighing fifty pounds and costing rather more. It is all a matter of deciding what impact it is required to achieve and what is necessary in order to achieve it. Given adequately experienced and able creative people, there is considerable scope for novelty and therefore impact, particularly in comparison with press advertising which is limited in size and material. In direct mail, one can select from a number of materials, choose from a variety of sizes, use three dimensions, and even sound, smell and chemical reaction. A further extremely useful aspect of mailing is that an actual sample can be sent out of the product itself.

The use of the mail is not fundamentally a requirement of direct mail. Circular distribution has already been mentioned though this is clearly more relevant to consumer promotions. Maybe the industrial equivalent is to use telex, or even fax, for distributing an advertising message. This is fast, accurate and likely to have high impact. Care needs to be exercised as recipients could regard this as intruding on their privacy, much as they react to telephone selling.

Whatever form a shot may take, however, it must be emphasized that it does not begin to achieve purchasing impact until it reaches the right person.

An undirected leaflet in a personally addressed envelope may be put in the right file in the mailing room, but without the envelope the leaflet is directionless and will end up who knows where? An individually typed letter addressed to ICI and starting Dear Sirs, may just as well not be sent at all. Similarly a letter to the Chief Buyer of Unilever is hardly likely to reach the person one is trying to influence. It is essential to determine carefully and precisely whom the message is to reach, whether by name or job title, then to address both the envelope and the enclosure to that person.

TIMING

As with press advertising there is an opportunity to achieve a cumulative build up of awareness by sending out a series of shots. The actual number will be determined by factors mentioned earlier. A further consideration is the period of time over which the campaign is likely to extend. If for a year, and if continuity is required, then it may emerge that a monthly interval is an optimum time. If for a longer period, say several years, then perhaps a quarterly interval is adequate, as with a house magazine. Even less frequent mailings can be effective: for instance a calendar or a diary once a year.

It may be necessary to achieve results quickly and in this case the campaign can comprise a series of rapid shots at weekly or even at daily intervals. When considering this kind of saturation it is useful to recall the personal nature of direct mail. One of the pitfalls, which is also one of the strengths, is the fact that the recipient of a direct mail piece tends, rightly, to regard it as an individual and personal communication from the sender. Consequently the receipt of five letters from the same firm on the same subject on five consecutive days may achieve impact, but may well alienate the prospect. Similarly a generalization which does not apply to a particular person in a press advertisement may well cause offence if written into a letter. For instance, a letter inviting an existing customer to try out a product which he or she has been using for years is a good way of losing the business which already exists.

In calculating timing it is useful to put oneself in the place of the buyer and consider the most likely reaction to a proposed plan.

A good deal of emphasis is sometimes placed on the best day of the week and the best time of the year to send out direct mail. It is argued for instance that Monday is a bad day both psychologically and because it is a heavy day for incoming post; also that Friday is a bad day because people's minds are turning towards the weekend. Another argument is that August is a bad month and, of course Christmas time is poor. In modern marketing there is little place for conjecture. It is the function of a direct mail practitioner to accept such theories as possible, but to test them, to verify them or reject them; Christmas time after all is a very good time for Christmas trees.

COSTS

Costs, absolute and relative, are vital factors when establishing the advertising and indeed the marketing mix.

A full page in a technical magazine for instance might cost £2000 given a circulation of 10000. This would be a cost per copy of 20p.

There may well be more than one reader per copy which brings the cost down to say 8p per reader. It is known, however, that a 10 per cent 'noted' rating is a reasonable average, i.e. only one in ten readers will actually notice the advertisement, and of these perhaps a third will read most of the copy. This can put the cost of real communication up to £2.40 per prospect.

Going to the other extreme, the cost of getting a selling argument across by means of a salesperson may well be £150 per prospect, or more. An exhibition may produce results at a lower figure, but both these situations afford the opportunity of face-to-face selling, which is likely to be more effective.

How does direct mail stand up in comparison with other channels of communication? Distribution of a cheap circular to households can be done at around 30p per unit. Using the postal services and a well-produced letter, maybe including a simple leaflet, the cost is going to be of the order of 50p. Thereafter the costs rise as the mailing increases in quality and sophistication.

If a campaign is designed largely to obtain sales leads a different set of figures will be obtained. It is not uncommon in press advertising of capital goods to find the cost of an enquiry ranging between £5 and £50. With direct mail a 5 per cent response where the unit mailing cost was 40p would result in a cost per enquiry of £8.

It may fairly be said that, all things being equal, there is not much to choose between press advertising and direct mail in terms of cost. If this is so, however, it is strange that so many promotional budgets allocate very much larger sums of money to press. One reason may be that direct mail is a good deal more complex and difficult to set up and that it is far more likely to go wrong. Another reason is simply that insufficient attention has been given to the value of this medium in relation to others and that its results have not been so carefully measured and analysed. And anyway it doesn't pay agencies a commission.

Setting targets

Before the position of measuring and assessing results can be reached, it is necessary to set targets. Just as, in an efficient business, management by objectives is an accepted way of operating, so in direct mail the starting point must be to define the objectives—in measurable, meaningful terms.

As with press advertising the objectives must be realistic. There will be occasions when an increase in sales can result directly from a mailing operation, but more often in industrial promotions the effect on sales is going to be indirect and less tangible. Thus it is necessary to set a target which can be more directly related. Perhaps the intention is to get sales leads which, in turn, will enable the sales force to convert them into orders. In this situation it may be unrealistic to measure the efficacy of the direct mail campaign in terms of sales. The product may not be right, or the price; alternatively the leads may not be followed up efficiently. If the primary objective is to secure sales leads, then the campaign must be assessed in these terms.

In the course of time it will be possible, for a given type of campaign, to establish norms of performance. These will vary considerably between one product group and another, and between markets, but even if a norm has not been established it is nevertheless valuable to set a figure against which performance can be measured.

A mailing campaign to a thousand prospects may take as an objective 'to secure a hundred sales leads'. This gives to the executive concerned, and the copywriter and visualizer, a clear statement of what the operation is all about. It also indicates to marketing and sales management exactly the role this campaign is intended to play. It facilitates a cost comparison with other media and this has a long-term value in shaping future media mixes. As the campaign proceeds it becomes apparent whether or not the objective is likely to be achieved or whether the operation needs to be strengthened, cut back, or indeed stopped, to avoid wasting money either because it is totally successful or a complete failure.

Obtaining sales leads is, perhaps, easy: a campaign designed to strengthen a company's reputation may be more difficult. This does not, however, lessen the need for setting targets. Indeed, with image-building campaigns, unless a plan is made beforehand to measure the results, it will be impossible to begin to evaluate the effect of the expenditure. In the case of such a campaign the objective must be quantified even if very broadly, for instance 'to be rated among the top three suppliers of industrial paints'. This will necessitate a minimum of two investigations: first to find out the present rating and then in due course the change in position after the campaign.

A campaign may set out to establish a realization among buyers that a certain brand-name connotes a particular product—and often a product with pre-defined benefits. This is a classic softening-up operation before the field force goes in, and calls for a saturation campaign which will continue until the objective has been achieved.

For every direct mail campaign then there must be a specific purpose, formally stated and in terms which can be measured. The methods of measurement to be adopted will be an integral part of the plan.

DIRECT RESPONSE MARKETING

There is some confusion as to the difference between direct mail (DM) and direct response marketing (DRM): indeed some people regard the terms as synonymous. This is unfortunate since they are fundamentally different.

Direct response marketing is an activity in which prospects are invited to place an order directly as a response to an offer in an advertisement or a direct mail shot. The order is placed directly with the marketing organization without a salesperson as intermediary, and it is dispatched directly to the customer by post or freight without the intermediary of a retail outlet. There is also another term in use, direct response advertising, which refers to any advertisement that seeks to secure an order directly.

Direct response marketing is said to be the fastest growing sector of marketing activities, and many examples are to be found in the Sunday colour magazines and in the Saturday editions of national newspapers. These, however, are all in the consumer goods field and so far there is not much evidence of its suitability for industrial goods.

A growing problem is the use of the terms 'database marketing' and 'direct marketing'. Users of the terms usually intend them to be synonymous with direct mail.

Checklist

1. Have the target audiences been defined?
2. Are adequate databases available?
3. Can the people be (a) named, or (b) designated?
4. Do you plan to use a direct mail agency. If so, have you checked (a) the origin and (b) the nature of their lists, and (c) whether they are up to date, accurate and comprehensive?
5. In producing the brief have you defined

    (a) The objective of the campaign?
    (b) The number of shots?
    (c) The form they should take?
    (d) Frequency and timing?
    (e) Use of reply-paid material?
    (f) A follow-up to a reply?

6. Is there a system for names to be deleted from the list as replies are received?
7. Have quantified targets been set?
8. Are the means for comparison of performance clearly specified?
9. Has the field force been given advance notice of the campaign?
10. Has consideration been given to an initial test mailing?

EXHIBITIONS

Exhibitions vary considerably in size and scope from a small show with perhaps twenty or thirty modest stands to vast international fairs with a thousand or more exhibitors covering a product range across the entire industrial sector.

The significance of exhibitions in the industrial promotional budget may not be great but, looking at some of the larger events, it is evident that the individual expenditure on many stands is of a high order indeed. While a budget of a hundred or so pounds may be possible with some of the smaller exhibitions, the costs rise easily into tens of thousands and more with the bigger shows.

It is strange to find that so little is known about the usefulness of exhibitions, that they are so often an expression of faith rather than fact, with such factors as size of stand and budget determined intuitively by some senior executive. Evidence of this is to be found by discussing the matter with exhibitors and is confirmed by the random way in which in one year a company invests in a substantial stand, next year pulls out altogether, then later comes back with an even larger display.

There tends to be a progression in the evolution of a particular exhibition rather like the life-cycle of a new product. Initially an exhibition satisfies a need which as it grows causes the exhibition to expand. This attracts more visitors and thus more exhibitors, producing a cumulative growth. A further variable at work is the force of competitive prestige. In order to impress customers, exhibitors vie with each other to have the grandest and largest stands and, as this factor develops, so the expense rises until a few of the leaders suddenly realize that the whole thing is uneconomical, and drop out. The example having been set, others follow suit, and the exhibition goes into a period of decline in which it may stagnate, disintegrate, fragment or disappear altogether.

There is probably more money wasted at exhibitions than in any other medium, a paradox since fundamentally the concept of an exhibition is to save money by getting face to face with large numbers of buyers in greater numbers per salesperson-day than could ever be achieved on the road.

The exhibition industry itself may be partly to blame. It breaks down into three broad groups: the organizers, the venue proprietors and the contractors.

Exhibitions are arranged by a wide variety of organizations ranging from commercial exhibition companies to trade associations, publishers and learned bodies. Their function is to hire a hall, then let out spaces to exhibitors at a rate which will bring a profit. Beyond this they may involve themselves in conducting pre-publicity and providing some service during the show. Only the most progressive organizers will set up facilities for providing intelligence for exhibitors on the number and nature of visitors, their length of stay, their attitudes towards different stands and exhibits, their wants and criticisms. Furthermore there is little effort to discipline exhibitors into containing costs by, for instance, restricting stand sizes or imposing shell schemes, as in common practice in the United States. Exhibition organizers sometimes play a passive and short-term role which is not helpful to exhibitors and in the long term does not help themselves.

Exhibition halls are often inadequate, and this, though perhaps not the fault of anyone in particular, points the need for exhibitors to assess carefully the value of each venue. Exhibition contractors, the people who construct the stands, are involved in very high labour costs, with the result that a stand built to last for a week will often cost more than a luxury house. There is considerable room for improving the cost-effectiveness of exhibitions and there is little doubt that the exhibition industry as a whole could make an important contribution. This is largely outside the control of an individual exhibitor, but this should not preclude collective action by groups of companies. Moreover, to be aware of areas of high expense at least enables a company to exert maximum control and scrutiny in obtaining good value for money.

Exhibitors

Before turning to the positive role of exhibitions in the marketing operation, it is unfortunately necessary to press this negative theme a little further by extending it to the exhibitor. Earlier in this book it has been pointed out that much in marketing communications has hitherto been intuitive, without any logical objective, and without any data to support decisions. Exhibitions are equally susceptible to this danger, as is borne out by a booklet from the Institute of Directors in which what it terms dangers and temptations to exhibitors are set out.

1. An exhibition should not be looked upon as an isolated event.
2. Never enter an exhibition—no matter how inexpensive it appears to be—unless it fulfils some clearly defined marketing objective.

3. An exhibition is not the occasion for giving a once-off opportunity to polish up a tarnished corporate image.
4. Prestige is never a sufficient reason for appearing at exhibitions.
5. Don't base exhibition plans on the theory 'if the competitors are there we have to be'.
6. Don't try one exhibition just 'to see how it goes'.
7. An exhibition should not be looked upon as an opportunity for senior members of the company to have a free holiday or a booze-up with their old cronies—it is an occasion for the people in the firing line, no matter how junior they may be, to do a hard-hitting job of work.
8. Don't exhibit at all if you have to do it on the cheap—in money or executive time. This is not to say that many exhibitions are not inexpensive—but be sure you assign adequate money for the job expected to be done.
9. Remember—it's ten times easier to start exhibiting than to stop, once you have an exhibition programme under way.

To the above 'rules' there are a number of other points worthy of consideration with a view to increasing the effectiveness of an exhibition.

10. Regard an exhibition stand as a three-dimensional advertisement.
11. Build in really effective corporate identification.
12. Pay special attention to lighting the key points of the stand and to the writing of copy panels.
13. Design a single focal point visually and in terms of traffic flow.
14. Allow for staffing at the level of approximately two people per 10 square metres.
15. Plan in advance for fast post-exhibition follow-up.
16. At each show make a formal evaluation of competitors' activities.

Inter-media comparisons

An exhibition is simply a channel of persuasion which is available as an ingredient in the marketing mix. It must therefore fit into the marketing plan and have a specific purpose, or not be used at all. It has certain characteristics which make it more or less attractive depending upon the requirements of the campaign. It is useful to examine these and in so doing relate them to other media with which it will be required to combine.

SELLING EFFICIENCY

Fundamentally an exhibition should be highly efficient in selling terms since it assembles in one place maybe tens of thousands of buyers who if they can be attracted to a stand will facilitate a 'call rate' far in excess of normal. A salesman on a stand may well talk to forty or fifty buyers in the course of a day—a factor ten times greater than the norm. And think of the psychological advantage of the buyer calling on the salesforce and asking for information. A recent study[1] showed that the average cost per contact was around £50, i.e. one third the cost of a sales call.

IMPACT

Compared for instance with press advertising, impact is obviously higher, since an exhibition has the opportunity to compress into one activity the whole selling operation—attention, interest, persuasion, desire to purchase and indeed the placing of an order.

DEMONSTRATION

Here an exhibition scores even over sales visits, since with heavy equipment in particular the opportunity exists to give far more comprehensive demonstrations than can ever be achieved by a travelling salesperson.

TIME-SCALE

This acts in two ways: firstly one may well have to wait a year or two for an exhibition to take place; secondly, setting this factor aside, an exhibition can provide the chance to influence a very large part of a market in a very short space of time.

MARKET PENETRATION

Having regard to the complex nature of the decision-making units in industrial companies, exhibitions often bring to the surface many of the hidden influences in the purchasing process—the engineer, chemist, designer, factory manager, as well as directors.

COMPANY IMAGE

The company can be presented in all its aspects at one and the same time, enabling a customer to see it as a whole—its products, manufacturing facilities, subsidiaries and associates, and most important its senior management.

MARKET DEVELOPMENT

A unique opportunity is presented for uncovering a wide variety of uses for products which lead to the identification of new markets. Similarly an interchange of views on products often leads to modifications which give rise to the development of new products.

COST

It is important to cost an exhibition fully, to add together rental, stand construction, staff, promotional material, entertaining, pre-publicity and so on. An unsophisticated show of a few hundred pounds can have a very high degree of cost-effectiveness. One costing say seventy or eighty thousand pounds needs a great deal of justification. The real cost however is the unit cost, that is, the cost per enquiry or the cost per contact and this in relation to the unit costs of other media.

Setting the objectives

These must be set down in writing as part of the overall promotional strategy and must incorporate targets that are precise, and capable of being attained and measured. For instance an exhibition may be chosen as the launching platform for a new product, say a piece of equipment for food processing. There may be 500 companies who could buy this product and, with perhaps four people likely to be involved in the buying decision, one arrives at a total of 2000 people to be contacted. The setting of the target will in fact be determined by the nature of the exhibition, in that a popular and well-established one may well be visited by representatives of half the industry or more whereas a smaller or untried one may attract only a very small percentage.

Further factors in setting targets in this instance are the interest of the product or service itself and the prestige of the company. These will determine the willingness of people to put themselves out to attend the show and visit the stand.

In the light of such factors and perhaps with previous experience the first target may be to make face-to-face contact with 500 people who represent potential customers and to secure an entrée for a subsequent sales visit. A secondary goal could be to obtain the general goodwill of the industry as a whole by distributing to interested parties 5000 leaflets describing a new piece of equipment.

Over and above the primary objective of an exhibition stand will be a number of supplementary requirements which should be catered for only so long as they do not act as a distraction or as a negative influence. The broad range of company activities may need to be put across to show how it backs up a new product. The extent to which modern plant and machinery is used may be another feature, with examples of accuracy, reliability and quality control. Provision may be made for conducting marketing research; perhaps entertaining facilities are needed for customers in other product categories.

At the other extreme, the need may be to provide first-class entertainment for only a small number of very large customers. Such an example could be

Table 6.1 Objectives of an exhibition

Whilst sales leads are the most popular goal, there are many other objectives as the following US research shows. Exhibitors went into exhibitions in order to:

Generate qualified leads	71%
Maintain an image	63%
Intensify awareness	60%
Establish a presence	56%
Introduce a new product	31%
Generate immediate sales	25%
Judge reaction to new product	13%
Provide dealer support	8%
Discover new applications	5%
Stimulate secondary markets	4%
Recruit distributors	3%

Table 6.2 Reasons for visiting an exhibition

As against exhibitors motives, the following were the reasons attributed to visitors for attending a show:

To evaluate new products	56%
To see specific products or companies	23%
To obtain product information	13%
General interest	10%
To attend seminars	6%

the Farnborough or Paris Air Shows where, frequently, there is little emphasis on products, but rather a very well set up 'soft sell' operation in which VIP customers are provided with pleasant facilities to relax and enjoy the display with hard business left to another time and place. The objective in this instance may be to provide an opportunity for 150 top customers to meet the chairman and to spend one of a number of agreeable afternoons with him.

Planning an exhibition

Having defined the objectives of an exhibition in quantitative terms it is necessary to build into the event a maximum of efficiency in order to achieve the required result at least cost. This can be planned by examining every stage in the development of an exhibition promotion.

Certainly a primary factor in participating in an exhibition is to capitalize on what may be described as a captive audience. The audience, however, is rarely captive in the sense that cinema viewers are; indeed their movements along a gangway are often fleeting and transitory; an attractive stand helps somewhat to overcome this.

It is worth while to regard the established visitors, who will come anyway, as a bonus which adds to the effectiveness of the operation, but the essential task for an exhibitor is to take all possible steps to ensure that his key prospective customers are notified in advance of what will be on show, how much their presence will be welcomed, and the ways in which they will stand to benefit.

An exhibition stand can justify a separate campaign of its own, designed to obtain visits by the right people defined in the marketing plan. This calls for the usual letter stickers, advertisement inserts, preview editorials and a plan showing where the stand is located, but this is what everyone else is already doing. A good deal more is required if the full benefits are to be obtained, and this calls for a campaign of its own using all suitable channels of persuasion—invitations from a director, backed up by personal contact from the sales force, special press advertising, a direct mail build-up and some special incentive.

The fact is however that many firms do little individually to publicize their events. Evidence of this is to be found in a piece of research conducted in the United States but with general application anywhere (Fig. 6.1).

Just what is required will depend on the objectives of the exhibition stand, and as has been said earlier these will be quantified, thus providing a basis for developing the campaign plan, and also eventually a mark against which the exhibition can be evaluated.

It is only when 'to have 500 potential buyers call upon our stand' has been written down and agreed that the size of the task becomes apparent. The exhibition campaign plan can only then be put in hand and tailored carefully to match the need—no more and no less.

SITE AND SIZE

An examination of any exhibition hall will bring to light the fact that some areas are popular while others are not. What is missing is factual data on the traffic flow at various places in a hall at various times. This is vital and one should look to exhibition organizers to supply such information. In its absence, it must rest with the exhibitor to extract his own information, such as traffic flow in main and subsidiary gangways, and in upper floors as compared with the ground floor. Interviews with visitors can for instance establish whether they visited the gallery, how much time they spent in the hall altogether and how valuable they found the exhibition. Research can easily be extended into determining what other channels of persuasion they are exposed to, for instance which trade magazines they read. Such information enables one to judge the relationship between a given exhibition and other media including, of course, other exhibitions.

Pre-show promotion techniques (83% of all companies did some pre-show promotion)

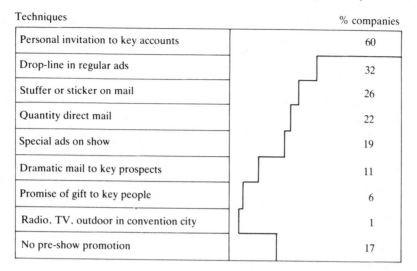

Techniques	% companies
Personal invitation to key accounts	60
Drop-line in regular ads	32
Stuffer or sticker on mail	26
Quantity direct mail	22
Special ads on show	19
Dramatic mail to key prospects	11
Promise of gift to key people	6
Radio, TV, outdoor in convention city	1
No pre-show promotion	17

Figure 6.1   Pre-show promotion techniques in the United States (*Source:* Trade Show Bureau Research Report Study No 4

As to the size of a stand, the answer is simply to make it as small as possible consistent with the laid-down objectives. Too much regard is probably paid to highly subjective comparisons with the size and appearance of competitors' stands, a factor which is probably much less significant to the visitor than the exhibitor. If, of course, the objective is primarily to impress upon people that a company is the largest and most important in the industry, then a large and impressive stand could be justified.

It is important to begin by listing what facilities are essential and what are the minimum areas required, rather than first determining the square footage and then fitting things in as best one can. The shape of available sites is often an important consideration, and the number of open sides can be a vital factor, if only because an island stand has up to four times the display area of a wall stand.

DESIGN

Closely related to size and site is the design of a stand: indeed it is difficult to see how a stand can be efficiently conceived without some regard first being given to layout if not design.

It has been said that an exhibition stand should be regarded as a three-dimensional advertisement. It follows that the design should be tested in the same way, having regard to the fact that its cost can well be considerably greater than that of an advertisement. What is the 'single selling idea', what eye-catching headline is needed, what should the body copy say, and who should write it, and what illustration should be used? It is strange that the layout of a stand, the words on copy panels and the products and illustrations are often left to in-company staff to determine and produce, whereas for an advertisement a whole battalion of specialists will be employed.

A number of skills therefore need to be brought to bear since a stand involves construction, décor, advertising messages or selling copy, display, as well as an optimum environment for face-to-face selling. Too often it is evident that only a number of these aspects has received adequate consideration, for example, the large number of people who will walk past the stand, but will not be prepared to step on it and thus become exposed to the attention of sales staff. For these people, usually the majority, it is vital that the design be in the form of a three-dimensional advertisement. It must incorporate a means of attracting attention, it must convey at a distance, and at a glance, a good selling message which will stimulate interest, and it must follow this with descriptive and selling copy which will cause a person to want to read more and to enquire for further information. To a person concerned with advertisement design, such an approach may be second nature and in any case there will be close co-operation with a copywriter whose very function it is to express selling messages in a crisp compelling manner. Exhibition designers may sometimes be primarily specialists in architecture and décor rather than advertising, and the copy is more often than not written by a sales manager or a member of the advertising department who would not lay claim to being an expert copywriter. Yet the space to be filled will cost considerably more than an equivalent press advertisement, or even a campaign.

The layout of a stand is critical to its success in terms of its laid down objectives. Does the stand need to be designed so as to attract a maximum of visitors to it? In which case it must be open and inviting. Does it alternatively have to function primarily as a meeting point for important customers who will relax and refresh themselves in the convivial company of senior members of staff? That may call for a largely closed-in stand where access is open to a carefully selected and screened number of people. Perhaps a major objective is to distribute a large number of leaflets to visitors, in which case it just isn't good enough to lay out the leaflets in whatever vacant space there happens to be. No, the whole stand design in that case must be centred around making it as easy as possible for the passer-by to pick up a leaflet. It's the equivalent of a reply-paid coupon in an advertisement.

For designers to have the best chance of producing a stand which will be effective it is important that their briefing should be brought fully into the overall objectives of the exhibition and be provided with a complete list of facilities required, products to be exhibited, displays to be featured, and finally every single word of copy with an indication of emphasis and dominance of each part.

The sequence of events which should be followed is agreement on layout, visuals, a model if necessary, then working drawings and specification. Each stage must be considered and approved in detail if extra costs are to be avoided. If top management are going to express a point of view, it is now that this should take place before any construction is started.

STAND ADMINISTRATION AND STAFFING

It will be found most effective to designate one senior executive as stand manager for the whole period of the show, and for that person to have a written brief. The job will entail achieving the written objectives and it is only fair therefore that he or she should be involved at an early stage in the development of the stand. Such a person will in effect be the captain of the ship, responsible for motivating sales staff, maintaining discipline, looking to stand cleanliness and maintenance, ensuring an adequate supply of literature, and the hundred and one things that go to make the stand a dynamic part of a marketing operation.

It is surprising how often the staff are not given an adequate briefing on their responsibilities and functions. It is enlightening to go to any exhibition and visit a series of stands in order to assess the level of sales service. It is unlikely that any attention will be given in anything other than a minority of cases and generally speaking the larger the stand the poorer the service. Yet it is elementary to include in the exhibition briefing the instruction (always assuming this is desirable) that everyone stepping on to a stand should be greeted with an offer of help, indeed that anyone even showing an interest from the gangway should be given some attention.

The failure of sales staff to perform effectively on an exhibition stand has been well explained in a feature published by *Industrial Marketing*.

> The sales situation at a trade show is the reverse of a field sales call—the prospect comes to you. You have a fraction of the normal time to present your facts. The salesperson has to make more presentations per hour than he or she might make in a day in the field.
>
> Trade show selling is a different sell, and many salespeople simply don't know how to sell in a trade show. They feel like salt water fish that have been placed in a fresh water lake and have difficulty adapting in order to survive.
>
> It's a frightening change. A rapid presentation style has to be adopted. An adjustment must be made to the environmental change. There is seldom the security of an appointment call or sales schedule. A change in priorities must be made. A seasoned salesperson with a good list of steady clients is suddenly faced with a new 'cold call' fear.
>
> Is it any wonder that when the sales rep's regular customer comes into the exhibit, the sales rep may expand the visiting time in order to avoid the unpleasantness of the trade show's difficult environment?

Exhibitionitis

This is an illness that everyone visiting an exhibition has had but without realizing that it had a name and was well recognized by exhibition professionals. It not only affects visitors, it can also play havoc with exhibitors.

Simply stated, anyone at an exhibition will, after the first hour or so, begin to feel weary of standing or walking to such an extent that his or her normal business drive will give way to an increasingly urgent desire to sit down.

This is an important threat, and an even more important opportunity. The stand can be designed in such a way that staff members can be seated without appearing to have withdrawn from giving service to customers. Alternatively a roster can be drawn up which allows for periods of relaxation. And then for customers a seating arrangement can be made such that without feeling committed or cornered a visitor can sit and relax while discussing his or her particular interest.

'Are you sitting comfortably?' is a slogan which is well worth considering seriously at any exhibition, large or small.

Budgeting

Arriving at an effective and yet economic budget for an exhibition is both difficult and complex. There are of course some short cuts but these do not necessarily produce the best results. They include:

1. What can we afford?
2. What did we spend last year?
3. How much are our competitors spending?
4. Percentage of anticipated sales.

These and other factors are all worthy of consideration, but perhaps the most logical approach is what is known as the task method of budgeting as described in Chapter 3. Here the 'task' to be achieved is analysed in some detail, i.e. a listing of specific objectives. Then in conjunction with the stand designer an outline is produced of what is essential for the achievement of those objectives. This outline covers stand location, size of stand, type of construction, style of presentation, special features and any other requirements. This then gives the minimum requirement and provides the basis of competitive quotations for stand construction.

From research conducted on behalf of British Business Press (1987) a very interesting breakdown of typical exhibition costs was produced. These are given in Table 6.3.

Memorability

Some very interesting work has been done in the United States on the

Table 6.3 Typical exhibition costs. Example 1 is a 30 m² shell-scheme stand, portable exhibits. Example 2 is a 60 m² purpose-built stand, heavy exhibits

	Example 1	Example 2
1. Stand space	3600	6000
2. Stand construction	400	6000
3. Transporting and erecting exhibits	200	1000
4. Stand graphics	800	1500
5. Furniture, flowers, power, telephone, drinks, cleaning, etc.	700	1200
6. Invitations/mailings to prospects	300	500
7. Catalogue and other advertising	1000	2000
8. Leaflets for distribution from stand	500	1500
9. Entertaining costs	500	1000
10. Staff travel subsistence	2000	4000
11. Temporary staff	200	400
12. Unforeseen extras	500	1000
13. Internal meeting hours	1000	2000
Total costs per exhibition	£11 700	£28 100

memorability of an exhibition stand.[2] Its purpose has been to measure just how long an exhibit will remain in the memory of a visitor: also to find what factors affect the degree of memorability.

As can be seen from Figure 6.2 an exhibit is remembered long after the event and indeed it can probably be concluded that exhibitions have a longer retention time than any other medium.

Memorability drops off to around 70 per cent at about five or six weeks but then increases to 75 per cent and remains at that level from eight weeks through fourteen weeks. Exhibitors probably are following up on their enquiries with literature and personal sales calls which reinforce the exhibit memorability.

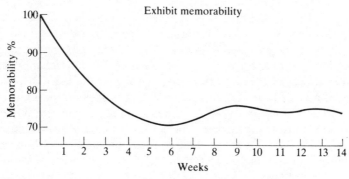

Figure 6.2 Exhibit memorability (USA Trade Show Bureau Report)

Stand staff performance affects memorability the most because the personal contact with visitors creates a strong impact. Stands achieving a high degree of person-to-person contact had higher memorability scores than others. Also the level of awareness of a company was a strong influence on the degree to which visitors remembered visiting an exhibit. In separate analyses of companies considered leaders in their industry or field and companies that spend more money on advertising, their level of memorability was considerably higher than the average.

The type of exhibit approach used is the third major factor affecting memorability. Exhibits using formal or informal product demonstrations generally had higher memorability than static displays.

Perhaps the most important message to come out of this piece of research is that an exhibition investment has a potential value for way outside the duration of the exhibition. The pre-exhibition opportunity to publicize a forthcoming event has always been recognized and exploited to some degree. It may be that exhibitors have not fully capitalized on the favourable opportunity for doing business that exists for many weeks after an exhibition has closed.

Exhibition data form

The exhibition data form (EDF) brings to business, industrial and technical exhibitions the independent, professional auditing procedures which have long been available to the United Kingdom press. Through EDFs, exhibitors have access to accurate, standardized information on exhibition attendance, stand space sold and other useful data on which to appraise exhibitions in the light of their own marketing objectives.

The EDF evolved from the activities of three organizations—the Audit Bureau of Circulation, the Incorporated Society of British Advertisers and the Association of Exhibition Organisers. The scheme is under the overall control of the Council of the ABC which is advised by a Joint Industry Committee (JIC) whose members represent both organizers and exhibitors.

The following details give the broad scope of the data forms. Further information can be obtained from the Audit Bureau of Circulation.

The exhibition data form applies to any business, industrial or technical exhibition which has been accepted for registration by the ABC. The form consists of a basic four pages—three subject to independent audit and one devoted to additional statements by the exhibition organizer. Where space allowed on the printed form is insufficient for the data provided, any section can be expanded and the form enlarged after consultation with the Bureau. All data submitted is subject to further verification by ABC before publication.

MAIN PRODUCT GROUPS/SERVICE

Exhibition organizers are encouraged to give as full a listing as possible of the main product groups and services that were exhibited. This provides a permanent record of the scope of each exhibition and a measure of the success of the exhibition in meeting its original objectives.

TARGET AUDIENCE

The target audience must be defined by the exhibition organizer in advance and the registered free attendance figure includes only those visitors who fall within the target group.

Research at exhibitions

Over and above measurement of the specific value of an exhibition, which is dealt with in the next section, there are many opportunities for research work during an exhibition. Quite simply it can be said that within an exhibition hall for a number of days will be a good sample of a particular market or market segment. There is thus an opportunity to ask questions and obtain answers about any aspect of market opinion, behaviour or motivation that one wishes to pursue. And this at relatively low cost and in a very short space of time.

What are the readership habits of this market segment for instance? A well-tried technique is to compile a short-list of the most likely publications and to make up a flip chart with the front covers of each publication on separate sheets. Interviewers can then stop people at random, or talk to visitors to the stand, asking them 'which of the following publications are read regularly?' Within a few days one has a profile of readership which is often quite different from an existing media plan based upon circulation data and/or intuition.

Another particularly useful research project for an exhibition is to market test a new product. Here the product is on the stand, having been well publicized in advance, and visitors are asked to comment on certain pre-determined criteria such as size, shape, weight, colour, speed, cost, accuracy, performance, and application. Product prototypes can obviously be evaluated in this way as indeed can mere ideas or concepts. The opportunity is particularly attractive to manufacturers of specialized products where their potential market is widely spread and could only be otherwise contacted at very considerable cost.

In general it can be said that whatever information is required about a market can be obtained from an appropriate exhibition provided due allowance is made for the sample not necessarily being representative of the total market.

Visitors on the whole do not seem to mind answering a modest number of questions: in fact many seem to enjoy it. It is important however to ensure that the exhibition organizers are kept fully informed of any proposed research work where this is to be conducted in the public gangway.

Exhibition evaluation

The setting of objectives and evaluation go hand in hand. Given an objective of securing 200 sales leads, evaluation at its simplest is to ask whether that number was achieved, and if not why not. It will readily be seen how important it is to quantify objectives from the outset.

It is obviously not possible to write down in detail all the ways in which an exhibition can be evaluated. And in any case this must depend on the objectives which were set for a particular exhibition. What must be said, however, is that having decided to make an investment in the form of an exhibition it would be the height of business folly not to make a determined effort to measure the return on the investment.

The question of evaluation is dealt with in a very useful publication by ISBA called *Guide for Exhibitors*.[3] Their many recommendations include:

1. Boxes for visiting cards.
2. Enquiry pads with room for literature/sample requests (literature must be sent out immediately while visitors interest is keen and a reply paid card should be included for further information).
3. Visitors book. Noting of general enquiries—not specifically recorded for follow up purposes. It is advised not to use visitors' books in Eastern European countries.
4. Noting names and number of delegates to lectures and/or film shows at exhibitions. Where one is selling over the counter the total sales less stand/ space cost give one the immediate answer.
5. Obtain from the organizers the total number of visitors to the show and compare this with previous years.
6. Note whether your presentation really does stop the crowd.
7. Note the level of activity on your stand compared to others in the near vicinity.

SALES LITERATURE

There are opposing schools of thought on the use of sales literature at exhibitions, some holding that if it is put out, people tend to pick it up indiscriminately, and that if it is not put out people are encouraged to make enquiries; others contend that the more literature distributed the better.

There are good reasons for producing something in the way of an exhibition 'give away' which should be displayed so that people have easy access to it, but which will also include the offer to send on, say, the main catalogue as a means of obtaining future sales leads. Since, however, much of an industrial marketing communications campaign is aimed at getting sales literature into the hands of prospective buyers, it is important that this opportunity be used to the full on a properly planned basis. A jumble of sales leaflets scattered around on a few tables can hardly be said to be maximizing a selling opportunity.

Private exhibitions

An important trend in this field is to mount an exhibition on an individual basis, sometimes to coincide with a public one in the near vicinity, sometimes entirely independently. A further variation is for a number of firms with complementary product ranges to combine and share expenses, a particularly attractive solution where they share common markets.

The reason for the development of private exhibitions lies partly in the spiralling costs of participating in a public exhibition and partly in the degree of attention which can be given to visitors in surroundings which are usually a good deal more comfortable than an exhibition hall, without the distractions of hundreds of other exhibitors, and avoiding the physical and mental exhaustion which most visitors experience at any major show.

Consider for example a medium-sized stand at a national exhibition. The total cost for an area of, say 100–150 m^2 may well be of the order of £50 000. Such an event if staged in a nearby hotel may provide three or four times the area for half the cost in a relaxed atmosphere, with far superior reception and entertainment facilities. Moreover, the layout could be such that each visitor is greeted personally, conducted around the entire display, and questioned in depth to find out particular interests and to determine future sales action.

Where a company has a limited market, large numbers of people at a public exhibition looking around for general interest can seriously impair the efficiency of the sales staff on duty. The staff at a private show are able to relax, are more likely to be able to carry out an effective selling job, and can give special attention to major customers and to the press, perhaps in a private suite adjoining the exhibition area. Furthermore, competitors cannot easily intrude to probe for details of new products and new selling approaches.

Partisans of the private exhibition will point to more and more advantages such as not having to contend with the difficulties of restrictive labour practices at exhibition halls, being able to set up a show at a time to suit oneself, not having to pay officials to obtain special services. Certainly there are important advantages.

There is, however, one basic benefit of a trade show that does not apply to a private one, namely that with very little effort on the part of an exhibitor a good proportion of a potential market may have the opportunity of coming face to face with one's products.

It would seem, therefore, that to justify a private exhibition instead of a public one, the potential market will be relatively small, say a few hundred, and certainly no more than a few thousand, with all the purchasing influences within that market well defined. Furthermore, there must be sufficient incentive to persuade buyers to make the effort of a special call, even though the venue is fairly close to the exhibition hall.

If, for example, a new company was launching a range of resistors which had a very wide potential application in the electrical and electronic industries, it would probably benefit by using the established audience of one of the major national or international exhibitions to secure a maximum of sales leads, and indeed to gain valuable market intelligence on the reaction to the new range.

Alternatively if the product was a new piece of equipment for carton manufacturers of whom there were only a few hundred prospects, and these very well defined, a private show might be much the most effective method of exhibiting.

Travelling exhibitions

There may be advantages in moving away from the idea of attaching a private exhibition to a public one, and simply setting up an exhibition in its own right. It might be in one location or, more likely, it would be staged in a number of places near the major potential sources of business. The operation can be efficient since, once the exhibition equipment has been assembled, it is a relatively easy matter to move on to another location. Hotels are generally co-operative in accommodating such ventures and provincial rates can be very competitive. A disadvantage is that a good deal of sales force time, and management, is tied down by these events, and this time must be justified by an adequate level of visitors of worthwhile calibre. Once again it is necessary to set targets, compare costs, and as soon as an operation begins to fail, either take corrective action or put a stop to the project.

Trailers and caravans can provide an alternative or sometimes a supplement to the staging of round-the-country exhibitions. They are also of particular value for export promotions. Indeed there is a good deal of scope for initiative in the field of travelling exhibitions, and the use of railways, barges, ships and aeroplanes has not been anything like exploited to the full. The sheer novelty of such ventures can do much to ensure the success of the operation.

Checklist

The checklist has been divided into two parts for convenience—pre-exhibition and post-exhibition.

PRE-EXHIBITION

1. Has a proposed exhibition been examined from the point of view of:
   (a) The likely audience to be reached
   (b) The extent of competition
   (c) Location and accessibility of the site
   (d) Promotional activities by the organizers
   (e) Entertainment facilities?

2. Does the exhibition form part of an integrated marketing plan?
3. Has a written objective been produced for the intended exhibition stand?
4. Have all the relevant people been brought into the planning of the exhibition, for instance; sales management, advertising agency, designer, copywriter, R&D and transport department?
5. Has consideration been given to:
   (a) Site, location and size
   (b) Display requirements
   (c) Own entertaining facilities
   (d) Sales literature dispensers
   (e) Exhibits
   (f) Construction
   (g) Stand management
   (h) Staffing
   (i) Planned approach to visitors
   (j) Sales follow-up?

6. Has pre-publicity been organized to ensure a maximum attendance?
7. Has special provision been made for receiving:
   (a) The press
   (b) Overseas visitors?

8. Has a detailed schedule been produced of all activities leading up to the show, including the necessary action for its duration, and termination?
9. In budgeting for an exhibition, have all the costs been included, for example sales staff's time, preparation of exhibits and their transportation?
10. Have you considered how best to exploit photography in:
   (a) Products
   (b) Product applications
   (c) Own factory and processes
   (d) News and events
   (e) People and personalities
   (f) Prestige?

11. Has the use of editorial publicity been established as an integral part of the organizer's press office operation?

POST-EXHIBITION

1. Was the attendance up to target in terms of total numbers, industry category, job status, buying power, etc?
2. What was the cost per 'sales call' or demonstration?
3. Were the numbers entertained satisfactory in quantity and quality?
4. Were any sales objectives met?
5. How many new sales leads were obtained and have these been followed up?
6. How much sales literature was distributed and did this meet the set targets?
7. Did you gain any new contacts regarding decision-makers 'behind the scenes'?
8. What did you learn about your competitors' activities?
9. Was editorial coverage up to target?
10. Were the exhibits delivered, installed and removed on time?
11. Was the stand construction completed on time and did it in every way function to your satisfaction?
12. How did the stand compare with competitors in overall effectiveness, in visitor traffic and in cost?
13. What new market/product knowledge did you gain out of the show?
14. Were you within budget? If not, why not?
15. How did all the above factors compare with the last time you were at this show, and with any other relevant exhibitions?

References

1. Centre for Leisure and Tourism Studies (London 1991).
2. The UK Exhibition Industry, The Facts, Exhibition Industry Federation, 1990.
3. ISBA (London 1993).

7.

LITERATURE

It is a common failing that people believe that others outside their company know far more about it and its products than in fact they do. They also expect customers to have a well-balanced and well-informed view of the company's business as a matter of course and to have an intense interest in even the most trivial aspects of a company's operations.

The preparation of a publications or literature strategy can do much to ensure that there is full information about every important aspect of a company's operations and its products or services.

Planning, production and distribution

It is an unfortunate fact that the publication of company literature is often *ad hoc*, unplanned, hurried, ill-conceived and sometimes quite inappropriate. To be effective and efficient, literature must be part of the marketing and corporate strategy. This means quite simply that every single publication must stem from a defined objective which starts with an outline of the audience to be reached, the method of distribution to be employed, and the basic message which it is required to deliver.

It is, however, wrong to suppose that given this start, the production of a well-conceived range of literature will solve the communications problems. It is more than likely that less than 25 per cent of literature, however efficiently distributed, is ever read at all, and certainly page traffic studies of magazines confirm this proportion. With these discouraging statistics, more and more importance centres on what is produced and its quality.

PLANNING

Publications in industry often run late, and even when a production schedule exists it is gradually compressed so that the final printing stage—in a sense the most important of all, and certainly the most expensive—is rushed to the extent that quality suffers and errors creep in. The reason is nearly always bad planning, or at least planning which has lost direction.

The first stage in effective planning is to ensure that the preparation of a piece of literature is carried out in exactly the right sequence. The objectives must be written and agreed before a writer is briefed. A synopsis or outline must be produced before the copy is started and, finally, every single word of copy must be approved before a designer takes over. This is not to say that the designer does not enter the procedure until this stage. The designer should be an integral part of the team from the outset and must work in closest co-operation with writer and executive. But layout, as a general rule, does not start until writing is both complete and fully agreed with everyone who is required to express an opinion.

Presentation of design must vary according to the nature of a job, but it is important in maintaining a time schedule that design work is progressive in the sense that ideas and treatments receive general agreement before the preparation of finished visuals, and policy matters such as style, visual treatment, size, colours, typography and so on are defined to produce work which will meet the specific objectives.

Following this sequence of operations is the type mark-up which must be read as an engineer would read a blueprint before production begins. It is wasteful and unnecessary to wait until proofs are available before deciding that 8 point is not really large enough or Times New Roman is too traditional a typeface. The proofs when they come should be an agreeable conclusion to a well-planned exercise. There should be no unpleasant surprises, no radical changes—the job should be exactly what had been envisaged throughout the phases of production.

The second stage in effective planning is to establish from the outset a realistic time schedule and to take steps to enforce it. This is easy to say but sometimes difficult to implement: nevertheless it must be done. If, from past experience, the managing director is likely to require a complete rewrite at a certain stage, the possibility must be included in the schedule, and to do so is probably the surest way of bringing home to him or her just what effect a change of mind can have on a project.

Table 7.1 may serve to underline the value of scheduling. It has been constructed as a typical time-scale for the preparation and production of a sixteen-page, three-colour brochure. Note that no provision has been made for the commissioning of special photography or technical drawings for instance.

There could well be situations in which a piece of print is required within a week or even less, but to work to high standards it is essential to allow adequate time for a publication which will, after all, last for perhaps a year and sometimes considerably longer.

PREPARATION AND PRODUCTION

The production of good industrial literature is often complex and almost

Table 7.1 Print schedule

Produce written objectives and obtain approval	1 week
Brief writer, obtain synopsis and get approval	2 weeks
Write copy	2 weeks
Obtain complete approval	1 week
Visual treatment	2 weeks
Finished visual	2 weeks
Final approval	1 week
Type mark-up and artwork	1 week
Proofs	2 weeks
Printing	3 weeks
Total—17 weeks	

always difficult. The subject matter is usually of a technical nature, it is specialized, and, moreover, must be written with an authority which demonstrates to the reader the expertise of the company issuing it. This maybe indicates that it should be written by an expert but the chances of the writing being interesting and dynamic are then frequently diminished.

Careful choice of the best available writer is therefore of paramount importance. If the technical nature requires that it be written by an engineer, then perhaps it will be necessary for it to be rewritten as a matter of deliberate policy by an expert and stylish writer. Similarly with design, when illustrations are of a highly specialized nature a visualizer will require considerable guidance by experts on precisely which items are of most importance.

In the production of literature there are a large number of variables which perhaps are not encountered with so much force in other media, for instance how many pages, what kind of paper, what size, how many colours, what style of design and typography.

It is reasonable to argue that having hired the best or most appropriate creative people to do the job, they should be left to get on with it. This will only be true if the initial briefing has been full and comprehensive.

Literature must fit into the general company style, shape and size; if not it should be different for a good reason. The creative team must know if cost is the overriding consideration, or if prestige; whether an item is to fit into an existing catalogue, be carried in the pocket, sent through the post or handed out by sales staff. The nature of the audience must be known: different styles will be required for addressing architects and archaeologists, artists and artisans, scientists and directors. Size of typeface and style becomes important depending upon age groups; but a good creative person if equipped with the right background information will be able to produce work which fits a particular audience's frame of reference.

Similarly the most appropriate printing process will tend to come out of the original definition of objectives, or if not here, from the visual treatment.

Interdependent with this will be the kind of paper to be used, number of colours, degree of finish and method of presentation.

A more difficult matter is in the choice of a printer. The variations which occur between one supplier and another in quality and delivery make price alone an unsatisfactory and incomplete basis on which to select a printer. The soundest basis is to build up a relationship with a few printers with whom the majority of business is placed, establishing from the outset that certain standards of quality, service and, most important, integrity, must be maintained and that any serious defects will result in a termination of the relationship. Even so, it will be necessary to put an occasional job out to tender in order that cost comparisons can be made.

DISTRIBUTION

Experience shows that much industrial literature is produced at considerable expense, then left substantially unused for a few years before being repulped as wastepaper. This underlines the need for a literature strategy which plans its audiences and methods of distribution.

There will no doubt be a primary audience. For example a leaflet about a new electronic device may be aimed primarily at all design engineers within certain defined industries. Secondary audiences may be the technical buyers and production engineers in the same factories. Other audiences for consideration will be the press, one's own staff, wholesalers and retailers or other end users. A prestige brochure, on the other hand, may be directed towards the senior management of customers and prospects, again to employees, but maybe also to suppliers and to shareholders.

A good general rule is that literature in the store room is wasted though, of course, it is necessary for efficient distribution to maintain adequate stocks to meet demand. Here it is most important to install an effective system of maximum/minimum stock control coupled with a procedure which ensures that before re-ordering takes places, the full 'pass for press' procedure is used to ensure that the reprint is completely up to date.

Prestige publications

Jargon in marketing has brought down upon itself connotations which are both unfortunate and inaccurate. 'Prestige', for instance, tends to be equated in the minds of many managements with waste of money. If, alternatively, such publications were described as 'image building', the reaction would be even less favourable.

The fact is, however, that when a company name is mentioned to a buyer, if she or he has heard of it at all, a certain image is conjured up. It may be favourable or unfavourable. Indeed it may be highly biased or completely erroneous. Yet is it possible to produce literature which if read will help to create the kind of image that a company hopes to possess. This, of course, presupposes that there exists a plan which defines the company image. Given this objective there are numerous types of publications which can be produced having a sound business basis other than just a general feeling that this is something which ought to be published.

A general company or corporate brochure, for instance, can bring together all the activities of a company expressed in terms which the key audience can recognize as valuable. Such a publication may be preceded by research to establish the level of knowledge about the company and where gaps exist. It is important to avoid being introspective and writing about the company for the sake of it. At the other extreme, if the capability of top management or the existence of modern buildings are outstanding, they are worth publicizing. The first step in such a publication calls for an objective analysis of a company's strengths in relation to competitors and the nature of the audience, and their interest.

A number of companies publish books about their histories, but the important question here seems to be 'who cares?' If the company has had an outstandingly interesting history there may well be justification for such a book. The growth and development may reflect very creditably upon the business as a whole; there may have been outstanding personalities in the business who are characters with an intrinsic interest of their own; there may have been a number of innovations which people in general do not know about—inventions, or new management techniques. On the other hand a company may be in a fast-developing industry where little regard is paid to the past and in which the future—long- and short-term—is all that seems to matter. Perhaps the criterion to be adopted is to demonstrate the need and value of such a publication, and if this cannot be done then not to publish.

Often a company will be in an industry which itself is of wide general interest and can therefore justify a special publication about it. Certain industries producing basic materials such as paper and steel come into this category, along with, for example, textiles, soap, aircraft, electronics, railways and very many others. Sometimes this aspect of literature is covered by an educational programme or classed under the heading of public relations. In the context of this chapter it is enough to apply the question 'will this help to achieve our defined overall objective?' Providing the answer is yes, then the job is worth doing.

It may not be inappropriate at this juncture to emphasize that much industrial purchasing is done on a subjective basis and that attitudes, as well as the placement of orders for capital goods, have an average gestation period of some years. The long-term building of a good reputation is therefore an important activity which is part of the marketing plan. It is no longer inevitable that providing a good product is produced a good reputation will follow without further effort. Customer satisfaction must not only be given, but must be seen to be given.

In much the same way as company publications about an industry can enhance a reputation, so also can literature dealing with other matters which bear on a company's activities. Statistics about an industry as a whole, for example, can prove to be of great value to buyers, suppliers and other interested people. If no other source of such data is readily available many people may take advantage of the statistics and in turn equate the value and reliability of this service with the performance of the company as a whole.

Some marketing principles may be misleading; for instance the proposition that one does not sell product performance, but rather consumer satisfaction, is fine but it can lead to missing quite real selling propositions. The fact is that, no matter how well a customer's identified needs are met by the specification of the product and its performance, there are intangible influences on all human behaviour which will affect decision-making. The task is to uncover these hidden motivations and to take action to satisfy them. Knowledge of the existence of very modern and sophisticated machinery may well be an important factor in a purchasing decision even though it actually makes not the slightest difference to the quality or performance of a product.

Technical publications

In the field of industrial marketing communications there almost always exists the need for technical publications which range from specification and data sheets to servicing and operating manuals. To have technical validity and authority these must be written by engineers, technicians or scientists who frequently do not wish to undertake the task and anyway are not able to express themselves clearly.

The result is often a compromise, the outcome of which is that the job is not as good as it might be. There are of course technical writers, but good ones are few and it is not a profession which attracts talented specialists. A solution which is often adopted is to sub-contract the writing to an outside organization which specializes in the production of technical publications. This can be satisfactory, particularly for the smaller firm which may not have a constant demand to maintain a well-balanced workload for its own technical writers. Considerable caution must be exercised in using an outside organization: quality and capability vary considerably, and there is often a high staff turnover which makes continuity of style and quality difficult.

As with many other publicity activities the right solution is perhaps to establish and then pursue exactly those services which are essential. It should then follow that a technical leaflet or a maintenance manual is no more an undesirable but necessary evil than the raw material from which the product is made or the machine that makes it. Thus, if the product warrants first-class materials it also warrants first-class literature and the rate for the job must be paid to the few good technical writers available.

Where a company has a wide range of complementary products it is usually necessary to provide a catalogue, with all the difficulties this involves. Catalogues are expensive to produce, impossible to keep up to date, and never meet the requirements of everyone. Nevertheless, with many technical products they are so essential a part of the marketing operation that they are used by the customer's design department to specify a certain type number, and thus predetermine the brand of product ultimately to be purchased. Interesting catalogue developments are taking place particularly in the development of microfilm storage units and various other systems of information retrieval, and there is every indication that this technique will continue to develop. A further but quite different system is one in which a specialist distributor arranges to send out staff to a given market on behalf of a number of clients and actually place into customers' catalogue files the latest material. This scheme is certainly working successfully in some fields, but its application may be limited.

Sales publications

Sales literature represents the opportunity for placing in front of a prospect the complete selling proposition. Even if such material will not always be read, it is nevertheless a good chance to set down in detail a considered view on the merits of the product and the satisfactions it will provide.

A disadvantage is that it is difficult to be specific to an individual's needs in the way in which a salesperson can. A salesperson, however, while having the chance to modify a presentation to suit the circumstances, and to counter objections and doubts by the buyer, does not have unlimited time during a visit and therefore may miss out certain features. Overall, the considered and consolidated argument contained in a piece of sales literature ought to be better than that of any one salesperson.

This is not to suggest the replacement of sales staff by sales literature. Rather it is to emphasize that in technical selling, sales literature has a powerful role to play providing it is carefully produced and used in a planned and purposeful manner.

A sales leaflet or brochure can be regarded as the back-up material to a salesperson's visit during which the buyer will have been taken carefully through each item, relating it to his or her special requirements. Such literature will not be simply an enumeration of product attributes, but a summary of the benefits to the customer. It should probably not be sent out in advance or in lieu of a visit, since it might enable a prospect to conclude that he or she did not require the product, thus creating an unnecessary sales block.

Alternatively, other forms of sales literature, such as direct mailing pieces which are designed simply to create interest but not to call for a yes/no judgement to be made, are an excellent preliminary to a sales call. The contents of a piece of literature or any other item of publicity should not be based solely on what a buyer wants to know. This is only the starting point. The contents must be planned deliberately to provide a prospect with what the selling company wishes him or her to know, no less and no more.

Various other items of print can come under the heading of sales literature. Some of these are covered under direct mail, and others under point of sale. Two that are not used as much as they might be are reprints of advertisements and of editorial mentions or articles. It seems likely that if an advertisement is worth while, it is wasteful to rely simply on its being seen in a magazine. From readership data, it can be reliably forecast that perhaps only a third of a potential market will ever notice it, let alone read it. The exposure must be increased if it is mailed out to the prospect list, and the cost of doing so is very low.

House magazines

In this section of the book dealing with marketing communications, consideration is given only to external house magazines (i.e. for customers and prospects) as opposed to those which are produced primarily for internal circulation to employees. Sometimes one magazine is produced to serve both functions, but it is rare for this to be successful since the interests of the two groups are so different.

External house magazines are certainly a valid means of persuasive communications: their selling role is sometimes rather remote and in fact more nearly related to a long-range image-building operation.

One of the difficulties facing a would-be publisher is that, once started, a house magazine is difficult to stop. As the cost of launching such a venture can be quite high a major policy decision is required at this stage. Again the solution is to define audiences and objectives and then to produce something which is modest and infrequent but can be strengthened if it succeeds.

The acid test must be whether it can prove to be of sufficient interest to cause recipients to look at it and even read it. Unless continuity of really interesting material can be assured it must become of declining value. It is akin to a new product launch without the possibility of a test marketing operation.

Against the idea of a house magazine is the situation that already too many trade and technical journals are produced commercially and this must restrict the available reading time by prospective buyers. Secondly, it is only natural that the sponsors of a house magazine will view it with a great deal more interest and initial enthusiasm than its potential readership. In the balance against the idea, much more than a printing operation is involved: this is publishing and it includes producing to a deadline and the most difficult matter of distribution—of a growing uncontrollable database which becomes out of date at a rate of at least 10 per cent each year and therefore requires very thorough procedures for maintaining its accuracy. The overall cost of a well-produced house magazine can become very high indeed.

If the advantages predominate, the job must be done well, since this magazine will contribute in very large measure to the image of the company in the minds of the readers.

There are often good reasons for placing the publishing of a magazine in the hands of an outside organization. This is clearly not so if the format is simply a few duplicated pages of 'company newsheet', but if the work is substantial it is difficult to justify employing a staff with adequate expertise to produce something which must compete with the best commercial journals. The very fact of having an independent editor will help to ensure that the subject matter is written to interest people outside the business, and without the kind of introverted jargon and detailed trivia which easily creep into an inside production.

Goals must be set, not only quantitative, but also in terms of reader interest. In Chapter 13 on media research, page traffic studies are dealt with. This same technique can be applied to house magazines to establish the percentage interest in each page, and in the magazine as a whole. The objective should be stated in terms of readership, not circulation. One goal, for example, may be to obtain a readership of say, 500 hospital engineers within a year of publication. A formal readership study may subsequently show that only 10 per cent of the circulation of 1000 is read, the remainder discarded. In such a clear-cut situation the course of action ought not to be difficult to determine; for instance, cease publication.

Checklist

1. Have you a long-term plan for literature?
2. Does this plan fit into the company marketing strategy?
3. In the preparation of a new piece of literature
    (a) Has the objective been defined?
    (b) Is the potential audience agreed?
    (c) Has the method of distribution been determined?
    (d) Has a production schedule been produced?
    (e) Does the schedule make provision for
        (i) briefing?
        (ii) writing?

(iii) visual treatment?
(iv) quotation?
(v)   finished visual?
(vi) artwork?
(vii) proofing?
(viii) revisions?
(ix) printing?

4. In briefing a designer has guidance been given on

   (a) Number and size of pages?
   (b) Paper and board?
   (c) Illustrations?
   (d) Style of design?
   (e) Number of colours?
   (f) Typeface and sizes?
   (g) Expense?
   (h) Printing process?
   (i) Quantity?

5. Has provision been made for (a) storage (b) stock control and continuous updating?

8

PHOTOGRAPHY

Still photography is part of the raw material which serves as the basis for promotion and other persuasive communications activities. A good deal of photography is carried out for a specific purpose and is used subsequently for other purposes. Much of the work, however, is done speculatively when the opportunity presents itself in anticipation of future uses.

Subjects

Consideration will be given later to the care which must be exercised in order to match the photographer to the job in hand. Before doing so, it is perhaps useful to examine some of the variety of subjects which can be included in what is part of the promotion programme. This classification of subjects is not exhaustive, but is presented rather to show that a disciplined and analytical approach is possible and indeed necessary even in such a creative area as photography.

PRODUCTS

It goes without saying that there are numerous products which, as such, cannot usefully be photographed—usefully that is in a promotional sense. A management consultancy may be said to fit into this category, and to a lesser extent industrial chemicals, or even for that matter steel strip.

In practice there are many products where illustrations are vital, for instance where appearance counts, as in packaging, and others which cannot be taken to a buyer because of size, as with heavy capital equipment.

Product photographs to a greater or lesser extent form the basis of press advertising, literature, sales aids, press releases, and direct mail, but there can be rather more to product photography than merely presenting a factual static representation of what the product looks like. There is much creative scope for interpretation by the photographer in order that the picture portrays the product benefit rather than only the product itself. Take, for example, a new type of fibreboard box designed to provide extra strength; itself a most mundane subject. Now stand an elephant on it and the picture may well prove to be of interest to a daily newspaper, and certainly to trade outlets. Another example might be a sheet of cardboard which is particularly water resistant. Here the product benefit could be demonstrated by constructing a boat from it and then photographing it being rowed across the Thames by an Olympic oarsman.

PRODUCT APPLICATIONS

It follows naturally from the above section that an outstanding way of showing product benefits is to photograph them in use. A radiation monitor maybe is not much to look at and could well be mistaken for a digital voltmeter or a pH meter, but when put into the radiotherapy unit of a nationally known hospital its use is immediately apparent, as well as the added value of implied endorsement by the user. An industrial pump designed to withstand the most rugged of conditions has difficulty in making this point until it is photographed *in situ* on a massive paper machine with water and stock jetting all over it.

To ask a photographer to produce a 'dramatic' picture of an industrial product may be a cliché (a dramatic cucumber was once called for), but a top-rate photographer with an adequate brief will produce photographs which sell the goods, sometimes more effectively than written or spoken words, since here is pictorial evidence of a product providing a service or satisfaction which is claimed of it. It is a credible demonstration of a manufacturer's claim.

INDUSTRIAL PROCESSES

It has been argued elsewhere in this book that the nature of the manufacturing process can be a powerful support to the selling proposition of a product. This factor can be utilized by building up a library of the principal or interesting features of a process.

In photographing the operations of a factory it is necessary in the first instance to produce a shooting schedule and to confirm this in advance with everyone likely to be involved. The works manager will be of special importance, since his or her staff will be needed to give maximum co-operation by repainting machinery, providing clean overalls, pacifying the operatives who are concerned at losing bonus pay, and providing electricians, labourers and technical advisers to help the photographer. It is a matter of communicating to staff that an industrial photograph is a far cry from a seaside snap and is making an important contribution to the future of the business.

Some photographers on a large assignment prefer to carry out an initial survey, sometimes with a hand-held camera, to ensure that possible difficulties are anticipated and that any major work the client needs notice of can be put in hand in good time. A photographer may, for instance, wish to work at night in order to have pure artificial light: this may involve bringing in a special night shift.

Top-class photographers have a creativity and sensitivity which enables them to give life to a piece of plant or machinery. More important even than clever composition and lighting, if the brief requires it, they can illustrate what a machine *does* rather than what it *is*. Furthermore a photographer can build in a feeling of quality and precision which turns a fundamentally passive situation into an active selling picture.

It is not enough to leave things to chance, and hope that the right result will emerge. The briefing for photography must state the specific merits that a series of pictures need to portray: whether it is cleanliness, scale of production, automation, efficiency of factory layout, craftmanship, scientific aids, or quality control.

NEWS PHOTOGRAPHY

This is a separate class of photography and needs certain qualities if it is to be useful—a sense of immediacy, a human interest, an unusual angle.

There is a great danger of producing cliché photography in many news situations—VIP shaking hands with managing director prior to a tour of works; a plaque being unveiled; the mayor shares a joke with one of the workers; or the chairman's wife cuts tape, presses a button or accepts a ceremonial key. These photographs are easy enough to take but are difficult to place with newspapers and tend to be repetitious and uninteresting even for a house magazine.

The best news photographs are probably not planned at all but come out of the persistent trailing of a tour party by a photographer with a news sense. Alternatively news can be created, as for instance when a boat was sawn in half, then stuck together and refloated, to demonstrate the qualities of a new adhesive.

PEOPLE

A basic library of portraits of directors and senior executives is necessary for any firm seriously engaged in marketing communications and public relations activities. This is good reference material and will be used for such events as new appointments and announcements, though such pictures serve little purpose sometimes other than to break up a page of type and provide a sense of satisfaction to the person concerned.

There are opportunities to go further than a straight portrait or a picture of someone sitting at a desk signing a letter or holding a telephone; a happy group of people clutching their cocktail glasses; or those frequently used groups of businessmen with their wives, all in evening dress, standing in the corner of a ballroom looking sometimes self-satisfied, and sometimes embarrassed.

There is now a healthy trend towards photographing people going about their business so as to get across their personalities, functions or features of the products or processes in which they are involved. This is valuable because it is both different and gives the photograph a positive role. It communicates something other than just faces.

PRESTIGE PHOTOGRAPHY

It is not easy to be specific about this since so much depends upon the circumstances. Often it is a matter of looking through photographs which have been taken for other purposes and selecting any which have additional merit. Photographs of industrial processes for instance, apart from showing the equipment and demonstrating its purpose, may be of such a quality in photographic or visual terms that they can be used outside their original intention. Many newspapers and magazines will accept such pictures with a small caption on an exclusive basis.

It is necessary to decide what aspects of a business are likely to be impressive in a general sense. The exterior of a new building, for instance, or an aerial view, a well-equipped surgery, or a fleet of vehicles with a new livery, advanced scientific equipment, or a computer: features of a business which are not directly relevant in a promotional context but tend to be creditable in their own right.

Photographers

Much emphasis has been laid on matching a photograph to its purpose. It follows that the means of achieving such an objective must be to match the photographer to the task. Just as in any other art form, each photographer will have certain strengths and weaknesses, special interests and capabilities. The strength of 'high quality' will probably be matched by the fact that the cost will be high. A photographer who excels at portraiture may be only average at industrial work or news photography.

COMMERCIAL PHOTOGRAPHERS

It is necessary then for a publicity executive to build up a knowledge of sources of supply of various skills and price ranges. Many of the best sources of supply are independent photographers with a small studio and processing unit. Their particular skill is one that is difficult to pass on to an assistant, or to a group of colleagues, and for this reason photographic units tend to be small. The disadvantage is that a one-man firm suffers from peaks and troughs in demand which will sometimes make it difficult to get a particular photographer on to an assignment at a given time. The sporadic nature of the business may also cause the charges to be high since the photographer must fix fees at a level which will cover the costs on a long term and continuous basis, even when there is little work going through.

A top-flight photographer may command a market price of £1000 a day, and in the context of the job to be done this may represent good value for money. The provision of a good set of photographs of a new £100m plant for example is worth every penny of the £5000 a week's assignment might cost.

There is, of course, room for competitive buying in photography. One of the customs of top photographers (and top designers) is that, apart from being able to command relatively high charges by virtue of their excellence, they sometimes base their fees on the use to which a photograph is to be put. Thus a photograph for record purposes may cost say £50 while the same photograph for an expensive series of newspaper advertisements may be billed at £500. Advertising agencies, particularly large ones, tend to be at a disadvantage here. A good example was of a photographer on a routine assignment at a fee of £500 a day, who was asked independently by the company's advertising agent to take a particular shot, while he was on the spot, for a press advertisement. He billed the agency £800 for the one shot and the art buyer considered he had obtained good value for money. The client took a different view. No doubt photographers will argue that the marketing men, for whom they do much of their work, themselves set product prices on what the market will bear and that they should not complain when they are given the same treatment. It is as well, however, to be aware of the situation.

The larger studios employ a number of photographers, perhaps half a dozen, and there are obvious benefits to be derived. The provision of a news service in particular tends to call for a pool of photographers to be able to meet sudden demands. Shared overheads may enable such units to function more economically, and a group of photographers can consist of a number of people who are specialists in their own right. On the other hand it is difficult for a client to build up such a personal relationship as when dealing with an individual and, since changes in personnel occur from time to time, a continuity of style, technique and quality can be difficult to maintain if there are several photographers on call.

STAFF PHOTOGRAPHERS

Bernard Shaw said: 'The golden rule is that there are no golden rules', and this certainly applies to dogmatism about staff photographers or indeed any creative staff. The odds are weighted heavily against staff photographers being at the very top of their profession. They cannot hope to be a specialist in all the categories of photography that will be required; moreover their skills will not match those of a £1000 a day person, or they would themselves be working independently.

Even a very capable staff photographer will tend to get into a rut if he or she always works for one firm, and it is unlikely that there will be the same freedom of creative expression as a freelance has since the work will be controlled by a direct-line boss. The day-to-day operations will be restricted by conventional working hours, by limitations of props and equipment and by general interference, however well-intended.

Nevertheless, for larger companies there is a real value in an internal photographic unit which can cope with the many routine photographic demands which arise. It can supply an essential and very economic service provided its limitations are recognized from the outset.

PROPS AND MODELS

It is so easy, and in industrial publicity so common, to think always in terms of getting work done 'on the cheap'.

If, for example, a home environment is required for a photograph, there is a good chance that someone's actual home will be used rather than a set built at £1000 to match the requirements of the assignment. Similarly it is much easier to look around for the prettiest secretary to stand in front of the camera rather than pay for an expensive model. For a small firm working on a tight budget these improvisations often make sound common sense, but one gets what one pays for, and there is little doubt that the quality of a photograph can be enhanced radically by the use of professional models and exactly appropriate props.

Expensive photography is not always so expensive as it seems since it rarely needs retouching, often finds many other uses, and projects a quality image which can be of a great benefit to both the product and the company.

Processes and production

Most industrial photography is in black and white. While there is a growing trend towards colour there is still little need for it in the majority of literature, direct mail or press advertising, and the requirements of exhibitions and public relations can usually be met with monochrome. The nature of the product can be decisive since a carton manufacturer or a printer may well have a very definite need for colour work, but by and large colour is unnecessary and indeed often unsuitable.

Types of cameras can surely be left to the photographer, although it is as well to be aware of the limitations of filmstock as regards size. For some years past there has been a good deal of controversy around the merits of sizes from 35 mm to 5 in × 4 in and even larger. While some industrial photographers still use large film stock, virtually none use 35 mm, and there is a general consensus that $2\frac{1}{4}$ in^2 is the most suitable. Certainly with fine-grain film and development, very considerable enlargements can be obtained up to 6 × 8 ft without the effect of grain becoming objectionable.

In commissioning photography it is as well to be aware of the importance of lighting, if only to understand and anticipate the needs of the photographer. The hand-held flash unit may be enough for news photography, but for product shots it is frequently necessary to employ a wide variety of sophisticated lighting techniques for the best results. In photographing industrial plant, lighting often becomes the most significant single factor, with high-powered lights located at strategic points often to the inconvenience of the work people. One of the greatest failings among clients is to arrange shooting schedules which do not allow enough time, people, mechanical handling, electricians and power supplies to do justice to the lighting.

SALES AIDS

Obviously black and white prints can be used by sales representatives and sometimes that is all they need. Colour photography here can come into its own since the additional cost may not be great against the realism of the picture.

Consideration should also be given to the use of 35 mm colour film for the provision of slides and film strips and for three-dimensional slides with a special viewer. These visual aids can provide the basis of a very effective sales presentation, sometimes at very low cost.

Checklist

1. Have you made budgetary provision for photography as a separate promotional element?
2. Have you considered how best to exploit photography in
   (a) Products?
   (b) Product applications?
   (c) Own factory and processes?
   (d) News and events?
   (e) People and personalities?
   (f) Prestige?

3. Have you (a) set up an adequate library of prints, (b) with suitable cross referencing? (c) Are there arrangements for updating this material? (d) And preventing people removing them?
4. In arranging a photographic session, is the photographer aware of the purpose and objectives, both (a) immediate and (b) long-term?
5. With photography inside factories and offices are the necessary line management, staff and works fully informed in order to obtain maximum co-operation?

9.

VIDEO FILMS & AV

The production of an industrial film is sometimes the most expensive single item in a publicity budget and yet, paradoxically, once produced it is often the least used because it has few or no pre-planned objectives. It may indeed prove to be the most expensive white elephant in the promotional field.

As with other media it is necessary to refer again to the marketing and promotional strategies which determine the need for a film or not. It is easy to think of good reasons to justify a film, having already decided to make one, but this sequence of thinking often leads to the film being the end in itself rather than simply the beginning of a promotional process.

'What is the objective?' This is the essential question, and the singular is deliberately used in order to avoid the other common failing in film making, that of trying to satisfy the interests of several different audiences with one and the same film. The result is generally a film of no special interest to anyone.

The objective, for instance, may be to demonstrate to farmers the versatility of a new tractor and its range of attachments, to help a salesperson to put across the selling proposition. From the definition of potential market in the marketing strategy, the precise nature of the audience will be known— say farmers having in excess of a certain acreage—and this will determine the method of film distribution and display.

There is usually a case for examining secondary audiences, but this must not cloud the principal objective. In the above example there may well be an overseas potential; schools, agricultural colleges and young farmers' clubs among others may be interested, but they must be regarded as ancillaries and of secondary importance.

Having set a specific objective, the next step is to restate it in quantitative terms, fixing not only a measurement against which performance can be judged, but also an assessment of value for money before production begins. Suppose the total potential market is 50 000 people, can a realistic target audience be set at 5000 a year? If that seems practicable, having regard to the methods of distribution available and the estimated life of the film, is the expenditure justified? The answer is often that, given planned distribution, the cost per viewer is very low. In the above example for instance, a film costing £30 000 would obtain an exposure in the first year at a cost of £6 per viewer. If distribution continued at the same rate for four or five years, the cost would come down to around a pound per head. At the other extreme, there are films which have been so little used that the cost per viewer has reached hundreds of pounds or even more.

Advantages and disadvantages

In terms of the 'impact diagram' in Chapter 2 (Fig. 2.2), the film can be regarded as one of a number of co-ordinated media which impress a common message upon the mind of a prospect. It is useful to consider the merits of a film in relation to other media.

IMPACT

This is clearly of a high order, arguably even higher than a salesperson's visit, due to the complete absence of distractions. This is not necessarily so, since there is no opportunity with a film for varying the argument to suit the circumstances, or to counter an objection. Obviously, however, a film has a much higher impact than press advertising.

COST

Initial costs very high, maybe between £10 000 and £100 000. Organizational and distribution costs must be added. Cost per viewer may be low.

COVERAGE OF POTENTIAL MARKET

Depends very much on how precisely the purchasing influences can be defined and how willing they are likely to be to view the film. This probably is the biggest problem and the biggest challenge.

COMPLEXITY OF SALES MESSAGE

In press advertising, for example, the sales message is subject to severe limitation. In a film there is virtually no limit and moreover the sales argument is presented in two forms—visual and audio—simultaneously and of course in colour.

SPEED

While films can be produced very quickly, it is usually unwise to do so.

Several months may be needed for production alone. Distribution may have to be spread over a number of years.

INTRUSION

Mention has been made with other media that a buyer may feel a sense of intrusion which can build up a resistance, for example in an intensive direct mail campaign. With a film he or she is likely to have gone to a showing as a matter of choice, and will probably at least start with a positive attitude of mind. Also films have a relaxing 'entertainment' connotation, arising from TV or cinema.

Film-making

The decision to make a film having been reached in principle there are a number of stages required in logical sequence to ensure an effective result. In the chapter on literature the need for such a procedure was stressed. In film-making it becomes even more important since changes made, particularly towards the end of production, can not only be very expensive, but can lead to the overall quality depreciating with serious results. It is assumed that the objective, audience and distribution procedure will have already been put down in writing and that the budget, type and length of film have been given some consideration.

The following sequence might then be:

1. Outline synopsis
2. Choice of film unit
3. Briefing
4. Treatment
5. Quotation
6. Script and visual interpretation
7. Shooting schedule
8. Internal organization and liaison
9. Rushes
10. Editing
11. Recording
12. Viewing
13. Completion

It follows that plans will be in train concurrently for distribution, and to secure adequate publicity for the film on its initial launching.

OUTLINE SYNOPSIS

It is usually the task of the marketing communications department, or maybe the advertising agency, to set down in more detail the points which need to be made verbally and visually in order to communicate the essential sales message.

It is useful at this stage to consider this not so much from a creative point of view, but rather as a factual outline of events which may or may not be in an acceptable creative sequence. This document will in due course be the basis of the briefing and with this in mind it can well be written while negotiations are proceeding with the film units which have already been short-listed.

From the outset it is essential to secure the active support of top management, and a realization that they will need to devote time at each critical stage to give a considered judgement which is unlikely to be changed. Approval of the outline synopsis is one such critical stage.

CHOICE OF FILM UNIT

Without wide experience in the film business it is wise to have the views and advice of other people who have been concerned in the recent past with the making of a film. A preliminary selection is not difficult as film units will usually have gained a reputation in a particular field of activity, or technique, or price range. It will then be advantageous to see a number of their recent productions and to judge these not only from the standpoint of entertainment, but also as audio/visual interpretations of the client's objectives.

This procedure should lead to the choice of one or two units that appear to meet the requirements. Full discussions must take place to give them the data they require for a quotation and to provide an opportunity of discovering whether a good personal rapport can be established and if they, as a unit, seem capable of understanding and interpreting what is required.

BRIEFING

There are a variety of ways of operating. One satisfactory procedure is to commission the chosen film unit to prepare a treatment and maybe a script for a nominal fee, with a full quotation to follow. The justification for this interim action is that to ask for a quotation before a full treatment has been prepared is rather like asking a printer to quote for a job before it has been designed.

The outline synopsis now becomes the basis of briefing the unit, which must be given every facility to ask questions and examine locations. This degree of co-operation will enable them to make the best possible creative contribution. If the film involves technical subject matter, a senior technical person must be assigned from the outset. If the factory is to be filmed, the factory manager must be fully involved.

The client company must treat the briefing as a most serious contribution to the subject. Thereafter the matter moves progressively out of its hands.

TREATMENT

This is the document in which the film-maker feeds back his interpretation of the client's briefing. It will be in effect an expanded and detailed synopsis with a written description of both visual and sound effects added. It will enumerate the various locations, the need for music, commentary and direct speech, and animation for instance.

In engineer's terminology this is the film's specification and blueprint combined into one. It should be read and agreed by everyone concerned and care exercised to ensure that the readers are well enough briefed, even with a verbal explanation by the producer, to understand fully the implications of each item.

QUOTATION

A 'treatment' can be costed accurately and, if the above procedure has been followed, the subsequent quotation is not likely to be very different from that which was foreseen. Items which are likely to have a significant effect on costs will have been discussed at an earlier stage, such as the extent and nature of animation sequences, special music to be composed and so on.

The contractual stage of the film and the detailed points in the contract are important to formalize; for instance, progress payments may be required, and provision for contingencies such as bad weather and lack of access to locations due to plant closedown.

SCRIPT

Good writers are not easy to find and it is worth paying for the best. An extensive briefing must be given to the writer and the script must be scrutinized together with the visual and timing schedules so that every single item is seen to fit. Any alteration hereafter can have most undesirable consequences in terms of both cost and quality.

SHOOTING SCHEDULE AND ORGANIZATION

Many people in a client's organization will need to be co-opted in order to ensure the smooth shooting of the film. The importance of management support has been stressed; it is valuable now to line up alongside the film unit a team of staff with executive authority over the whole internal operation—

to plan the organization and liaison in detail and to anticipate difficulties before they arise.

RUSHES

As the shooting of the film progresses, each sequence will become available for viewing and it is at this stage that the technical advisers should be brought in to ensure that pictorially there is nothing inaccurate.

EDITING AND RECORDING

There is little that can be contributed by the client at this late stage: in fact, the results will probably be better if the experts are allowed to get on with it. The client may want to hear the recording to be reassured that the right emphasis is given to certain passages in the script or that technical words are pronounced correctly.

VIEWING

The final viewing will be to a mixed audience of all those concerned in the client's organization, and they must decide that the result is right from their viewpoint, at least in technical and factual terms. From this stage the film goes to processing, and production is complete.

Distribution

Just as with press advertising there is an inclination to concentrate the main effort on the creation and production of an advertisement and to neglect media selection, so with films there has been a tendency to disregard the need for a plan of action to make maximum use of them commercially. In other words, the production of the film becomes almost an end in itself.

There are many channels of distribution available and it is to be hoped that the distribution plan and budget will have been drawn up and approved well before the film in completed. Such channels include:

1. Cinema circuits
2. Television
3. Film libraries
4. Trade and other associations
5. Clubs and organizations
6. Customers and prospects
7. Central Office of Information
8. Client-sponsored local film shows

9. Education establishments
10. Part of individual sales presentations
11. Exhibitions and conferences

Re-examination of the target audience will help to determine which methods of distribution are likely to be most effective. From the moment a film is completed it is starting to become out of date; therefore action must be prompt and it must be intensive.

Distribution can be expensive, as well as the maintenance and administration that must accompany it; nothing can be worse than a film arriving late, damaged, or even just not rewound.

In promotional terms, a film represents an opportunity of breaking new ground, influencing new people, and getting across a message often with greater impact than can be achieved with other media. The film, however, must not be expected to do this task alone. It must be supported, perhaps with a brochure highlighting the main features, or with posters and handbills, product displays or instructional charts. A personal introduction or demonstration is also very useful.

A film is only one part of the sales promotion armoury and should be treated as such by being linked with other media. It should be advertised. It will clearly be reviewed in a house magazine. If the subject justifies it, say a steel strip mill, the film may be mailed direct to the top fifty prospects throughout the world. The opportunities are limitless.

Pre-distribution publicity

A major event, such as the completion of a new video or photographic film, provides the opportunity for good deal of pre-distribution publicity, valuable both for general public relations and also to help to stimulate the demand for showings.

A particularly useful way of introducing a film is in a series of previews. The first will usually be for the press and provides the chance for journalists to meet company management as well as the film unit itself. Film reviews in the press can lead to a useful demand and, if the reviews are complimentary, they can be used to form the basis of promotional material.

Following the press reception, there are a number of events which should be considered. Important customers will feature largely when planning such functions, and if staged at a high level in congenial surroundings a good deal of hard business can be generated at them. Particular people will have special interests in a film: suppliers of equipment that was featured for instance; general suppliers to the company; officials of trade associations; and of course employees, particularly those who have co-operated and appear in the film.

Finally, pre-release publicity can spread across the entire selling function so that for a period the film is being promoted by the sales force, direct mail, inserts in advertisements, mention in the house magazine, envelope stuffers and so on until every prospect viewer is thoroughly informed and interested to see it.

Film strips and slides

This chapter would be incomplete without mention of the opportunities provided by film strips and slides, and also, the declining use of photographic film.

The oldest technique here is film strips which go back almost to the beginning of film itself. The process simply involves a series of individual frames, usually on 35 mm stock, each of which portrays part of a story sequence. The setting up of a complex piece of equipment may be the subject, or a comprehensive series of applications in diverse fields. There are also valuable opportunities for a film strip in the educational field and in training for internal staff or for distributors or users. An advantage can be to combine the visual sequence with a taped commentary. This provides a very neat package of a small roll of film plus a cassette which can be used independently of one's own staff, and indeed can be mailed around the world. The cost of a film strip can be held within a few hundred pounds, and additional copies are easy and inexpensive to obtain. Two disadvantages should be considered. The sequence of events is fixed and may not be suitable for every audience. More important perhaps is the fact that a special projector is required, and not all audience groups will have ready access to such equipment.

Colour transparencies are the basis of 35 mm slides which can be put together to form a programme in a similar way to a film strip but with the special advantage of flexbility. Slides can be changed, updated, omitted or used in a different sequence to suit the circumstances. With modern projectors, usually widely available, there are few problems likely to be encountered in setting up for a presentation. Specialists in AV programmes have developed techniques involving multi-projector images coupled with integrated soundtracks which provide an impressive show. As with still photography it is important not to fall into the trap of expecting such a programme to be produced for a few tens of pounds. Top-quality photography is essential and, if sound is to be used, a thoroughly professional recording. Even so, there is no doubt that if the subject is suitable for this form of treatment it can be produced for very considerably less than a film.

Checklist

1. Has the objective been set?
2. Has the target audience been defined?
3. Have the relative merits of video and photographic films been carefully assessed in relation to the objective and audience?
4. Have the methods of (a) distribution and (b) presentation been decided?
5. Has provision been made for checking and maintaining copies?
6. Has the budget been agreed together with the type and length of the film required?
7. Has a comprehensive production schedule been (a) produced, and (b) distributed to every person likely to be affected?
8. Has a date been put on each of the following stages?
   (a) Synopsis
   (b) Choice of film unit
   (c) Briefing
   (d) Treatment
   (e) Quotation
   (f) Signing of contract
   (g) Approval of script and visual interpretation
   (h) Shooting schedule
   (i) View rushes
   (j) Approval of complete film
   (k) Press show and launch
   (l) Publicity
   (m) Distribution
9. Has consideration been given to film strips and slides?

10

EDITORIAL PUBLICITY

As a preliminary to this chapter it is necessary to discuss a term in publicity which is possibly misunderstood more than any other, namely PR. What does it mean and arising out of this just what are the functions of a PRO and a press officer?

The first point is of course that PR can mean either public relations or press relations—two quite different functions. Furthermore, either may or may not be viewed in the context of the marketing function or of the business as a whole.

In this book the term public relations is used in its widest context, that of building and sustaining good relations between an organization and its various publics which include customers and prospects equally with employees and shareholders. The means by which good public relations are maintained include press advertising and direct mail just as much as editorial publicity.

The term press relations is used here to indicate the building up of good relationships between an organization and the various journalists who are likely to be concerned with it in order to secure good editorial publicity about any aspect of a company's operations, whether news about products, or new management techniques or strikes. It should also be noted that 'media relations' is being used increasingly to replace 'press relations'. This is in order that radio and TV shall not be overlooked. Similarly 'news release' may replace 'press release'. On the other hand there continue to be 'press officers' who in turn hold 'press conferences'.

In this chapter the subject of editorial publicity is dealt with only in so far as it contributes to the promotion of sales and is strictly within the confines of marketing activities and objectives.

Of the channels of persuasion which are available to bring to bear a sales message upon the mind of a prospect, the editorial columns of the press, television and radio are powerful media to include and integrate in the overall marketing communications mix. Again it is important to start with objectives and where possible to quantify these, both in order to determine the amount of effort needed to achieve the target, and as a means of subsequently measuring performance. It is not good enough to aim at 'securing a maximum of editorial coverage about a new type of industrial fire extinguisher'. It is necessary rather to define all the audiences which represent buying influences, to categorize and enumerate them, then specify which should be the target of an editorial message covering the new product. From this point the publications needed to make contact with this audience can be listed and a strategy developed for obtaining editorial coverage.

For example, suppose there are a total of fifty publications reaching the potential market for fire extinguishers of 50 000 people. The duplication of readership can be determined from readership surveys (see Chapter 13) as will be the average page traffic of the types of publication in question. It may be that by a combination of data, experience and judgement, it is concluded that to register with 75 per cent of the total potential market, editorial mention must be secured in twenty of the publications. If the news value is high this may be easy to achieve. If not, then perhaps some special activities will be necessary to create interest amongst the journalists. Alternatively the answer may be that the objective is not capable of achievement through editorial publicity, in which case other channels of persuasion must be strengthened in order that the total marketing communications impact provides adequate support for the selling effort.

The media, be it national, local, technical or special interest, is concerned primarily with providing information of interest to its readers or audiences, within of course the framework of a given editorial policy. The editor's job is to provide editorial material which will result in the readers' approbation and will influence the prestige of the publication. In due course this will influence its circulation, readership and thus advertising revenue. Editors can select from a wide range of sources: items of news, features, specialized stories, off-beat pieces, illustrations and so on. They must provide a good editorial mix. The function of a publicity executive is to think in terms of the ultimate audience, and to write in a way that will fit in with editorial criteria. To do otherwise is both a waste of time and an insult to the intelligence of an editor. The goal which must be aimed at then is to write a story which an editor will regard as a worthwhile item for his publication and which at the same time does a first-class selling job.

Editorial subjects

Approaching the matter with a journalist's eye, there are often too many subjects in industrial publicity: too many for the available staff to write about and, more important, too many for the press (particularly the monthlies) to assimilate. For many companies, having a variety of product lines and markets and applications, it is not difficult to produce, say, one story a week. It is expecting too much of the trade press to hope that all these will be published; even weeklies and dailies have many hundreds or thousands of other sources of news to call upon and regardless of any other consideration they must maintain a good editorial balance.

Thus the release of stories, even very good ones, may have to be rationed and this leads to the discipline (so often missing in press relations activities) of advance planning. It should be possible for the executive concerned to have an outline plan of releases to the press covering at least several months ahead. Obviously unforeseen news stories will emerge but this does not invalidate the need for planning the basic framework of editorial publicity. Within the marketing communications strategy it is known well in advance which products are to be promoted and when. It follows that editorial stories would be planned to coincide with publicity in other media. A new product, for example, only becomes news when it is released to the outside world. It might have been produced months before and indeed been in service on a restricted basis for weeks, but it is only news as and when a company decides to make it so.

NEW PRODUCTS AND SERVICES

When exactly does a product or service qualify to be called new? It could be argued that for a firm producing plastic bottles or mouldings, every new order is likely to be a new product. But there may be a thousand of these each year. The criterion then should not be, is it new, but does it have news value? A small modification to a well-established moisture meter which results in an improvement of accuracy from ± 5 per cent error to ± 2 per cent has a far greater news value than a new style of lettering on a plastic bottle, even though the moisture meter can hardly claim to be a new product.

The degree of news value must also be assessed, since this will determine the way in which the story is written and presented. For example, the substitution of nylon bearings for metal in industrial castors has news value, though somewhat limited, whereas a process control system to automate a paper mill for the first time in the world is likely to justify major international press coverage.

When integrating editorial publicity with other promotional activities, it is important to emphasize that an item is only news as long as it is not known. Pre-planning must ensure that advertisements do not start appearing before an editor has had the opportunity to publish the contents of a press release.

PRODUCT AND SERVICE APPLICATIONS

Even where a product range is not undergoing a continuous change, a good basis for industrial and business news is the variety and novelty of product applications or new uses for a service. A thickness gauge may be developed and established for use on steel strip. Adaptations may well lead to its application in measuring paper, plastics, rubber, foil and fabric. A radiological dosemeter may seem to lack a very broad audience interest, but applications could well include detecting radioactive minerals in Cornwall, equipping a civil defence force in Sweden, finding a lost isotope through police action, or locating the blockage in a sewer.

The difficulty with application stories is to find them, and there is no easy solution here. The answer lies in the progressive building up among company staff of an awareness of the value of such stories. This is a target at which publicity executives must aim. It can be aided by continually probing and asking questions, by participation in sales conferences, by visiting customers, and by subsequently distributing press cuttings to all concerned. Top management can help by indicating that they regard time identifying and sifting out application stories well spent. This attitude of mind is easier to cultivate if such stories are planned to fit into the overall strategy. The possibility of a substantial financial incentive to employees contributing stories should be considered.

NON-PRODUCT INNOVATION

If a piece of editorial publicity is to contribute directly to the promotion of sales, it follows that it must have a direct reference to whatever is being sold. There are, however, a number of editorial subjects which, while not having a direct selling value, act as a reminder of the company and its products. Many innovations fall into this category, such as the installation of a new type of machine to produce a product not only faster but to closer tolerances, or a more efficient way of storing a product, or a way of processing waste to enable it to be reused. These items do not offer a 'consumer benefit' but they have reminder value coupled with a contribution to the building up of company reputation which is probably one of the set objectives of the public relations campaign.

OTHER NEWS ITEMS

Appointments of new people, staff promotions, new literature, exhibitions, large contracts, new factory openings, visits by VIPs, setting new records (the thousandth order), anniversaries—all these items can be turned with advantage to assist the promotional campaign. Even staff achievements are worth publicizing, like registering patents, lectures, learned papers or even election to the local council.

No listing of news subjects can be comprehensive: rather it is necessary to build up a news awareness throughout the company, a process which is helped a great deal by a perceptive reading of periodicals as well as talking to journalists and continually monitoring their needs. For example, in Chapter

8 we mentioned a very boring but very strong fibreboard box that had been taken into Billy Smart's Circus where an elephant stood on it. The resulting photograph was used not only by the packaging press, but also by the nationals.

FEATURE ARTICLES

Over and above news stories there are many opportunities for having a single subject dealt with in depth, either by offering a journalist exclusive coverage of some item, or by getting a member of staff to write an article dealing with a subject more extensively than is possible in a press release.

Many feature articles which have no direct sales connection fall into the category of public relations but others can be quite deliberately part of the sales plan. For instance, the complexities of the production process, the planning and launching of a product and the marketing research which preceded it.

The big problem is always to find someone with the time and ability to do the writing, maybe one or two thousand words, or even more. For a busy and senior executive to find the time is partly a matter of motivation. Apart from the 'ego trip' it is worth considering actually paying a fee for the job. In addition to this, many publications will also pay a fee for a contributed article, in which case the writer benefits from two sources. Not all people have the ability to write well for the press. In this case the publicity executive may take on the task of editing or rewriting. Alternatively it may be necessary to employ an outside specialist writer; for instance a freelance journalist. Even so the effort and the expense will be well worth the publicity which will be achieved.

Press (or news) releases

THE PRESS LIST

Before beginning to write a press release it is essential to define the audience to whom it is addressed. This may be for instance the decision-makers in a particular market segment plus a number of other categories who are known to have an influence on purchasing decisions. A useful starting point is to compile a list of all publications and other media which can conceivably be interested in news from the company or organization, and use it as the basic checklist for each proposed press release.

Over a period of time the list will be extended by the inclusion of contacts such as freelance journalists, trade organizations, specialist news agencies, house magazine editors, named journalists with a special interest, as well as overseas publishers and agencies. Names will be deleted as publications change or the business is modified.

WRITING THE RELEASE

Editors receive far too many press releases for them to handle or sometimes even read, and few hit the mark. Most often, releases are introspective about 'me' and 'us' and 'how proud we are' rather than about 'you' and 'how your company stands to benefit'. They are acceptable neither to the reader nor to the editor.

It follows that writing a press release is not a job which can be delegated to a junior. Securing adequate editorial publicity is a major part of a publicity programme and needs to be placed in the hands of a specialist. The publicity value of a press release is to be judged on the same terms as an advertisement in the same medium. A release of high interest value may result in an area of editorial space equivalent in impact to several pages of advertisements. The same technique and effort is justified for a press release as for an advertisement.

On the actual writing of the release, the maxim should be: 'If in doubt, leave it out', but generally a story should run to between 100 and 300 words. It should be written in the same style as a journalist would write it, i.e. giving the news as it will interest the reader. And it should be written in a factual, authoritative manner; it should be lively and interesting, but without the smallest trace of the hard sell.

A good rule to follow is to adopt the style of the inverted triangle with the really important news at the top and the supporting information coming further down. This enables a news editor to sub from the bottom and still leave intact the main thrust of the story.

Structure

As with any piece of writing, it must have a beginning, a middle, and an end.

1. *Headline*   This is vital. It is the signal to the journalists which must at a glance cause them to pause and read on rather than discard the release into the bin. So put in the essential news in three or four words. And play it straight. Other journalists will not use your headline. If they did, they might find some competitive journal doing the same thing to them, so they just won't take the risk.

2. *1st paragraph*   The release stands or falls on the first paragraph. It must therefore contain the main news angle written from the reader's point of view, not from yours. The basic marketing concept—identify the consumer benefit.

3. *2nd and 3rd paragraphs*   If these are necessary, then they are there to elaborate on the main story already told in the first paragraph. But even so, they must give the highlights only of what you are trying to put across. It is not nearly so interesting to the reader as it is to you.

4. *4th paragraph*   Consider putting in a quote from someone in authority, preferably outside the organization and therefore more credible.

5. *5th paragraph*   Include facts and data here such as price, delivery, the date an event will happen, and so on.

6. *Further information*   Always offer this: give two names to contact, with office and home telephone numbers.

Points to note

1. Keep sentences short; avoid jargon and abbreviations.
2. Have a clear attractive layout, typed double-spaced, on one side only.
3. Send the release only to publications that will really find it of interest.
4. Use a photograph wherever possible and always caption it so that the caption can be seen at the same time as the photograph.
5. Any amplification of the story should be on a separate sheet or accompanying publication which can be used or discarded depending on its relevance to the journalist.
6. Ask journalists to criticize your releases. That's the way to learn.

DISTRIBUTION OF PRESS RELEASES

Press releases should be used as a channel of advance information to a wide range of people over and above the press. These should include:

1. Staff/works notice boards
2. Reception
3. House magazine
4. Salesforce
5. Top management
6. Service engineers
7. Overseas agents
8. Outside services (e.g. advertising agencies)
9. Distributors
10. Opinion formers (e.g. local MPs)
11. Trade Association
12. Customers (selected releases)
13. Shareholders (selected releases)
14. Solicitors/bank managers/auditors (selected releases)

PHOTOGRAPHS

Most press releases should be accompanied by a photograph. The reasons are varied. A photograph can illustrate special features: it helps to result in an editorial which is different and stands out; it may secure additional column centimetres; lastly it may be published even though the release is ignored.

Something has been said in an earlier chapter on the way in which photography is used in publicity. A paradoxical situation often exists between photography for press advertisements and photography for press releases. In the former the contents and composition are given considerable thought and closely debated by creative people at the agency even before a visual reaches the client who once again examines and scrutinizes the material. A photographer is commissioned, briefed, directed by a visualizer, possibly accompanied by the copywriter or the creative director, and fifty or sixty shots are taken. From these maybe half a dozen enlargements are examined until the desired visual solution is found.

Unfortunately the procedure for a press photograph is likely to be very different—a print from the file, or a quick shot by the work's photographer with a word from the press officer as a briefing. This makes no sense at all since whether a picture is used by an editor or not will depend in large measure upon its excellence and, after all, the illustrations both for advertisements and editorial are seen by the same audience. Second-rate photographs are a very false economy.

TIMING

Editorial publicity must be timed to fit the promotional plan but it must also fit in with the publishers' requirements. Copy dates in industrial publicity range from a few hours for nationals to a month and even more for some periodicals, and this is one of the reasons why it is sometimes necessary to place an embargo on publication. As an example of the need for planning, a press release on one particularly important news event, concerning the opening of a new factory, had to be supplied to a quarterly magazine two months in advance in order that the editorial mention should coincide with the coverage to be given by the dailies.

If the time of appearance of an editorial item is of special importance, a close study is necessary of copy dates of all the major publications involved, perhaps coupled with a personal contact with the editors concerned.

Press receptions

A major piece of business or industrial news will frequently be publicized by holding a press reception, or by taking the press to the factory, or alternatively to see a product being used by a customer. Such an event usually does not involve a very high expense in relation to the overall selling cost, or indeed the value of the resulting publicity.

A press reception enables a subject to be explained in depth and with greater impact than can be achieved by a press release. It enables senior company officials to make personal contact with journalists, to their mutual benefit, and in particular enables an enquiring reporter to get an individual angle on a story which will be much appreciated. Questions are facilitated and these help to avoid misunderstandings, while at the same time a good deal of general company philosophy rubs off on to one of the most influential of a company's publics, the press. Probably most important of all is that for an hour or so, maybe even a day, each journalist is thinking and acting within the company's environment. The company therefore becomes more than a mere name; it assumes an identity, a personality. This is an investment for the future which will have continuing repercussions and almost certainly affect the way in which press releases and other contacts are received subsequently, generally for good.

Journalists, however, do not have unlimited time and cannot be expected to react favourably to giving hours to a reception where it is dramatically announced that the southern area sales manager has been promoted to national accounts manager. Receptions must be reserved for worthwhile events judged in the terms of editors and their audiences.

Personal relationships

Journalists have a difficult task in sorting the multitude of news items which pour into them: in deciding which represent genuine news, which make technical sense and are appropriate to their readers' interests, and which should be set aside because they are merely product puffs, misleading or badly written.

It is valuable for publicity executives to build up good personal relationships with members of the press, not in order to influence them into accepting poor-quality material, but to keep them accurately informed about progress and developments in their section of industry. Journalists rely heavily on such personal relationships; they provide a means of obtaining news from a source on which they can rely both for accuracy and speedy action.

There are occasions when the press should meet senior executives of a company: a personal interview can be interesting editorially and valuable in promotional terms but as a general rule the press officer must be sufficiently senior and well-informed to deal with the press as an executive voicing the view of the company. If this is not so a journalist could be justified in regarding the latter as an obstacle in the communications process rather than an instrument.

A few executives still hold the view that even though editorial publicity may be useful, journalists themselves cannot be trusted. There are hair-raising stories about badly reported events, breaches of confidences and the need for advertisements as bribes. No doubt such things have happened but they are now mostly part of the folklore of the past. Journalists by and large are trustworthy and sincere professionals. Where they get a story wrong or report on a company unfairly it is generally because the firm failed to supply adequate material. There is a need, however, to beware of what might be termed the 'gutter press'.

Measuring results

Every release to the press must be scrutinized in terms of each and every publication's needs. Therefore, a presupposition in the measurement of results is that most publications receiving a release may be expected to carry the story. It is tempting to send a standard press release to an entire mailing list in the hope that one or two extra mentions might be gained in this way, but this is clearly lazy and expensive and the press quickly learns to ignore the sender. One method of measurement is to determine the percentage of publications using a story, expressed on a base of the total number circularized. One hundred per cent response is sometimes attained but 50 per cent can be regarded as a good achievement. Twenty per cent or lower implies that the release was sent to too many publications or was wrongly written: at any rate it points to the need for enquiry. If a publication consistently fails to use a company's material, there should be an adequate record system to indicate this fact and the editor should be contacted diplomatically to find out why.

Measuring results in terms of sales leads can be misleading. It is well known in technical journalism that reader enquiries can be increased significantly by the simple expedient of missing out certain key data, thus forcing people to write to a company to obtain it. It is true that this provides sales leads and might meet a company's short-term requirements, but reader enquiries will tend to be, say, in tens, whereas readership of an item may well be in thousands, or considerably more. Looking at this particular matter in reverse, if an editor puts himself out to cover a story in depth and publishes a comprehensive feature article, few enquiries may be generated, yet the value of the editorial is many times greater than a short column mention. If response were to be the criterion, the opposite conclusion might be reached.

A technique which is used extensively, but has been subject to a good deal of criticism, is to measure by column centimetres. The disadvantage is that to add the number of centimetres in, say, *The Financial Times* to that in *Production Equipment Digest* is like trying to add apples and pears. This is certainly a valid limitation. Nevertheless, for a given firm or a particular campaign, the results can be sufficiently homogeneous to be assessed in this way. A refinement which is sometimes adopted is to express column centimetres in terms of equivalent advertising space, and this may well provide useful information on value for money spent.

As a research exercise an investigation of reader impact may be made following a particular piece of editorial publicity. This can hardly be a continuous measure of editorial efficiency since the expense would be too high. Where a certain item of news is restricted to editorial publicity only, the percentage audience reached of a defined potential market can be measured by carrying out a subsequent recall research.

Press cuttings

To carry out an editorial publicity campaign without evaluating the press cuttings is rather like an artillery bombardment without observation of the fall of shot. Not all mentions will be identified, but this can be partly made good by using two cuttings agencies, and by following up publications where no mention is recorded to find out what the reason might be.

Press cuttings can be circulated with effect among top management and sales staff. They are often of great interest to employees in general and can be used in house magazines. They may even form the basis of sales literature. Moreover the widespread circulation of cuttings, apart from improving morale, enables employees to see for themselves the type of story which interests the press and stimulates them to originate ideas for further stories.

Limitations and advantages

While it is by no means true that editorial publicity is free publicity, the fact is that it is not only very good value for money but that it is also in some respect the most effective form of publicity available. Its particular strength derives from the implied endorsement of the publication in which a particular item appears, or, if not endorsement, at least an apparently independent appraisal of a product or service now being offered. As against this, an advertisement for the same product will be seen as partisan and much of its message will be discounted for this reason. And quite apart from credibility it is known from page traffic studies (see Chapter 13) that editorials have far more readers than advertisements: maybe as many as a factor of five. A further benefit to come from editorial publicity is the opportunity for inexpensive reprints, and quotations of extracts.

There are a number of important limitations, the most significant of which is the uncertainty of when a particular piece of news will appear, whether in fact it will ever appear at all, and if so whether it will be an accurate representation of the story. In an extreme case it could well be a negative report and cast doubts upon the value of a product. It is difficult to see editorial publicity as the main component of a promotional campaign since once a story has been reported it cannot be repeated, whereas a requirement of a campaign is likely to be continuity over a protracted period of time, and to satisfy this requirement is going to call for the deployment of a multi-media mix.

Checklist

1. Has the use of editorial publicity been established as an integral part of the marketing communications operation?
2. Is there a plan of action covering the same period of time as the marketing strategy?
3. Have quantified objectives been set for editorial publicity?
4. Are the sales staff aware of the value of this form of publicity, and the extent to which they can contribute?
5. Have press lists been drawn up which relate specifically to (a) the company's activities (b) its markets and (c) its products?
6. Has attention been given to the importance of producing press releases which are tailored to the needs of the particular audience and media concerned?
7. Is photography used wherever possible, and is the same attention given to its creative treatment and production as for press advertising?
8. Are press releases timed so as to fit in with (a) editorial press dates and (b) the overall promotional campaign?
9. Have good personal relationships been built up between the relevant journalists and the key company staff?
10. Has provision been made (a) for measuring results and (b) for corrective action to be taken if necessary?
11. Are press cuttings used as a means of evaluation?
12. Are they comprehensive?
13. Are they circulated to personnel who might be interested?

OTHER MEANS OF PROMOTION

In this marketing communications section of the book, the reader has been taken progressively from the initial strategy through each major channel of persuasive communications—press advertising, direct mail, exhibitions, literature, photography, videos and editorial publicity. One of the problems facing publicity executives is that as each of these media is used more efficiently, its competitive edge is blunted. Maybe this is countered by ingenuity in creative presentation, but nevertheless competition is intense. An advertisement is fighting for attention amidst thousands of others; an exhibition stand may be in a hall amongst hundreds of others, an editorial mention is only a drop in an ocean of words.

The impact of a sales message depends a great deal upon the novelty with which it is presented, but novelty becomes increasingly hard to find as a particular medium is more widely used by industrial advertisers. Each seeks as a result to find more unconventional ways of presenting a message. For instance, the first time a national newspaper was distributed at an exhibition with a special front page entirely devoted to one of the exhibitors it must have created a remarkable effect, as no doubt did the first aerial advertisement to be towed behind an aircraft.

This chapter examines some of the lesser-used industrial publicity techniques as well as some of the peripheral activities which tend to be classed under the publicity function. It cannot hope to be exhaustive, but it will underline the importance of applying creative imagination to new or less used techniques which can give a powerful stimulus to a campaign or even becomes its focal point.

Television advertising

For many years television has been used for industrial advertising, but only for a minority of products. Since it is a mass communications vehicle it follows that it is appropriate only where relatively mass audiences are required. Most industrial campaigns are aimed at audiences of 10000 or less: television tends to be more suitable for audiences of 100000 or more. The exception is in the USA where the wide variety of channels provides cost-effective advertising opportunities.

There are of course many countries around the world in which television is the major medium but it is largely suitable for consumer products where the target audiences are in the millions. Even so there are a number of industrial categories where television has proved to be useful, if only sometimes because of its novelty value.

The cost of advertising on commercial television

Because commercial television offers a range of rates dependent upon supply and demand it is difficult to provide exact costs. However, a network 30 second *peaktime* commercial in the UK could cost in the region of £40000 if that spot got a TVR (television rating—i.e. percentage of viewers) of 30.

Channel Four allows, on its own, new advertisers with limited budgets to experiment with television advertising. That is not to say that Channel Four is not a medium in its own right. Equally, advertising on ITV 1 need not be a prohibitively expensive exercise. Buying a campaign which does not depend on high-demand peaktime spots may reach exactly the target audience that a business advertiser wishes to reach.

How to advertise on television

The advertiser will obviously consult with his agency initially from a budget point of view. He will then establish the creative approach and the weight of the TV campaign, the latter, of course, being directly related to budget. With the advice of copywriters and the TV production department a commercial is generally fed out to an independent production house at an agreed cost. Alternatively, if industrial advertisers do not have an agency they may go direct to the television company who will advise and help make the commercial. In this case it is common practice for the advertiser to use a time buying shop at no extra cost.

THE COST OF MAKING A COMMERCIAL

While a commercial may cost as little as £100 it is likely that larger sums of money will be involved. Below are some UK ball-park figures on just how much it can cost to advertise on television.

1. *5 or 10 second commercials—£200–£2000*   Within this price range, production values will range from the most basic and cheapest slide presentation of a simple message with a station announcer's voice over it, to a multi-slide presentation accompanied by pre-recorded sound on a separate audio cassette. At the upper end of this price bracket, a director and/or producer should also be provided, as well as some editing facilities.

2. *5 or 10 second commercials—£2000–£5000*   Advertisers requiring high production values can add extra facilities such as special visual effects, or the addition of music, pack-shots of the product; studio use plus colour camera, as well as more of the director's and producer's time.

3. *30 second commercials—£5000–£15 000*   Productions within this range will enable the advertiser to be more ambitious in his presentation. A budget at the top end should be adequate to cover a full day's studio use, editing time, special effects, casting, lighting, make-up and art direction, simple set construction and props, and all necessary crewing and transportation and artwork costs and insurances.

4. *30 second commercials and longer from £15 000*   Commercials that require location shooting, as well as studio time, synchronized sound, the use of several artists as well as the necessary technical and staffing facilities, can be expected to cost anything from this figure up to £40–£50 000. Many factors determine price: the stature of the lead artist or artists; the cost of music; where and if location shooting is required; the complexities of set design; how much editing time is needed—and so on.

5. *Repeat fees and other ancillary costs*   In addition to the performance fee paid an artist or artists to appear in a television commercial, 'repeat' fees are due to performers when the commercial is transmitted. The scale of these fees is related to the area(s) in which the commercial is shown, and to the number of times it is repeated.

Radio advertising

Radio is a mass medium in much the same way as television and newspapers. It has a variable audience profile as does television and there will be times when listeners will comprise a higher than usual AB content. Even with this narrow profile, use of radio will be a blunderbuss approach to communicating with businessmen, though there are certain time slots in which listeners become highly segmented, and the opportunity to reach businessmen can be available for instance during the immediate pre- and post-work driving hours.

   The geographical segmentation which can be achieved with local radio stations may be of interest if a firm is setting about a moving sales campaign or road show: it can also help on the rare occasion when test marketing an industrial product. Generally its usefulness is in direct proportion to its number of prospects, i.e the total number of companies who may buy a product multiplied by the average number of people in the decision-making units. On a national scale it is probably not worth while for target prospects less than the order of 100 000, though in many other countries radio has for ng had an important role to play in what might be regarded broadly as the rate communications function.

On the credit side, a radio commercial is fast to produce and relatively cheap. Small slots of time can be bought to give tactical support to the sales force. And there are minor spin-offs like reaching out to non-buying audiences (which even so are important in PR terms) such as employees and their families, shareholders, local communities, opinion formers and potential recruits—schools.

A starting point after obtaining audience profiles at various times of day is to conduct a small research amongst existing customers. Get the sales force to ask people they call on for a week if and when they listen to local radio.

Sponsorship

A major new activity in the promotion of companies and products is sponsorship. Simple and effective, this can involve paying for or subsidizing such things as sports, the arts, books, conferences, exhibitions, flower shows, ballroom dances: the list is endless. A clear distinction must be made with patronage which can be applied to any of these activities, but is concerned only with giving support to the event regardless of any possible reward or benefit. Sponsorship on the other hand is the deliberate financial support given to an event in order to achieve a specific commercial objective. Typical objectives might be:

1. To increase brand awareness among customers.
2. To improve perception of company in terms of modernity, warmth, concern etc.
3. To increase goodwill and understanding among trade customers.
4. To enhance company's image in local community.
5. To raise employees' morale and company loyalty.
6. To create favourable awareness of the company among young potential future consumers.

The staging of numerous 'high visibility' sponsorship schemes by major consumer goods companies tends to imply that there is little going on in the industrial sector. The opposite is probably the case: it is simply that they tend to be specialized, or educational, or at a local level. So their visibility is not very great but in practice they not only do a useful job, but are also very cost effective.

The whole business of sponsorship has been very well summarized by the Incorporated Society of British Advertisers in a booklet[1] which puts up 10 points:

1. Sponsorship is a tool of company communication. Its prime purpose is the achievement of favourable publicity for the company or its brands within a relevant target audience by the support of an activity (or some

aspect thereof) which is not directly linked to the company's normal business.

2. It should not be confused with patronage, advertising or sales promotion, although they have some elements and objects in common. Sponsorship can prove an important additional ingredient in the marketing communication programme.

3. Sponsorship provides great flexibility—*in the choice of activity sponsored*; the arts, sport, leisure, social or communal activities; *the form the sponsorship may take*—tournaments, events, support of teams or individual competitors; *scale of participation*, from international golf to awards at the local flower show. Terms, conditions and level of financial contributions are invariably open to negotiation.

4. Sponsorship is normally undertaken for one (or more) of the following reasons:
   (a) To enhance the company name/brand image.
   (b) Improve trade relations.
   (c) Foster company's 'good citizen' image.
   (d) Boost employee morale.

5. Sponsorship is unlikely to achieve significant results used on a 'one-off' basis. It should be regarded in the long term, both in setting objectives and budgets. (The possibility of escalating costs should be borne in mind, as should the 'risk' factor in sponsoring a team or individual over a lengthy period.)

6. Setting realistic objectives is imperative; both when deciding the area, nature, level and duration of sponsorhip, and in formulating strategy once participation has been decided upon.

7. Sponsorship is a business deal; a written contract is essential. It is important to establish a good relationship, with mutual recognition of the responsibilities and expectations of both parties.

8. The full benefits of the sponsorship will be achieved only if it is integrated with the company's other publicity activities; e.g., advertising, PR, sales promotion, staff and customer relations etc.

9. Procedures should be established for the control (including budgetary), monitoring and evaluation of the sponsorship programme.

10. First-time sponsors should consider obtaining advice and guidance— from relevant statutory bodies and/or a specialist consultancy or agency.

Sponsored books

The sponsored book is an excellent method of promotion and, if the editorial ᵗᵐe is carefully devised in association with a publisher, it can prove to be a ⁿcant instrument of marketing policy. The book usually relates to ⁿatter close to the firm's products or markets and should be practical and authoritative. (*The Industrial Applications of the Diamond* by N. R. Smith, Director of the diamond tool specialists, Van Moppes and Sons Ltd is a good example.) The author is usually a senior member of the firm and his or her name appears on the title page, linked with the name of his/her company. This is the only reference to the firm but all examples, pictures etc. are drawn from the firm's products and customers. The firm underwrites the cost of the book but takes an agreed percentage of revenue from all copies sold. It can thus be a self-liquidating exercise, but if it is not, there is always some financial return as libraries take the book, and the promotional cost is low. It should also be remembered that a published book is the most permanent and deeply penetrating method of communication yet devised.

Telemarketing

A new range of uses for the telephone has grown up over the past few years and looks likely to develop further. Already in the United States direct marketing by telephone is said to have exceeded that by mail. In a United States survey of industrial companies two-thirds of the respondents said they used the telephone for selling or lead generation.

In the United Kingdom the use of the telephone for selling has been slow to get off the ground due perhaps to the reaction by customers that such calls are intrusive and an unwarranted, and certainly undesirable, invasion of their privacy.

The function of telemarketing has grown in the United States into a highly disciplined activity by people having a natural aptitude for telephone conversation. They are well trained and usually work to a structured brief on what to say.

One of the most useful applications of the telephone in marketing is in market research where at least simple answers can be obtained in a very short space of time. There is little doubt however that other business uses of the telephone will expand. Campaign evaluation for example is worth considering as are readership surveys in relation to business people and industrial decision-makers.

Posters

Little use is made of posters in industrial publicity, and this may be a good reason for using them. They represent a first-class medium for getting across the basic sales message but the problem is in finding suitable site locations. Some obvious opportunities exist: exhibition halls, conferences, key railway stations, airports and even railway and underground trains. There are the company's own vehicles, sites adjacent to exhibition halls and hotels where visitors are likely to stay, taxis or even sandwich-board men. Posters can be used as direct mail pieces: they even occasionally reach the office wall if the design is outstanding enough.

Point of sale

Many industrial products, especially components, have a retail market and, however small, this is worth supporting. Consideration can therefore be given to showcards, dispensers, display units, give-away leaflets as well as posters. Point of sale material can also be of value in industrial merchandising, for instance, by agricultural merchants, electrical contractors or industrial wholesalers.

Packaging

With very many consumer products, food, toiletries and cigarettes, packaging may lay fair claim to be at least as important as the product itself. Apart from other factors, it preconditions a buyer to adopt a favourable attitude towards the contents: it is a vital part of building up a favourable brand image.

Professional buyers are not immune to subjective forces. A well-packaged or presented product will have the edge on one for which no trouble at all has been taken. It is equally true as with consumer goods that an over-packaged product may set up a resistance.

Most industrial products must be packaged in some way. A wooden crate with wood wool packing can be improved by including around the product a well-fitted polythene bag with a brand name on it. In place of a cardboard box an attractively printed carton can be used. Functional packaging also has a part to play: shrinkwrapping of gear wheels to prevent corrosion, a dust cover for an inspection microscope, expanded plastic case inserts for delicate machinery. A well-produced and appropriate piece of packing confirms the supplier's belief that his product is good enough to be carefully protected.

Gifts

The question of giving business gifts is more likely to set a boardroom alight than the most expensive advertising campaign. Does it establish a dangerous precedent? Will competitors follow suit? Where should the line be drawn and what of those who do not receive a gift, or worse still, get one this year but not next? These questions are answered only by a careful consideration of what to give, how and when to give it, and what repercussions are likely.

There can be few guidelines on gifts since the circumstances vary so much. The criterion is: does the gift make a maximum contribution to the promotion of sales at minimum cost? If to emboss the trade mark will provide additional publicity, for example with an item to stand on a desk or hang on an office wall, then it should be used. If it is likely to be out of place, say on something for the home, then it should not be used. Guidance on what not to give can usually be found in the multitude of business gift catalogues. The items in these are most likely to be what other firms will be choosing and there is a limit to the number of penknives and desk diaries that a buyer can absorb. Choose then something novel, something that sells, is appropriate and in good taste.

Christmas cards

These are included under sales promotion rather than under public relations, because they can be regarded as contributing to the selling effort. Where firms use Christmas cards as another direct mail shot to all and sundry there is a strong case for supposing that they are likely to be either ineffectual or even considered in bad taste and therefore counter-productive.

In industrial selling, however, a close personal relationship is often built up between a buyer and a salesperson—to their mutual advantage—and here an exchange of Christmas cards can surely be regarded as part of the building up of good relationships, and in so far as they contribute to efficient selling, an element of a sales promotional activity.

Brand-names

All products, including industrial, must have names. The buyer, and the user, must identify it and if the selling company does not provide an adequate name or identity, the buyer will invent one.

Furthermore, all products have an image. This may have evolved, or come by chance, or it may have been deliberately planned and promoted. The inescapable fact is that whenever a product is named to a buyer it conjures up a certain image which may be good or bad, cheap or expensive, reliable or unreliable. The brand-name itself is not necessarily a significant factor in determining the image of an industrial product. This would be too much to hope for, rather the image will be created by the product itself in the long run. However, it is the case that a product needs a name to identify it and to enable a buyer to recall it when making the purchase. The essential requirement is that it should be memorable, and the simpler the name is the better, both in the number of letters and the ease of pronunciation.

In determining a brand-name for an industrial product there would seem to be little point in basing it on, say, the raw materials from which it is made, or the process, or the town, or a nearby forest or river. There may be some advantage in a name which emphasizes the 'customer benefit', but if this leads to a word which is exotic, complex and highly contrived, it is better to abandon it and try for something simple. It is possible to aim for both but it will be hard to improve on such classics as OXO or KODAK.

Sales aids

The marketing services or publicity department often finds itself closely involved in a number of sales activities such as sales training, sales conferences and sales manuals. This is to be welcomed since it helps to weld the two functions. These, however, are not considered to be a major part of the promotional operation and for this reason are not dealt with in any detail. They are mentioned, however, because it is important that they are not overlooked in the overall marketing mix. Two matters which perhaps can be considered within the publicity framework are sales aids and samples.

Progressive sales managers will devote considerable time in training their sales staff to present the benefits of a product to a buyer, to overcome points of resistance and to close the deal. In this process a variety of aids can be deployed with advantage.

The product itself is the obvious choice together with the facilities to demonstrate it. This may be a demonstration caravan or a well-fitted show case. Where a product is not demonstrable, use can be made of a photograph album, a slide projector or a self-contained video unit. Samples of raw materials, for instance, need to be more than just a handful of pieces of sheet metal; these can be presented in such a way as to project their selling features attractively.

A sales presentation requires the skill of a stage show. The development of the argument needs to be planned, using the salesperson to the full, but support needs to be given with every appropriate visual, audio and three-dimensional aid. Pre-presentation material should be sent in advance to prepare the prospect, and the follow-up should make full use of sales literature, advertisement reprints, press cuttings and any other promotional material.

Whatever material is used, it should be geared to the sales arguments and method of visual presentation being used elsewhere, to achieve maximum integrated impact.

Stickers, stuffers and mailings

Correspondence from a company provides at least three opportunities for introducing, or at least reinforcing, a sales argument.

Suppose, for instance, that a new brand of heat-resisting paint is being launched and that all the conventional media of a major campaign are being brought to bear on the potential market. For a specified period of time and with suitable phasing, the brand-name together with the main slogan can be printed on to a mini-leaflet and stuffed into every envelope leaving the company; a small sticker can be affixed to each letter sent out; finally at very low cost all envelopes can be franked with a few key words. In themselves these are small actions, but viewed as a whole they help to give cohesion to a campaign, and have an impressive effect both on potential buyers and one's own staff.

Signboards

Signboards outside a factory are often overlooked, or left to the initiative of an architect or factory manager. A solution is to place the responsibility for company signs firmly on the publicity department. These may include large illuminated signs and neon lights, and range down to signposts and notice boards.

Seminars

Although perhaps part of educational public relations, seminars can have a direct selling function. Indeed in some branches of business, such as hi-tech and financial services, they have become a major selling activity. One company took over the Festival Hall to present a technical seminar on a new range of components having certain novel features. Not only did they fill the hall with prospective buyers, they also charged an entrance fee, and made a profit.

Summary

Finally, an interesting though dated indication of the usage of 'miscellaneous promotion items' is given in a publication by Metalworking Production[2] in relation to a segment of the engineering industry (see Table 12.1).

Checklist

1. Are novel means of sales promotion encouraged in order to get the edge on competition?
2. Is 'brainstorming' or other techniques used in which people are able to suggest the most unlikely ideas, without fear of criticism, in order to maximize on creative initiative?
3. Does such creative expression extend past headlines, copy angles, sign-offs, slogans and symbols, to include the medium, e.g., size and shape, material, colour, texture, feel, smell, wrapping and presentation?
4. Specifically, has consideration been given to:
   (a) TV and radio?
   (b) Sponsorship?
   (c) Telemarketing?

Table 11.1   Expenditure on miscellaneous promotional items

	Percentage
Regular press handouts	54
Christmas gifts	48
Christmas cards	45
Films	34
Calendars	30
Coloured slides and viewers	17
Mobile display vans	8
Diaries	8
Point of sale display panels	6
Press conferences	6
Private film shows/cocktail and theatre parties	4
Technical posters and wall charts	3
Advertising gifts and novelties	3
Works exhibitions and novelties	3

(d)   Seminars and conferences?

(e)   Christmas cards?

(f)   Calendars and diaries?

(g)   Point-of-sale material, posters, or wall charts?

(h)   Sponsored books and pamphlets?

(i)   Outgoing mail, stickers, stuffers, franking?

(j)   Sales aids, manuals, conferences, slides, films?

(k)   Brand-names and symbols?

(l)   Packaging and presentation?

References

1. *Guide to Sponsorship* (ISBA 1990).
2. *Special Report on the Buying and Selling Techniques used in the British Engineering Industry* (McGraw-Hill).

Part 3
RESEARCH

INTRODUCTION

During the past twenty years or so a great deal of progress has been made in applying research techniques to aspects of marketing. Initially this was concentrated in the consumer sector since it was here that the money was most readily available, and in a sense this was an easier area to investigate. The movement into industrial marketing was slow, and often inadequately based because of low budgets, and this in turn resulted in inaccurate results, discouraging further research and leading to yet lower budgets.

Persistence on the part of certain leading companies, publishers, and in particular a few specialist industrial research agencies, has led to a breakthrough to such an extent that sophisticated techniques are nowadays being applied to the marketing of industrial products and services. It may well be that in the future, expenditure on industrial marketing research will exceed that on consumer research.

The distinction should be drawn between market research and marketing research, particularly in the context of his book. Market research is concerned with the investigation of markets, their size, location, purchasing power, growth, capital structure and economics. This is only one aspect of the matter. Marketing research can be regarded as the application of research techniques to any facet of marketing including the market. Thus new product research, concept testing, attitude and motivation studies, patterns of buying behaviour, structure of decision-making units, are all part of the growing science of marketing research. Into this category fit media research and campaign evaluation, the subjects of the next two chapters.

Research processes are not infallible. The aim of any research activity is to reduce to a minimum the areas of uncertainty surrounding management decisions. The application of research techniques, and the use of scientific disciplines do not of themselves eliminate uncertainty. They merely provide a degree of precision to some of the criteria upon which marketing and other business decisions are based. The tendency in some quarters for marketing research to be regarded as wasteful or misleading is more often due to a blind reliance on, or a misinterpretation of, research data than the data itself being at fault. The solution lies in using professional expertise not only to conduct the research but also to interpret its significance.

12

MEDIA RESEARCH

Press advertising

Press advertising represents the largest single item in the industrial publicity budget.

In Chapter 4 emphasis was laid on the need for accurate media selection and the criteria which should be considered were broken down into fourteen categories. Some of these do not require research to evaluate them, for instance 'frequency' or 'special services from publisher'. Others require accurate data for intelligent decisions to be made.

CIRCULATION

It is necessary to be sceptical when considering media data and to examine closely the basis upon which it has been arrived at. Take for example total circulation. If a figure is quoted by a publisher, but unsupported by his membership of the Audit Bureau of Circulation (ABC) an advertiser must draw his own conclusions and at least be doubtful. A good deal of pioneer work has been done by *British Rate and Data* (published by Maclean Hunter) in insisting on data meeting certain standards before they will publish it.

Given that a total circulation figure is validated either by ABC or by postal certificate or perhaps some other acceptable audit, the question arises 'what precisely does this figure mean?'. This at least is an assurance that a certain number of copies went out through the post. But to whom did these copies go? Did they ask for them? And did they pay for them? Suppose in a specialized field there are 4000 separate identifiable purchasing units, and suppose a journal can prove that its specialized circulation is 4000, this is by no means a guarantee that it is addressed to 100 per cent of the market. Where the market for a particular publication is not homogeneous, the variations in coverage between one segment and another can be so great as to make a total circulation figure comparatively useless. Some progress has been made in the UK in providing details of circulation by means of the Media Data Form. This enables an advertiser to obtain reliable information on methods of circulation (free, subsidized, or full price), circulation to overseas countries and often a breakdown under United Kingdom geographical regions.

When a breakdown of industries or of occupations is in question, the situation is different. In the first place, such data on the Media Data Form is not audited and it is an unfortunate fact that from some publishers the figures can be little more than uninformed or approximate head-counting. Even where the job is done thoroughly and professionally by a publisher, there are real difficulties in knowing just how to categorize a given recipient, and in how much detail. Since, however, the usual reason for an analysis being required is to enable comparisons to be made between different, competitive publications it is necessary to note that such data is presented in a form which makes a comparison possible only in very few instances.

One basis which is used by publishers for circulation analysis is the Government *Standard Industrial Classification*. This breaks down the whole of British industry with a great deal of detail and provides explanatory notes on what is meant by each sub-classification. This does not enable a conglomerate to be easily classified, but for many requirements it is a valuable starting point.

Finally, it must be appreciated that circulation is continuously changing, with perhaps 20 per cent a year new registrations, offset by 20 per cent lapses. A judgement based on circulation this year, even if it is right, may be wrong after the year has elapsed. It is surprising that to meet the apparent demand of big advertisers, publishers devote their energies increasingly to expanding circulation as an end in itself, when the factor which really has any relevance at all is readership. This, also, should not be regarded as an end in itself since finally it is the impact of an advertisement which really counts, and this will be dealt with in the next chapter on campaign evaluation. In the meantime, there are several techniques which can be employed to measure readership.

TOTAL READERSHIP

Any readership survey is liable to considerable errors from differences in interpretation as to what constitutes 'readership' and how individual respondents react to the term. Accepting an initial margin of error, however, a good deal of progress can be made in measuring the usefulness of a journal in terms of readership as opposed to circulation. The same criticism of total readership applies as with total circulation, namely it tends to be of use only in a homogeneous market, for example hairdressers or market gardeners.

A study of the number of people reading a publication in comparison with its circulation is often most revealing. For instance a magazine distributed only to members of an association or institute may have fewer readers than its circulation because not all members will spend time reading something they receive as a part of their membership. Furthermore they probably do not bother to take it into the office and circulate it. Against this, many publications exist which can fairly claim a readership of eight or more people per copy. Controlled circulation journals probably do not achieve such high reader/copy ratings, partly because they tend to send out individual copies as a matter of policy. Indeed this may be regarded as a strength since, if speed of communication is important, it is not in the best interest of an advertiser to use a publication which takes a month or two to reach out to all its readers.

A research into journals covering the instrumentation and automation industries gave a dramatic example of the differences which can occur between circulation and readership and resulted in quite different asessments in terms of 'cost/1000'. Table 12.1 is an extract from this survey.

Table 12.1   Cost per 1000 circulation compared with readership

Journal	Circulation	Estimated readership	Cost/1000 circulation	Cost/1000 readership
C	10 400	9 700	£6	£6.6
A	11 500	42 000	£7	£1.9
D	8 000	28 000	£7.9	£2.2
F	9 200	8 700	£10.7	£11
E	5 000	27 000	£13.4	£2.5
B	16 300	47 000	£16.5	£5.7

One of the problems facing a researcher into readership by industrial and business personnel is to determine a satisfactory definition of the 'universe' and then to find a reliable method of sampling. Table 12.1 was produced from a series of interviews at an exhibition that, because of its size and importance, could be regarded as counting among its visitors a representative cross-section of the whole industry being surveyed. Such an assumption is of course an immediate source of bias and must be considered when assessing the results.

The use of the interview is particularly important in readership surveys since readers are unable to distinguish between one journal and another without aided recall. The above survey used a flipchart with the front covers of each journal. As can be seen, the ranking order of publications in terms of cost/1000 circulation changes radically compared with cost/1000 readers.

An early survey into the horticultural field concentrated on two magazines *Grower* and the *Commercial Grower*. Initially a postal questionnaire was used and a result obtained. The question then arose of possible confusion of names, as a result of which an interview research was conducted that proved that the original results were quite incorrect.

A more recent study 'Engineering Publications in the UK' by Maclean Hunter, provided a comparison between circulation and readership as shown in Table 12.2.

Without a careful scrutiny of the sample base and the methods involved in obtaining and processing the data, it is not reasonable to take the figures as they stand in Table 12.2 and draw specific conclusions. What can be demonstrated is the extent to which a schedule drawn up on the basis of circulation can be wrong compared with a readership base.

Table 12.2   Readership compared with circulation

	Readership	Circulation	Readers/copy
Engineering	105 000	20 045	5.25
Mechanical Engineering News	89 000	71 767	1.24
The Engineer	87 000	37 964	2.29
Engineers Digest	46 000	15 568	2.95
Engineering Today	44 000	50 932	0.86
Chartered Mechanical Engineer	39 000	47 962	0.81

SEGMENTED READERSHIP

Here the objective is to find the readership habits of a specific group, usually a company's potential market, or a segment of it. Very often a company's own mailing list is not acceptable as being representative of the potential market: it may be for this reason that press advertising is being used to reach purchasing influences which are unknown. Each problem tends to be entirely different, and sampling methods need to be individually planned.

An example of the use of a segmented readership analysis was a survey of buyers of paperboard for carton and box-making. In this case, an examination of the total readership of the packaging press would have been meaningless since the number of converters of cardboard adds up to hundreds, while the number of users of packages as a whole amounts to tens of thousands. The result showed that the most popular and large-circulation journals scored badly, and of course they were expensive whereas certain minor journals did well. The budget was cut by 75 per cent.

DUPLICATION

When compiling a schedule to obtain maximum coverage or 'reach' it is important to examine the overlap of various publications, that is the extent of readership duplication. Researches into this aspect of readership have enabled schedules to be cut significantly, or alternatively for expenditures to be concentrated into significantly fewer publications, achieving much greater impact. A good deal of work on this has been carried out by a leading advertising agency on behalf of its clients. For one product the media department had identified some one hundred journals which, at least from the publishers' claims, could be considered as possible advertising media. A survey showed that one journal alone covered 89 per cent of the potential market while the second most important rated 68 per cent. Added together they amounted to 93 per cent, an exceptionally high coverage by any standards and well above the average. It is interesting to note that the sixth journal out of this massive list scored only 26 per cent.

A similar study carried out by an electronics company showed that there was no gain in advertising in more than three journals since the addition of a fourth added so little additional coverage as to be worthless.

A body of evidence begins to appear which leads to the conclusion that the law of diminishing returns applies in media scheduling wherever more than just two or three publications are available to reach a given market. The same results come from research into American business publications and the graph in Figure 12.1 is typical of many such investigations. As can be seen, if duplication of readership is not required there is little point in advertising in more than three publications—in a homogeneous market.

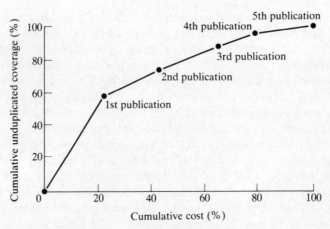

Figure 12.1   Cumulative readership—law of diminishing returns (*Source:* McGraw-Hill Report 1120.4)

It is interesting, though not surprising, that the law of diminishing returns in cumulative audience coverage also applies to consumer publications. In a survey of United Kingdom newspapers a similar phenomenon was to be found, as shown in Table 12.3. In this example, the addition of *The Times* to

Table 12.3 Cumulative unduplicated readership

Publication	Cumulative unduplicated readership by businessmen (%)
Sunday Times	39
Daily Telegraph	55
The Financial Times	60
The Times	62

the schedule would add only 2 per cent to the number of businessmen having the opportunity to see (OTS) a particular advertisement.

EDITORIAL EXCELLENCE

This must be regarded as a highly subjective area and one which must pay regard to the views of experts in the subject matter of a particular journal. With subscription magazines it might be considered that circulation is some

Table 12.4 Editorial page traffic

Editorial item	Interest rating (%)
Comment	60
Planning for decimals	91
Mechanical accounting	
Background to reappraisal	53
Visible record accounting computers	44
Special purpose accounting computers	36
Machine detail chart	26
Business man and machine in the 70s—a 2-day seminar	36
Design flow chart	22
Eat, drink and be wary	43
The greatest show on earth	32
Computerscope	
IBM announce magnetic tape keyboard peripherals	19
Insurance moves into real-time	14
A score for Scottish Honeywell	13
Mintech guide to installing a computer	17
The computer bureau scene	
Jobs for the boys	16
Fast start for Inter-Bank	10

measure of the value readers put on the editorial. This concept is clouded by the variety of circulation techniques used, though readership figures tend to overcome this difficulty.

One interesting research technique, which follows the Starch method in the United States, is the measurement of page traffic, i.e. the percentage of readers who claim to have read or noted a particular advertisement or editorial item. A few British publishers are using this technique and although the results must be regarded as being approximate, a good measure of consistency has appeared in relating one type of editorial item with another. Making comparisons between journals is a more difficult task but is not impossible.

An extract from a survey of *Business Systems and Equipment*, published by Maclean Hunter, is reproduced in Table 12.4.

Another type of study on editorial excellence was carried out in connection with *Travel Agency*. This showed that respondents spent an average of 1 hour 12 minutes reading the journal, and that 68 per cent claimed to read every issue: 24 per cent most issues.

A further study[1] looked at the place where journals are read and as is seen in Table 12.5 there can be a wide variation between one journal and another. The journals were all connected with civil engineering. The abbreviations are of the names of the journals. In the case of *NCE*, most of the recipients had the journal mailed to them at home which accounts for its high 'at home' rating.

Table 12.5 Where journals are read

	NCE	CN	CJ	CE	CP&E	PMJ
At home	78%	32%	22%	9%	18%	14%
At work	25%	63%	72%	75%	76%	83%
When travelling	—	—	1%	—	1%	—
Other	1%	10%	6%	16%	5%	3%

Another hitherto ignored factor about readers is their age. Figure 12.2 comes from Cahners Publishing Co. in the States and portrays a fairly typical spread of ages. It is worth noting that the average age was 45 but that varied from one job category to another. Clearly this factor is important for copywriters since it will determine the style of writing.

JOURNALS' REPUTATION

Over and above the intrinsic editorial value, a journal acquires a certain reputation which to some extent reflects on advertisements placed in it. It may be claimed for instance that the quality image of *The Times* tends

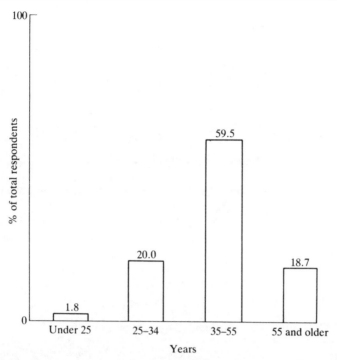

Figure 12.2   Age of recipients of business magazines (*Source:* Cahners Research No. 536.1)

subconsciously to enhance the view a reader takes of a product advertised in it.

There are a variety of techniques which can be used to evaluate 'journal reputation', each depending upon the particular circumstance. An interesting use of a semantic scale has been employed to compare a number of electronic journals. The following is an extract from the questionnaire:

> How would you rank the journals listed below for their conciseness, up-to-dateness, etc.?

> Here are a set of scales (Figure 12.3). We would like you to mark them as follows: if you find, say, *Wireless World* eminently concise, just as you would like it in fact from this point of view, then tick the scale in the space next to the word 'concise'; if you normally find it extremely long-winded, then tick the other end. You may feel, however, that the magazine ranks somewhere between these extremes; if so, then place your tick accordingly.

A survey into the printing industry was conducted in order to establish readership among managing directors of printing houses. Additionally the question was asked 'which single journal do you find most valuable?'. The point here is that there will sometimes arise a situation in which two journals

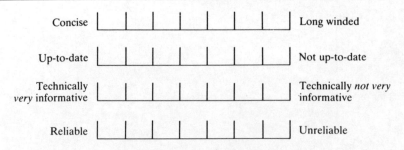

Figure 12.3   Semantic rating scale

score equally well in readership rating and even in segmented cost/1000, but their reputations may be of a different order.

One company asked readers which journal they would look through first if they were looking for a particular component. While the readership figures varied by up to a factor of two or so, the responses to this specific question were quite significant. A selection is reproduced in Table 12.6 to show the effect.

Table 12.6   'Journal preference' for a particular purpose

Publication	Read regularly (%)	Look at first for a particular component (%)
B	59.0	53.9
D	48.4	67.5
A	48.3	8.2
G	41.6	—
E	34.6	18.3
F	29.5	13.9
C	28.9	4.9

SPECIAL SERVICES TO PUBLISHERS

Some publishers recognize that it is valuable to assist the industries they cover by providing information which, even if not related specifically to the publications themselves, helps their clients to produce more effective advertising. Such a service is not in itself a reason for placing advertising in a sponsoring magazine, but it is reasonable to assume that publishers who try to meet the needs of their clients with supplementary research data might well concern themselves in a similar way with ensuring that their journals are written and distributed with competence and care. One particular service which has been developed extensively is to access the circulation list for direct-mail purposes. This can be a very valuable supplementary channel of communication.

Other media

In dealing with each of the major channels of persuasion in previous chapters, emphasis has been laid on the need for measuring results. This is in effect post-research. The object of media research is pre-research or, alternatively, research which, even if after an event, can be applied to future or similar cases.

Attempts have been made to assess the value placed on various media by buyers and it is surprising to find how few people are prepared to admit to being influenced to any degree by advertising, particularly men.

A survey in the *British Printer* asking printers which means of communication they found the most valuable source of information produced the result shown in Table 12.7.

Table 12.7   Influence of various media on British printing by company size (%)

| | *Total* | *Number of employees* | | | | |
		1–24	*25–49*	*50–99*	*100–199*	*200+*
The trade press	36	28	47	48	50	60
Calls by representatives	40	47	36	31	19	19
Exhibitions and trade fairs	10	8	7	18	25	12
Letters and brochures sent to you through the post	15	19	10	8	9	9

It is interesting to note how the trade press rating changed according to size of company. Indeed the whole mixture changed with company size, which points to another variable in market segmentation and the need to evaluate media against a specific segment whether this be product group, application group, size group, geographical group or whatever.

A similar investigation was included in the *How British Industry Buys* survey from which Table 12.8 was extracted.

Again it is interesting to note the variations which occur between different management functions in a company.

EXHIBITIONS

There is considerable scope for the provision of more data on exhibitions particularly authenticated information which is relevant to an advertiser's needs. Some organizers already record information about visitors as they

Table 12.8 Influence of various media on different types of personnel in British industry.* (*Source:* Hugh Buckner, *How British Industry Buys*)

	Board (general management)	Operating management	Prod. engineering	Des. and dev. engineering	Maint. engineering	Research	Buying	Finance	Sales	Other
Catalogues	39	36	45	64	34	64	52	32	44	76
Direct mail	12	9	14	6	31	21	23	14	5	27
Sales engineers' visits	66	61	60	67	78	64	64	60	73	40
Advertisements in trade press	14	32	28	22	21	15	12	23	24	24
Exhibitions	15	17	11	11	47	15	9	19	14	12
Demonstrations by manufacturers	50	41	35	26	37	21	37	38	45	22
Other	6	4		6			5	5	35	

*In industry, personnel with these functions consider, in the percentages shown, these factors to be among the two most important when obtaining information on products. For example: in industry generally board members, who play more than an occasional role in purchasing, in 66 per cent of cases consider sales engineers' visits to be among the two most important methods of obtaining information on products.

enter the exhibition hall. This will lead to exhibitions becoming more effective selling functions and in the long term will benefit the whole exhibition industry. Much remains to be investigated: corridor traffic for instance, the value of an island site or one near an entrance, the gallery versus the ground floor, and shell stands as against elaborate tailor-mades.

As has been indicated, research data on exhibitions are hard to come by, and do not yet represent a consolidated body of evidence. An example of useful information comes from a study of the International Electrical Engineers Exhibition. This showed that visitors stopped or talked at an average of 14 stands, and spent an average of 5.3 hours at the exhibition.

A more recent research showed that 61 per cent of visitors attended the International Wire Exhibition in Basle for more than one day as shown in Figure 12.4. The arithmetic average time spent in the exhibition halls was 5 hours per day, and the average length of stay for all visitors was 2.2 days. The number of stands visited varied widely between 2 or 3 and 30 in any one day: the arithmetic average was 13. The same research investigated the show's value or usefulness. On a scale of 1–7 where 1 represented the lowest

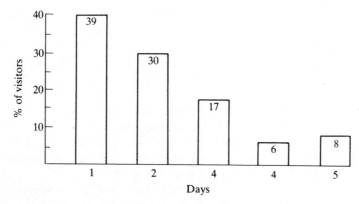

Figure 12.4 Length of stay at exhibition (*Source:* Mack-Brooks Research Report)

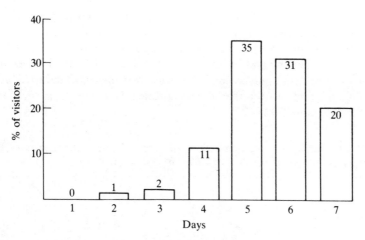

Figure 12.5 Exhibition visitor preference (*Source:* Mack-Brooks Research Report)

perceived value of the exhibition according to the visitor and 7 the highest, the results were shown as in Figure 12.5. Eighty-six per cent rated the exhibition above average and the arithmetic mean was 5.6.

Matching the market

The usefulness of media information—who reads what, who sees what, who is influenced by what—presupposes that a company is able to define its potential market with an adequate degree of accuracy.

A good deal of work has been done in examining who in a firm is responsible for buying decisions and it is evident that there may be up to a dozen people to be reached and sometimes more. An investigation in depth into a large manufacturer established that while a 'yes' decision could be made by four people, a decision not to purchase a given raw material could be made on the basis of a negative report from any one of twenty-three people. Yet the salesperson concerned saw no more than two people.

A frequently quoted average is eight people per company, and this, when multiplied by the number of manufacturing units in Great Britain (in excess of 50 000), brings the number of people involved in industrial purchasing to nearly half a million. And in matching media to market, the industrial press alone consists of over 2000 different publications.

Even so, there is nothing special about the job of matching which cannot be carried out by a normally competent marketing team given adequate support from published and commissioned research and subsequent statistical analysis.

There are two useful reference works which are of particular significance. The first is the *Standard Industrial Classification* which categorizes in some detail every trade and industry, and second the work pioneered by the Institute of Marketing and Industrial Market Research Ltd, which examined in considerable depth purchasing influence across the whole industrial sector, revealing a number of hitherto unquantified characteristics such as the example shown in Table 12.9.

Table 12.9 Purchasing 'decision-makers' showing who decides which supplier gets an order (%) (*Source:* Hugh Buckner, *How British Industry Buys*)

	Board (general management)	Operating management	Prod. engineering	Des. and dev. engineering	Maint. engineering	Research	Buying	Finance	Sales	Others in company	Others outside company
Plant equipment	44	28	10	7	3	—	19	1	—	2	—
Materials	17	25	5	6	1	4	52	1	1	1	1
Components	10	25	6	9	4	4	39	1	1	1	—

The extract from the Buckner study given above has been further amplified by a research now published periodically by *The Financial Times*, entitled *How British Industry Buys*.

A further piece of research on decision-makers is to be found in *Modern*

Purchasing on the influence of purchasing managers in the procurement of a variety of products and services and this is shown in Table 12.10. As can be seen the purchasing authority of buyers appears to be very limited.

Table 12.10   Purchasing responsibilities of buyers. (*Source: Modern Purchasing*)

Product	Actually selects supplier (%)	Has no influence (%)
Computer hardware	8	36
Air freight services	16	50
Vending machines	20	45
Floor cleaning contractors	26	48
Calculators	28	13
Cars	28	29
Fuel oil	44	16
Cartons	63	7
Stationery	74	8
Ball point pens	77	9

Research techniques

The techniques for media assessment are not excessively complex, difficult or expensive: nor are the results any more or less approximate than those from other types of research. It is perhaps surprising that this sector of marketing research has not expanded more rapidly, since the savings which can be achieved are both immediate and large. Given the lack of suitable information on all types of media it must follow that any promotional budget which does not make provision for some form of readership or comparative research is not likely to be utilizing its expenditure to the full.

Commenting on the opportunities in assessing advertising effectiveness Aubrey Wilson, a pioneer in this field, had this to say:

Advertising results, even the most enthusiastic supporters concede, are still largely unpredictable. Thus advertising poses one of the most difficult areas for manage-ment decisions and, therefore, one in which the accumulation of any knowledge is disproportionately valuable. Mistakes in advertising strategy and technique are costly and difficult, if not impossible, to rectify and expenditure is almost invariably irrecoverable. A misplaced purchase of a machine tool or vehicle will at worst, yield the second-hand value of the product. Not only can nothing be saved from unsuccessful advertising but often additional monies will be needed to correct the errors made. For these and other reasons advertising research is taking on a new importance as industrial advertising begins to take an increasing part in industrial marketing operations.

Checklist

1. Are your target audiences defined in sufficient detail to enable media readership to be compared with them?
2. Have you made an assessment of each proposed publication in terms of

    (a) Circulation—total and segmented?
    (b) Readership—total and segmented?
    (c) Cost per reader?
    (d) Rates—possible reductions?
    (e) Authenticity of any research data?
    (f) Editorial quality?
    (g) Journal's reputation?
    (h) Method of circulation?
    (i) Frequency of publication?
    (j) Readership duplication?

3. Have you set aside a budget for media research to supplement the available information?
4. Is there evidence to justify using more than three publications to reach a particular audience?
5. Are the publishers you are patronizing prepared to co-operate by way of (a) page traffic studies, (b) split-runs and (c) mailing list?
6. Have you established the relative importance of each channel of communication with your particular potential customers?

References

1. Survey of purchasing and readership (Research Services Ltd).

13

CAMPAIGN EVALUATION

Campaign evaluation can be difficult and expensive, but this is by no means inevitable. It is true that some campaigns cannot be measured in total, but this does not mean that measurements cannot be made of some of the component parts, which will result in an improvement in cost-effectiveness.

The position has been well stated by L. W. Rodger[1] whose comments on advertising could be taken to apply to the whole range of promotional activities.

> The advertising budget probably represents the largest amount of money disbursed by manufacturers with no precise measure of what it can be expected to achieve. The spending of large sums of money on advertising without some system of accountability can be compared to conducting a business without a book-keeping or accounting department. Advertising accountability has lagged far behind general management accountability in that the latter is held responsible for accomplishing certain specific and usually, measurable results in relation to money spent. Sound business operation demands that expenditure and results be related. The idea of holding advertising accountable for accomplishing certain sales results is certainly not new. But there is now a growing body of expert opinion that the sales criterion, as applied to advertising in isolation, is based on a fundamental misconception.

Rodger goes on to develop his theme on the criteria for evaluating a campaign in terms which are relevant to the media and also capable of implementation.

> Advertising is a means of communication. Its results can only be measured in terms of communication goals, in terms of the cost per advertising message delivered per customer for a given result. In other words, according to Colley, 'an advertising goal is a specific communication task, to be accomplished among a defined audience to a given degree in a given period of time'.

Lack of progress in the development of campaign evaluation is generally to be put down to the lack of defined specific goals, or alternatively to the setting of goals that are invalid.

It is not only the number of individuals in a company who contribute to a purchasing decision who must be considered, but also the many factors which are likely to influence each person's judgement on where an order should be placed. Typical influences give an idea of the complexity of the operation:

1. Used it in my previous firm.
2. Saw it at an exhibition.
3. Salesman convinced me of its quality.
4. I'd heard of the company's name.
5. Read about it in the press.
6. My MD knows the supplier's MD.
7. Swiss machines are always more reliable.
8. This firm was the only one to supply enough technical data.
9. I always get a bottle of Scotch from this firm.
10. All our other machines are this make.
11. Recommended by a friend.

The list is endless and highly subjective, notwithstanding the usual test of 'price-delivery-quality-service' which so many buyers like to believe is the sole basis for decision-making.

To take expenditure on advertising, or sales promotion, or even on the overall marketing function, and expect to be able to relate it precisely to sales (that is purchasing) is clearly unrealistic. It is made more complicated by the fact that for many industrial products, the gestation period between the original enquiry and an order is often more than a year. One authority has estimated an average time lag, depending on the product, of between one and four years.

Component research

If all influences cannot be researched in total, it is necessary to examine each 'component' of purchasing influence and decide whether it is amenable to scientific evaluation. From the various 'channels of persuasive communications' many criteria, some more detailed than others, can be tested. Copy-testing an advertisement, measurement of product awareness, brand-name research, product-company association, attitude studies, and finally, measurement of communications goals are some examples which can be examined here.

An examination of the sales communication process in Figure 13.1 well illustrates how very simple it is to consider each stage from advertisements to repeat business. Clearly each block is amenable to some form of evaluation and a relationship can be established with the next in the process. But equally it can be seen how easy it is for extraneous factors to invalidate conclusions based solely upon such a simplistic flow diagram. If the product performance is unsatisfactory, or the price or delivery, then the conversion factor between quotation and first order will be affected. If competition suddenly becomes

Figure 13.1 Sales schematic diagram

fierce, conversion from enquiry to sales call may change. There are, then, factors quite outside the marketing communications area which prevent a valid relationship between advertising and sales being established as a basis of campaign evaluation.

An analysis of the communications process can be taken further and broken down into more components in order to make monitoring more effective and accurate. Figure 13.2 as a model is perhaps a somewhat academic approach and has been devised quite deliberately in this way so as to allow readers to adopt a system of their own in more practical terms.

In Figure 13.2, known as Sequential Advertising Measurement, the starting point is with the 'message' (selling proposition) which is then formulated into a 'creative expression' (e.g. advertisement), which appears in a 'medium' (journal) and achieves 'attention' (page traffic noting) and 'impact' (recall). This then changes the 'attitude' of a prospect which arguably changes his or her 'behavioural intent' (what is to be purchased) and ultimately leads to a certain 'behaviour' (the order). Fulfilment of the order leads to 'contentment' as a result of acquiring the 'product' which has a 'performance', representing to the customer a 'benefit' which is the basis of the selling proposition, i.e. the 'message'. And so the circuit is complete.

Now the proposition is that each block can be taken in turn, objectives set,

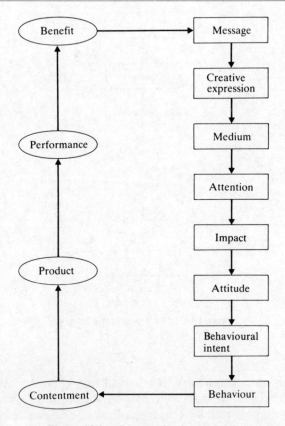

Figure 13.2 Communications model

quantified, measured and adjusted. The diagram has been converted into a table referred to as an Ad Evaluator Checklist, and showing nine discrete stages together with suggested sources of data.

From Table 13.1 a somewhat alarming calculation can be made of communications efficiency. Suppose each stage is 80 per cent efficient, and this is surely unlikely, then the cumulative efficiency of this particular communications system would be 17 per cent. This compares interestingly with a classical work on this subject in which messages from top management to shop-floor operatives were received by only 7 per cent. This was referred to as a 'somewhat opaque situation'.[2] Maybe advertising executives would do well to face up to the opaque screen which screens their products, their messages and their company.

Table 13.1   Seventeen possible sources of data for the evaluation of advertising within a sales context

Communication component	Data source
1. Customer benefit/message	1.1 Customer needs and wants—group discussion 1.2 Syndicated research
2. Creative expression/advertisement	2.1 Ad. pre-test—group discussion 2.2 Brand name pre-test
3. Transmission/medium	3.1 Readership research
4. Attention/interest	4.1 Page traffic 4.2 Read-most rating
5. Impact/action	5.1 Enquiries 5.2 Recall 5.3 Brand awareness
6. Attitude	6.1 Company/brand reputation
7. Behavioural intent/procurement motivation	7.1 Brand preference 7.2 Test market
8. Behaviour/1st order	8.1 Sales statistics 8.2 Competitor research
9. Satisfaction/repeat purchase	9.1 Sales statistics 9.2 Sales reports

Advertising testing

There are a number of techniques in common usage:

PAGE TRAFFIC

A first requirement of any advertisement is that it should be seen or 'noted'. In the United States it is not uncommon to use Starch ratings obtained by questioning readers by personal interview, on which advertisements they can remember (by 'aided recall'). In the United Kingdom the same idea has been tried by a number of publishers, but usually using a postal questionnaire.

The technique is to send out a second copy of a particular issue, say two weeks after publication, asking a sample readership to cross through any advertisement which they recall having noted in the original issue. An alternative approach is to ask respondents to indicate which advertisements they found of interest.

Such a technique may appear to be subjective and approximate, but a high enough degree of consistency is obtained to enable an advertiser to draw the conclusion that a particular advertisement is not performing as well as is required. Table 13.2, extracted from an interest rating survey by *Modern Purchasing*, indicates the kind of results that can be obtained.

Table 13.2   Advertisement page-traffic. (*Source: Modern Purchasing*)

Product type	Advertisement size	Interest rating (percentage of respondents finding an advertisement of interest)
Raw material	1 page black and white	20.3
Raw material	1 page black and white	5.9
Raw material	¼ page black and white	12.7
Raw material	2 pages black and white	12.7
Electrical goods	1 page 2 colours	3.4
Industrial fasteners	½ page black and white	14.4
Industrial fasteners	1 page 2 colours	6.8
Machinery	2 pages black and white	8.5
Tools	¼ page black and white	16.9
Exhibition	Inset black and white	17.8

In the issue in question, the highest rated advertisement was for storage equipment, a single page which scored 33.1 per cent. It is, however, by no means unknown from other researches for advertisements to score zero, but this does not necessarily mean that the advertisement itself is useless. It may only be in the wrong publication. But it does mean that it is not doing its job.

It is interesting to compare such ratings with those obtained from editorial items. Referring again to the *Modern Purchasing* survey the average score for recall of advertisements was 9.9 per cent whereas for editorial items a figure of 41.4 per cent was obtained.

From data made available by publishers, notably Maclean Hunter, some interesting facts emerge. For instance in Figure 13.3, the percentage of readers showing an interest in a particular ad can be compared with the interest ratings for editorials. The interest profile for ads peaks at around 8 per cent (arithmetic mean is 9.9 per cent), while editorials cover a very wide span, from 10 to 90 per cent, and peak at 35 per cent.

This data comes from an examination of seven different researches covering three particular non-competing business publications and encompasses an evaluation of 484 ads. This number is regarded as sufficiently large for further analysis which at least can be said to be indicative of trends.

Take as an example the widely held assumption that an advertisement will do better if it is positioned facing editorial instead of being drowned in a sea

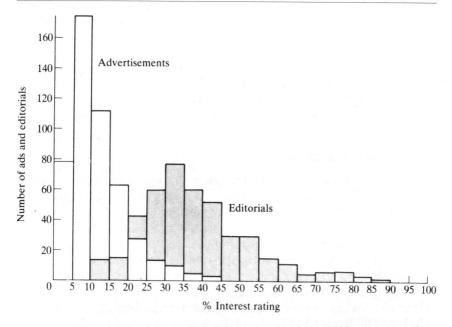

Figure 13.3 Advertisement ratings compared with editorials

of other ads. In terms of interest created, there was no significant difference between the 250 ads involved in this study.

Another commonly held view is that the addition of a second colour will increase the effectiveness of an advertisement. To throw some light on this factor, the ads in the above survey were further analysed and while a few two-colour ads achieved the highest individual scores, the overall effect was of no difference.

This of course does not reflect the attitude or image created, but merely the interest. Even here, the scope of the survey is not sufficiently broad to enable firm conclusions to be drawn. It does, however, call into question the blind acceptance that a second colour must produce better results.

Even when small advertisement spaces are used, it seems that some good performances can be obtained. There is a similarity between interest ratings for quarter pages as against half-page ads. From this it would seem that providing the subject is right, and creatively expressed, the size of the ad doesn't make too much difference.

There must come a stage at which the dominance of an ad is determined by size. Evidence of this comes from a comparison of the average score for two-page and larger ads with the average figure for all ads. The larger ads achieved something like twice the effect of the average.

In order to draw some conclusions about those advertisements with the highest scores, a detailed examination was made of the top 67 ads—those scoring 20 per cent and over. The two highest (over 40 per cent scores) were both two-page black and white, but more than half were single page, of which the bulk were one-colour. The majority of the DPS ads were here, but so also were eight small ads. At the other extreme, several ads received a zero rating and back covers in particular did not seem to do too well.

ADVERTISEMENT READERSHIP

'Noting' an advertisement is only the first step. The Starch research goes on to question which advertisements were read. The criterion is actually to have 'read most' of the copy. Whereas figures for noting an advertisement may range between 10 per cent and 30 per cent, the number of people claiming to have read most of an advertisement is more likely to be only a few per cent. Paradoxically, there are sometimes instances of an advertisement getting a relatively low 'noted' score, but a high 'read most' figure.

Studies in the United States indicate no difference in 'read most' as between back and front of a magazine, but bleed ads score 25 per cent higher (McGraw-Hill Report 3066).

ADVERTISEMENT RECALL

Another type of recall test can be to mail out a copy of one specific advertisement as part of a questionnaire and ask the question 'Do you remember seeing the enclosed advertisement?'. This has the merit of assessing the overall effectiveness of the advertisement, having regard to all the publications where it appeared. For example, a research in connection with printing machinery determined that 30.1 per cent respondents remembered seeing the advertisement and 69.9 per cent did not. A similar investigation for computer equipment obtained a recall of 34.6 per cent and a negative response of 65.4 per cent. From such tests, over a period it is possible to determine the effectiveness of one advertisement against another, and the degree of penetration being achieved.

An alternative technique is to telephone a sample of readers and ask questions about a particular advertisement. One such research for a dictating machine produced recalls over a period of time ranging from 40 to 60 per cent.

ADVERTISEMENT ENQUIRIES

In Chapter 4 on press advertising the use of enquiries or sales leads was discussed as a means of advertisement evaluation. This can be a valid criterion and indeed it may be argued that it matters little what 'attention' an advertisement scores; what really matters is what action follows. If action in the form of enquiries is what is required of an advertisement, then this is a reasonable argument, provided the quality of the enquiries can be measured.

ENQUIRIES RELATED TO SIZE

A little publicized but immensely important piece of research was conducted by Cahners Publishing Co. in America. The first, No. 250.1, produced the information shown in Figure 13.4. The data came from an analysis of 500 000 enquiries and can therefore claim a reasonable measure of statistical reliability. It shows that size of advertisement has surprisingly little effect on the number of enquiries generated, and certainly nothing like a linear relationship.

The next step is to plot this data against cost per enquiry (see Fig. 13.5) whereupon it is shown that enquiries from whole page ads cost more than double those from small sizes.

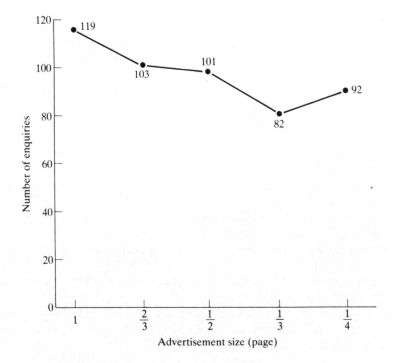

Figure 13.4 Enquiries by advertisement size (*Source:* Cahners Research Report No. 250.1)

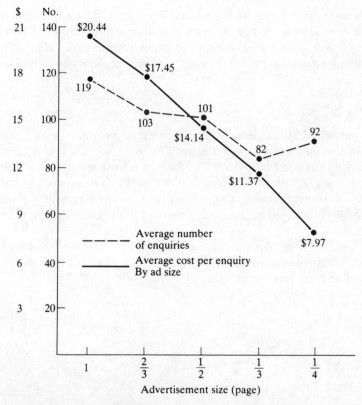

Figure 13.5   Cost per enquiry

Other Cahners Researches show that:

1. Advertising readership (as against enquiries) is not influenced by the use of coupons (Cahners 114.1).
2. Copy set in reverse (white upon black) is read at a 10 per cent slower rate than black on white (Cahners 1310.1).
3. Type set in lower case is read 13 per cent faster than that set in all capitals (Cahners 1310.4).
4. From a survey of 35 journals the average readership per copy was three (Cahners 412.0).
5. Cover ads receive a higher recall by an average of 40% (Cahners 116.1B).
6. Readership of ads increases as size increases in spite of figures shown earlier relating to enquiries (Cahners 110.1B).

With some product groups, particularly where repeat business is rare, a series of ratios can be established which, if constant, can enable a campaign to be assessed very effectively. For instance, given the average cost per enquiry, the average conversion into a quotation, the average number of quotations per order and the average value per order, an advertising budget can be calculated directly from the sales budget and targets set for each stage in the process so that any failure in performance can be pinpointed, and corrective action taken. However, few product groups are so simply constituted as to enable this procedure to be implemented with any degree of certainty.

10 RULES FOR SUCCESSFUL BUSINESS ADVERTISING

A piece published by the American journal *Business Marketing* led to the following checklist for a successful business ad. The basis of this evaluation is that there are just ten criteria for evaluating an advertisement. Each one of these has been given a 'weighting' so that marks can be awarded under each head from zero to whatever is the numerical figure given as a maximum. These maxima have been allocated in such a way that when added together they equal 50. Thus if the eventual score for a given ad is doubled, then the figure is in effect a percentage.

1. Attention Value (9)
The successful ad has a high degree of visual magnetism
On average, only a small number of ads in an issue of a magazine will capture the attention of any one reader. Some ads will be passed by because the subject matter is of no concern. But others, even though they may have something to offer, fail the very first test of stopping the reader in his or her scanning of the pages.

Ads perish right at the start because, at one extreme, they just lie there on the page, flat and grey, and at the other extreme, they are cluttered, noisy and hard to read.

An ad should be constructed so that a single component dominates the area—a picture, the headline or the text—but not the company name or logo.

Obviously, the more pertinent the picture, the more arresting the headline, the more informative the copy appears to be, the better.

2. Instant Message (5)
The successful ad selects the right audience
Often, an ad is the first meeting place of two parties looking for each other.

So there should be something in the ad that at first glance will enable readers to identify it as a source of information relating to their job interests—a problem they will have or an opportunity they will welcome.

This is done with either a picture or a headline—preferably both—the ad should say immediately to the reader, 'Hey, this is for you.'

3. Familiar Terminology (2)
The successful ad invites the reader into the scene
Within the framework of the layout, the art director's job is to visualize,

illuminate and dramatize the selling proposition.

And the art director must take into consideration the fact that the type of job a reader has dictates the selection of the illustrative material. Design engineers work with drawings. Construction engineers like to see products at work. Chemical engineers are comfortable with flow charts. Managers relate to pictures of people and so on.

4. Promise Specific Benefit (4)
The successful ad will promise a reward

An ad will survive the qualifying round only if readers are given reason to expect that if they continue on, they will learn something of value. A brag-and-boast headline, a generalization, an advertising platitude will turn readers off before they get into the message.

The reward that the ad offers can be explicit or implicit, and can even be stated negatively, in the form of warning of a possible loss.

The promise should be specific, the headline 'Less maintenance cost' is not as effective as 'You can cut maintenance costs 25%.'

5. Factual Back Up—Case History—Endorsement (3)
The successful ad backs up the promise

To make the promise believable, the ad must provide hard evidence that the claim is valid.

Sometimes, a description of the product's design or operation characteristics will be enough to support the claim.

Comparisons with competition can be convincing. Case histories make the reward appear attainable. Best of all are testimonials; 'They-say' advertising carries more weight than 'We-say' advertising.

6. Logical Progression of Argument (2)
The successful ad presents the selling proposition in logical sequence

The job of the art director is to organize the parts of an ad so that there is an unmistakeable entry point (the single dominant component referred to earlier) and the reader is guided through the material is a sequence consistent with the logical development of the selling proposition.

A layout should not call attention to itself. It should be a frame within which the various components are arranged.

7. Simple Writing Style—Short Words and Sentences (2)
The successful ad talks 'Person-to-Person'

Much industrial advertising, unlike consumer goods advertising, consists of one company talking to another company—or even an entire industry.

But copy is more persuasive when it speaks to the reader as an individual—as if it were one friend telling another friend about a good thing.

First, the terms should be the terms of the reader's business, not the advertiser's business. But more than that, the writing style should be simple:

short words, short sentences, short paragraphs, active rather than passive voice, no advertising cliches, frequent use of the personal pronoun 'you'. A more friendly tone results when the copy refers to the advertiser in the first person 'we' rather than in the company name.

8. Readability (8)
Successful advertising is easy to read
This is a principle that shouldn't need to be stated, but the fact is that typography is the least understood part of our business.

The business press is loaded with ads in which the most essential part of the advertiser's message—the copy—appears in type too small for easy reading or is squeezed into a corner or is printed over part of the illustration.

Text type should be no smaller than 9 point. It should appear black on white. It should stand clear of interference from any other part of the ad. Column width should not be more than half the width of the ad.

9. Action (7)
Successful advertising emphasises the service, not the source
Many industrial advertisers insist that the company name or logo' be the biggest thing in the ad, that the company name appear in the headline, that it be set in bold-face wherever it appears in the copy. That's too much.

An ad should make readers want to buy—or at least consider buying—before telling them *where* to buy.

10. Corporate Benefit (8)
Successful advertising reflects the company's character
A company's advertising represents the best opportunity it has—better than the sales force—to portray the company's personality—the things that will make the company liked, respected, admired.

A messy ad tends to indicate a messy company. A brag-and-boast ad suggests the company is *maker*-orientated, not *user*-orientated. A dull-looking ad raises the possibility that the company has nothing to get excited about, is behind the times, is slowing down.

What we are talking about is a matter of subtleties, but the fact remains: like sex appeal (which is not easy to define), some companies have it, some don't. And whatever it is, it should be consistent over time and across the spectrum of corporate structure and product lines.

Evaluation

To evaluate an advertisement, award a rating against each of the ten points above up to a maximum of the score shown in brackets e.g. (8) award any figure between 0 and 8 depending on your judgement of how effective the ad is against that particular point.

Then add all the scores together, and double the result. This is now the %
rating of the ad. Clients must set their own standards but here is a suggestion:

82–100%	Outstanding
72–80	Very good
52–70	Acceptable
0–50	Send it back

Product awareness

How aware is a potential market of a product's existence? A conventional
questionnaire can ask respondents to list the 'top three industrial floor
cleaners'. Such an open question will enable a manufacturer to determine
whether his product is top of the list, rates number three, or perhaps does not
appear at all.

A campaign may very well have as an objective to raise the level of
awareness from sixth position to being among the top three. The plan of
action will estimate the cost of achieving this result and will indicate the time-
scale. By monitoring progress, it can be determined to what extent a
campaign is achieving its objective. This procedure is particularly useful for a
new product launch since at the outset product awareness will be zero, and
by progressive researches the real value for money derived from promotional
activities can be gauged with accuracy.

This is still of course 'component research' since a product can be pushed
up to the top of the awareness charts and still not sell, but at least one factor
has been identified. The market knows about the product and further
investigation must now be made to establish why sales are not being
achieved.

An example of product awareness, and indeed company awareness comes
from an American study of a campaign for Sta-flow, a plastic produced by
Air Products. Table 13.3 shows how after an advertising campaign product
awareness increased from 0 to 23.8 per cent and in Table 13.4 company
awareness increased from 4.8 per cent to 64.3 per cent.

Table 13.3 Product awareness

	Pre-ad mentions (%)	Post-ad mentions (%)
Lexan	85.6	88.1
Noryl	80.8	52.4
Cyclolac	77.9	81.0
Tenite	53.8	90.5
Sta-flow	0	23.8

Table 13.4   Company awareness

	Pre-ad mentions (%)	Post-ad mentions (%)
GE	79.8	85.7
Eastman	74.0	90.5
Borg-Warner	62.5	73.8
Mobay	53.8	76.2
Air Products	4.8	64.3

Attitude studies

A natural sequence is to determine the attitude of the buying public to a product. This may come from questionnaire research—'which is the most reliable voltmeter?', 'which is the least reliable?', 'which is the best value for money?'—and so on. A technique often used in the consumer field for motivation research is focused group discussion. This can be applied to industrial matters by getting together a group of buyers without disclosing the precise nature of the question to be answered, or indeed the name of the company concerned, and starting discussion of the subject in general with a group leader guiding the conversation towards the topics being researched.

Such a study was conducted to determine the attitude of packaging buyers to *solid* fibreboard cases and why it was they preferred to buy *corrugated* fibreboard cases. The fact emerged that the buyers did not know the difference between the two products and as far as they were concerned simply bought fibreboard cases. This led to a campaign to identify solid cases as a specific product with certain outstanding qualities. Research was undertaken before and after the campaign to measure the level of knowledge which buyers had of the benefits associated with solid cases.

Product–company association

The question of which supplier comes first to mind when a buyer is seeking a given product can be explored by postal research. A question such as 'which first three company names come to mind when considering the purchase of ...' generally produces an answer. This kind of research is especially useful since not only does it enable a company to determine its own position in the market, but also shows up the relative position of its competitors.

Thus in a campaign to promote a new quality of raw material a company was able to see its product–name association creep up from 3 per cent to 18 per cent in a year, while its principal competitor dropped from 16 per cent to 8 per cent. Clearly the campaign was achieving a tangible effect.

A problem related to product–company association is brand-name–

company association. It is not uncommon in industrial marketing to come across a 'Hoover situation' in which a brand-name becomes generic, and applicable in a buyer's mind to any one of a number of suppliers. If this happens unknown to the company it will in the long run nullify the value of the brand-name.

Brand-name research

A campaign may be required to establish a new brand-name, or to reinforce an existing one. In the first instance, research techniques can be applied to the selection of a new brand-name.

If a brand-name is designed to conjure up a certain image a number of possible names can be put to a sample of respondents to comment on what connotation they would associate with each name.

It is useful to make such an investigation a personal one, and invite people to speak each name. This will produce another valuable indicator, whether or not each word is easily readable, and if so whether it is pronounced as intended.

The memorability of a brand-name is particularly important, and this again can be measured. An example was a new material for which a short-list of three names was produced. These were each printed on a card, and one hundred people interviewed. The procedure was to ask each person to look at each name in turn, while it was exposed for a standard time. No reason was given for the request. One week later each individual was re-interviewed and asked to write down the three names. The results were that one name had a much higher recall factor than the other two, and over one-third of the respondents could recall the name exactly as it was shown to them.

The next step with the brand-name adopted was to launch a campaign to establish it. At the outset, the level of knowledge in the potential market was zero, but research was conducted to discover which was the leading brand-name for that particular product group. After an extensive campaign of six months, further research showed that the new name had already secured top place in the ratings. It is significant that the sales of the new product, a basic raw material, were at that time not more than a few per cent of the market whereas the brand-name preference had a rating of several tens per cent. This is to be expected with such a product where long-term contracts inhibit a rapid change in the purchasing pattern. The campaign was in fact a success measured in communications terms: had sales in the short term been used as the criterion, it would have been regarded as a failure.

Image research

A less tangible objective is the establishment of the right image for a company or brand. It is doubtful whether many companies have defined formally and in exact terms the precise image they wish to project and yet they will have an image, whether they like it or not, and moreover will not infrequently spend a good deal of money to enhance what has been referred to as their prestige.

The fact that all organizations have an image is indicated by a panel research which asked buyers to discuss certain companies and how they viewed them in terms of price, quality, delivery and so on. The research company inserted a 'control' name, that is of a company which did not exist. Many of the discussion group were found to have decided views on its image, even though the majority registered that they had never heard of it.

An example of formal research into the public's attitude towards a company was exemplified by one very large manufacturing group which was number two in size in its particular industry. It was a public company and was beginning to realize that apart from the effect on sales, there were such matters as raising loans, and the value of shares to be considered in connection with the expense of promoting a company name. Initially research showed that it was hardly known at all to the publics the company considered to be important. The company agreed to spend a large sum of money on prestige advertising, but in order to obtain tangible value for money, it set the objective 'to be listed among the top three' in response to the question 'name the leading company in the industry'. Two years later the objective was achieved.

The test in any campaign is whether or not value was obtained for the money spent—whether the objectives were achieved, and if not why not. For an organization not to bother to measure the result of its expenditure on advertising and promotion is simply neglect of managerial responsibility.

Checklist

1. Does your promotional budget include a sum for campaign evaluation?
2. Has each of your campaigns a specific objective which is capable of being measured?
3. Has provision been made for continuous checks to be made to ensure that results are being obtained?
4. Is there a system for feedback of results to enable changes to be made to a campaign in sufficient time to achieve the final objective?

References

1. L. W. Rodger, *Marketing in a Competitive Economy* (Associated Business Programmes, London, 1974), p. 216.
2. R. W. Revans, *Science and the Manager* (MacDonald, London, 1965).

Part 4

PUBLIC RELATIONS

14.

PUBLIC RELATIONS

The fundamental difference between public relations and press relations (or editorial publicity) is that editorial publicity is a medium just as much as press advertising and exhibitions, while public relations is an element of publicity dealing with all the many publics which can be involved in influencing the operation of a business from whatever point of view, sales or otherwise. It includes customers and prospects, but here the concern is not so much to be directly involved in selling, but rather to project the corporate image, and create a climate in which the selling operation can be conducted with greater efficiency.

In broad terms the public relations function is to establish and maintain a mutual understanding between an organization and its publics, to communicate a company's views, objectives and purposes, while at the same time monitoring, feeding back and correcting the publics' attitudes and reactions. The publics with which an organization may be concerned include the following:

1. Customers and prospects
2. Employees and trade unions
3. Shareholders and 'the City'
4. Suppliers
5. Local communities
6. Opinion formers
7. Specialized groups
8. Government departments
9. Local authorities
10. Educational bodies
11. Pressure groups
12. International bodies
13. People in general.

In developing a public relations programme the procedure follows the development of a marketing strategy, namely to produce an overall plan with written objectives broken down now under publics instead of products and market segments. The methods of achieving these objectives may utilize the same media and techniques as are used for marketing communications. Press

advertising, direct mail, photographs, editorial publicity all have contributions to make to the public relations programme but there are a number of
differences in detail and a number of techniques not usually dealt with under
marketing communication.

Having widened the scope of public relations beyond its more common
'press officer' context, to be effective the executive responsible for it needs to
be an experienced publicity person rather than the conventional ex-
journalist. His place in the management structure needs to be examined in
this new light, and this is dealt with under Publicity organizations, Chapter
15.

Public relations activities need creativity. Frequently, to secure the greatest
impact, the techniques require novelty and need to be adapted to the
particular audience, the subject and the existing climate of opinion. There
will therefore only be general guidelines and examples here.

PR activities are broken down under the key publics to whom they most
often refer, though any one activity may influence more than one public or
indeed all of them.

Customers and prospects

In considering public relations activities aimed at influencing customers and
prospects, it is inevitable that there will be an overlap into what may be
considered the sales promotional area. For instance, is prestige advertising
PR or marketing communications? This question also applies to editorial
publicity about new appointments, technological advances, large contracts.
Indeed the closeness of these facets of publicity would tend to indicate the
need for some form of central control.

Overall, one may say that public relations is concerned with creating a
favourable image, or, to use a less emotive word, a favourable reputation.
Evidence of the value within a marketing context is provided by Dr Theodore
Levitt in his study *Industrial Buying Behaviour* for the Harvard Graduate
Business School:

> One of the venerable questions in marketing, and particularly the marketing of
> industrial products, is whether a company's generalised reputation affects its ability
> to sell its products. With the great flood of new products in recent years, the
> question has been focused more sharply around the extent to which a company's
> generalised reputation affects its ability to launch new products. While nobody
> claims that a good reputation is an adequate substitute for a good product
> supported by a good sales effort, the question remains as to what contribution a
> good reputation can make to a good selling effort. Thus, all other things being
> equal, does a relatively well-known company ... have a real edge over a relatively
> obscure company? Would it pay for a relatively obscure company to spend more
> money to advertise and promote its name and general competence or to spend more
> on training its salesmen?

Following this question, the study goes on to identify sixteen areas in which a good reputation can be shown to have a positive benefit. It concludes: 'Having a good reputation is always better than being a less well-known or completely anonymous company.'

The emergence of reputation as a factor in the marketing mix leads onto the extension of the classical 4 P's into Five. The fourth P of promotion (which more properly anyway should be 'perception') now has to be considered as those activities which are involved with the product (brand image) and those concerned with the company (corporate image). It can be said then that whether or not a product is purchased is dependent on five factors—the product, its price, its availability, the brand image and the corporate image. Each one of these variables can act in a positive or negative way but the nett effect must obviously be positive for a purchase to take place. Thus a product might be very good (positive) but the price rather high (negative) and not too readily available (negative). The brand name might be unknown (negative) but the manufacturer highly regarded (positive). The product benefits and corporate image in this case must clearly be strong enough to overcome the 'price', 'place' and 'brand image' barriers.

The attractiveness of the total product offering is diagrammatically illustrated by the example below which demonstrates both the polarity of

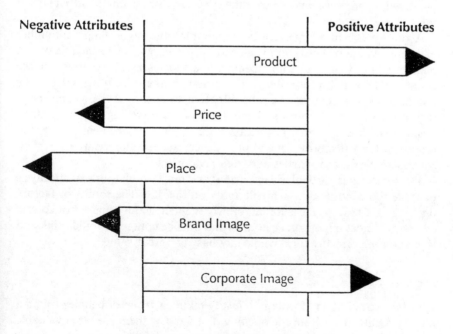

Figure 14.1 Five Marketing Variables

each factor (positive or negative) and the intensity of each. A series of such diagrams facilitates the comparison of all competitive products in a market segment, and highlights their strengths and weaknesses.

Such an analysis enables a strategy to be selected for increasing market share of ones own product simply by considering which one (or more) of the five factors is likely to be the most cost-effective in beating the competitors.

Alternatively one can look at a constant market share but a trade off of one factor against another one e.g. price could be increased but corporate image strengthened without loss of sales. In so far as PR is the function which builds reputation or corporate image it can be seen then to have a direct correlation to sales and hence to profit.

Some of the special PR opportunities which can be used for public relations purposes with particular relevance to influencing customers and prospects are discussed below.

FACTORY OPENINGS

The building of a new factory or a major extension provides the opportunity to generate enthusiasm and goodwill as well as publicity in the press and on radio and television.

For any large-scale operation it is essential to produce comprehensive plans well in advance, and six months is not an over-estimate particularly if there is a VIP opener.

Arrangements in a large factory are complex and involve a great number of people whose co-operation is essential. It is important to include on the planning board of a factory opening, the most senior executives of the company. Personal responsibility is essential for the efficient running of the operation: key executives must be allocated to such matters as transport, security, catering, cleaning and painting, press, unveiling, public address system, signboards, first aid, publications, gifts or mementoes, special treatment for VIPs, protocol and precedence, trades union relations, technical explanations, tour parties and even lavatories!

The rehearsal is particularly important and must simulate as realistically as possible the conditions which will apply on the day. The results of factory openings are hard to measure but clearly the fact that a hundred or so of a company's most important customers and outside contacts should think and talk about a company for a whole day has very great value.

FACTORY TOURS

One does not need an 'opening' to justify taking a group of people around a factory. Quite apart from the opening of a factory, there are often valuable opportunities in organizing a regular programme of visits or tours.

If done they must be done well: planning and execution must be immaculate, and visits must not interfere with production.

Care is necessary to ensure that tours are not too much about the company and its processes but rather tailored to the interests of a particular group. People are impressed by a programme which avoids delays or too much walking: also an adequate number of guides are necessary to ensure personal attention.

For important groups a great deal of benefit can be obtained by arranging for some unusual feature, such as a special train or chartered aircraft. People visiting a factory must be made to feel they are really important, which of course they are.

CONFERENCES

An opportunity sometimes occurs during a trade exhibition for a member of staff to contribute at an accompanying conference on aspects of a company's activities. Even if there is not an official conference it may be useful, while customers are concentrated in one place, to stage a conference either concerned solely with company interests, or perhaps sponsored by the company. A variation on a conference is a seminar which can deal in depth with some aspect of a company's activities, maybe from a more academic point of view.

Again if a number of customers and prospects are known to be spending some time, maybe overnight in a city, this is an opportunity to offer some completely social function, the contacts from which will pay off handsomely in terms of strengthening personal relationships.

The cost of such functions may seem high but this is often apparently so of other public relations operations as well as exhibitions and advertising, but if an investment is needed in order to develop a business then the investment should be made. Investment in PR may be intangible, but so is the investment in machinery which will stand idle if the orders are not forthcoming. It must be clearly understood that PR is not free or cheap publicity: it can be very expensive: it can also be very worth while.

Employees and trade unions

While the task of dealing with employees falls to line management, public relations executives should occupy a primary role in the means of communicating with workers and staff and also in anticipating and interpreting their reactions.

INFORMATION

Notice boards are the traditional medium for communicating with employees. They are often poorly designed, badly sited, inadequately lit, and frequently contain a hotchpotch of out-of-date, poorly duplicated notices in language which is difficult to understand.

It is surprising that since so much industrial unrest is due to misunderstanding, greater attention has not been given to communicating information accurately, effectively and speedily. One reason is that line managers regard themselves as the proper channel for communications and are sceptical of the value of PR here. Certainly they must not be short-circuited, but their efforts can benefit substantially from support from other channels of communication.

Notice boards have a part to play, but responsibility for their presentation and maintenance should rest with the public relations department.

Other methods of communicating with employees do not differ fundamentally from those used to influence customers. Direct mail can be used, literature suitably written and designed, stuffers in wage packets, posters, display units and exhibitions, open days, receptions and lunches. The formula is similar since the objective is the same: to influence people and to inform them with impact of the facts. The difference is often that customer publicity tends to be handled by professionals, and employee publicity by people whose skills lie in other parts of the business.

A particularly interesting comment on employee communications came from a UK survey by *International Management* magazine. This concluded that: 'Audio visual aids are an effective way for a company to communicate with its employees. Yet this is the method least used.' The survey measured the cost-effectiveness of different methods of communications. It found that although slide presentations, overhead projectors, films, and video tapes are all highly effective ways of passing information to workers, these methods are rarely used. Notice boards are widely used, it said, but are generally ineffective.

More than half of the companies surveyed communicate corporate policy and objectives to employees through the annual report or a popular version of it. These methods scored low in effectiveness.

The survey also found that employment policies and procedures seldom are passed along to workers during induction programmes.

The report suggested that companies publish more frequent and relevant news sheets for individual plants or units, rather than company-wide magazines.

HOUSE MAGAZINES

These are essentially part of the process of feeding information to employees, though in fact they can achieve much more by building up a corporate spirit and a feeling of unity.

A firm employing one or two hundred people does not need a house magazine, though an occasional newsheet from the chairman is often appreciated. With larger organizations a magazine of some sort is a useful vehicle for providing information and building up goodwill amongst employees. No doubt there are publications which are welcomed, and secure a fairly high readership rating. The editing of these publications is not the job for a part-time amateur nor should it result in a highly polished magazine which sets out to compete with professional glossy monthlies. It should have written objectives, a carefully planned editorial and a presentation which is compatible with the audience it is addressing. Readership research can be applied here with considerable effectiveness.

PRODUCTIVITY AND SAFETY

Effective communications are necessary to get across to employees ideas on safety, productivity, cleanliness, tidiness, good attendance, personnel late-ness, and indeed many aspects of management. Line or staff specialists, maybe the safety officer or the company doctor, will provide the ammuni-tion, but the firing of the bullets can only properly be the function of the public relations department who will call upon conventional publicity media to achieve the result. A works or a shop seminar on safety, or a specially designed campaign incorporating leaflets, films, posters and displays, are as valid on the shop floor as the market-place.

INDUSTRIAL DISPUTES

There are occasions in a company when an industrial dispute arises, and when there is a need for swift and decisive action not only in negotiations, but in communications.

It is all too common that the press is able to get hold of a story from the employee's side so much more easily and quickly than from the management. This is understandable, since an employee has to refer to no one in expressing a point of view whereas a company official has to exercise great care to ensure that he or she is putting across company policy and is doing it in a way that cannot be misinterpreted.

Though situations are diverse it is possible to lay down general procedures which provide machinery for handling the press during a dispute.

The press officer must be fully informed of a dispute as soon as it arises, or even if it is anticipated, so that he or she has the opportunity to gather the necessary facts and to advise on a plan of action. Whether to say nothing, a little or a lot; whether to be conciliatory or vigorous—these are matters which cannot be left to develop at random during a press interview.

If the press and the public (including shareholders, customers and employees) are to get a balanced view, it follows that an authoritative statement by the management is necessary. Such a statement can be prepared in advance and issued to the press, preferably in writing. Where supplementary questions are asked, these should be noted, and answers written down, considered, and then read back to the press. In practice an experienced press officer can write out likely questions and produce in advance answers which are unambiguous and in accordance with company policy.

The use of a public relations executive in this way calls for a person of ability and seniority coupled with a close involvement in top management thinking.

Shareholders and 'the City'

Public companies need to pay high regard to the way in which any story about their activities is likely to cause repercussions on the stock market.

Financial PR is not random action to keep bad news from the press and inflate good news. It calls for careful planning and involves a range of activities, including press advertising, literature, financial and policy statements, shareholders' meetings and the annual report. Advance planning will ensure that each opportunity is exploited to the full.

The overlap with other key publics should not be forgotten. Employees read annual reports, and take pride in the company they work for. Customers and suppliers have an interest in such information.

Share values and the response to an issue depend largely on financial criteria, but a company's reputation can have a significant bearing on the matter. Press releases dealing, for example, with winning important contracts will be designed initially to influence potential customers, but they also contribute to the building up of a firm's image with investors, stockbrokers and bankers.

Economic and industrial journalists probably have most influence in interpreting a company and its policies to the public, and relationships of mutual understanding must be cultivated. Journalists can, after all, only report on events in the light of their own personal knowledge and experience. A very useful operation in this respect is to arrange for groups of journalists to meet informally from time to time with members of a company's top management. Such functions should not be centred around a particular news item, but be planned deliberately to exchange views and impart information of a general nature. It does no harm, either, for top management to understand and respect the requirements of journalists.

Suppliers

Suppliers make up one of a company's key publics. The building of a good business relationship depends in part on an understanding of one another, and the respect of suppliers for their customers can be valuable. Suppliers, after all, have preferences among their customers and these can well lead to benefits in terms of service, delivery and even price.

A further factor is that suppliers have many contacts within their trade and their views often reach a wide variety of influential people. Their recommendations count in building up a company's reputation.

Local communities

Much of the strength of a company lies in the quality and attitudes of the people it employs. Local communities are a major source of recruitment at all levels, and local public relations activities can be a source of encouragement to potential employees. Existing employees, too, like to feel that the firm they work for has a favourable reputation in the locality, is known to have enlightened management policies, and is providing a useful service to the community.

A company also depends a great deal on the local authority, on councillors and permanent officials, especially when acquiring new premises or expanding its operations. It needs good relations with public utilities, with the police, educationalists, local organizations, and other businesses in the area whose co-operation is sometimes of considerable value in matters of common interest whether rateable values, rates of pay or the sharing of a common bus service.

A firm which sets out to play a part in the life of a local community has much to gain for little investment, though its obligations cannot be satisfied simply by sponsoring a football match or contributing to a charity or two. Senior people from the company must take a genuine interest in local affairs and be seen to be doing so.

Opinion formers

This is one of the 'jargon terms' of public relations practitioners. The thought behind the term is that within a community there are certain people who by reason of their function or position are likely to be able to exert a special influence on public opinion. The contention is that general opinions are formed or changed by people whose views are respected. A teacher or a youth leader for example may have a specially high influence on young people, while other typical opinion formers include members of parliament, academics, top business men, clergymen, local community leaders and lawyers.

Having defined what amounts in selling terms to the potential market, it remains to plan the action necessary to direct an adequate level of persuasive communications at them in order to achieve the desired effect.

It is true that such an operation can be expensive and also that the results are difficult to measure. More than usual judgement must be exercised in order to equate the investment to the likely return in terms of impact upon sales, finance, recruitment and all the many activities which contribute to a company's profitable existence.

Specialized groups

In most organizations a situation arises which requires a special group of people to be informed or persuaded in order to understand fully a company's point of view.

This was the case when radioactive isotopes were first introduced into industry for measurement and control. There was concern about radiation hazards among safety officers, trade unionists, government departments and members of parliament. In particular there was the suspicion that material passing in front of an isotope could itself become radioactive. This was scientifically unfounded but nonetheless had to be treated as a serious potential point of sales resistance. A good deal of scientific publicity and official backing was required at a number of levels in order to overcome what were quite genuine and serious fears.

Another interesting problem confronted a certain manufacturer who relied on large quantities of waste paper as a basic raw material. One major source of supply, the housewife via refuse collection, began to decline. There were a number of specialized groups to be informed of the importance of saving paper, and of its value to the economy. The housewife was the primary source, but her co-operation was of no avail unless the dustman kept paper separate from other refuse. Here it was necessary to influence the public cleansing officer who controlled the dustmen, the local authority committee and even the mayor. Other sources of supply were youth organizations, who could raise funds by collecting waste paper, and industrial concerns like printers who as a matter of course were large producers of waste.

A solution to the shortage of waste paper could have been to increase the price paid for it until supply caught up with demand, but the cost would have been very great and in turn would have been passed on to the consumer. In the event a major public relations campaign was mounted to reach all the interested groups. For housewives, conventional consumer media were used such as television, radio, posters, door-to-door circulars and talks to women's groups. The annual conference of public cleansing officers included in their programme a visit to a factory to see waste paper being used. The Lord Mayor of London held a reception, which every London mayor attended, and heard of the national need for waste paper. A novel feature which caught the imagination of journalists was an exhibition of waste paper which involved dumping several tons of it in the middle of the Savoy Hotel. A pop song was written and recorded, a film made, schoolchildren were informed, and the network of publicity spread to the key publics likely to affect the situation.

When a company decides to move from one location to another, a very well-planned public relations campaign is required not just to employees, but more important to their families. In setting up a new factory there are often local community interests that must be considered. Largely it is a matter of informing people well in advance and of giving them an opportunity to express their views. They will want to know how it will affect them personally, for instance will there be opportunities for employment? Will there be undue smell or noise, or an increase in traffic? Will it disturb a local bird sanctuary? And so on.

A feature of public relations in connection with specialized groups is the tendency to wait for a situation to arise before taking action. This is sometimes inevitable, but a plan to maintain good relations and provide an adequate flow of information to such people on a continuous basis can function even if at a relatively low intensity. Indeed, such a procedure will do much to avoid crises arising which require crash action, usually expensive, and sometimes too late.

People in general

'How do we want people to see us?' This is a question that a company should ask itself periodically, and work out an answer in some detail and in writing. This will then become the foundation of public relations policy.

Consider how an impression of an organization is formed. Is it through a salesperson, or a buyer? Perhaps it is through the receptionist or a van driver? Maybe it is the letter heading or the exterior of a building: perhaps what appears in the press as editorial or advertising. Whatever the medium and whatever its primary purpose, it also has a public relations connotation.

An important factor is 'house styling'. The process begins with the name of the company and its subsidiaries. The name should be simple, appropriate, easy to pronounce, memorable and, of course, registerable. Is a trade mark or symbol necessary? If there is a house colour, is it useful and is it the most effective colour?

If a 'style' is to be established to what should it apply? A designer must know this before starting work, and the items may include letter headings, invoices, order forms, visiting cards, vehicles, notice boards, advertising, products, company ties and even security police cap badges. There can be many complications and arguments for deviation from the standard specification, and much expense in implementation, but in practice the introduction of a new house style can lead to considerable economies. Standardization of paper sizes and of forms can save hundreds of pounds. A change from embossed letterheads to litho printing, a reduction in the number of colours on vehicles, the elimination of copperplate visiting cards, provide opportunities for savings, especially where a company has grown up over a number of years and each element of the business has been developed on an individual basis.

Message sources

At this point it might be useful to consider all the message sources which go together towards the growth of perception in a person's mind. First there are all those 'active' sources such as press advertising, exhibitions, direct mail, and so on. With these there is a tactical objective eg to generate sales leads. In addition to this, however, there will be created an impression of the organisation itself—its corporate identity. Then there are 'outside' message sources. These are a matter of what other people say about an organisation. They are probably the most important source of all eg what customers say about your products—third party endorsement. Then one must consider 'people' message sources. What do all the employees have to say about their employer? And the employees need to be broken down into specific groups in order that subsequent action can be taken. Finally there are all the many message sources which are referred to as 'passive' because they have a different purpose other than sending a corporate message. The following list gives some idea of the range of opportunities to co-ordinate action to improve reputation, sometimes at very little cost.

ACTIVE MESSAGE SOURCES (PROMOTIONAL)

1. Press advertising
2. TV
3. Radio
4. Outdoor
5. Public Exhibitions
6. Private Exhibitions
7. Films, video and A.V.
8. Demonstrations and visits
9. Sponsorship
10. Telemarketing
11. Sales leaflets and brochures
12. Business gifts
13. Directories and year books
14. Educational packs
15. Sales calls

16. Merchandising
17. Point of sale
18. Sales promotion
19. Envelope franking, letter stuffers and stickers etc
20. Sales aids
21. Direct Mail
22. Seminars and conferences
23. Press Releases
24. Press Receptions
25. Press visits
26. Parliamentary and other lobbies
27. Charity Support
28. Feature Articles

OUTSIDE MESSAGE SOURCES

29. Agents and Distributors
30. Customers—Specifiers, Authorisers, Purchasers
31. Users
32. Media/Journalists
33. Trade Associations
34. Consultants
35. Local Community
36. Competitors
37. Suppliers

PEOPLE MESSAGE SOURCES

38. Company VIP's
39. Sales Force
40. Service Engineers
41. Telephonist
42. Receptionist
43. Employees in general
44. Spouses and friends
45. Shareholders
46. Applications for Jobs
47. Handling complaints
48. Membership of Trade Associations
49. Membership of Learned Institutes
50. Attendance at Conferences
51. Chairing Committees
52. Public Speaking

53. Local Community Activities
54. Social Activities

PASSIVE MESSAGE SOURCES

55. Annual Report
56. Sales Letters
57. Company Name
58. House magazine/newsletters
59. Sales office back-up
60. House style
61. Packaging
62. Labels
63. Telephone Contact
64. Business cards
65. Specification sheets
66. Test certificates
67. Instruction manuals
68. Service manuals
69. Delivery notes and invoices
70. Cars, delivery vehicles
71. Price list/credit facilities
72. Pre-sales service
73. Christmas cards
74. Telex
75. Facsimile Messages
76. Telephone Directory entries
77. Trade mark
78. Calendars
79. Diaries
80. Wall Charts
81. Photographs
82. Showrooms
83. Appearance of factory
84. Location
85. Ties and emblems
86. Brand names
87. Logotypes
88. Royal Warrant
89. Queen's Award to Industry
90. Reception area
91. Notice boards
92. The product—quality, appearance etc

93. Delivery promises—reliability
94. Group Name
95. Nationality
96. Range of Product/application
97. Guarantee cards/trading terms
98. Samples
99. Job titles
100. Visitors/entertaining

Corporate relations

The need for a planned programme of corporate relations stems not from some new management concept but from the fact that organizations are finding, somewhat to their dismay, the need for a formalized corporate strategy. This need is being interpreted in a number of ways, but simply stated is that it is no longer good enough to take random actions for long-term effect: rather it is necessary to give mature consideration to future objectives and the means of achieving them. Such objectives will incorporate financial investment, labour force and staffing, marketing aspects, production, research and development, and of course profit. This is no more than a move from past practices in which future events were just allowed to take their natural course, to a position in which a company sets out deliberately to move to a predetermined position. The weakness of any attempt at corporate planning is that unforeseeable events are bound to cause the objectives to be changed, but this is no reason for not taking action to influence the course of events so as to hit the desired target as closely as possible. Corporate relations are but one of the management functions which can be used to help achieve this goal.

The need for corporate goals and for a strategy to achieve them stems from a growing number of influences, external and internal, which if ignored may well undermine the profitable development of a company and indeed threaten its very existence. The increasing tendency by governments to impose controls is a major factor as are international regulations at one extreme and a vigorous consumerist movement at the other. Thus trade barriers and constraints, scarcity of raw materials, inflation, high taxation, are factors which play a larger part in the development of business. Equally the growing interest by employees and trade unions with their sometimes massive influence must be taken into consideration in any future planning.

In this section an examination is made of corporate relations from the point of view of *what* they are, *why* they are necessary, to *whom* they should be addressed, *when*, and *how*. Finally, the all important question of the results that might reasonably be expected of such an activity.

First *what*. Corporate relations is a term used to signify the deliberate attempts by an organization to maintain the best possible relations with each and every identifiable group of people whose interests and activities may be supposed to have an effect, for good or ill, on the prosperity and progress of the business. Such an operation is intrinsically linked with communications in both directions since without communications of some kind it is difficult to see how any change or impact can be obtained. It is important at the outset to realize two things. First that no matter how efficient any corporate communications system may be, it will be of no avail unless the object of the communication is sound. In just the same way no amount of advertising will ever sell an unsatisfactory product. The second point to be made is that every single means of communication must be considered for possible use, not just the classical PR media such as press releases, factory visits, booklets and special events. Corporate relations then are the building up of a good *reputation* with a company's many and varied publics. An old-fashioned term sums it up very well—*goodwill.*

Clearly the kind of activity being described is going to cost money. Hence the need to ask *why?* The plain fact is that all companies have an image whether they like it or not, or even if they are totally unaware of it. That is to say that a company is perceived by people in a variety of ways, depending upon the messages, conscious or unconscious, they have received about it. And the perception varies from one public to another. Customers may view a supplier as a thoroughly reliable and trustworthy organization with which to do business, whereas its employees may take the very opposite view.

The reason *why* corporate relations are important is that it is only when relationships are positive and sound that the most effective and efficient business can be conducted. For example is it reasonable to expect the best possible applicants for a job with a company which has a very poor reputation as an employer? It may be argued that in such a case the simple solution is in changing the conditions of employment so that they are really attractive, but this is overlooking the essential ingredient of corporate communications for if people are unaware of a situation they cannot react to it. And if, as often happens, they are misinformed about it the opposite result to what was intended may be the outcome. The reason why corporate communications are important is that in one direction a company is receiving messages about itself from all the interested publics, and on the other hand it is sending out messages to those same people to ensure that they are fully informed, that they understand and that they are convinced. The reason *why* thus is in order to establish and maintain a series of relationships in which business can be conducted most efficiently.

The *when* of corporate relations can be dealt with simply. A reputation is with a company all its life. It's no use having a corporate relations function, and a corporate communication programme for a couple of years and then closing it down. People's memories and attitudes are dynamic and will change over time. A company must decide whether or not it is really serious in the matter of building its reputation, and if it is, and it wishes to maintain it, this can be achieved in one way only, and that is by a continuous programme of activities. It should also be borne in mind that the time-scale to achieve any major change is likely to be of the order of years rather than months, so advance planning is required as well as continuity.

Turning now to *how* corporate relations are to be achieved, this of course is where the difficulties arise and where the answers tend to become diffuse, uncertain and even contradictory. In outline it can be said that the starting point is to draw up plans, both strategic and tactical, to set objectives, to measure results, to co-ordinate all related and parallel activities, and to ensure that an adequate administrative and professional facility exists to guarantee proper execution.

STRATEGIC PLANNING

The key to successful strategic planning for good corporate relations is in the setting of comprehensive objectives. Two examples have been chosen to illustrate this point. First a major multinational corporation which listed five aims:

1. To increase the share of people's minds available to the company.
2. To engender favourable attention and acceptability from its diverse publics.
3. To explain the realities of the company's social and economic contributions to the countries where it did business.
4. To state the case for business in general and MNCs in particular.
5. To correct some of the myths and refute irresponsible allegations.

The programme which evolved consisted of a package of five interdependent activities, each mutually supporting, making its own unique contribution, but working to the same plan and objectives. The elements of the package were an advertising campaign, a public information brochure, an external house magazine, a press relations programme and the establishment of a speakers' panel, and the complete programme was based on a publicly stated philosophy of openness, frankness and fact.

The second example is for a well-known company in the high technology business. The programme had five objectives:

1. To extend the company's corporate identity and to enhance/improve attitudes held towards the company among the defined target audiences.
2. To establish and promote the company as a leader and innovator in advanced technology.
3. To promote the company's capabilities and achievements in selected areas of advanced technology.

4. To create a high level of awareness and knowledge among target groups in prospective market areas for the technological excellence of its products.
5. To create a favourable attitude among target groups so that divisional marketing activities for particular products or systems could be carried out more effectively.

The main thrust of the campaign to achieve these aims was a most adventurous press campaign of very large advertisements in the colour supplements, backed by supportive advertising in 'management newspapers' and the specialist press.

TACTICAL PLANNING

It is not sufficient to produce one major homogeneous campaign and leave it at that. It is vital to examine each and every other sector of communications with its own specialized objectives, audiences, messages and media in order to ensure that these contribute also to the common objective of the company's reputation. In this way marketing communications, employee communications, a safety campaign, city and financial news, and all the rest add together to make up a synergistic whole. It can be seen that organizationally there is a need for the provision of top management direction to ensure the proper orchestration of all the many parts which are being conducted on a day-to-day basis.

The second part of tactical operations relates to what might be termed 'reactive activities'. This is where over and above the carefully constructed ongoing campaign there arise events which, if not handled properly, can work against the corporate objectives or alternatively fail to give the potential support that may otherwise be achieved. Examples may be in an industrial dispute where bad handling can undo much of the goodwill which might have been built up over a period of years. It is necessary then to develop a programme for crisis management in which plans are laid down for handling any particular contingency that may arise. Equally, but in the opposite direction, failure to exploit fully the securing of a major overseas contract is a loss in terms of the very favourable light in which such an achievement can be shown to the target groups that together make up the corporate public.

Such contingencies cannot by their very nature be incorporated in any plan, but the organization must be sufficiently flexible to be able to react fast to each of these as they occur and to have in mind not just the event itself and how to solve or exploit it, but also the overall objectives.

The most important factor here is to be pro-active rather than reactive.

CORPORATE RESEARCH

Early in the growth of the marketing concept and of corporate planning, communications activities were characterized by 'prestige advertising' and by a narrow form of public relations which relied mainly on what was loosely termed 'press relations'. It was unusual to have specific goals, and large sums of money were invested to put out almost self-congratulatory messages about oneself without much regard to the interest of the audiences or indeed what the effect on them might be. Companies indulging in these activities became sceptical of their value and as economic conditions became tougher any attempt to buy prestige declined.

The growth of corporate affairs as a function, and corporate relations as an activity, has been accompanied by the precise setting of objectives in quantified form, and by a programme of research to ensure that any investment will achieve tangible results. Business people have begun to demand that expenditure in this area should be accountable and the effects measurable.

The starting point of any properly constructed programme of corporate communications is to make bench-mark measurements against which progress can be compared as the campaign proceeds. It is no use making such measurements at the end of a campaign as by that time it is too late to take any corrective action. A company may decide that it wishes to increase the level of awareness among certain discrete publics and at the same time gain an improved attitude towards itself and its products. Sample groups from each segment must be chosen and an assessment made of their current level of awareness and the nature of their attitudes. Only with this information can an effective plan be drawn up. From this a budget is set with the task to move from a current level A to a targeted level B in a given period of time. Using the same audience segments, methods of sampling and questioning techniques, research must be planned at intermediate stages in order to find out whether the results are on schedule, in advance of it or behind it. Variations can be made at this stage in order to bring the campaign back on to course and the changes may be simply in the direction of the campaign, or it may be necessary to increase expenditure, or for that matter cut it back. So the operation breaks down into four stages—set objectives, quantify, research, verify.

BENEFITS

A well-constructed and properly funded corporate relations programme can lead to many benefits of which the following are but a few of the more obvious examples.

1. Increased market reputation and market share

2. Happier and more satisfied employees
3. Rise in share prices
4. Greater productivity
5. Favourable government support
6. Better quality applicants for jobs
7. Improved treatment from suppliers
8. Better understanding by, and less criticism from outside pressure groups

While benefits will accrue to any company the chances are that the larger the organization, the greater the need for a formalized corporate communication policy. This applies with even greater effect where the products concerned fall into the category known as 'undifferentiated'. With little to choose between one brand and another—for example with petrol, oil, banks, cigarettes, detergents, what are the real determinants of a purchasing decision? There is a good deal of evidence to suggest that the customer will go for the brand or name he or she knows best and for which he or she has the greatest regard. Where products are intrinsically the same, the most important factor must become that indefinable property which lies behind the product—its reputation. And this applies with equal force to industrial products and services as to consumer ones.

It is now well established that there is a correlation between 'familiarity' and 'favourability'. ie the better known an organisation the more likely it is that people will wish to do business with it—to buy its products, work for it, or become shareholders. This relationship is well illustrated by Figure 14.2.

From all this discussion there are two laws which can be propounded:

The Corporate Image Law
The stronger the corporate image, the higher the price the customer is prepared to pay and the greater the effort he is prepared to make to acquire the product.

Law of Favourability
The stronger the familiarity with a brand or company, the greater the inclination to make a purchase or do business.

At the end of a chapter on public relations, it is relevant to stress that the greatest single factor in a business is the people who work for it. It is true that sophisticated communications techniques must be used to make the company's operations clear to the world. But paramount in relations with the public is the chief executive and an enthusiastic staff and workforce. The public relations practitioner will only succeed in projecting what exists. If a company deserves a bad reputation, no amount of public relations expenditure will eliminate it. The only remedy is to concentrate on the source of the trouble.

Finally, the ultimate goal of public relations is to increase profit. As such it is just another form of investment as in plant and machinery.

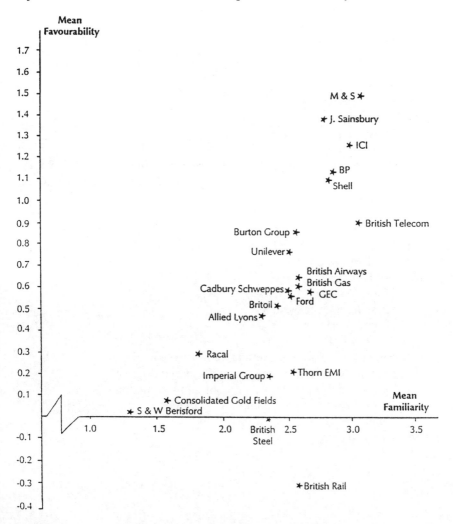

Figure 14.2   Familiarity and Favourability

Checklist

1. Has the difference between public relations and press relations been established? Do top management understand this?
2. Has a plan of action been drawn up to influence the following audiences?
   (a)   Customers and prospects

   (b) Employees and trade unions
   (c) Shareholders and investors
   (d) Suppliers
   (e) Local communities
   (f) Opinion formers
   (g) Government departments
   (h) Local authorities
   (i) Educational bodies
   (j) Specialized groups
   (k) Pressure groups
   (l) International bodies
   (m) General public
3. In drawing up such a forward plan, has each medium been considered, i.e. in addition to editorial publicity—press advertising, direct mail, exhibitions, literature, films and so on?
4. In addition to conventional media have opportunities under the following headings been examined?
   (a) Factory openings and tours
   (b) Conferences and seminars
   (c) Speakers panel
   (d) Notice boards
   (e) Closed-circuit television
   (f) House magazine
   (g) Factory signs
   (h) Employees' clothing, overalls, uniforms, badges
   (i) Meetings between journalists and top management
   (j) Sponsored events—local, national and international
   (k) Involvement in local community activities
   (l) Demonstrations
   (m) House styling

Part 5

PUBLICITY ORGANIZATIONS

MARKETING ORGANIZATION

There has been considerable change in the past decade in the position of the marketing communications function in relation to the top management structure of a company. The most significant development was that publicity in the industrial field achieved recognition as a serious and valuable operation, albeit as a part of the selling activity. A typical company organization chart (Figure 15.1) in the classic tradition was:

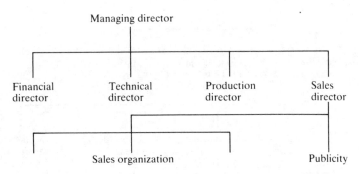

Figure 15.1   Company organization chart 1 (sales orientation)

This scheme was usual whether the company was large or small, and would range from large publicity departments with managers responsible to sales directors, to small operations in which the chief sales executives handled the publicity themselves.

In changing from a sales- to a marketing-orientated organization there have been, and still are, a number of interim stages in which for instance the publicity manager reports to the managing director who (unknowingly) thus assumes the function of part-time marketing director. Sometimes a marketing director was appointed, but placed alongside a sales director, with the inevitable clash of interests. This is not to say that a company cannot operate efficiently and effectively without conforming to some theoretical ideal structure. Each situation requires its own solution having regard to variables such as the size of the company, the nature of its products and market, and inevitably the capabilities and personalities of the people it employs.

Figures 15.2, 15.3 and 15.4 represent typical organizational structures for industrial companies which are marketing oriented, have 'own products' but vary considerably in size. Such a company, as in Figure 15.2 may employ a few hundred people and have a turnover of 10 million pounds. Here the sales manager is very much out in the field with accounts of his or her own. The marketing communications manager would in some cases have no more than a good secretary as an assistant, and would not only handle advertising and public relations, but also arrange whatever marketing research was required. Marketing planning would be the job of the marketing director who, as the company developed in size, might add a marketing executive as an assistant but in a staff rather than line capacity. Much of the publicity work would be bought in, and in a small company this is far better than employing a number of specialists with a corresponding increase in semi-fixed overheads.

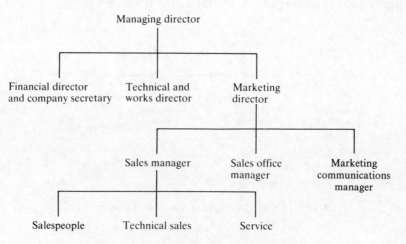

Figure 15.2   Small company organization

Figure 15.3 represents a company with a turnover of say 50 million and employing a thousand or more people. A new title has been introduced, 'marketing services manager', a function designed to supply every service required by the marketing operation. There is still no separate marketing planning function, but this takes place within the marketing services department under the direction of the marketing director. No independent provision is made for product development, but depending on the nature of the business the function is shared between the technical department and the marketing services department.

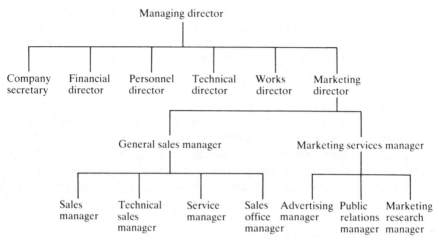

Figure 15.3 Medium sized company organization

The three functions under the marketing services manager then break down as follows:

1. *Advertising*
   (a) Press advertising
   (b) Exhibitions
   (c) Direct mail
   (d) Literature
2. *Public Relations*
   (a) Public relations
   (b) Press relations
   (c) House magazines
   (d) Videos
   (e) Photography
3. *Marketing Research*
   (a) Market research
   (b) Product research
   (c) Product testing
   (d) Attitude research
   (e) Campaign evaluation

Whether to put videos under public relations is simply a matter of which category films most often tend to fit in a particular company. As the company develops within this structure, the number of specialists can be increased so that there will be an exhibitions manager, a press officer or a photographer under public relations, and a statistician or economist under marketing research.

Where there is a wide variety of products in a company of this size, an alternative is to break down the marketing services department into product or brand specialists. This has the merit of getting greater knowledge of products and markets amongst the individuals handling the promotions, but these same people now need to have a very broad experience of every aspect of persuasive communications.

In Figure 15.4 the overall company structure has been omitted to look in more detail at the marketing function. This scheme is more appropriate for a company with a turnover of many millions of pounds. Here the strength of a centralized structure can be seen in that it is possible to deploy a number of specialists who concentrate exclusively on one aspect only of marketing. One person or even a department will be concerned specifically with the search for new products: similarly with the planning of marketing operations and the development of marketing strategies. Research and economics have been taken outside the marketing services function, which is now concerned principally with making a direct contribution to short- and medium-term marketing operations. The 'brand manager' concept is introduced in the form of product group executives and they, in turn, can call upon specialists in particular media to contribute to their operations.

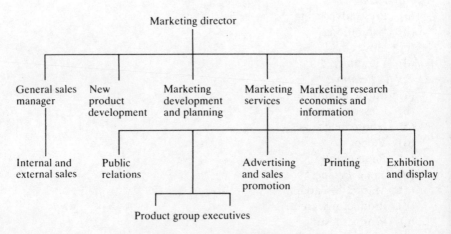

Figure 15.4   Large company organization

It is arguable whether public relations should be allowed to go so far down the line as shown in this structure. An alternative is to make this directly responsible to the marketing director, and with a connecting link to the managing director.

It may be necessary to have a number of sales managers reporting to the marketing director. When the span of control begins to become too great a marketing manager can be introduced to administer the other marketing functions. No provision has been made in any of the structures described for the 'creative' function. It has been assumed that outside agencies will be used and that the need for visualizers and copywriters will not arise. This will be discussed in the next part of the chapter.

A matter of continual debate in larger companies is whether to centralize marketing communications or to split it up amongst the operating divisions, each with its own publicity department. It is probably not important, providing those operating the business believe strongly and enthusiastically in the system they are using. This is often borne out by the changes recommended by management consultants. Frequently if publicity is centralized, consultants recommend decentralization and vice versa. Both systems work. If anything the balance must be slightly in favour of central control since the increasing use of sophisticated marketing techniques calls for specialists who cannot be justified, or indeed fully utilized, by a small organization.

A final point to be made emerges from research by the author and that is the significant replacement of sales directors by marketing directors. It is also noticeable that increasingly advertising and PR functions are being merged under the umbrella of someone at board level with a title like Corporate Affairs Director. Where this happens the responsibility and authority for advertising and related functions rests with just this one person—which is a good reason for having him or her. In the majority of cases however the advertising manager, or equivalent, has the responsibility but not the authority. Research has shown that only 37 per cent of publicity managers can approve an advertisement and only 12 per cent a campaign. In 75 per cent of the cases authority for approving an advertisement had to come from at least one director.

In-house services

It is now necessary to consider briefly each of the marketing communications functions and how, if at all, a publicity department should set itself up to handle them. An examination of such departments shows a wide diversity of views, with some industrial companies making do with a very modest staff, and others employing tens and sometimes hundreds of people.

A good basic rule for the creation and development of a publicity department is to keep it as small as possible. The reason for this is twofold. Specialist services are almost always available from outside agencies and they are often of better quality than an internal department can provide. Secondly, if a company goes through a difficult financial period it is sometimes forced to make drastic cutbacks in current expenditure, and such economies are inevitably made in activities which will have the least deleterious effect *in the short term*. These are generally publicity and R&D,

often with results which are later regretted. The comments which follow are of a general nature and it is to be expected that there will be exceptions which work extremely well.

PRESS ADVERTISING

Few firms produce their own press advertising, and thus there is rarely a case for a company to employ its own advertisement visualizers, typographers and artists. Far better ones are available outside, and certainly no top-grade creative person will stay for long with an industrial company. Even if that person is brilliant to start with, this will soon wear off without the variety, challenge and stimulus of an agency or studio atmosphere.

With technical copywriting there is a strong body of opinion that an agency cannot produce adequate copy, and that it takes longer to produce the brief than to write the copy oneself. This is not only untrue: it is nonsense. Writing is a highly skilled and creative function, which requires a top-rate craftsman. Few advertising managers (or sales managers) would claim to have this facility. It is true that most advertising agencies find technical copywriting difficult, and that many are incapable of doing it. The solution is not to do it oneself, but to change the agency.

The production side of press advertising, voucher checking and so on is usually handled well by an agency, and there can be little justification for a publicity department being involved in this.

MEDIA PLANNING

Agencies are in a difficult position on press media planning. They cannot obtain adequate data from publishers, and clients as a rule are unwilling or unable to allocate adequate funds for a thorough investigation to be undertaken. Some agencies are breaking new ground in this respect and much progress will be made over the next ten years but, in the meantime, the solution seems to be to encourage the agency media department in every possible way, but for the publicity department to retain a strong measure of control and scrutiny.

As regards the media mix outside press advertising, most of the 750 or so agencies in the United Kingdom have good experience of press media, and some of literature and exhibitions, but for other media few have strong enough all-round experience to compete with a company's own publicity department, particularly in the specialized industry and product groups in which a firm is operating.

DIRECT MAIL

This is usually most efficiently directed and executed within the publicity department. Partly the reason is that many agencies are not set up to process this medium: partly because the maintenance of lists can usually best be handled at the client end: partly because action is usually required at a moment's notice: partly because this is very much a personal means of contact from supplier to customer.

A sales letter, for instance, is usually something which a sales manager or an advertising manager can do better than a copywriter. This is not to contradict the argument in favour of professional writers for press advertising: it is a matter of horses for courses, and the professional in sales letters is, or should be, a sales manager.

Direct mail is, of course, not confined to writing a letter, and there is a good deal of outside creative expertise from advertising agencies, art studios, freelancers or direct mail houses, which can be used with considerable advantage.

The lead and initiative should, however, rest with the publicity department.

EXHIBITIONS

These must be a co-operative effort. Only rarely can an outside consultant or agency know enough about a company to be able to handle the whole process from the initial briefing to the final opening. This is particularly true in view of the company changes in policy and personnel which may take place over the period of planning an exhibition. Moreover a stand is a highly complex publicity medium and should be produced as an environment where company personnel will be required to sell actively and efficiently.

It is equally rare that a company employs people on its staff who have adequate knowledge of design, writing, architecture, décor and construction to be able to do the job independently.

The answer is to organize a joint effort, but to do this formally with each element of the job analysed, isolated and planned so that the appropriate specialist is used for the appropriate job, and then integrated into the whole. Figure 15.5 is a simple diagram that can be used as a starting point for a more detailed network which will incorporate a time-scale.

LITERATURE

Organizing literature usually involves another compromise. Few publicity departments can carry out the visualizing, and few agencies or outside consultants are capable of writing the text. The final difficulty is that very few publicity departments are able to write the text either, unless they are large enough to justify the employment of specialist writers.

There are agencies who employ writers able to do the complete assignment, and there are freelance writers who can sometimes be used. Technical

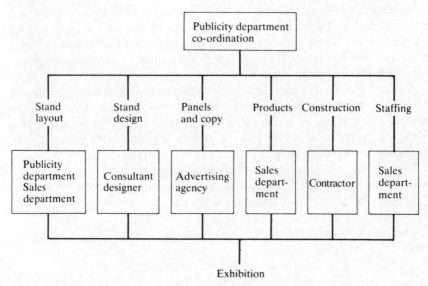

Figure 15.5   Planning for an exhibition

journalists can be hired on a freelance basis and generally produce good work. Alternatively, someone inside the company may write the basic text to be passed on to a professional writer for finishing.

On the production side there is not much to choose between using an agency or having a specialist on the staff of the publicity department. If the workload is steady and sufficiently great, it pays to employ a full-time executive: if not, an agency will probably do a first-class job, but will charge anything between 15 per cent and 25 per cent of the total print bill for the service. For the smaller company, many printers have their own designers, or maintain a close contact with a design unit. This can be satisfactory, especially if the work is not too detailed or specialized but the disadvantage is that it lengthens the chain of communication.

For house magazines, the solution is to appoint a professional editor. Whether that editor should be on the company's staff is immaterial provided he or she is capable and is given a wide degree of freedom to implement editorial policy within the budget.

PHOTOGRAPHY

To have a staff photographer is a decided advantage providing this does not mean that every photographic job must be handled by him or her. Some photographers specialize in creative work, others in industrial work, portraiture, news, landscape, advertising, and it is too much to expect to find all these skills in one person employed as a member of staff. Alternatively, much company photography required quickly, or for record purposes, or at little expense can best be done by a staff photographer.

PRINTING

No matter how many, or how sophisticated, the offset litho machines a company installs, they cannot replace outside printers. With a larger firm, a print department can make great savings on forms and routine internal jobs. Even some external work is acceptable for certain purposes— a news-sheet, manuals or an exhibition handout for example. Outside this, however, for sales literature, it is unusual for a company to be able to produce work of acceptable quality or even at competitive cost.

FILMS AND VIDEOS

Hardly a firm in the country is equipped with its own film unit. A video-camera has some use for sales and the management training, and perhaps for other internal communications, but not much else. If films or videos form a large part of a company's publicity programme it is essential to have an executive on the staff with specialist experience or alternatively to take counsel with experts at the advertising agency.

The essential function for the company is to make active provision for the promotion and distribution of films. This cannot be farmed out, notwithstanding the existence of one or two distribution libraries. These provide a good physical distribution service, but films are made to be shown actively to specific audiences, and this will not happen unless a company plans for it and sets up the necessary organization.

With the emergence of video recording there has been a swing back to using in-house facilities which with care can result in very competently produced programmes. This however is more in a technical sense than creative where the services of an outside specialist are vital.

EDITORIAL PUBLICITY

It is difficult to justify employing an agency for editorial publicity as distinct from public relations. The preparation of press releases and of press conferences calls for a professional executive, but the degree of in-company knowledge, contacts and accessibility required favours the employment of a staff person. Furthermore, the press tend to prefer to deal direct with a company since they need answers with both speed and authority. An agency or a consultant is at an inherent disadvantage in this respect.

An outside PR organization has contacts as part of its stock in trade of course, but these can be matched in time by most companies themselves and with greater effect.

PUBLIC RELATIONS

Even the best of public relations practitioners, after immersion in a company environment for a few years begin to acquire a biased point of view. They are, after all, subordinate to the management they are advising and must exercise a certain caution in giving advice which in turn is not always regarded as highly as that from an outside source.

There is much to be said for retaining a public relations consultancy to give top-level advice, to work in conjunction with a company's own PR staff and to be available to provide assistance for special events which are outside the scope, capacity or experience of staff executives.

The staff person has an important function, and as already indicated, should have direct access to the chief executive. The range of public relations activities, however, is so broad that an agency can usually bring to bear a good deal more experience on a problem than a staff executive who, as time goes on, becomes more and more specialized, and operates within a restricted environment.

MISCELLANEOUS PUBLICITY ACTIVITIES

All manner of miscellaneous activities fall to a publicity department, and rightly. The publicity staff are the company's experts in communications whether internal or external, and should be used as such. Sales conferences, gifts, Christmas cards, samples, factory signs, notice boards—all these and more fall to the publicity department to organize. Some limits may be necessary, particularly as when the department is asked to produce raffle tickets for the sports club dinner, and the procedure here is to require that some estimate should be produced of how much it costs to use an in-house service for some of the smaller items which could just as easily and effectively be produced elsewhere.

PLANNING AND BUDGETING

This task cannot be delegated. It is in fact the single most important job of a publicity department, and the only one which emphatically cannot be 'put out'.

The one key function of a company's publicity department is to operate within the framework of the marketing strategy, to plan, budget, administer, monitor and to assess the overall range of publicity activities.

16.

PUBLISHERS

Publishers of periodicals merit special attention since they play such a significant role in industrial publicity. The United Kingdom is unique in this respect, both in the number of publications (2000 trade and technical), and in the share of publicity budgets allocated to press advertising (about 40 per cent). Even if the average circulation for a journal is taken at a modest 5000, with 2000 publications, this would amount to 10 million copies per month (or whatever period) and multiplied by the 'pass-on' circulation, perhaps five per copy, this results in a total potential readership of 50 million. Clearly there is much duplication in the figure of 50 million.

Quantity, however, is not necessarily a sign of strength: indeed the number of periodicals currently being circulated is likely to prove to be the weakness of the publishing industry, in that there is a limit to the amount of reading time that any one person has. Nevertheless, considerable sums of money are invested in press advertising; one estimate puts it at well in excess of £1000 m a year, and this is adequate justification for a detailed examination of publishing.

Development of the press

There have been three distinct phases of development that have taken place over the past decade or so, and these are very akin to the changes that were earlier outlined for products in relation to marketing development, i.e. product orientation followed by sales orientation and marketing orientation. In the publishing world it is possible to restate these developments as journal orientation, circulation orientation and audience (or readership) orientation. It is necessary to look into each of these phases since many publishers are still heavily entrenched in the first two stages.

Each stage of development tends to be characterized by the nature or function of the person at the head of a publication. In the first phase it is the editor who is primarily responsible for laying down policy. In the second phase the advertisement manager emerges as the principal executive. Finally, and some companies have moved well into this position, the senior executive is a general manager or publisher who can call upon all the modern marketing services to assist in the promotion of his or her product.

This leads to an alternative method of identifying the phase of development reached, by asking 'what is the product that a publisher is marketing?'. In the first phase the answer is a journal: in the second, it is circulation that is being sold. In the third phase the product being marketed is an audience or a readership—vastly different from circulation. Apply the classical question 'what business are we in?'. The answer is surely not writing (phase 1), or publishing (phase 2) but communications. It is only by accepting this concept that periodicals can maintain their predominant position in the publicity mix.

Publishing organizations

A good deal of change has taken place, not only in the emergence of a marketing concept, but in rationalizations and amalgamations which have facilitated the implementation of a marketing approach. The three organization charts (Figs 16.1, 16.2 and 16.3) represent the three phases of development, and while it may appear that they cover respectively small, medium and large operations, there are examples of the smallest of publishers being completely marketing-orientated and the largest still operating around the journal-production concept.

Many publications exist today which fit into the pattern outlined in Figure 16.1. Some are extremely successful in financial terms: others may even be satisfactory communicators. The basis of operation is that the editor produces an editorial mix intuitively which he or she has found over a period of time to be successful in terms of paid-for circulation. Advertisers, if they have liked the appearance and contents of a publication, have been welcome to participate providing they did not get in the way of the editorial. It was commonplace, and is still not unknown for publishers in phase one of development to be unwilling to disclose even their total circulation let alone other data. The product is the journal.

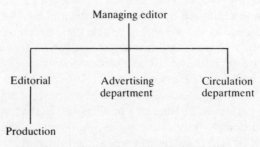

Figure 16.1   Publishing organization—phase 1

The editorial department here decides on editorial content regardless of any other considerations. It will usually control layout and presentation, production and sometimes circulation and distribution. The advertisement department is concerned with selling space, and indeed in the absence of adequate information to reinforce a sales argument, many space representatives are, through no fault of their own, little more than collectors of orders for space. At best they are salesmen of the old school whose success depends upon their personality and their ability to capture the confidence of a prospect—but in themselves rather than their product.

This over-simplification does not imply that a given management structure automatically places a publisher among the has-beens, nor that a managing editor is incapable of comprehending and implementing the marketing concept. There are exceptions as always with general rules and procedures.

The organization in Figure 16.2 may not appear much different from that of phase 1, but there is a higher degree of specialization, and the addition of some central services.

Figure 16.2   Publishing organization—phase 2

The differences lie not so much in the organization chart as in the significance of each of the functions in the business operation. A director at the head is to signify that it is an all-round business executive who lays down policy and makes decisions, and that these are on a commercial basis. The editor is rated level with the other departmental heads, and the advertisement manager, for instance, can expect to have as much influence on the make-up and presentation as the editor. Significantly, circulation is treated as a separate and important function with paid-for circulation giving way to free distribution if this is considered necessary to secure business.

Central services are an indication of the growth of publishers into larger units which can provide specialized facilities such as an art department and publicity. Further developments of central services take over responsibility for printing, sometimes distribution and even production and circulation.

Adopting the phase 3 concept of the 'product' being an audience and the 'benefit' exposure or access to that audience, it follows that the product development function in publishing is concerned with maintaining the right readership to meet the advertisers' needs (see Fig. 16.3). While many products in industry remain static, at least for a short period of time, and therefore may not require development, in publishing, the audience is in a continual state of change. As new readers register, and people move jobs, the audience mix will become unbalanced and therefore in effect a different product which may not be wanted by advertisers.

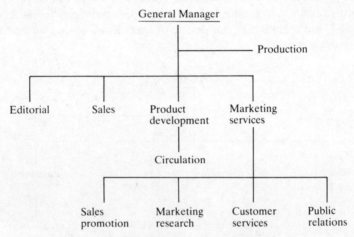

Figure 16.3   Publishing organization—phase 3

The 'market' is of course the potential advertisers, and so the starting point in the development of a product in publishing is to assess the market's needs i.e. what audience does it wish to reach. This requires to be broken down into segments which will relate to, for example, industrial classification, job category, geographical location and size of firm. From this point it is necessary for the editorial team to devise an editorial mix that will appeal to the audience which emerges, and for a method of circulation to be set up which will reach it.

In marketing services, the research people will be monitoring the success of circulation, and the interest of readers in the editorial. They will study the impact of advertisements, the number of 'pass-on' readers and various other factors of importance to advertisers such as the value of different positions in a journal, the influence of colour, bleed and so on. This data will provide the ammunition which will be fired first by the sales promotion department and then by the sales force. Public relations will take as its task the building of good relations and a good understanding with all the publics of a journal including readers, advertisers, distributors, contributors, trade associations, suppliers and shareholders.

Customer services is a function which is not yet fully established in publishing. Each journal has certain strengths which derive from being in its particular business. Some of these strengths can be marketed in one form or another to existing and prospective customers. For example, a journal's circulation list can be hired out as the basis of a direct mail operation. The editorial team have technical knowledge which can be applied to the staging of seminars and conferences. The editors are writers, and some of this talent can be expanded into writing house magazines, leaflets for clients or film scripts. Publishers are also in a good position to sponsor exhibitions. 'Customer services' will also include carrying out specific assignments for customers, such as working with them to measure the total effectiveness of a campaign. Split runs for instance are easy to arrange, but few technical publishers offer this facility, let alone promote it as a sales feature.

Production is shown as a central service. So probably should be marketing services unless the idea of product groups is adopted. In this case, a number of complementary journals are marketed within one product group. The editorial teams need to be separate, but the sales force and all the other functions can be operated to serve all the publications in a group. This method of operation is particularly suited to larger organizations: indeed with large numbers of publications, it becomes necessary in order to maintain a workable span of management control.

Departmental functions

EDITORIAL

It has been said earlier that press advertising is 'too cheap'. This is evidenced throughout all departments in a publishing organization, but no more so than in the editorial department. Considering the national importance of technical journals in disseminating information on new developments in industry and commerce, it is disconcerting to find the conditions under which the editorial side is often forced to work because of the limited finance available to it. An editorial team often consists of little more than an editor and an assistant, and sometimes works under conditions of employment which are not attractive to specialists of stature and calibre. A comparison with the situation in the United States where there are relatively fewer publications, shows that an editorial team may be made up of a dozen or so specialists, each a respected authority in his or her own right.

Inadequate staffing leads to a high proportion of technical journals which are produced largely from press releases selected almost at random and mixed in with contributed articles from sources that may or may not be authoritative, dealing with subject matter that tends to be determined by the contributors rather than defined as part of a planned editorial programme.

There is also a lack of research data to assist editors who therefore do not acurately know for whom they are writing: nor are they accustomed to having a feedback on which items are of interest to readers and which are not. Editors of most journals have to operate largely on the basis of experience and intuition.

ADVERTISING

Many publications function with only an advertisement manager and a secretary to sell their advertising space. Others have one or two space representatives. A commission system is usually built into the salary structure so that when a journal does well (often a matter of chance) high incomes can be obtained, and when it does badly the advertisement staff are underpaid. Opportunities for promotion have tended to be few, though this is changing as publishing groups grow and encourage interchanges between publications.

Publishers have difficulty in recruiting sales staff of high quality, and it is argued by many space buyers that representatives have little or no influence on the choice of media in an advertising schedule. The lack of media data is obviously a contributory factor here.

CIRCULATION

The traditional circulation manager on a subscription magazine may be little more than a senior clerk, sending out occasional mailing shots to prospective subscribers, attending trade exhibitions and dealing with renewals and the paper work involved in handling thousands of low value accounts. It is not generally realized that the cost of securing renewals is usually as high as the total net income from subscriptions; that is to say, it makes no difference financially to a publisher whether it sells a publication or gives it away.

Circulation departments are changing and some of the more advanced publishers are utilizing the most sophisticated equipment and techniques to secure at least the right circulation mixture, if not the right readership.

PROMOTIONS

In general, little effort is put into the promotion of either advertisement sales or circulation. This is rather strange when it is considered that the publishing industry represents the largest single item of promotional expenditure among its clients. Very few magazines use any form of advertising themselves, neither for that matter do they invest in any of the other channels of persuasion to any marked degree.

Lack of promotional activity is often an indicator of lack of anything to promote. Where this is not the case, an increase in sales promotion would help the publishers by making their marketing operations more efficient, and it would help the advertisers by providing them with more information.

PRODUCTION

Few publishers are themselves involved in the business of printing. Their production side then comprises one or two people concerned with bringing manuscripts to the galley stage, and pasting these up with illustrations according to a laid down design formula for the make-up of the journal including the disposition of the advertisements.

Methods of circulation

There are a number of basic methods of circulation, each with variations and each having advantages and disadvantages. Broadly it can be said that methods fall into two categories, paid-for and free.

PAID-FOR CIRCULATION

It may then be supposed that a paid-for readership is by definition an interested one, and indeed this is still arguable. There are two factors which operate against it from an advertiser's point of view. Firstly, many readers receive their publications from within their company, and therefore to them they are free. Secondly, a company tends to have an internal distribution list which often means that some readers receive a magazine weeks or months after publication, by which time it may not be of any great interest. Publishers of subscription journals will argue that the in-company distribution of their publications represents a strength in that it results in a readership many times greater than circulation. It could, however, be a weakness.

A special category of paid-for circulation is when a subscriber receives a copy of a publication as a result of being a member of an institute or association. Here there is often no pass-on readership: indeed it is not unknown for real readership to be somewhat lower than total circulation.

The problem with subscription journals is that since anyone can buy them, the publisher cannot, or does not, control who receives them, and therefore is not able to direct the circulation into those areas which are wanted by the advertisers. The circulation therefore is random, often highly fragmented and as a result sometimes not commercial. There are also real difficulties about determining where copies go, particularly if they are obtained through newsagents or bookstalls.

FREE CIRCULATION

The first journal to receive popular acclaim in the field of free circulation was *Industrial Equipment News*. Nowadays a good proportion of trade and technical publications are distributed free of charge either in part or in entirety.

The term 'controlled circulation' needs to be examined since the degree of control is entirely at the discretion of a publisher. The result is that in some instances it is applied only in a very loose sense and is often under the jurisdiction of a relatively junior employee. The fault lies as much with the advertisers, as with publishers, for not taking a stronger line and applying a greater degree of scrutiny.

At the lowest level there are journals which are simply sent out to a mailing list, with no requirement for readers to register or to qualify. Publishers may argue that such circulation is controlled since they control who they send it to. For instance, they may take the published list of members of an association and mail personal copies to each member. A refinement could be to eliminate people working for companies employing less than 100. Mailing lists can be purchased from specialist sources—some advertisers are willing to make their lists accessible, for instance, but it is important to realize that such mailing lists for a free circulation journal are never likely to be as good as those which a firm can produce for itself. Special caution should be applied to journals which overnight increase their circulation by a significant number, for instance, from 5000 to 7000. This can be, and is, done quite simply by finding some additional source of names and adding it to the existing list. Alternatively, by sending to the same companies on the lists, but instead of addressing one copy to the buyer, to address two copies one for the buyer, one for the works manager. There is maybe a case for doing this, but the advertiser is well advised to scrutinize the details of the circulation methods adopted.

A number of free circulation journals require a reader to register and to be in one of a number of defined categories, for example to exercise a purchasing influence. Such registration ensures a measure of interest in a journal but if copies are sent only to those taking the trouble to register, the coverage of any one market is no longer 100 per cent. A further problem with registered readers is that they seldom cancel or transfer their application when they change jobs or retire. This leads to publishers inadvertently sending sizeable proportions of their circulation to dead-end addresses or recipients who no longer have any interest or importance. Moreover, there is no practical way in which an applicant's form can be authenticated by a publisher, and so the validity of a circulation even of 'applied-for' journals depends upon the validity of the data supplied by the readers, who tend to inflate the importance of their position as a means of obtaining a personal and free copy of a journal.

A method known as rotating circulation is a lesser used practice but poorly regarded. The technique is to build up a list of, for example, 50 000 firms, then send each consecutive issue to a different 10 000 until after five monthly issues all the mailing list has been covered. This tends to bring high enquiry response rates initially and enable a publisher to make claims about his circulation which may be misleading.

In general the concept of free circulation publications is based upon the sound marketing philosophy of defining a market then going all out to achieve a maximum share of it. Many magazines in this category have achieved outstanding success and are firmly entrenched as valuable advertising media. Readership researches confirm that they are hitting the target. While they do not get the same pass-on readership as subscription journals, they have the merit of going directly to the person most concerned who is able to give his immediate attention to it.

The editorial format which has become associated with free-circulation journals is perhaps unfortunate in that the concentration on new products, sometimes to the exclusion of features, confuses the issue and has led to the assumption that maximum reader response comes from free journals and that serious articles in depth are published only in subscription journals. This is not inevitably so: either editorial treatment or a mixture is suitable for either type of circulation.

HYBRIDS

Almost all circulations are hybrid in the sense that there are a proportion of copies which are free and a proportion which are charged at a lower rate than usual. Perhaps what is not realized is that many formerly paid-for journals have been forced by competition to inflate their circulation, and that this has been done by giving away copies. It is not unknown for a journal to have as many free copies as paid-for, but to trade under the heading of a subscription publication.

Authentic data

Publishing has been described as 'the last refuge for a gentleman', but this is not always true. Advertisers have been misled deliberately by some publishers who have blatantly said one thing and done another. This situation is changing fast under the influence of various organizations, notably the Audit Bureau of Circulation, but there are still many publications which are not prepared to submit their circulations to the independent audit which an industrial advertiser requires.

The Media Data Form represents a valuable step forward and its continued development will do much to increase the efficiency of media selection and thus advertising efficiency. In the meantime the growing demand from advertisers for data has led to a variety of publishers' information being supplied, and experience has shown that some of this is irrelevant, inaccurate or misleading. Circulations are known to have been quoted well in excess of the total market, and in excess of the print order. Circulation breakdowns by category have been known to be closer to wishful thinking than the actual facts of the case.

As always, the buyer would do well to exercise considerable caution, and adopt a tough line with suppliers who will not supply the service that is required.

17.

ADVERTISING AGENCIES

Advertising agencies still suffer from their origin as agents for publications, selling advertising space to 'clients' in consideration of a commission from the media owners. From that point the situation developed to where agencies competed with each other by offering free services, primarily the creation of advertisements for their clients who not unnaturally accepted the services and asked for more. Gradually agencies identified themselves with clients rather than the media they represented until they cut adrift completely from individual publications and set up exclusive relationships with their clients, the advertisers. It was, and still is, difficult for them to be completely independent and objective in their relations with the media since the press (and TV) continued to pay a commission whereas certain other media, for example exhibitions, did not. Thus many supplementary services were provided for clients but were paid for out of commission from press advertising. The merits or demerits of this situation are examined later, but it explains why many agencies are still oriented around 'above the line' advertising, while their clients are often heavily involved in other forms of persuasive communications.

Agency organization

There are over 700 advertising agencies in the United Kingdom split in numbers about evenly between London and the provinces. Since the larger agencies are almost exclusively in London this is where the greater majority of advertising agency activity is concentrated.

Agencies vary from those consisting of one or two people, with a turnover of a few hundreds of thousands of pounds, to very large businesses employing hundreds and sometimes a thousand or more people and having turnovers of many millions. In comparing such turnovers with other businesses it should be remembered that profit margins are of a relatively low order, usually little over 1 per cent. It is true of any business that its strength lies first in the calibre of the people it employs, and this is especially so in agencies since that is all they have to offer—there is no plant and equipment to make good the deficiencies of human beings and relatively little in the way of scientific research, quality control and inspection to safeguard the quality of their output.

The organization of agencies is extremely varied in detail. There are some structural characteristics which can be isolated, and these are indicated in the following examples which are examined from the point of view of handling industrial accounts.

SMALL AGENCY

The organization shown in Figure 17.1 might be typical of an agency employing up to around twenty-five people and having a turnover of up to and over five million pounds. It is more than likely that the managing director will handle one or two accounts himself or herself, as indeed may the creative and production directors. This would leave each account executive with maybe £200 000 of billing. The primary business of this kind of agency is likely to be heavily directed to trade press advertising but it often possesses special skills in the particular requirements of its clients, perhaps in sales literature or direct mail. It will be necessary to utilize outside services even for creative work, and the amount of effort available for media planning, at least in the media department, will be small. There is no built-in provision for press relations, exhibitions or research. The span of control is already approaching a maximum especially if the managing director is handling accounts personally as well as running the business.

The number of clients, product groups and campaigns will probably be small, and most people in the agency will know and care about most of the clients. The staff will therefore be sensitive about the needs of clients and the organization will centre around these needs rather than expecting clients to fit into a rigid procedural pattern. The following are some of the advantages and disadvantages which may apply from a client's point of view.

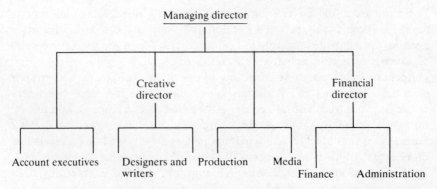

Figure 17.1   Small agency organization

1. Advantages:

   (a) Attention from top management
   (b) Quick response to needs
   (c) Short chain of command
   (d) Attention to personal details
   (e) Ease of identifying with clients' business
   (f) Often locally situated

2. Disadvantages:

   (a) Lack of specialists
   (b) Difficulty in getting top calibre people to work in a small agency
   (c) Tendency to 'sameness' in creativity
   (d) Over-dependence on a single person in the handling of an account
   (e) Lack of breadth of knowledge resulting from small number of accounts

MEDIUM AGENCY

Such an agency may well be set up primarily with a view to handling industrial accounts and will employ people with appropriate talents and interests. The total number of employees may be a hundred or more with a billing of several tens of million pounds.

The organizational chart (Figure 17.2), shows a logical progression from Figure 17.1, with client service breaking into groups under the overall control of a director. Each group will contain three or four executives and be self-contained except for central services which may or may not include produc-

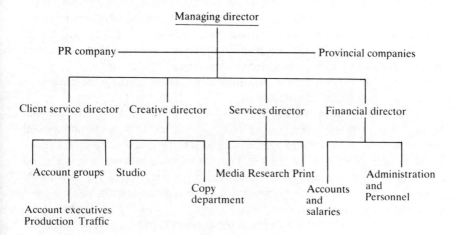

Figure 17.2 Medium agency organization

tion and traffic. It is a matter of opinion whether there is benefit in the creative unit being centralized or integrated within each group. Whichever way it goes, however, it is important to have a creative director who can not only supply ideas and creative stimulus, but also ensure the maintenance of creative standards.

A feature in this size of agency is that it can justify the employment of specialists in media, research and print, as well as having associated companies to handle press relations and perhaps exhibitions, artwork, photography and so on.

1. Advantages:
    (a) Stable business of substance
    (b) Top people are likely to be able and experienced
    (c) Large number of account executives with a wide range of industrial experience
    (d) Availability of specialists
    (e) Access to associated services

2. Disadvantages:
    (a) Lack of personal attention from the top
    (b) Longer chain of command
    (c) Difficulty in getting instant response and attention
    (d) Extended and diffused internal communications

LARGE AGENCY

The kind of structure which may exist in a very large agency which, in addition to handling major consumer accounts, will also make provision for industrial advertising, is shown in Figure 17.3. It is most likely that one or more account groups will set out to become a small industrial agency within the parent company. There will be a group head with a number of account executives (usually with some assistants) and probably a number of creative people as well as production and traffic assistants, and in the case of a technical group a media specialist.

To this extent, the technical group may look similar to the small industrial agency: it is probably even treated as a 'profit centre'. The differences will come largely in the variety of specialists and services that can be called upon. Furthermore there will be all the benefits of a large company—a good reference library, a management and staff development plan, a cinema or projection room, and maybe a computer. Most agencies of this size have not just overseas connections, but overseas companies with good communications, and the means of producing campaigns that can be readily projected on an international basis.

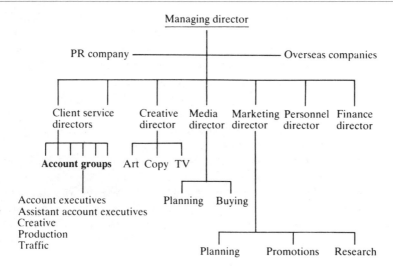

Figure 17.3   Large agency organization

1. Advantages:
   (a) High calibre people at the top
   (b) Sophisticated consumer techniques which can be adapted for industrial advertising
   (c) Capacity to think big
   (d) Can provide virtually every service from within the company
   (e) Creative excellence

2. Disadvantages:
   (a) The industrial side may be regarded as the poor relation
   (b) Service is usually expensive
   (c) Work takes longer to produce, due to lengthy communications and internal procedures and disciplines
   (d) Staff are usually not so technical and have difficulty in interpreting a brief, particularly as regards copywriting
   (e) Smaller clients have to fit into agency organization rather than the agency changing to suit a client

Agency procedures

It is useful to examine the stages through which a typical job is likely to pass. It will be seen that, except in a small agency, there are a large number of people likely to be involved in the processing of a single advertisement. The question of effective communication becomes vital to ensure that the initial message and purpose is not lost or blunted, but rather sharpened and refined.

It is not always appreciated by the client how important the brief is to the agency. This, after all, is the raw material from which the advertisement or campaign is to be constructed. Inadequate briefing may be compensated by the persistence and tenacity of agency staff, but this is often the cause of high charges and jobs which are regarded as unsatisfactory by the client. The client must put as much into preparing the brief for the agency as the agency will subsequently put into its proposals. Briefs should be in writing in order to exclude the possibility of misunderstanding. A good starting point is to ensure that everyone in the agency who is involved should have had a thorough background brief.

Figure 17.4 shows the likely steps within an agency in the formulation of a campaign plan. Though appearing as a series of discrete steps, there is always a good deal of intercommunication throughout the preparation of a campaign. Media is very much influenced by research: the account group will

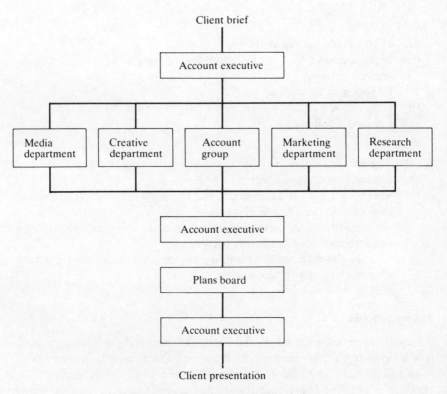

Figure 17.4 Agency procedural chart

have strong ideas of its own, and creative ideas will interact on almost every aspect of the campaign.

Points to be covered in agency background brief include:

1. Strategic and corporate objectives
2. Marketing objectives
3. Communications objectives
4. The market
5. The market need
6. The product
7. Competition
8. Price
9. Selling platform
10. Distribution channels
11. Pre- and post-sales service

First there is the brief from the client giving the objectives and requirements. The account executive is responsible for interpreting these to the various agency departments that are likely to be involved. The account group is shown as a separate function in this operation since while the account executive will bear the main load, there will usually be executives both junior and senior to him or her who will contribute to the plan. Research may be necessary to assist media planning and to provide intelligence for the marketing department. Creative personnel will not begin designing advertisements at this stage, but they should have the opportunity to express an opinion on whether press advertising is an appropriate vehicle from their point of view, or whether for example, three dimensions are required: if press advertising then does the nature of the objective indicate a need for double-page spreads, half pages or inserts? This will interact with media planning who may be concentrating on national dailies while creative want four-colour reproductions on art paper. The marketing department will examine the brief in a rather broader context and may be questioning the client's advertising brief in relation to its own marketing plan. There may be a call for a higher concentration on certain market segments—a proposition which if accepted will invalidate much of the media planning and perhaps throw the whole job back into the melting pot.

The planning of a campaign within an agency can be looked upon as a very intensive 'think' workshop: almost a long-drawn-out brainstorming session.

After the plan is agreed, it has to be implemented, and Figure 17.5 shows the stages through which a press advertisement is likely to pass.

This somewhat complex chart is an outline of what is probably a minimum of activity for an advertisement which develops without complication. At any stage there is likely to be a 'rejection' which can put the whole project back to an earlier stage, or even back to the starting point. The visual may be rejected

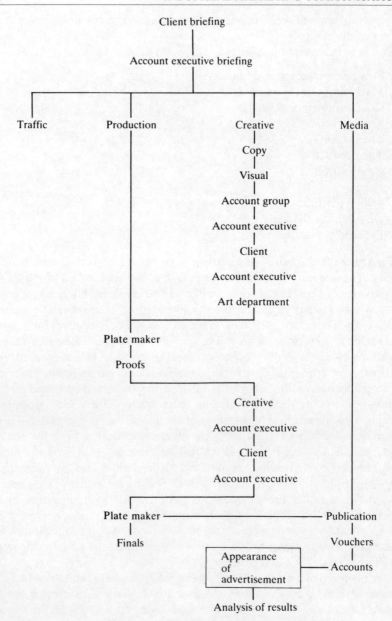

Figure 17.5   Advertising progress chart

by the creative head or by the group head or account executive. At the client end there may be two or three, or more, people who need to express an opinion. The artwork and sometimes the type mark-up may go through the same process, and the proofs may be subject to a number of revisions before everyone is satisfied. In the process of creating an advertisement there may well be two dozen or more points of decision-making before it is finally 'passed for press'. It will be seen that there is an uncomfortable similarity between this operation and a game of snakes and ladders!

Departments and functions

The functions and departments within an agency have been outlined, and their interrelationships examined. The roles of the principal ones are now considered in more detail.

ACCOUNT GROUP

Since there may or may not be an account group as such, it is the account executive who is considered principally under this head.

There are unquestionably some account executives (or supervisors, or associate directors) who are little more than message carriers between the agency and the client. At best such people might be regarded as liaison men or women. In industrial advertising, this is an unacceptable situation. The executive is the key person in the whole operation. He or she must understand fully the client's needs and interpret them with precision to the supporting staff at the agency. Thereafter the account executive must maintain a close watch on every stage of development, exercising direction and control where necessary, while retaining the respect and confidence both of the client and the agency personnel: he or she must mediate, persuade and enthuse colleagues, be a combination of diplomat, wet nurse, salesperson and dictator, and above and beyond all that must be a first-rate all-round industrial marketing executive.

MEDIA DEPARTMENT

Apart from routine functions such as collecting rate cards, specimen and voucher copies, and checking invoices, the media department has two main operations, planning and buying. Both of these are important and call for a good deal of expertise.

The lack of adequate data on industrial media (by which is usually meant only press and, where applicable, television) is such that media planning is often highly superficial. General experience of industrial media is not enough in view of the large number of publications, and the large number of different products and markets which are all part of determining the media mix. A fully effective media planning operation is therefore likely to involve a good deal of investigation and research by very able specialists.

Media buying is not such an intangible business, but it is one in which significant sums of clients' money can be saved by careful planning and investigation coupled with ruthless negotiation and bargaining.

CREATIVE DEPARTMENT

This will usually comprise a mixture of writers, designers and typographers whose collective creative talents need to be welded into a cohesive team which will interpret product benefits into a visual selling proposition having impact upon potential customers. It is from this department largely that the spark of genius is needed to lift an advertisement out of the ordinary and into the outstanding.

It is basically 'ideas' which emanate from a creative department, not words and pictures. Its work therefore must be judged in terms of creative expression of a client's goods rather than by the graphic excellence of a final proof.

RESEARCH DEPARTMENT

Too little research is put into industrial publicity, due often to the reluctance of clients to invest money in what at first sight seems a non-productive activity. Nevertheless agencies are developing their research facilities which are being concentrated into media, advertisement and campaign evaluation.

Research departments are also able to carry out desk research themselves into markets both to supplement clients' own activities, and to provide data for the planning of campaigns within the agency.

MARKETING DEPARTMENT

Such a department usually exists only in the medium to large agencies, though some marketing expertise is usually available from other staff within an agency. There is also a trend to combine research and marketing into one 'planning' group.

Any agency marketing function can operate where the client has only a limited operation himself, or it can supplement it, or operate it as a second opinion. Furthermore it can work in conjunction with other agency departments during the preparation of an advertising plan. This will help to ensure that the advertising fits into the overall marketing strategy.

Often a marketing department will be a strategic point in an agency where the communications mix can be formulated, and it is not uncommon for this department to be responsible for 'below the line' activities, that is those that do not bring a direct media commission.

PRODUCTION AND TRAFFIC

This is usually a central agency service but is sometimes carried out within an account group. The function, however, is to translate the 'creative' specification into printing plates. That is to take the design, artwork, copy and type mark-up; order plates and setting, obtain proofs, see to their progressing and eventual distribution.

Coupled with the production is the overall progressing of a job which begins when space is booked and goes on continuously, monitoring every stage until the advertisement appears and the invoices are cleared.

These are important services and are usually carried out very well by agencies: far better than a client could hope to do.

PRINT DEPARTMENT

A number of agencies providing a service for industrial accounts have found that there is a demand for sales and technical literature which can best be handled by a separate print department. This will usually include posters, showcards and sometimes direct mail.

The writing and design work for literature will often be carried out by the main creative department, or perhaps by freelance people. The print department is then a specialized production unit which includes the function of print buying. Though the cost incurred may seem to be high, the result will usually show a good standard of professional workmanship.

PUBLIC RELATIONS

Most agencies do not have a public relations department, but rather an associated company which is thus enabled to take on business from companies not necessarily clients of the parent agency.

Editorial publicity in support of an integrated campaign will, in these circumstances, go through the separate company. Indeed, even where an agency has an integral PR department, it is more than usual to find that a separate executive has to be briefed on editorial publicity. Where this happens it is time wasted for a client, since the basic information is the same regardless of the medium. The selling platform, the product benefits, the creative expression, must be the same if a campaign is to have overall cohesion and impact.

EXHIBITIONS AND DISPLAY

As with public relations, it is not uncommon for exhibitions to be handled by an associated company. The same comments therefore apply as those on public relations.

One agency has a philosophy that an exhibition is only an advertisement with a third dimension. There is much to commend this attitude since many of the criteria for a good advertisement apply also to a good exhibition stand, for example stopping power, easy to read headline, punchy copy, and so on.

Methods of remuneration

As distinct from consumer accounts, which usually obtain their agency's services entirely out of the 15 per cent media commission, industrial advertising is usually undertaken only on the basis of an added fee. This may be to 'plus-up' all media commission to an agreed level, or it may be a flat rate per annum with or without media commission rebated. In between there are almost infinite variations, adjustments and understandings which enable an agency to recoup its expenses, though it is sometimes not realized how unnecessarily expensive the more complex payment systems are.

It is necessary to be clear about the method of remuneration for an agency. While, in the past, an agency was a representative for journals and newspapers, it was logical that it should be remunerated by a commission from the publishers.

If, however, an agency is operating on behalf of advertisers there can be no logical justification for payment other than from the clients it serves. The amount of space booked is quite irrelevant to the amount of work that is done by an agency either in terms of publicity as a whole or even press advertising alone. The creative time, the media planning time, the space booking time, the production, are the same whether for a 25×20 cm space in a plastics magazine or in a national daily. They are still the same if there is one appearance, or ten, and they are not much different whether they appear in one publication or a hundred. Furthermore, how can an account executive justify taking a briefing for a piece of direct mail when he or she is being paid out of commission from a magazine, for example?

Publications will continue to offer commission since in doing so there is a built-in attraction to agencies to place their business with them as opposed to other media. Agencies for their part are content to leave matters as they are since they can argue that only by using a 'recognized' agency can a client recoup the commission.

This is unsound practice from every business point of view and encourages inefficient operations and biased recommendations. The only basis upon which agency services can be justified is to pay for work done which, if not satisfactory, can soon be rectified by finding another supplier. It is difficult to see how the ending of the commission system could do other than benefit advertisers.

In the meantime it may be useful to give a detailed explanation of how agencies commonly 'plus up' their charges.

When an advertising agency places an order for an advertisement with a media owner, it will be charged the rate-card (gross) figure less an agency commission, commonly 15%. Thus the client would pay £1000 for instance, but the agency only £850, ie it receives a commission of £150. This applies to all 'above the line' media such as press, TV, radio and posters. N.B. Trade and Technical journals only pay 10%.

For non-commissionable services (below-the-line), an agency usually adds a sum as a handling fee. A bill for printing sent by a printer to an agency or consultancy will often be increased by 17.65%. This may seem a very odd figure, and not many people know why. The reason is very hard to justify but comes about as follows:

£1000 + £176.50 = charge to client £1176.50 (gross)

Note: 15% (the usual agency commission) of £1176.50 is £176.50 which when subtracted from the total leaves £1000.

So the charge of 17.65% (of the nett) enables the agency to recoup what would have been 15% of the gross figure had there been a media commission.

Client–agency relationships

This is a problem which is written and talked about whenever advertising people meet.

It may be that the method of agency remuneration leads to clients being apathetic towards the quality of service derived from an agency, and this apathy encourages unwillingness to provide the material necessary for an agency to do a good job. The view often expressed by clients that an agency cannot produce good technical or industrial material is matched only by the view from the other side that clients seem incapable of providing a thorough and comprehensive brief. This is a failure in communications, and the failure is allowed to continue because neither side considers the real cost involved. The only other possible explanation for this communications gap is that the people concerned are inadequate, and if this is so, the solution is to employ people who are capable of doing the job properly.

If clients can obtain several designs and copy platforms 'free' they will not feel under pressure to ensure that they are precise in their briefing, nor will they put themselves out to spend time gathering background material which will enable agencies to hit the mark first time. Similarly there is no great pressure on account executives to put undue effort into projects since, if clients do not approve the first attempt, they can always have another. If, on the other hand, every advertisement design and copy was charged at market price, perhaps £300 or so, and similarly every redesign, the whole procedure would necessarily tighten up considerably.

Over and above any considerations of the method of payment, most agencies can and will provide almost any service for which clients reasonably ask, providing there is a margin of profit. It rests then with the clients, who after all are the buyers, to demand the best standard of professional service, but to be prepared to pay for it. The mutual respect and confidence which must exist to obtain the best results will follow automatically.

Choosing an agency

The first question to be answered is why an agency should be necessary at all. The fact that almost all industrial advertisers use an agency does not necessarily prove that they are right.

The worst reason, but probably a common one, is that it is to obtain the benefit of the publishers' commission. The right reason has been summed up in an IPA publication.[1]

> The agency's most valuable asset is it objective and professional viewpoint. The analysis and assessment of a client's problems together with the unbiased, unemotional appraisal of specific market conditions, make a real contribution to efficient marketing and effective advertising.

An objective assessment of the need for an advertising agency leads to consideration of precisely which activities require servicing. This can then become the basis on which a choice is made. In other words a 'services specification' is required that will act as a coarse screen to filter out those companies that do not match requirements. Then their level of performance can be examined.

The objective assessment must come before involvement with the personalities concerned. Next comes the cost of the service, and the best value for money.

Finally, but in the end most important, are the personalities involved. The finest brains and the most businesslike organization are of little avail unless it is possible for the principals on both sides to establish an easy rapport which will enable them to work together as a team. The key figure here is the account executive who will ensure that the client receives the service he or she needs and demands. A weakness in creativity within the agency, for example, can be overcome by an effective account executive who will possibly insist on freelance services being used. As against this an excellent creative team will find it difficult to produce effective advertising if the account executive is inadequate.

Perhaps it is appropriate at this stage to refer again to the role of the marketing communications manager. To obtain effective publicity, the manager must not only be professionally capable, but must be given real responsibility and authority. It follows that the appointment of an advertising agency is the responsibility of the Marketing Communications (Marcom) manager. The marketing manager will certainly be involved, and is right to express his views, but the decision to hire and fire should rest with the chief publicity executive. The results, good or bad, become his or her personal responsibility with all the advantages this brings. (See also Chapter 18.)

Checklist

In evaluating your present agency, or in making an assessment of a new one, have the following criteria been examined?

1. Agency management structure
2. Internal procedures
3. Basis of remuneration
4. Internal method of costing, plussing-up and charging: allocation of overheads
5. Legal and financial status: major shareholders: issued capital: turnover
6. Clients—names, industry groups, billings, number of years, with named contacts for references
7. Experience in relevant industries and markets
8. Quality of advertisements in relation to brief of

    (a) Copywriting
    (b) Headline
    (c) Sign-off or action
    (d) Visual
    (e) Campaign continuity
    (f) Measurement of results

9. Campaign assessment in relation to brief of

    (a) Campaign plan
    (b) Copy platform
    (c) Media mix
    (d) Visual continuity
    (e) Measurement of results

10. Media services and expertise in

    (a) Press
    (b) TV
    (c) Direct mail
    (d) Merchandising
    (e) Packaging

    (f) Point of sale
    (g) Sales literature
    (h) Technical publications
    (i) Exhibitions
    (j) Photography
    (k) Press relations
    (l) Public relations

11. Research

    (a) Advertising
    (b) Media
    (c) Campaign
    (d) Market
    (e) Product
    (f) Other

12. Overseas connections
13. Provincial branches
14. Personal compatibility with and professional capability of

    (a) Account executive
    (b) Account director
    (c) Creative head
    (d) Media manager
    (e) Research and/or market head
    (f) Managing director

Reference

1. *Industrial Marketing and the Advertising Agency.*

18

OUTSIDE SERVICES

A changing feature of marketing activities is the extent to which outside services are used, as opposed to internal staff. This is partly due to a desire not to have a marketing department which is larger than absolutely necessary; due to the increasing specialisation of the marketing function, and the need for professional practitioners in each of the specialised areas. There are no absolutes in the sense of right or wrong, and perhaps it is best to first consider the strengths and weaknesses in very general terms.

Strengths and weaknesses

The first strength to consider of an advertising agency, a PR consultancy, or some such outside service is that it is likely to be far more professional than any in-company department. Whatever its size, the service will comprise a group of people whose sole activity is, and has been, in this one specialisation. And every day they are handling a range of clients with various objectives, plans, budgets, activities and evaluations. There is also the synergistic inter-relationship of the 'account-handling' staff who can refer to one another in arriving at solutions to their problems.

A second strength is objectivity. Outside advisers have no personal involvement; indeed, that is one of their weaknesses. They can look upon marketing problems and solutions completely dispassionately, uninfluenced by any of the factors which impinge upon an employee of a firm; 'what the boss thinks', or 'we tried it once, and it didn't work', will not cut much ice with a consultant. It might be said that client corporate culture will not necessarily have an over-riding effect.

A third strength is the credibility of an outside organization, particularly if it is being paid a handsome fee. 'A prophet is without honour . . .' certainly applies to the way in which top management sometimes react to the recommendations of outside consultants as opposed to their own staff. It may not even be that the outside proposals are all that different to what has been said for years, but somehow the outsider seems to act as a more credible message source.

Finally, in the list of strengths, an outside service provides for a client company an expandable work force which can be increased or decreased substantially at very short notice. This is important in that no marketing campaign ever runs smoothly without peaks and troughs. There are frequently times when a much greater effort is required, just as there may crop up the need to stop an activity completely. The budget may have been cut for advertising, or all the campaign objectives are achieved prematurely. An agency will just stop work temporarily, whereas if such work is being carried out by one's own staff, what are they going to occupy themselves with now.

To counter the strengths of outside services it is necessary to consider their possible weaknesses, the first of which might be that their time is limited for any one client. They have other clients, each with their own priorities. Whereas with an in-house function, a particular issue can be given a high priority like 'do it now', it may not even be possible to communicate with the client contact person, let alone obtain some service.

A second weakness, particularly in industrial marketing, is that the staff of outside agencies often seem to have merely superficial knowledge of the client's business, its markets or its products. How often does one hear of agencies submitting copy which has to be completely re-written, or of a press release which has to undergo the same treatment? It may be due to inadequate briefing, poor communications, incompetence or lack of time, but it certainly happens.

A third factor is that outside services almost always seem to be far more expensive than expected. This is probably because the wrong criteria are used for comparison. A comparison might well be made between a PR consultancy with an average charge-out rate of £100 an hour, and an in-house person at £25000 pa which works out to £100 per day. This must be an unfair comparison since no overheads are included, but, in any case, an outside consultant can be hired in small increments as opposed to inside staff where one has an additional whole person or nothing at all.

A final weakness of outside services is that staff turnover seems always to be very high. No sooner has an account handler grown accustomed to the needs of a client, than he or she leaves or is transferred to another account. This leads straight away to the work being superficial which, in turn, must add to the expense.

There is thus no clear cut answer in favour of or against a particular company using outside services. All that can be said is that their use is growing and that they are progressively becoming more and more capable. For efficient service it is necessary to pay special attention to the choice of an outside service, to its adequate briefing and, where necessary, to its evaluation.

It is useful at this stage to review the range of services on offer. Emphasis will be given to advertising agencies simply because they are the most frequently used service of all. Second place will be given to PR consultancies, and thereafter all the others.

Advertising agencies

For the manufacturer of industrial products or for the supplier of services to business organizations, a special kind of advertising agency is required. Not everyone will agree with this proposition. Indeed, there are many who hold that since the advertising principles are the same for both consumer and industrial products, the practice is also the same and, therefore, any well set-up consumer agency can perform a thoroughly good job for an industrial client. There are three reasons why this is not the case.

1. Many industrial products and services are complex and specialised with the result that executives who are fully immersed in consumer products have difficulty in understanding the client's language, let alone interpreting it into a compelling and believable selling argument.
2. For the most part, the media is entirely different. Consumer marketing expertise in relation to television, newspapers and posters is of no value when what is needed is a broad knowledge of technical journals, exhibitions, literature, direct mail and the like. A further limitation is that consumer media planning is based upon extensive readership and market data. In the industrial sector the lack of information puts actual experience of industrial media at a premium.
3. Advertising budgets are relatively low, which leads to the necessity of charging a substantial fee, or alternatively providing a lower level service.

What are business to business agencies?

Quite simply these are what used to be called Industrial Agencies, but with a new name. There is good reason for this change in title since the expertise is not only in understanding industrial products, but more importantly the nature of the markets in which they are sold. And for the most part these markets are businesses or organizations. Indeed, there are some consumer products which also sell to industry, and here the expertise of a business to business agency is an important asset.

Otherwise the agencies operate as any other with a full service on offer, covering research, planning, creative, media and all the necessary administrative back-up. How do they differ?

BUDGETS

In industrual marketing, the balance between the cost of the sales force, product development, pre and post sales service, and advertising is quite different to consumer marketing. Advertising budgets are relatively small and considerable ingenuity is required to stretch them sufficiently to achieve the maximum effect. If budgets are small then income from media commission is even smaller. Thus a business to business agency has to be geared up to operate efficiently on a relatively low income. In many cases clients find it to their advantage to operate on a totally different financial basis, namely of paying an annual fee based upon the actual service provided. This has the advantage of ensuring that agency recommendations are totally unbiased, and even more importantly the agency is fully accountable for all the expenditure it incurs on a client's behalf.

PLANNING

The first and vital stage of any advertising campaign is to produce the advertising plan. This requires an intimate knowledge of the marketplace. Industrial markets are not only extremely complex, but they also differ widely one from another.

The purchasing decision for a consumer product is relatively simple. When a company makes a purchase, however, the 'decision making unit' is likely to be made up of technical specialists, purchasing executives, end users, and often several or even all members of the board. Identifying these purchasing decision makers calls for an in-depth knowledge of industry and how it operates. Purchasing motives are also different. True, there are people involved who will each have personal reasons for wanting to make a purchase, and these may well be as subjective as any consumer purchase. But over and above these are objective and rational factors, with the buyer often in a position to evaluate fully and at length the performance of the product in question. The total number of prospects may number a hundred or so, and the value of the transaction may be of the order of hundreds of thousands of pounds. All these factors require advertising to be planned in a completely different way for it to be really effective.

MEDIA

Since the markets are often numerous, and highly segmented, and since the managers making the decisions are likely to have completely different functions, it follows that matching the media to the markets is an intricate and specialised task. There is no room for the 'blunderbuss' approach of mass media; rather it is necessary to engage in precision targeting to ensure that advertising messages really do get through to the right people. A much wider range of media needs to be considered—trade and technical journals, management magazines, institution publications, sales literature, direct mail, seminars, conferences, exhibitions, sales aids, private shows, audio-visual material, editorial publicity, and so on. There needs to be within the agency a sufficient body of knowledge and experience to ensure that the most effective media mix is produced, having regard to the strengths and weaknesses of each medium.

CREATIVE

The creative magic is every bit as important in industrial advertising. Indeed, the creative opportunities from using such a wide variety of media are immense. But the creative inspiration must come across as authoritative and genuine, which calls for a knowledge on the part of the creative staff of the interests, motivation and terminology of the prospective customers they are addressing. In addition, there must be a realisation that the product benefits are likely to differ as between the financial director, the works manager, the purchasing officer and the chairman. Not only the media, but also the message, must match the market.

OBJECTIVES

Whereas in consumer advertising the primary objective may be to secure an increase in sales, in industrial advertising it is rarely that simple. More likely it is called upon to supply technical information and to generate enquiries. This can be followed up by mail, telephone and personal calling which will lead to a sale, but often after many months of careful negotiation. So the specific objectives are likely to be different.

TOTAL COMMUNICATIONS

The full service business to business agency plays an important role in a company's marketing operation, and for this reason its executives must have not only the necessary advertising skills, but also a working familiarity with the client's operations and the markets which they serve. More than that, it is not good enough to be restricted to the few major media channels which will suffice for a consumer campaign. It must be able to provide both counselling and executive action in any relevant channel of communication, no matter how unusual or difficult or financially unrewarding.

Media independents

These are a small number of organizations, sometimes known as media brokers. These companies set out to do no more than look after the advertising media interests of clients, ie excluding services in marketing, creativity (copy and design), research, production, etc. They are staffed by specialists in media and, thus, are able to provide a service, some say unequalled, in media planning and, in particular, media buying. They obviously have more muscle than any individual client when it comes to negotiating rates with the media. In relation to the needs of industrial advertisers, budgets are not usually high enough to make them interesting to a media independent, and they are probably not as knowledgeable about industrial media as the client himself.

Design studios

There are probably a thousand or more design studios, many of which will be individual consultants. They commonly provide design for a wide range of activities including press advertising, literature, direct mail shots, letterheads, packaging, etc. Some of these businesses provide a broader 'creative' service, including creative ideas and copywriting. They are sometimes referred to as 'creative hotshops'. Design studios will not usually be geared up to handle media planning or buying, neither should they be expected to have any kind of marketing expertise.

PR consultancies

The term PR has been used deliberately in the sure knowledge that it is ambiguous. A number of outside services offer and provide a public relations service, whilst a rather larger number offer press relations and nothing much more. The first step, then, is to decide exactly which service is required. If it is simply free editorial publicity that is required, the operation is very simple. Items of news and interest are found and delivered one way or another to the press to cover as they think fit. This is a vital, and probably the most cost-effective channel of communications in the industrial marketing plan. But it is not public relations. This is all about building a corporate reputation and developing efficient two-way communications between an organization and its public. The latter will, of course, include customers and prospects, but they will also take in employees, shareholders, suppliers and, in fact, all the relevant stakeholders of a business.

PR consultancies are not, of course, consultancies at all. Some of them may set out to offer the kind of advice one might expect to receive from a consultant, but most of them are in the business of providing an executive service, just as an advertising agency or any other outside service. This raises an important issue since some client companies with particularly technical products or specialised services, may find that they are far better at putting together effective press releases and building up good relationships with industrial editors. But they can hardly fail to benefit from strategic PR advice and assistance in developing and implementing a PR plan.

Nevertheless, a PR consultancy will have all the strengths and weaknesses described earlier. One can add to this a further benefit if it is needed. That is creativity. It is a fact that coverage in the press is dependent on the newsworthiness of the stories put out. With many firms in the technical/industrial/business fields, stories from new products alone provide more news than any one publication would be able to take in. Not much creativity is needed. With many consumer products, however, very little ever changes, and thus one needs a PR consultancy with lots of bright ideas on how to create news which will, in turn, publicise a product. There are, of course, numerous industrial products where things don't change too much—in basic raw materials, for example.

Most of the characteristics which have already been put forward in relation to advertising agencies are equally relevant to PR consultancies. There are about the same number of each in the UK, and they range from one-man/woman businesses to medium-size companies employing a few hundred people. There are some which specialise in industrial/business accounts, some consumer and some generalist. There are account handlers also, but here there is a difference in that these people have fewer back-up staff to call upon to help them. For instance, they mostly write their own copy, something which an agency contact person would never do. The other significant difference is that agencies are at least partly paid for out of media commission, whereas consultancies have no other income than the fees they charge.

PR distributors

A fast growing service sector is in providing distribution services from client or consultancy to the media. Activities can then be concentrated into preparation and writing of press releases, features and the like. Meanwhile their distribution can be left to specialist agencies who will provide a great deal of helpful reference, for example the names of the multitude of contacts to whom stories should be sent. This applies to the entire range of media—newspapers and magazines, as well as TV and radio.

Marketing consultancies

These are simply specialised management consultancies who, typically, are engaged on an ad hoc basis by a client company who requires top-level advice on some aspect of marketing. A major company will use the services of a marketing consultancy as an extension of its own marketing department; in effect, it buys in some extra time for a specific task. Alternatively, the client may require a second opinion on some aspect of strategic marketing. For the smaller client company, however, a marketing consultancy is often brought in to provide a level of marketing expertise which is not available amongst the permanent staff. It is not usual for a marketing consultancy to undertake executive work as against giving advice and drawing up, for instance, a marketing plan.

For some years now marketing advice has been available under a scheme subsidised by the Department of Trade and Industry (DTI). Here clients can commission a government-listed consultancy to spend anything from five to fifteen days producing a marketing plan of action, and 50 per cent or more of the consultancy's fee will be paid by the DTI.

Direct mail houses

The whole direct mail process, which is growing in popularity, starts with the creative process of copy and design, then moves on to the provision of a suitable database. This is followed by the logistics of putting the scheme together and mailing it, and finally taking in the responses and handling them. Some direct mail houses will lay claim to handling the entire operation, and in consumer marketing this might be so. Chances are that in the field of industrial marketing, both the overall direction and also a great deal of the action will need to be handled by the client company itself.

The direct mail house excels when it comes to expediting the mailing. The mechanical processes of labelling and stuffing have been automated and can be carried out very efficiently and economically. It may be that creative services and the provision of lists had best be found elsewhere.

List brokers

These days, mailing lists or databases come from many sources including directories, journals, and company customer lists. List brokers make a business out of having access to large numbers of specialised mailing lists, which they will access for a handling fee. It is almost never possible to buy a mailing list, either direct from the original source or from a broker. Rather, lists are for hire and are supplied in such a way (eg direct to a mailing house) so that the hirer cannot get sight of the names and addresses.

As regards the quality of mailing lists, bitter experience leads one to the conclusion that considerable caution should be exercised when hiring lists. Many are considerably out of date and can result in major losses. If at all possible in industrial marketing communications, companies would be well advised to build their own mailing lists, and also make provision for keeping them up to date.

Telemarketing

Telemarketing is a fast-growing outside service in the UK, both for direct selling, market research, and other activities. It is well-established in consumer marketing, but in the industrial sector it has two disadvantages. The first is that it is probably unable to cope adequately with products, markets, or subjects which are technical. Secondly, it is likely to prove to be very much more expensive than an in-house exercise.

Other services

1. The outside service which almost all companies use is printing. There is always the option of putting printing through an advertising agency or PR consultancy, but the great disadvantage here is that of expense. The best solution is to build up an ongoing relationship with a particular printer who one learns to trust, both in terms of price and expertise. Even so, it is important that jobs should be periodically put out to competitive quotation.
2. Exhibitions are another activity in which outside services have a role to play. Choice of exhibition and location in the hall are matters which just have to be looked after by the client company itself, but when it comes to stand design and then stand construction, it is mostly beneficial to use outside services but always going through the procedure of competitive quotations.
3. The growing importance of audio-visual material has led to the growth of specialist outside services here. This is important since it is difficult for the non-specialist to produce material which is up to the required professional standard. Care must be taken to shop around for a supplier who can meet the requirements of the budget, since many AV suppliers are accustomed to doing business with clients in consumer marketing where budgets are higher, eg by a factor of ten or more.
4. Market Research is an activity for which very few firms employ a specialist. As a result, any major research is usually contracted out whilst much minor research work is conducted in-house, but, even so, this can be much better than no research at all provided that one is aware of the possible shortcomings. It is worth bearing in mind that a good number of research consultancies specialise in industrial and business markets and products.
5. A final outside service which is mentioned for the sake of completeness is that of commando sales. Here one can hire an outside sales force to supplement one's own. Such a facility is often used for a product launch so as to get to a large number of customers in a short period of time. As with telemarketing, the limitation lies in the ability of the sales force to take in the technicalities of an industrial or business product. This is essentially a consumer service.

Using outside services efficiently

Particular reference here is made to advertising agencies and, to some extent, PR consultancies. The key to obtaining efficient service has to lie in the quality of the brief from the client company. It is convenient to consider the briefing as having two stages—the tactical brief, and the background brief. It is important that the tactical brief should be well thought out and should cover the complete story or message to be put across, together with a fine definition of the target audience. This should be in writing, and should have been approved by everyone who has a say in the matter. It is just not good enough to wait until the advertisement is proofed, or the press release written, before getting approval since this is a waste of time and, thus, money. Indeed, poor briefing is one of the reasons why agencies and consultancies are sometimes accused of being over-expensive.

Over and above ensuring that a sound tactical briefing system is in place, it is necessary to ensure that all the involved personnel have a thorough knowledge of the company. This calls for a comprehensive background brief.

CHOOSING OUTSIDE SERVICES

The most difficult outside service to choose is probably an advertising agency, followed by a PR consultancy. These two will be looked at in some detail.

The first and most important step is to draw up a specification. This must outline the complete range of activities which you will require, together with the 'profile' of the ideal organization, eg location, size, other clients, method of charging, etc. The choosing process can then be examined in three stages—coarse screening, fine screening, and the pitch.

The coarse screening stage starts with the identification of, say, a dozen agencies which would appear to be candidates for further scrutiny. Obvious sources of names are one's existing file of likely agencies that have sent in details over the past few years. To this can be added any that one has heard about in a favourable light, and any which may be recommended by colleagues and acquaintances. The really serious work, however, must be done with a directory, which might be the *Advertiser's Annual* or, alternatively, the quarterly (small) edition of *BRAD* (British Rate and Data). In both these publications there is a comprehensive list of advertising agencies together with their clients. It is relatively easy to identify those which are likely to have ongoing knowledge of at least the relevant markets, if not products, providing they are not competitive. Alternatively, there are one or two companies who specialise in agency selection, such as The Advertising Agencies Register. Another important source of information is the IPA

(Institute of Practitioners in Advertising). For existing advertisers, of course, it is worthwhile consulting advertisement sales representatives, many of whom have an intimate knowledge of agencies with expertise precisely in the areas in which one has an interest. Thus, one compiles a coarse screen list of candidate agencies. Write a personal letter to the managing director, together with the specification, asking if there would be any interest in taking on a new account. At this stage it is best to keep a distance away from a dozen or so candidates and get them to outline their suitability by post. This avoids lengthy meetings and, from experience, it is usually found to be easy to make a rough choice from the information which will be supplied. The objective here is to arrive at three or four agencies which, on the face of it, might be able to handle your account.

With the short-listed agencies the fine screening is reached. The first step is to visit each and receive a 'credentials' presentation. This is where the agency will put up its very best work for inspection. For some this will be the most important part of the selection process, since this is work actually completed together with some indication of the results achieved. There is no reason why the clients themselves should not be contacted in order to get their opinions on the campaigns which have been presented, not to mention for some comment on the agency in question. The next step will be for the agency to visit you and to meet all the various people they would have to do business with, should they be appointed.

For the agencies which survive the fine screening stage comes the pitch. Here a detailed brief is given on some real marketing communications problem, or even the entire company programme for the next year. Each agency is given a fixed amount of time to come up with their proposals—the overall plan, media, budget, and, very often, first creative thoughts. In some cases, a nominal charge will be made. On the basis of such a series of competitive presentations, probably to a number of senior company managers, the final choice will be made. For industrial advertisers, some thought must be given to the validity of the final selection process. Can a candidate agency really gain an adequate knowledge about a client company in the few weeks allowed to it to make a presentation which will do justice to the problem? Or will it lead to the very weakness that many agencies are accused of, namely, of being superficial and lacking in technical knowledge? It is for this reason that the credentials presentation is so important.

The choice of a PR consultancy follows exactly the same path, but with a few inor differences. At the coarse screening stage, the directories to use are the *Hollis Directory* and the *PRCA Year Book*. Advice on matching a consultancy to a client specification can be obtained from the PRCA (Public Relations Consultants' Association), and from the IPR (Institute of Public Relations).

The agency audit

This talks about an agency audit, but it is every bit as relevant to a PR consultancy. In order to measure, or audit, performance it is necessary to draw up a list of criteria against which performance is to be measured. The following is an example:

1. Creativity/Design
2. Copywriting
3. Campaign planning
4. Remuneration and costing
5. Market/Product knowledge
6. Media planning
7. Media buying
8. Research and evaluation
9. Pro-active/reactive
10. Maintaining dates
11. Personal relationships

A meeting is then convened, and the agenda will be to go through each item giving what amounts to a largely subjective assessment of performance over, say, the past year. The agency, of course, has the opportunity to give comments and explanations, but it will end up with a good knowledge of how the client views its services. It now sets about making whatever changes are necessary. The point is that it is far better to get the agency to come into line with client requirements, rather than dismiss it and have to go through the lengthy, and uncertain, process of finding a replacement. Come the second year, or the second audit, this should be no more than fine-tuning. But if any of the previous shortcomings have not been rectified, then obviously there is going to have to be some serious discussions. If an agency is really on the ball, its reaction to an agency audit will be to ask for a client audit. And maybe that would be a useful action.

Finally, an agency audit should not be regarded as entirely negative. It is as much an opportunity for praise as it is for criticism. In practice, it turns out to be a bit of both. Its merit is that it is quick, effective, and costs nothing.

ABC   Audit Bureau of Circulation.

Account executive   An executive in an advertising agency, or other such organization, responsible for the overall managing of a client's requirements. Sometimes known as account supervisor, account manager or account director.

Advertising   The use of paid-for space in a publication, or time on television, radio or cinema, usually as a means of persuading people to take a particular course of action, or to reach a point of view.

Advertising schedule   Schedule of advertisement insertions showing details of costs, timing, and nature of the media and the bookings in them.

Artwork   The pictorial or illustrative part of an advertisement, or publication, in its finished form ready for production, e.g. a retouched and masked photograph.

Attention value   The extent to which an advertisement can secure the initial attention of a reader.

Attitude research   An investigation, often by personal interview or group discussion, of the attitude of people towards an organization or its products.

Base line   The wording or typesetting at the bottom of an advertisement, including the company's name and address often in a standard form or house style.

Below-the-line   A term frequently used to define non-commission-paying promotional media.

Bleed   An advertisement or printed page which utilizes the entire page area, i.e. extends into the margin.

Block   A plate of metal (or rubber or plastic), engraved, moulded or cast for printing.

Blow-up   A very considerable enlargement, say, of a photograph or illustration.

Brand name   A distinctive name by which a product or group of products is identified.

Brief   Summary of facts, objectives and instructions relating to the creation of a campaign, an advertisement, or any other element of a marketing mix.

Brochure   A stitched booklet, usually having eight or more pages, often with a prestige connotation.

Caption   Short description relating to an illustration or diagram.

Catalogue   Publication containing descriptions or details of a number or range of products.

CC   Controlled circulation.

Circulation   The total number of copies distributed of a periodical or publication.

Clippings   See 'Press cuttings'.

Column centimetres   Measurement of area derived from the width of a column of type, in a publication, multiplied by its depth.

Controlled circulation   In which the method of circulation is controlled by some specific criterion relating to the status of the reader, and for which no charge is made.

Copy   Text or written matter for reproduction.

Copy date   Date by which advertising or editorial material should reach a publisher for inclusion in a particular issue. (See also 'press date'.)

Copy platform   The main copy theme of an advertisement.

Creative   Relating to copy and/or visual content of an advertisement or similar promotional material, or to a department in an advertising agency in which copywriting and design are carried out.

Cut-out half tone   Printing block or area of a plate in which the background to an illustration has been cut out or eliminated.

Data sheet   Leaflet containing factual information and data about a product and its performance.

Decision-making unit   Group of people who together contribute to a decision on whether or not, and what, to purchase (DMU).

Distribution The means by which goods are moved from the place of manufacture to the point of purchase.

Double-page spread Two facing pages in a publication, combined into one integral advertisement; strictly speaking should incorporate the gutter.

DPS Double-page spread.

DRM Direct-response marketing—selling by means of press advertising or direct mail which invites a direct placement of orders without further negotiations or intermediate channels of distribution, e.g. retail outlet.

Dummy A made-up or faked version of a proposed publication.

Electro A duplicate of an original block: produced by electro-chemical deposition of metal on to a matrix.

Embargo In relation to press release, a time or date before which a particular items of news must not be published.

Facia In exhibitions, the headboard above a stand, usually giving the identity of the exhibitor.

Facing matter An advertisement which appears opposite editorial matter in a publication (abbreviation FM). In newspapers, a more common term is 'among matter'.

Final (proof) A print taken from the plate or forme of an advertisement as it finally appears.

Fine grain Descriptive of a photographic emulsion or the developer used to process it: results in a negative which can be enlarged to a high degree without showing excessive grain.

Forme Frame in which type matter and blocks are assembled for letterpress work.

Four-colour set Set of plates, one for each of the four colours (red, yellow, blue, black) used to produce a 'full' colour print. Term sometimes refers to set of colour proofs.

Full plate Photographic print 8 in × 6 in, sometimes known as 'whole plate': similarly 'half plate' is 6 in × 4 in.

Galleys Rough proofs of typesetting taken prior to the make-up of pages.

Give-away A cheap promotional piece, often a leaflet, which can be handed out to all and sundry. Sometimes known as a 'throw-away'.

Gutter The margin of a page adjacent to the fold in a publication, the vertical centre of a double-page spread.

Half plate   Photographic print or negative, 6 in × 4 in.

Half tone   Describes a printing block or plate of a tonal illustration, the reproduction of which is facilitated by breaking up the continuous tones to leave a series of dots which pick up the ink.

Handout   A cheap leaflet for handing out at an exhibition, for example.

House magazine   A periodical published by a company. Usually in one of two forms, external for customer readership, or internal for employees.

House style   A characteristic and standardized graphic form which is applied throughout a company to such items as letterheadings, publications, advertisements, vehicles and even packaging and product design.

Image   The mental impression which a person has of an organization or its products.

Impact   The force with which a selling message registers in a person's mind.

Insert   A piece of sales promotional material placed into the pages of a publication. Can be either loose or bound in.

Keyed advertisement   An advertisement designed to cause an enquirer to indicate the source of his enquiry by quoting a code number, or a particular 'department'.

Layout   Accurate position guide of an advertisement or piece of literature.

Leaflet   Printed sheet of paper: maybe folded to make into four pages, or stitched with another sheet to make into eight. Term usually applies to publication with fewer than twelve pages. See also brochure.

Letterpress   Form of commercial printing in declining use. Consists of raised printing surfaces upon which ink is deposited, and subsequently transferred to paper.

Line block   Printing block for reproducing line illustrations (letterpress). Face of metal is solid without any half tone or screen.

Litho   Short for lithography, a form of printing from a flat as opposed to a raised surface. Ink impression is obtained by chemical treatment of surface such that certain areas retain ink while others reject it.

Local press   Local newspapers, usually covering a borough or rural district. Published once or twice a week. See also provincial press.

Logotype   Commonly used to describe a company symbol, badge or name style.

Mailing list   Classified list of names and addresses suitable for sending mailing shots.

Mailing piece Letter, leaflet or other article sent through the post on a widespread basis.

Mailing shot A single mailing operation. Two mailings to the same list would be referred to as a two-shot campaign.

Manual Printed document of any number of pages, usually containing specific instructions, e.g. sales manual, operating or servicing manual.

Market A collective term embracing all the people or points of purchase for a particular product both actual and potential.

Market penetration The extent to which market potential has been realized. Market share.

Market research Investigation into the characteristics of a given market, e.g. location, size, growth, attitudes. See also marketing research.

Market segmentation The breakdown of a market into discrete and identifiable segments, e.g. types of company, industries, geographical location; also types of product requirements.

Marketing The complete series of operations which ensure a compatibility between customer demand and product performance, and which results in customer satisfaction coupled with an adequate level of profit. The operations which may be encompassed by the term marketing include product development, marketing research, advertising, promotion, sales and service.

Marketing mix A planned mixture of all the elements of marketing in such a way as to achieve the greatest effect at minimum cost.

Marketing research Any research activity that provides information relating to the marketing operation. While embracing market research, it also includes media research, motivation studies, advertisement attention value, packaging effectiveness.

Marketing services All those activities which are required to service a marketing operation, other than those which are concerned directly with the sales force and the sales office.

Marketing strategy A written plan, usually comprehensive, of all the activities involved in achieving a particular marketing objective, and their relationship to one another in both time and magnitude. Will include short- and long-term sales, production and profit targets, pricing policy, selling strategy, staffing requirements, as well as the whole marketing mix and expense budgets.

Matrix Paper or plastic mould from which duplicate printing blocks are produced. See 'Electro' and 'Stereo'.

Mechanicals/mechanical production   The processes required to achieve the desired reproduction of an advertising message.

Media commission   Commission allowed by publishers, poster, radio and television companies to recognized advertising agencies in consideration of the space or time they book on behalf of their clients.

Media Data Form   An established format for presenting audited data regarding a publication so as to facilitate comparison.

Medium   A channel of communication, e.g. a magazine, a television station, an exhibition, direct mail. Plural media, often used to refer specifically to periodicals.

Merchandising   The techniques for promoting sales at the point of sale.

Motivation research   Investigation of motives behind purchasing decisions. Often linked with the technique of small group discussions.

National press   Newspapers, daily or Sunday, having a mass circulation throughout the country.

News release   See 'Press release'.

Offset litho   See 'Litho'. Offsetting is merely part of the process by which the image on the plate is transferred to a rubber sheet which then prints onto the paper, thus avoiding a mirror or reverse reproduction.

Opinion formers   Groups or categories of people who because of their status or position are considered to exert more than usual influence on the views of others.

Overlay   Transparent or translucent sheet of paper laid over one piece of artwork carrying further artwork which is to be reproduced in a different colour; or for protection or to facilitate instruction on how it should be used or modified for production.

Page proofs   Proofs of a leaflet, brochure, booklet, magazine or similar publication taken at the stage when pages have been made up.

Page traffic   Number of readers of a particular page in a periodical, expressed as a percentage of the total readership.

Paper setting   The setting of an advertisement by the printer of a periodical, usually free of charge. See 'Trade setting'.

Pass for press   Final approval of a publication before printing.

Persuasive communications   Any form of communication which is intended to persuade, e.g. advertising, editorial publicity, speeches, films.

Plate   Printing block or litho plate.

Point of sale (point of purchase)   The place at which a sale is made, also refers to publicity material used there, e.g. posters, showcards, display units, leaflets (POS and POP).

PR   'Public relations' or 'Press relations', see below.

PRO   Public relations officer—an executive responsible for planning and implementing the public relations policy of an organization.

Presentation   A meeting in which proposals are put to an audience in a planned and usually formal manner.

Press   All periodicals whether national, local, trade or technical.

Press cuttings   Excerpts on a particular subject cut out from any kind of periodical. Used as a monitoring device to indicate the extent to which a subject is receiving publicity.

Press date   The date on which a publication or a section of a publication is due to be passed for press.

Press reception   A meeting to which press representatives—editors, journalists, reporters—are invited in order to be informed of an event, and to have the opportunity of questioning or commenting.

Press relations   That part of public relations activity aimed at establishing and maintaining a favourable relationship both with and via the press. Also referred to as media relations.

Press release   Written statement describing an event which is considered to be of sufficient interest to readers for an editor to publish some reference to it. Sometimes referred to as a news release.

Press visit   Visit by members of the press to a place of interest to them usually coupled with a special event such as an official opening of a factory.

Production   Putting into film form illustrations or words with a view to printing, e.g. plate making, filmsetting. Also the management of all mechanical processes required to achieve the reproduction of an advertising message.

Proof   Preliminary printing by any process to facilitate checking and approval prior to final printing.

Provincial press   Newspapers, usually daily, circulating in a restricted geographical region, e.g. a city or county.

Public relations   The conscious effort to improve an organization's communications, relationships and reputation with such publics as employees, customers and shareholders.

Public relations consultant   An individual or consultancy employed by an organization to advise and/or act on its behalf in the field of public relations.

Publicity   The process of securing people's attention and imparting a message. See also 'Advertising', 'Public relations' and 'Sales promotion'— all of which fall to some extent within this term.

Quantify   To express in measurable terms relating to quantity.

Rate card   Document issued by publishers or advertising contractors showing the charges made for various types and sizes of advertisement.

Readership   The number of people who read a publication as opposed to the number of people who receive it, or the number of copies printed or distributed.

Repros   Good quality proofs of typesetting usually for use in making up artwork, or in enlarging for display purposes. Also known as repro-pulls.

Rough   An illustration or design in rough form.

Run of paper   The positioning of an advertisement in any part of a periodical, as against a specified or premium position (ROP).

Sales forecast   A projection of likely sales, given certain defined criteria and making certain defined assumptions. Often based upon historical data. Not the same as sales target.

Sales promotion   Any non face-to-face activity concerned with the promotion of sales, but often taken to refer to 'below the line' activities.

Sales target   A set sales objective—a positive statement of intent, as against a sales forecast which arises out of a passive acceptance of anticipated criteria.

Same size   Relating to a piece of artwork which is the same size as the reproduction for which it is to be used (SS).

Sample   In research that specified subdivision of the universe (see below) deemed to be adequately representative of the whole and therefore to be interviewed or questioned.

Scamp   See 'Rough'.

Service fee   Charge made, usually on a predetermined annual basis, by an advertising or public relations agency for the service it is required to provide.

Shell scheme Standard design of booth provided by the organizer at an exhibition.

Sign-off Slogan at the end of an advertisement or piece of sales promotional material.

Silk screening Method of printing by which ink is forced through a fine silk mesh on which have been superimposed opaque areas representing the reverse of the design and through which ink will not pass.

Single column centimetre Standard measurement in newspapers and magazines based upon the depth of type matter contained in a single column (SCC).

Split run In which a publication is printed and distributed in two parts, facilitating the comparison of two advertisements.

Squared-up half tone Half-tone plate in which printing area is in the form of a rectangle. See 'Cut-out half tone'.

Standard industrial classification Comprehensive listing of industries and services, published by Her Majesty's Stationery Office (SIC).

Stereo Duplicate printing plate cast in metal from a paper or flong matrix.

Sticker Label, poster, or other printed sheet intended for sticking on window, letter, envelope or other medium for display purposes.

Stuffer Piece of publicity matter intended for general distribution with other material such as outgoing mail or goods, e.g 'envelope stuffer'.

Symbol Distinctive sign or graphic design denoting a company or a product. Often a pictorial representation of a company or product name. See 'Logotype'.

Task method A means of establishing a campaign and a budget by relating it to the objective to be achieved rather than for instance the amount of money arbitrarily available to be spent.

Technical press Periodicals dealing with technical subjects. Usually grouped together as 'trade and technical', or business—referring in effect to all non-consumer publications.

Test-marketing A method of testing out a marketing plan on a limited scale, but simulating as nearly as possible all the factors involved in the full campaign: usually carried out in a restricted but representative geographical location.

Trade press Strictly, referring to periodicals dealing with particular trades. See also technical press.

Trade setting Typesetting by a trade house directly for a client or agency, as against setting facilities by a publisher. See also 'Paper setting'.

Traffic Relating to the operation in an advertising agency of scheduling and controlling all stages in the preparation of a project. Relates commonly to production.

Two-colour The number of colours used in an advertisement or publication. Usually black plus one other.

Type area The space which is available on a page in a publication for printing.

Unique selling proposition A customer satisfaction or a product benefit which is unique as a selling argument (USP).

Universe In research, the total market—or other unit to be investigated.

Visual Artist's impression of an advertisement or other piece of publicity material. See also 'Layout'.

Voucher Free copy of periodical sent to advertiser or organization as evidence of an advertisement having been published.

Web offset A method of offset-litho printing in which the paper is fed into the press from the reel as opposed to sheets.

READING LIST

Marketing

Crouch, S., *Marketing Research* (Heinemann, London 1985).

Davidson, J. Hugh, *Offensive Marketing* (Gower Publishing Company, Aldershot, 1987).

Delozier, M. Wayne, *The Marketing Communications Process* (McGraw-Hill, Maidenhead, 1976).

Hart, N. A., *Effective Industrial Marketing* (Mercury Books, London, 1993).

Hart, N. A. and Stapleton, J., *The Marketing Dictionary* (Butterworth-Heinemann, Oxford, 1992).

Kotler, T., *Marketing Management* (Prentice-Hall, Hemel Hempstead, 1991).

Advertising

Broadbent, S., *Spending Advertising Money* (Business Books, London, 1984).

Broadbent, S., *Twenty Advertising Case Histories* (Holt, Rinehart & Winston, Eastbourne, 1984).

Director's Guide, *Choosing and Using an Advertising Agency* (Director Publications Ltd, London, 1985).

Public Relations

Bernstein, D., *Company Image and Reality* (Holt, Rinehart & Winston, Eastbourne, 1984).

Hart, N. A., *Effective Corporate Relations* (McGraw-Hill, Maidenhead, 1987).

Haywood, R., *All about PR* (McGraw-Hill, Maidenhead, 1990).

Howard, W., *The Practice of Public Relations* (IM/Heinemann, London, 1985).

Research into industrial advertisers and their advertising agencies

As part of the work necessary to producing an update of this book, a research was conducted into advertising and related practice from both the points of view of advertisers and agencies. The results, which are given in the following pages are compared with those of the previous research in 1977 (shown in brackets). This is the third such research, the first one having been carried out in 1970.

METHOD

A questionnaire together with a covering letter and reply-paid envelope was sent to 500 industrial and business-to-business companies with advertising spends of the order of £500,000 and above. A similar number was sent to advertising agencies with industrial clients. The letter to clients was sent by Kogan Page, the publishers, and the one to agencies by the Association of Business Advertising Agencies.

A 20 per cent response was obtained to the client letter, and 8.2 per cent from the agencies. In the latter case, however, the submissions provided evidence in relation to 563 clients.

Acknowledgement is given to Primary Contact Limited and to the Association of Business Advertising Agencies for their help and assistance in carrying out this survey. Also to Kogan Page Limited for the administering back-up.

SUMMARY

1. 20 per cent of industrial advertisers no longer use an advertising agency compared with 9 per cent fifteen years ago.
2. Clients are increasingly favouring paying agencies on a fee basis rather than media commission.
3. Agencies are not seen to be providing such good services in direct mail and PR as in press advertising.

4. Client companies are changing their advertising agencies much more frequently than in the past, eg over three quarters of the respondents had changed their agency once or more over the past five years.
5. A new and burning issue with advertisers these days is to get value for money from their advertising agencies.
6. Client companies are spending more of their budgets on direct mail (up 56%) and public relations (up 40%) and less on press advertising (down 18%).
7. Over two thirds of advertisers now arrive at their budgets by relating them to the 'task' to be achieved.
8. A new job title has emerged to replace advertising manager (down from 53% to 24%). This is marketing services manager, or marketing communications manager. Meanwhile, sales directors have almost totally disappeared.
9. 83 per cent of agencies claim to offer media relations or PR, compared with 56 per cent in 1977.
10. The account executive gets involved in the majority of media planning decisions (67%) whereas the client is said not to be involved.
11. Most ads have to be seen by a director of a client company (73%) before they are allowed to appear.
12. Few clients appear to give completely adequate briefing to their agencies (31%) but their overall knowledge of marketing has improved (59%).

Results of advertiser survey

1a. Do you use an advertising agency?
     YES 80% (91%)
     NO 20% (9%)

Comment: This is a major change, and one large enough to be statistically significant. No doubt due in part to client companies becoming aware that they can obtain media commission just as well as can agencies.

1b. If yes, is your agency:

industrial (or business) only?	24% (13%)
mainly industrial (or business)?	26% (38%)
about half industrial (or business)?	28% (34%)
mainly consumer?	22% (15%)
an incorporated member of the Institute of Practitioners in Advertising?	38% (69%)

Comment: Three quarters of British advertisers use an agency with some kind of industrial bias. There is a surprisingly low score for the IPA. This might be simply that the client companies are unaware of their agencies' affiliations.

1c. Aproximately how many personnel has your agency? Would it be nearer to:

     10—20% (20%)
     20—24% (23%)
     30—28% (28%)
     60—12% (21%)
     100 or over—16% (8%)

Comment: Overall there has been remarkable little change since the last survey. Three quarters of industrial clients are using advertising agencies employing fewer than thirty staff. This compares with the original research in 1970 when the ratio was 50:50.

1d. Does your agency have overseas connections?
     YES 71% (53%)
     NO 29% (47%)

Comment: Clearly agencies have been gearing up for overseas requirements of clients. Even so it is interesting to note how many clients have overseas campaigns but do not use the overseas connections of their agencies.

1e. Does it handle your export advertising?
     YES 51% (45%)
     NO 49% (55%)

2. If you are not in the London area, do you prefer using:
     a London advertising agency—25% (30%)
     a local advertising agency—75% (70%)

Comment: A fairly substantial vote in favour of local agencies, particularly when compared with the first report in 1970 which gave a 50:50 balance.

3a. Do you pay your advertising agency a service fee?
     YES 45% (58%)
     NO 55% (42%)

3b. If so, is this a:
     flat sum fixed annually—75% (34%)
     fixed percentage on annual expenditure on space—25% (66%)

Comment: Fewer clients pay a service fee (or don't realise that they do) but there is a growing tendency to pay this as a fixed fee rather than a percentage.

4. Do you favour remunerating an advertising agency by:
     a flat annual fee—41% (21%)
     commission or commission plus related fee—59% (79%)

Comment: Whilst over half the clients still favour the commission system there is a very clear movement away from it. The number of clients preferring to pay a flat annual fee has more than doubled since the last survey.

5. Are you satisfied with the calibre of your agency personnel?

      YES 95% (92%)

      NO 5% (8%)

This must come close to a universal satisfaction. It is a marginal improvement on the previous survey which in turn was a higher figure than the original one.

6. Is your account executive a director or associate director of your agency?

      YES 83% (80%)

      NO 17% (20%)

Comment: A slight increase but of no statistical significance.

7. Does the agency's creative team have direct contact with you as much as you would like?

      YES 83% (86%)

      NO 17% (14%)

Comment: There is obviously still a feeling amongst a minority of clients that they should have a greater opportunity for contact with the creative people. But no significant change since the last research.

8. Would you indicate your assessment of your agency's service in relation to the following activities, scoring 5 if completely satisfied and 0 if the service is unsatisfactory or non-existent.

NB The following scores represent the arithmetic average of the responses, and are listed in descending order of preference.

Television	4.00
Press advertising	3.92 (4.20)
Media buying	3.90
Photography	3.87 (3.90)
Public exhibition stands	3.75 (3.80)
Sales literature	3.72 (4.00)
Media planning	3.70 (3.80)
Market research	3.70 (3.30)
Data sheets	3.50 (3.50)
Promotional planning	3.50 (3.50)
Media relations	3.44 (3.60)
Direct mail	3.26 (3.60)

Comment: A number of other services were included in the questionnaire but have been omitted from the summary due to the relatively small numbers of responses.

There is no general conclusion to be drawn on changes since the previous research. There is, however, a clear indication that the greater majority of the services provided are rated by the clients as satisfactory or even better. At the bottom of the list is media relations and direct mail, both having dropped from last time. Two factors are thought to have contributed to this state of affairs. One is the increasing use of the two functions, and their sophistication leading to higher expectations. The other is the greatly increased number of specialised agencies providing the two services and offering maybe a higher standard of performance.

9. Approximately how many changes of agency have you had in the last 5/10 years?

	5 years	10 years
No change	22% (47%)	5% (24%)
One change	49% (38%)	38% (50%)
Two changes	22% (6%)	32% (11%)
Three or more	8% (9%)	24% (15%)

Comment: Three quarters of the respondents had changed their agency at least once in five years compared with only half in the previous survey. And in ten years 95 per cent registered one or more changes compared with 75 per cent. This represents a major change in the frequency with which agencies are fired. Looking in further detail at the figures, nearly a third of the respondents changed two or more times in five years (compared with the earlier figure of 15 per cent) and over ten years well over half had made that number of changes (compared with a quarter).

10. Have you ever dismissed an agency? If so can you say why?
>   Most people had dismissed an agency some time in their professional career, and there were three outstanding reasons. In order of importance these were:
>   Poor account handling and service
>   Poor value for money
>   Low quality work

Comment: These were the same reasons as given in the previous research.

11a. What factors would be most likely to influence your choice if selecting another agency?
>   Four factors were way ahead of any others. In order of importance:
>   Creativity
>   Personal chemistry/service/professionalism
>   Knowledge of markets
>   Value for money

Comment: Value for money has appeared for the first time in any of these studies.

12. Approximately what is your expenditure on all forms of marketing communication (excluding staff overheads)?
>   The question was broken down into five expenditure groups ranging from 0 to £500 000 and above. 65 per cent of respondents were spending in excess of £500 000.

13. Approximately what percentage of your appropriation is allocated to the various media?

Press advertising	33% (40)
Direct mail	14% (9)
Sales literature	28% (27)
Exhibitions	13% (15)
Public relations	13% (9)

Comment: Whilst sales literature and exhibitions remain about the same as the previous study, some major changes have occurred with the other media. The biggest change is in the use of direct mail which has increased by 56 per cent. This is closely followed by public relations, up by 40 per cent. Press advertising has declined from occupying 40 per cent of the budget to 33 per cent, a drop of 18 per cent.

14. Is your marketing communications budget arrived at as a percentage of sales turnover, a calculated cost related to objectives, or an arbitrary sum fixed on past practice?

% sales turnover	4% (17)
Cost related to objectives	68% (53)
Arbitrary sum	14% (30)
Other	14% (NA)

Comment: The 'other' category was included this time since a number of respondents used a mixture of methods to arrive at their budget. Apart from that however, there has been a massive change away from 'arbitrary sum' to what is now known as the 'task method' of budgeting. This is an obvious pointer to the increasing professionalism of managers responsible for compiling budgets.

15. Your position within the company?

Marketing manager (or director)	29% (12)
Marketing services manager or marketing communications manager	28% (NA)
Advertising manager	24% (53)
Other (including MD)	19% (16)

Comment: Since the last survey two new titles have emerged, namely marketing services manager and marketing communications (marcom) manager. The title 'sales promotion manager' has disappeared. The use of 'advertising manager' has halved, and only one of the respondents had the previously popular title of publicity manager.

16. To whom at board level does the marketing communications function report?

Managing Director	46% (33)
Marketing Director	36% (35)
Sales Director	4% (23)
Other	14% (9)

Comment: The most interesting item in the responses to this question is the almost total demise of the sales director as someone with a controlling interest in marketing communications. The increasing involvement of the chief executive is another interesting feature.

From answers to other questions it is clear that the title of sales director in itself has almost disappeared, though there are still a few examples of 'sales and marketing director' for people who have yet to accept that sales is a subset of marketing.

Results of agency survey

1. On which of the following activities do you provide a comprehensive service?

Sales literature	100%	(93%)
Press advertising	96%	(100%)
Media evaluation and selection	96%	(98%)
Media buying	96%	(N/A)
Technical data sheets	91%	(60%)
Direct mail	87%	(85%)
Promotional planning	83%	(90%)
Media relations	83%	(56%)
House journals	83%	(48%)
Market research	74%	(N/A)
Photography	70%	(76%)
Public exhibition stands	65%	(76%)
Private exhibitions	57%	(75%)
Video production	57%	(N/A)
Sales promotion	57%	(N/A)
Sales conferences, symposia	48%	(55%)
Television	30%	(N/A)

Comment: A very comprehensive range of services is still being offered, and the results of the research are much the same as in the last investigation. Video production and television have appeared for the first time, and three services have increased substantially—media relations, house journals and technical data sheets.

2. In the scheduling of trade, technical and business media, who is mainly responsible?

The agency	82% (67%)
The client	4% (0%)
About equal	14% (33%)

Comment: Even more agencies than before take the view that they are the predominant force in media planning.

3. If mainly the agency, is the planning done by:

Media department	33% (39%)
Account executive	24% (9%)
A combination	43% (52%)

Comment: The account handler appears to be playing a larger role in deciding upon the media to be used.

4. What sources of reference do you use in planning media on a scale of 0–5 per cent?

	Average
Calls by representatives	3.0 (2.8)
Media data forms	3.7 (3.3)
British Rate and Data	3.4 (3.8)
Rate cards	2.6 (2.6)
Other	5.0 (N.A.)

Comment: The change here is that media data forms have a higher respect than previously, but that agencies are apparently relying upon their own investigations and experience rather than material supplied by the publishers.

5. In how many of the following is the Advertising (Marketing Services, etc) manager able to take a decision:

Reject an ad	52% (52%)
Accept an ad	43% (42%)
Reject a schedule	50% (49%)
Accept a schedule	48% (39%)
Reject a campaign	44% (37%)
Accept a campaign	32% (27%)

Comment: Whilst there is a strong similarity between some sets of figures, the authority of the advertising manager, or equivalent, has clearly increased. This might indicate that the function of advertising has increased in the eyes of top management.

6. In how many of these does an ad have to be approved by:

Client's MD	39% (25%)
Another director	34% (38%)

Comment: It might be concluded here that CEO's are taking a more personal interest in advertising but this conflicts with the previous assumption regarding the authority of the advertising manager. It may well be that the advertising manager is taking greater control of campaigns and schedules, but when it comes to the final appearance of the ad someone more senior wants to become involved.

7. From what number of clients do you receive a completely adequate briefing in relation to:

Campaigns	31% (51%)
Individual ads	41% (56%)

Comment: The respect of agencies for their clients seems to have declined even further.

8. How many clients would you say have a thorough understanding of the value of:

Industrial (business) advertising	52% (50%)
Marketing	59% (40%)

Comment: Notwithstanding Question 7, clients are perceived to have a significantly better understanding of marketing. The overall conclusion has to be that whilst clients are sound enough on broad marketing matters, they are less so when it comes to advertising, and even less so on the more detailed aspects of the advertising process.

9. How many clients pay a service fee?   46% (28%)
Comment: There is some doubt about the answers to this question since some clients pay a service fee in addition to the agency taking a commission. However the change is sufficiently large to be considered significant. Obviously a service fee of some kind is becoming more popular.

GW00597721

"The
guidebook
that pays
for itself —
in one day"

TEXT BY

CHRISTINA PROSTANO
CHARLES W. WALDRON

Publisher Information

NEW YORK FOR LESS

First published in Great Britain in 1997 by Metropolis International (UK) Limited, a member of the New York Convention & Visitors Bureau.

Discounts by Metropolis International (UK) Limited. Text by Christina Prostano and Charles W. Waldron. Principal photography by Debra Sweeney.

ISBN 0-9525437-8-8

COPYRIGHT

Copyright © Metropolis International (UK) Limited, 1997.

for less, for less logos and *for less guidebooks* are trademarks of Metropolis International (UK) Limited.

All rights reserved. No part of this book may be reproduced or utilized in any form or by any means, electronic or mechanical, including photocopying, recording or by any information storage retrieval system, without permission in writing from the publishers.

DISCLAIMER

Assessments of attractions, hotels, museums and so forth are based on the authors' impressions and therefore contain an element of subjective opinion which may not reflect the opinion of the publishers.

The contents of this publication are believed to be correct at the time of printing, however, details such as prices will change over time. We would advise you to call ahead to confirm important information.

Care has been taken in the preparation of this guidebook, however, the publisher cannot accept responsibility for errors or inaccuracies that may occur.

The publisher will not be held responsible for any loss, damage, injury, expense or inconvenience sustained by any person, howsoever caused, as a result of information or advice contained in this guide except insofar as the law prevents the exclusion of such liability.

PUBLISHER

Metropolis International (UK) Limited
222 Kensal Road
London W10 5BN
England

Telephone:
+44-(0)181-964-4242

Fax:
+44-(0)181-964-4141

E-mail:
metropolis@for–less.com

Web site:
http://www.for–less.com

FOR LESS TITLES

FORTHCOMING

Contents

for less guidebooks . . .

New York for less is part of a revolutionary new series of guidebooks. Unlike "budget guides", these high quality guidebooks are designed to enable <u>every</u> visitor, however much they anticipate spending, to explore and to save money at the <u>best</u> places.

For less guidebooks save you money by providing you with specially negotiated discounts at hundreds of top attractions, hotels, tours, restaurants, shops, theaters and other venues.

These unique discounts ensure that, unlike any other guidebook, for less guidebooks really do "pay for themselves - in one day".

Over 100,000 people from 30 different countries have already saved money with *for less* guidebooks. If you look through this book you will quickly understand why *for less guidebooks* are becoming the natural choice for the intelligent traveler.

Customer Satisfaction Card

We want your comments so that we can continue to improve this book. On page 287 you will find a customer satisfaction card that you can mail back to us (at no postal cost) from anywhere in the world.

. . . *for less* guidebooks

For less guidebooks have been designed to make visiting a city as easy and pleasant as possible.

The simple, attractive, area-by-area format ensures that you can focus on enjoying the city and do not waste time puzzling your way through a complicated guidebook.

The substantial discounts are easy to obtain and can cut the total cost of a stay for an individual, a couple or a family by over 20%.

For example, each of the restaurants offers 25% off the total bill (including <u>all</u> food and beverage costs) at <u>any</u> time.

Uniquely, each *for less* guidebook comes with a fold-out city map, divided by neighborhood. This large map links to hundreds of mini-maps in the guidebook, enabling you to find exact locations quickly and easily.

How to Use *New York for less*

New York for less has been created to enable visitors to save money by obtaining discounts at the best places in New York City. All discounts are applicable for up to four people for up to eight consecutive days. Each page is color coded as follows:

Attractions and Museums	Tours
Hotels	Restaurants
Shops	Nightlife and Performing Arts

Before you use the card, you must complete it by following the instructions on the inside front cover. The card should always be presented when you request the bill (check) and before payment is made.

Discounts apply whatever method of payment you choose, however, *New York for less* cannot be used in conjunction with other offers or discounts.

Throughout this book, you will find the *New York for less* logo. Every time it appears, it indicates that you are entitled to a discount.

Use of the card or vouchers must conform to the instructions on pages 7 and 8 and to the specific instructions set out in each entry.

All organizations offering discounts in this guidebook have a contract with the publisher to give genuine discounts to holders of valid *New York for less* cards and/or vouchers.

CREDIT CARD SYMBOLS USED

AM = AMEX
VS = VISA
MC = MASTERCARD
DC = DINERS CLUB
DS = DISCOVER

Care has been taken to ensure that discounts are only offered at reputable establishments, however, the publisher and/or its agents cannot accept responsibility for the quality of merchandise or service provided, nor for errors or inaccuracies in this guidebook.

The publisher and/or its agents will not be responsible if any establishment breaches its contract (although it will attempt to secure compliance) or if any establishment changes ownership and the new owners refuse to honor the contract.

For post-publication updates and amendments to the discounts offered you should call (212) 465-7369. For any other information please call Metropolis International at (212) 587-0287.

How to Obtain Discounts...

ATTRACTIONS AND MUSEUMS

To obtain discounts at attractions or museums you have to either show your card or hand in a voucher which you will find at the back of the book. When you hand in the voucher you should circle the number of people in your party and also show your card.

At most attractions, discounts are available off the adult, child, senior and student prices. Children are usually defined as under 12, seniors as over 65.

An index of attractions, museums and galleries that offer *New York for less* discounts is on page 260.

Empire State Building

HOTELS

For details of how to book hotels see page 32.

TOURS AND TRANSPORTATION

New York for less offers you discounts on transfers into Manhattan from J.F.K. and LaGuardia Airports (see page 18).

New York for less also offers large savings on car rental (page 241), bus tours (page 219), helicopter tours (page 222), walking tours (pages 223-224) and cruises (pages 218-221).

Cruise on the Hudson

To obtain the discounts, you must book as instructed in each tour's entry. You cannot book through a travel agent, hotel concierge or other intermediary.

RESTAURANTS

New York for less entitles you to a flat 25% off the total bill (check), including food and beverages, at 90 restaurants in Manhattan listed on pages 264-265.

The price indicated is not a fixed or minimum price. It is only a guide to the average cost of a meal. It is based on a typical two-course meal for one person without an alcoholic drink. You are entitled to the discount however much you spend.

Dining on Union Square

So that the service is not reduced by the discount, it is recommended that you tip on the total amount of the bill, before the discount is applied. A standard tip in New York City is 15-20% of the bill.

SHOPS

New York for less offers a 20% discount at 70 Manhattan shops, listed on pages 262-263. To obtain the discount, simply show the card before you pay for the goods. Discounts on goods already reduced in price or on sale are at the discretion of the shop's management.

Soho shopping

Lincoln Center

Broadway theaters

Travelex

DIALING IN THE U.S.

Unless otherwise noted, all phone numbers listed in this book are within the (212) Manhattan area code. When a phone number is listed with an area code, such as (800) it should be prefaced by the number 1. See page 258 for more dialing information.

. . . How to Obtain Discounts

NIGHTLIFE AND PERFORMING ARTS

New York for less offers you discounts on tickets for Broadway theater productions (see page 215).

Unfortunately, we cannot guarantee that you will be able to obtain discounts at particular performances, as certain shows are frequently sold out.

FOREIGN CURRENCY EXCHANGE

With the voucher on page 283, you can change money commission-free at branches of Travelex / Mutual of Omaha listed on page 255.

Their rates are competitive and you will save 100% on the transaction charge.

TELEPHONE CALLING CARD

Your *New York for less* card is also a calling card. Best of all, you receive $8 worth of free calls when you activate it. You can use it for all international or domestic calls. Calls are billed to your credit card and there are no connection charges.

It is easy to activate: simply dial toll-free (freephone) 1-800-642-7410 and wait approximately 20 seconds for an operator (ignore the instruction to enter your card number and PIN).

Give the operator the last 8 digits of your *New York for less* card (which will form your calling card number) and details of your American Express, MasterCard, Visa or Diners Club. You will then be given a secret Personal Identification Number (PIN) which should always be dialed after the 8 digit calling card number.

To make a call, follow the instructions on the back of the card. If you encounter difficulties, just stay on the line and an operator will assist you at no extra charge.

Some hotels even charge you for making toll-free calls. To avoid this, use your calling card at any public telephone.

You can continue to use your card to make phone calls anywhere in the world, forever. You will be amazed how much money you save.

For example, a five-minute call from New York to Britain will cost up to $20 from a hotel phone, $6.15 from a public telephone and just $4 with the *New York for less* card.

This calling card service is operated by Interglobe Telecommunications (International) PLC (☎ *44-(0)171-972-0800*).

Introduction

Introduction to New York

"The skyline of New York is a monument of a splendor that no pyramids or palaces will ever equal or approach." – Ayn Rand

Clustered together on the tiny island of **Manhattan**, like tall trees in a dense forest, New York's skyscrapers symbolize the energy, the dynamism and the unlimited possibilities that this great city seems to hold.

Aerial view of Manhattan

But it is on the streets below, in the shadows of the giant buildings and inside the busy offices, bustling shops and glamorous restaurants, that the vitality of the city and its people can be felt.

Perhaps no other city embodies the spirit of the 20th century as completely as New York. From the **Statue of Liberty**, to the **Empire State Building**, to the yellow taxi cabs, its images have been captured on film so often that, for many people across the globe, they now represent America and the American way of life.

And yet, it is only in the last 200 years that New York has transformed itself from a small town on the edge of an empty continent into a major metropolis.

REFLECTIONS

"New York is a different country. Maybe it ought to have a separate government. Everybody thinks differently, acts differently. They just don't know what the hell the rest of the United States is." – Henry Ford

Founded by the Dutch as a trading colony, it was the capital of the United States for the first year of the new republic's life. However, it was as a commercial center, a place where business comes first, that New York established its pre-eminence.

Statue of Liberty

With it gleaming corporate offices and **Wall Street** banks, its position as one of the world's foremost financial and business centers is secure. But New York today is about much more than business. The city is a mecca for fashion, art, theater and music that has few, if any, equals. It is also home to some of the world's largest and most diverse ethnic

Introduction to New York

communities. A giant melting pot that sometimes seems as though it might burst at the seams, New York

is perhaps the most diverse city in the world. Here the rich rub shoulders with the poor, and the cultural elite ride the subway with beggars.

Criticized for their brusque manner, New Yorkers have a reputation for being rude. People here undoubtedly have a tendency to speak bluntly and rarely waste time getting to the point. But

Hot dog vendor

although you may well see New York cabbies yelling at each other through their taxi windows, you will also find open-minded, friendly New Yorkers who will be happy to help as you travel about their city.

The diversity of the population contrasts with the remarkable symmetry of the streets. Thanks to the **Randel Plan**, devised in 1811, everything north of 14th Street fits into a uniform and easily comprehensible grid, with the avenues running north-south and streets running east-west.

To the visitor, New York may seem overwhelming. Yet, to New Yorkers, the city is divided into distinctive and definable neighborhoods each with their own history and style.

View of New York from the Empire State Building

The busy streets of **Midtown**, with their notorious traffic, contrast with the quiet residential areas of the **West Village**, while the status-conscious shops of the **Upper East Side** are a world apart from the bohemian chic of the **East Village** or the historic streets of **Lower Manhattan**.

New York is far from being a purely urban landscape. In addition to its many small parks, it has one park of unparalleled size and magnificence: **Central Park,** New York's green playground. On a Sunday afternoon in summer, a visitor could be forgiven for thinking that the whole city was rollerblading, cycling or jogging around it.

Introduction to New York

No matter how long you stay in New York, you will never exhaust the possibilities that await you. Indeed, more than 30 million visitors come here each year to experience its endless opportunities. You can view Manhattan's impressive skyline from the Empire State Building, tour the city in a double-decker bus, row a boat in

Winter in Central Park

Central Park, ice-skate at Rockefeller Center and still only scratch the surface of what this city has to offer.

In addition to world-class museums such as **The Met**, **Guggenheim**, **MoMA** and the **American Museum of Natural History**, New York has incredible restaurants, hotels, shopping and nightlife. Its **Broadway theaters**

New York Marathon

have been drawing crowds for nearly a century and its dance clubs prove that, when Frank Sinatra sang of "the city that never sleeps", he was telling the literal truth.

New York is in a constant state of flux. Barely a day goes by without a movie or theater premier, a new restaurant or shop being launched or an art exhibit opening. Whenever you come, there is likely to be something special happening. From the Macy's Thanksgiving Day Parade to the New York Marathon, the city's seasonal events will enrich your visit.

New Yorkers who have spent their whole lives here, still sometimes find themselves on a city block where they have never been before, or stumbling upon an unknown shop or restaurant that soon becomes a favorite. It is this marvelous variety, the sense that you can never get the measure of New York that makes it such a fascinating place to live or visit.

For most visitors, the 13 mile (22km) island of Manhattan (taken from the Algonquin Indian name 'Mannahatta') *is* New York. However, of the 7.3 million residents, over 80% live in the outer boroughs of Brooklyn, the Bronx, Queens and Staten Island.

Introduction to New York

While lacking the glamour of Manhattan, each of these
is filled with a wealth of colorful neighborhoods and
exciting attractions.

Brooklyn, which was originally a
separate city, is connected to
Manhattan by the spectacular Brooklyn
Bridge. The Brooklyn Promenade, a
short walk from the bridge, provides
magnificent views of Lower Manhattan
and New York Harbor. Brooklyn
Heights, with its brownstone homes,
tree-lined streets and excellent
restaurants, bars and shops is fun to
explore. Brooklyn is also home to a collection of
ethnic enclaves including the Russian community at
Brighton Beach.

Yankees' 1996 World Series victory parade

For years, the South **Bronx** has been a byword for
urban decay and inner-city blight. The North Bronx, in
contrast, has a number of interesting attractions,
including the New York Botanical Garden and the
Bronx Wildlife Conservation Center, the largest zoo in
America.

The Bronx even has its own Little Italy, arguably more
authentic than its Manhattan counterpart. However,
its outstanding attraction is
probably the New York
Yankees baseball team,
whose die-hard fans could
not have been more pleased
by their victory in the 1996
World Series.

Queens is brimming with
dynamic and diverse ethnic
communities. In the largely
Greek area of Astoria, the
American Museum of the
Moving Image is worth a visit.
Also stop by the Flushing
Meadows-Corona Park which
was the site of both the 1939 and 1964 World's Fairs.

Macy's parade

The other New York City island, **Staten Island**, is a
short and pleasurable ferry ride from Lower
Manhattan. For just 50 cents round-trip, the Staten
Island Ferry offers breathtaking views of Lower
Manhattan, the Statue of Liberty and New York
Harbor. Places of interest include the Staten Island
Zoo, Richmondtown Historic Restoration and the Alice
Austen House.

REFLECTIONS

"That enfabled rock, that
ship of life, that
swarming, million-footed,
tower-masted, sky-soaring
citadel that bears the
magic name of the Island
of Manhattan."
– Thomas Wolfe

New York: Area by Area . . .

LOWER MANHATTAN

New York's old city mixes historic sights dating back to the early 17th century, with the modern financial institutions of Wall Street. Some of New York's top attractions are also located in the area, including the World Trade Center, South Street Seaport and Battery Park, where you can catch the ferry to the Statue of Liberty and Ellis Island. The combination of history and great sites make this one of the best places to begin sightseeing in New York.

SOHO, CHINATOWN AND THE LOWER EAST SIDE

Soho and Tribeca are filled with trendy shops, chic restaurants and art galleries. Unique to the area, cast-iron buildings house dramatic loft spaces which have become some of Manhattan's most expensive pieces of real estate. Further east, Chinatown, Little Italy and the Lower East Side are ethnic enclaves known for their authentic eateries and markets.

GREENWICH VILLAGE

Buzzing with activity, "the Village" is divided into the West and East Village, both filled with popular shops, bars and restaurants. In the West Village, Christopher Street is the center of New York's gay community. The East Village is the nucleus of the city's bohemian life. Its main street, St. Mark's Place, is crowded with funky boutiques and inexpensive restaurants.

CHELSEA, GRAMERCY AND THE FLATIRON DISTRICT

West Chelsea has recently become a center for art, as many new galleries have opened in its warehouse-sized buildings. There is also a thriving dining and nightlife scene. The heart of the Flatiron District revolves around the sophisticated bars and restaurants along Park Avenue South. Don't miss a trip to the top of one of the world's most famous skyscrapers – the Empire State Building.

. . . New York: Area by Area

MIDTOWN WEST

Midtown West is best known for its Broadway theaters. Centered around this hub of activity are many of the city's major hotels. You will also find the majority of Manhattan's theme restaurants and top attractions like Times Square and Rockefeller Center. For museum-goers, the Museum of Modern Art (MoMA) is a must-see. Fifth Avenue, the dividing line between Midtown West and East, is a shopper's paradise.

MIDTOWN EAST

Cleaner and quieter than its western counterpart, Midtown East is home to some of America's biggest corporations, housed in the enormous skyscrapers that comprise a large portion of Manhattan's famous skyline. On Fifth Avenue, there are designer shops and department stores like Saks Fifth Avenue and Tiffany & Co., as well as St. Patrick's Cathedral.

UPPER WEST SIDE AND HARLEM

Lincoln Center, New York's foremost performing arts complex, and the American Museum of Natural History are the main attractions on the Upper West Side. Apartments along Central Park West are some of the grandest and most sought-after in the city. Further north, Harlem has a large African-American and Latin-American community. One of its star attractions is the illustrious Apollo Theater.

UPPER EAST SIDE

The Upper East Side is Manhattan's most exclusive residential area. Elegant townhouses and luxury apartment buildings fill the blocks near Central Park. On Fifth Avenue's Museum Mile, you can find some of the world's finest museums, including "The Met" and the Guggenheim. Nearby, The Whitney is located on chic Madison Avenue, home to many of Manhattan's most luxurious shops and designer boutiques.

Before You Go. . .

WHEN TO GO

New York's climate can vary dramatically, from extremely hot and humid summers, with temperatures reaching 95°F (35°C), to cold and snowy winters, with temperatures plummeting well below 32°F (0°C). Fall and spring are generally mild and perhaps the best time to visit. You will, however, find a multitude of activities and events throughout the year. See page 250 for a full calendar of seasonal events and activities.

Virgin Atlantic Airlines

VISAS AND ENTRY REQUIREMENTS

All visitors must have one, all or a combination of the following in order to enter the U.S.: a valid passport, a visitor's visa and a valid onward passage ticket (such as a return airplane ticket). Presently, passport holders from the UK Canada, New Zealand, Japan and all western European countries (with the exception of Ireland, Portugal, Greece and Vatican City) are not required to have a visa if staying for less than 90 days. All other travelers must have visas. For more information, contact your local U.S. embassy or consulate.

Upon entering the country, customs allowances are limited to 200 cigarettes (or 50 cigars or 4.4 pounds (two kilograms) of tobacco), two pints (one liter) of alcohol and gifts worth no more than $100 (after that you must pay tax). In addition, no plants, fruit, produce or meat are allowed through customs at all.

Broadway Theaters

MONEY

The American currency is the dollar ($), divided into 100 cents (¢). Major credit cards, especially American Express, MasterCard and Visa, are accepted practically everywhere (including supermarkets and drug stores) and can also be used for cash advances at automated teller machines. Credit cards also offer the benefit of advanced bookings for everything from movie tickets to hotel accommodation. Traveler's checks are accepted in many stores and restaurants when accompanied by a photo identification. For commission-free (no transaction charge) currency and traveler's check exchange at Travelex (see page 255 for New York locations).

. . . Before You Go

New York is a relatively expensive city and the average daily tourist budget, excluding accomodation but including entrance prices, meals, transportation and entertainment, is approximately $70 per person.

HEALTH AND INSURANCE

It is advisable to take out travel insurance before your departure. In addition to baggage loss and trip cancellation, you will want to be sure that your policy provides adequate medical coverage, since U.S. medical care is notoriously expensive.

Central Park in the fall

PACKING FOR NEW YORK

A warm coat, gloves and scarf are necessities during the winter. In the spring and fall, a light jacket or heavy sweater is appropriate. Summers can be very hot and short-sleeved shirts and shorts are sensible and acceptable attire at most attractions and restaurants. Electricity throughout the U.S. is 110 volts (at 60 hz) with two-pronged plugs. If you have electrical accessories with different voltages, you will need to purchase a travel plug adaptor and electric current converter.

BOOKING A HOTEL ROOM IN ADVANCE

New York hotels tend to be more expensive than in many other U.S. cities. When choosing a hotel, you might first think about a price category, then consider in which area you would like to stay. On pages 33-46, you will find a comprehensive listing of quality hotels that can be booked at discounted rates using *New York for less.* You will also find a wealth of information to help you to choose something that will fit your needs and budget. It is strongly recommended that you book your hotel well in advance, particularly if you are traveling during the height of the tourist season when many hotels are completely sold out.

Lobby in the Tudor Hotel

BOOKING THEATER TICKETS IN ADVANCE

If you are interested in seeing a particular show, it is best to book as far ahead as possible. With your *New York for less* card, you can obtain substantial discounts on tickets for top Broadway productions and you can purchase your tickets in advance by phone, with a credit card (see page 215 for details).

Arriving in New York . . .

CHANGING MONEY AT THE AIRPORT

Although credit cards are widely accepted in New York, you will need some cash for transportation, entrance prices and snacks. You can change money at Travelex branches at J.F.K, LaGuardia and Newark Airports (see page 255 for a full listing).

J.F.K. Airport

GETTING FROM THE AIRPORT

J.F.K. AIRPORT

From **J.F.K.**, **Carey Airport Express** is a frequent shuttle service between all J.F.K. terminals to **Port Authority Bus Terminal** and **Grand Central Terminal** in midtown Manhattan. From Grand Central, a free shuttle service drops customers off at most midtown hotels. Buses pick up passengers outside the baggage claim area at each airline terminal, departing every 15-30 minutes from 6am to 12midnight every day. The ride takes 45-60 minutes and costs $13 one-way (reduced to $10 with voucher on page 286) and $26 round trip (reduced to to $20 with voucher on page 286). Unless you have already arranged transportation back to the airport for your departure, it is recommended that you purchase a round-trip ticket when you first arrive.

LaGuardia Airport

Alternatively, you can take a free airport shuttle to the Howard Beach subway station where you can catch the **A or C subway** to Manhattan. Shuttles and trains depart approximately every 15 minutes. The ride takes about 50 minutes and costs $1.50. A **taxi** from J.F.K. to midtown Manhattan takes 35-60 minutes depending on traffic and costs $30 plus tolls and tip.

LAGUARDIA AIRPORT

Carey Airport Express also provides service between **LaGuardia Airport** and **Port Authority Bus Terminal** and **Grand Central Terminal** where the free shuttle connects to most midtown Manhattan hotels. Buses depart every 15-30 minutes from 6.45am to 12midnight daily from outside the baggage claim area at each airline terminal. Tickets cost $10 one-way (reduced to $7 with voucher on page 286) and $20 round trip (reduced to $14 with voucher on page 286). The trip takes 30-45 minutes.

. . . Arriving in New York

Alternatively, a **taxi** costs $15-25 plus tolls and tip and will take 20-40 minutes.

From **Newark Airport**, **Olympia Trails Airport Express** (☎ *964-6233)* departs every 15-30 minutes, stopping at the **World Trade Center**, **Port Authority Bus Terminal** and **Grand Central Station** in Manhattan. The ride takes 30-45 minutes and costs $7. A **taxi** takes 20-45 minutes and cost $30-45 plus tolls and tip.

GETTING AROUND NEW YORK

New York is a relatively compact city which makes sightseeing fairly easy. Careful trip planning will allow you to do the majority of your sightseeing on foot, once you have reached a particular destination. This book is organized by neighborhood so that you can make the best use of your time.

Bus Tours - Taking a guided tour on a double-decker bus is the best way to orient yourself while visiting New York's major sights. The biggest company to

operate bus tours is **New York Apple Tours** (page 219) which offers a discount to *New York for less* cardholders.

Subway - Operating 24 hours a day, seven days a week,

Inside the subway

the subway is the fastest and easiest way to get around New York City. Trains run frequently (every 3-5 minutes during the day) and less frequently late at night. The one-way fare is $1.50 (no matter how many times you change trains) and can be paid with a MetroCard or a token bought at any subway station.

Bus - Most buses run 24 hours a day, seven days a week. Traffic can make bus travel slow and inconvenient during the day, but can be a good alternative to a taxi in the evenings. The fare is $1.50 and can be paid with a MetroCard or a token.

New York City bus

Taxi - The ubiquitous yellow cabs are easily recognizable. They are available when the center light is on, but not when the "Off Duty" side lights are on as well. Daytime traffic make cab rides a fairly expensive method of transportation, even for short distances.

Planning Your Trip . . .

New York has so many sights and attractions that it can be rather overwhelming for a first-time visitor. This section will help you plan your trip by highlighting some of the best things to do and see in the city.

IF YOU HAVE ONE DAY

A carriage ride in Central Park

Sightseeing – Start the day by taking the New York Apple Tour (page 219) double-decker sightseeing tour to the Statue of Liberty. Stop off at the World Trade Center (page 57) and admire the view from the observation deck on the 108th Floor. If you have time, walk to the South Street Seaport (page 54), Trinity Church (page 58) and New York's financial center, Wall Street, all within a short distance of each other.

Lunch/Dinner – New York has more than 17,000 eating establishments, serving a vast array of international cuisine. Choose from the many restaurants listed in this book and receive a 25% discount off the total bill.

Lower Manhattan view from the Staten Island Ferry

Museums – Continue the bus tour to the Upper East Side to the Museum Mile (page 182), one the most famous art districts in the world. The Metropolitan Museum of Art (page 184) and the Solomon R. Guggenheim Museum (page 186) are only two of the many prestigious institutions that are worth visiting on this stretch of Fifth Avenue.

Broadway shows – After an early dinner, take in a Broadway show in the Theater District (page 132).

Empire State Building – After the theater, head to the Observatory at the top of the Empire State Building (page 116) to witness the extraordinary view of the Manhattan sky at night.

IF YOU HAVE TWO DAYS

In addition to slowing down the pace of the previous itinerary, a second day in New York will give museum-goers a chance to visit the exceptional collections at the Museum of Modern Art (page 134) or the

. . . Planning Your Trip

American Museum of Natural History (page 164).
Later, take a walk through Central Park (page 205).
The park's main attraction, Wollman Memorial Rink
(page 208), is a great place for ice-skating and
rollerblading.

IF YOU HAVE THREE-FOUR DAYS

Soho and its surrounding areas are an excellent
place to explore. Wander through the galleries
and fashionable boutiques before heading to
nearby Chinatown, Little Italy or the Lower East
Side where you can indulge in the ethnic foods
for which these neighborhoods are best-known.
Before the sun sets, take a walk across the
Brooklyn Bridge for a breathtaking view of the
Manhattan skyline.

IF YOU HAVE A WEEK

Visitors fortunate enough to have a week in New
York will begin to discover the full range of what New
York has to offer. An excellent way to experience the
city and all its curiosities is by investigating its
distinctive neighborhoods in-depth.

Brooklyn Bridge

1. The Municipal Art Society (page 224) sponsors a
series of walking tours which focus on the
architecture, history and sites of some of Manhattan's
more interesting neighborhoods.

*Greenwich Village
townhouses*

2. Historic Greenwich Village
(page 93) is a picturesque,
yet dynamic area. Its
charming old-world streets
contain historic brownstone
houses, contemporary
shopping, dining and
nightlife opportunities.

3. For an excellent dinner
and a view of the island of
Manhattan you will never
forget, take a World Yacht
Dinner Cruise (page 221).

4. New York City's outer boroughs, often overlooked by
visitors, contain an array of historic and cultural sites
and attractions. Stroll along the Brooklyn Promenade
(page 226), directly across the river from Manhattan,
catch a baseball game at Yankee Stadium (page 232)
or take a ride on the Staten Island Ferry (page 61) for
great views of Lower Manhattan, the Statue of Liberty
and New York Harbor – for just 50¢.

If You Do One Thing . . .

These ten ideas may not be the most famous or popular destinations, but they are an honest selection of personal favorites.

If you visit one attraction:

Empire State Building Observatory (page 116)

If you go to one museum:

The Frick Collection (page 188)

If you take one walk:

Path along the Hudson River (page 63)

If you go to one nightclub:

Webster Hall (page 216)

If you take one tour:

Big Apple Tours' Statue of Liberty Express (page 219)

If you go to one restaurant:

Liberty Cafe (page 67)

If you go to one store:

Macy's (page 146)

If you take one excursion:

Rent a car and drive to Philadelphia (page 243)

If you go to one brewery:

Commonwealth Brewing Company (page 142)

If you visit one church:

Cathedral of St. John the Divine (page 170)

History of
New York

History . . .

The history of New York began long before the arrival of European settlers. The **Algonquin** and **Iroquois Indians** inhabited the region until the mid-1600s when they were forced out of the area by colonizing Europeans.

Purchase of Manhattan from the Indians (1626)

The first European settler to arrive in what is now New York Harbor was **Giovanni da Verrazano**, in 1524. Eighty-five years later, in 1609, **Henry Hudson**, working for the **Dutch East India Company**, sailed his ship, the *Half-Moon,* up the river that today bears his name.

In 1624, the **Dutch West India Company** established a permanent colony on Manhattan Island as a trading outpost and named it **New Amsterdam**. **Peter Minuit**, the colony's first governor, bought the island of Manhattan from the Indians for $24 worth of beads, blankets and trinkets in 1626.

During the 1640s, the Dutch, who had already started enforcing harsh laws towards the natives, launched a two and a half year war against them.

DeWit View (ca. 1672)

Peter Stuyvesant became governor in 1647 and implemented a strict plan to restore order and civility in what had become an unruly and lawless town. To keep warring Indians away he ordered a ditch to be dug and a wall to be installed at the present location of **Wall Street**, then the city's northern border. He remained governor for 17 years, during which time the settlement doubled in size and trading flourished.

New Amsterdam was seized by the English in 1664 and renamed **New York**, in honor of the king's brother, the Duke of York.

Dance on the Battery in the Presence of Peter Stuyvesant (1838) by A. Durand

In 1733, **John Peter Zenger** started a liberal paper called the *New York Weekly Journal*. His famous trial, on a libel charge, helped establish the American ideals of freedom of speech and freedom of the press which were later embodied in the **First Amendment to the Constitution**.

... History ...

The colonists set up the **Continental Congress** in 1774. Soon after, **Thomas Jefferson's Declaration of Independence**, extolling the virtues of a democratic government, was adopted. Delegates from the Continental Congress, preparing for a revolution, asked colonists to band together and refuse to pay taxes.

In 1776, 200 British ships entered New York Harbor and the **American Revolution** began. During this time, New York suffered from violence, over-crowding and starvation. After much bloodshed, British troops finally surrendered and began to withdraw from the colonies.

Pulling down the statue of George III at Bowling Green, July 1776

Initially, New York was named the first capital city of the newly formed **United States**. On April 23, 1789, **General George Washington**, hero of the American Revolution, was elected the nation's first president.

Portrait of George Washington (1796) by Gilbert Stuart

Following independence, New York City began to flourish, and by 1850, the **Irish Potato Famine** had sparked a wave of **immigration** that brought the city's population to 300,000.

From 1855 to 1890, the number of immigrants who entered the U.S. via New York City totaled 8 million. To accommodate this influx, **Ellis Island Immigration Station** was built in 1892. After having seen nearly 16 million people pass through, it was finally closed in 1954.

The influx of cheap labor helped put turn-of-the-century New York City at the forefront of technological and industrial achievements, ushering in the "**Golden Age**". In the 1860s, the first **elevated trains** appeared, further expanding New York's geographical boundaries, while mansions were built on upper Fifth Avenue, overlooking the newly created **Central Park**. **Thomas Edison** first provided electricity to the general public in 1882 and soon thereafter New York watched in awe

City Hall Park, early 1800s

...History...

the completion and dedication of the **Brooklyn Bridge** and the **Statue of Liberty**. By 1900, the construction of the city's **subway** had begun.

Central Park Summer, Looking South (1865) John Bachmann

During this period, banker **J.P. Morgan** and industrial tycoons **Cornelius Vanderbilt**, **Andrew Carnegie** and **John D. Rockefeller** monopolized the industry and wealth of the country and made names for themselves as the "**Robber Barons**". They went on to fund universities, libraries, museums and public institutions of all kinds, many of which still bear their names.

Immigrants on Battery Park, 1901

In 1917, America entered **World War I**. The eventual victory over Germany in 1918 introduced America as a world power while the country, and New York City in particular, profited immensely.

In 1920, the **women's suffrage movement** won the right to vote. At the same time, **Prohibition** gave rise to speakeasies – illegal drinking establishments run mainly by gangsters. **Jazz** flourished at nightclubs such as the **Cotton Club** in **Harlem** where **Duke Ellington** and **Cab Calloway** were regular performers.

The prosperity of the "**roaring 20s**" was followed by the **stock market crash** of October, 1929, and the **Great Depression**. Banks closed and people across the country lost their jobs and their homes.

Subway construction workers in a tunnel

President Franklin D. Roosevelt introduced the **New Deal** in an attempt to restore and revitalize public life by creating new jobs. At this time, great projects like the **Empire State Building** and **Rockefeller Center** were completed.

In 1933, **Fiorello LaGuardia** became mayor. Known for his stance against corruption and well-respected by

. . . History

the people, LaGuardia was re-elected twice. He led New York out of the Great Depression and through to the end of **World War II**.

The Second World War was as good to New York as the First had been. Government spending increased, jobs were created and New York Harbor filled with ships, soldiers and supplies bound for Europe.

New York skyline in 1932

During the 1950s, **Beat culture** became the latest in a long list of counter-cultural movements that have made New York a haven for progressive and radical thinkers. Nonetheless, the conservative influence of 1950s mainstream America was still dominant in New York.

In the 1960s, the struggle for racial equality led by African-American, Latin-American and other ethnic groups impacted the culture. **Equal rights** and **Anti-Vietnam demonstrations**, such as those at **Columbia University**, were in the nation's spotlight.

The early days of the Flatiron Building

Tired of the chaos and crime, many middle-class families moved to the suburbs. The departure of workers and businesses took its toll on city coffers, which reached the point of near-collapse in the mid-1970s.

Federal and state loans were reluctantly granted and the **Municipal Assistance Corporation** was established to keep the city's expenditures in check. Mayor **Ed Koch**, elected in 1978, took control of city finances and remained in office for three terms.

In the 1980s, New York experienced another economic and building boom. The "yuppie" emerged as a symbol of wealth and excess typified by public figures like **Donald Trump**.

Hard-nosed lawyer and federal prosecutor **Rudolph Guiliani** became New York's mayor in 1994 on a platform of reducing crime and improving New York's quality of life. Although many people fear that he is attempting to suburbanize New York and strip it of its uniqueness, the crime rate, at least, has fallen to half its previous level.

Trump Tower: a tribute to the wealth and excess of the 1980s

Timeline . . .

1524 Giovanni da Verrazano becomes the first European to land on Manhattan.

1609 While on a voyage for the Dutch East India Company, Henry Hudson sails into the bay and river that now bear his name.

THE DUTCH ARRIVE

1624 The colony of New Amsterdam is founded by the Dutch.

1626 The first governor, Peter Minuit, purchases the island of Manhattan for the equivalent of $24 worth of trinkets.

1628 The Reformed Dutch Church is the first religious organization to be established in Manhattan.

1647 Peter Stuyvesant becomes governor. He establishes order in the chaotic, lawless city.

1653 New Amsterdam is declared a town and receives a charter. A protective wall is erected to control the fighting with neighboring Indians.

1654 Jewish settlers arrive in New Amsterdam for the first time.

1661 Poor civic management and wars with the Indians lead an unstable New Amsterdam to the brink of bankruptcy.

THE BRITISH ARRIVE

1664 The English invade and seize New Amsterdam, renaming it New York after the Duke of York, the King of England's brother.

1674 The Treaty of Westminster grants the colony of New Amsterdam permanently to the English.

1700 The population of the city reaches 20,000.

1725 William Bradford establishes New York's first newspaper - the *New York Gazette*.

1733-1734 John Peter Zenger founds the *New York Weekly Journal*.

1754 King's College, the city's first college is founded. It later becomes Columbia University.

1763 The 1763 Treaty of Paris ends the French and Indian War (also known as the 7 Years' War). The British are victorious and take control of the thirteen colonies.

THE AMERICAN REVOLUTION

1776 The Declaration of Independence is read in Bowling Green and the American Revolution begins. British ships are sent to New York Harbor.

. . . Timeline . . .

1783 On September 3, the 1783 Treaty of Paris is signed. The colonists are victorious and England recognizes the independence of the thirteen colonies.

1789-90 New York is capital of the United States.

1789 The Constitution of the United States is ratified and General George Washington is elected as the first president.

THE NEW REPUBLIC

1811 John Randel devises the street "grid plan" for the future growth of New York City.

1812-1814 The U.S. declares war on Britain. British ships are positioned in New York Harbor in order to block and isolate the city from trade. City Hall is built.

1825 The Eerie Canal is opened, leading the way for New York to become an important trading port.

INDUSTRIAL GROWTH

1828 South Street Seaport becomes the center of New York's growing maritime trade.

1858-1876 Central Park is constructed.

1860 Abraham Lincoln is elected President.

1861-1865 The Civil War. The Union (North) wins and slavery is abolished. President Abraham Lincoln is assassinated.

1868 The "El", New York's first elevated railway and the precursor to the subway, is erected.

1870 The Metropolitan Museum of Art is founded. Work on the Brooklyn Bridge begins.

1882 Thomas Edison's electrical plant, located in Lower Manhattan, offers electricity to the public for general use.

1883 The Brooklyn Bridge is completed and opened.

1886 The Statue of Liberty is unveiled and New York hosts its first "ticker tape parade" on lower Broadway.

MASS IMMIGRATION

1892 Ellis Island is opened as an immigration station and remains so until 1954.

1898 Brooklyn, the Bronx, Queens and Staten Island become part of New York City – making it the world's largest, with a population of more than 3 million.

1900 Construction of the subway begins.

1902 The Flatiron Building is erected and, at 21 stories, is the world's first skyscraper.

. . . Timeline

1907 Metered taxis are introduced on the streets of New York.

1917 The United States enters World War I.

1920 The women's suffrage movement wins the right to vote. Prohibition laws are introduced.

THE GREAT DEPRESSION

1929 Wall Street crashes and ushers in the Great Depression. MoMA opens its first exhibition.

1931 The Empire State Building is completed and becomes the world's tallest structure.

1939 The World's Fair, held at Flushing Meadow Park in Queens, attracts over 44 million visitors.

1941 America enters World War II.

POST-WAR NEW YORK

1946 The United Nations charter is signed in New York.

1947 Jackie Robinson of the Brooklyn Dodgers is the first black player in major league baseball.

1959 The Solomon R. Guggenheim Museum opens.

1962 Lincoln Center for the Performing Arts opens.

1964 Race riots occur in Brooklyn and Harlem. The Beatles play Shea Stadium in Queens.

1964-65 The World's Fair is held on the same site in Queens as it was in 1939-40.

1973 The World Trade Center is completed in Lower Manhattan.

1977 A blackout lasts for 25 hours throughout the entire city.

1978 Ed Koch is elected mayor and begins economic turnaround.

1983 Trump Tower is completed by real estate developer and consummate yuppie Donald Trump.

1986 The stock market crashes again.

1990 New York's first black mayor, David Dinkens is elected. Ellis Island reopens as an immigration museum.

1993 Terrorists attempt to blow up the World Trade Center. Rudolph Guiliani is elected as New York City's first Republican mayor in 28 years.

1996 New York Yankees win the World Series. President Bill Clinton is re-elected for a second term.

Hotels

HOTEL FACILITIES

In addition to the
amenities represented by
the symbols below, all of
the hotels listed on the
following pages have
en suite showers and
baths, air conditioned
bedrooms, satellite or
cable TV, wake-up calls,
laundry facilities and non-
smoking rooms (available
upon request).

 Minibar

 Tea/coffee facilities

 Room service

 24-hour room Service

 Radio

 Direct dial telephone

 Hairdryer

 Room safe

 Babysitting service

 Disabled facilities

 Business Center

 Fitness Center

 Swimming Pool

Booking a Hotel Room

New York hotels are notoriously expensive by
international standards. In association with New
York's top hotel booking service, Quickbook, *New York
for less* offers you up to 50% off the published room
rates at over 40 hotels.

In order to obtain the *for less* discount, you must book
your rooms through Quickbook. From outside the
United States, telephone (212) 686-7666 or fax
(212) 779-6120. Within the U.S., dial toll-free 1-
888-NYForLess (1-888-766-6692). Bookings made
directly with hotels or through other booking agents
(such as tour operators, tourist authorities or travel
agents) will not be eligible for the
New York for less discount.

Because New York is extremely
busy at particular times of the
year, and hotel accommodation
can be difficult to find, it is
recommended that you book well
in advance.

Quickbook operators

The $ symbols by each hotel's entry indicate the
standard double room rates, <u>before</u> the *New York for
less* discount. $= under $149, $$= $150-199, $$$=
$200-249, $$$$= $250-299, $$$$$= over $300.

The first thing to do after you decide how much you
would like to spend is to decide in which area you
would like to stay. Most hotels in Manhattan are
located either in Midtown East or Midtown West. (See
pages 14-15 for a summary of New York's areas.)

As long as your card is valid on the first night that you
intend to stay in the hotel, you can stay as long as you
like at the discounted rate (subject to room
availability).

The stars under each hotel's name give an indication
of the quality of the hotel:

★★ : Basic amenities such as *en suite* bathrooms, air-
conditioning, TVs and radios.

★★★ : Full reception services, more formal restaurant
and bar arrangements, additional amenities.

★★★★ : More spacious accommodation offering high
standards of comfort and food. The range of services
includes porterage, room service, formal reception and
often a selection of restaurants.

★★★★★ : The majority of rooms are of the highest
international standard.

Soho Grand Hotel

★★★★

310 West Broadway
Soho

$$$

Opened in 1996, this stylish hotel is located in the heart of Soho. Rooms feature two-line phones, cable TV, mini-bars and in-room safes. Services include a fitness room and transportation to the Financial District. *(367 rooms)*

Southgate Towers

★★★

371 Seventh Avenue
Chelsea

PRICE CATEGORY

$$$$

Located across from Madison Square Garden, every room in this this all-suite hotel features a kitchen with a microwave and refrigerator. Services include business and fitness centers. *(522 suites)*

Rihga Royal

★★★★

151 West 54th Street
Midtown West

PRICE CATEGORY

$$$$$

This 54-story luxury hotel has nearly 500 deluxe suites. Each has superb amenities including VCRs, electronic safes, televisions, phones and mini-bars. A full service restaurant is located on the ground floor. *(496 suites)*

Best Western Woodward

★★★

**210 West 55th Stree
Midtown Wes**

The Best Western Woodward is located in a Beaux Ar
landmark building in the Theater District. Room
feature modern conveniences and new bathrooms. You
stay also includes continental breakfast. *(200 rooms)*

Doubletree Guest Suites

★★★

**1568 Broadwa
Midtown Wes**

This all-suite hotel is located near Rockefeller Cente
and Radio City Music Hall. Each suite contains a livin
room, dining area with full kitchen, and bedroom as we
as two TVs and three phones with voice mail. *(460 suite*

Hotel Gorham

★★★

**136 West 55th Stree
Midtown Wes**

This small luxury hotel has recently undergone
complete multi-million dollar renovation. Rooms ar
suites feature minibars, refrigerators, two-line phone
fax machines and in-room safes. *(122 rooms)*

PRICE CATEGORY

$$

PRICE CATEGORY

$$$

PRICE CATEGORY

$$

Hotel Metro

★★

45 West 35th Street
Midtown West

Hotel Metro has been recently restored in an Art Deco style. Continental breakfast is included with each stay. The 14th-floor terrace provides great views of the Empire State Building. *(174 rooms)*

PRICE CATEGORY

$$

 Mansfield

★★★

12 West 44th Street
Midtown West

This 1904 hotel is dedicated to Broadway actor John Mansfield who once lived on this block. Rooms include complimentary breakfast and feature hard-wood floors, marble baths, cable TV, VCR and CD player. *(126 rooms)*

PRICE CATEGORY

$$

Michelangelo

★★★★

152 West 51st Street
Midtown West

The Michelangelo is a first-class luxury hotel. The spacious rooms come with a complimentary breakfast and each features a marble foyer and Empire, Art Deco or Country French décor. *(178 rooms)*

PRICE CATEGORY

$$$$

PRICE CATEGORY

$$$$

PRICE CATEGORY

$$

PRICE CATEGORY

$$$$

Millennium Broadway

★★★★

145 West 44th Street
Midtown West

Floor-to-ceiling windows in each guest room look out onto the Theater District. Rockefeller Center and Fifth Avenue are all within walking distance. Amenities include multi lingual voice mail and child services. *(638 rooms)*

New York Marriott Marquis

★★★★

1568 Broadway
Midtown West

This 50-story hotel towers above Times Square. Rooms feature individual climate control, dual telephones and coffeemakers. Four eateries include The View – a revolving rooftop restaurant. *(1,911 rooms)*

New York Renaissance

★★★★

714 Seventh Avenue
Midtown West

Located in the heart of Times Square, this high-rise hotel provides quality accommodation and service. The rooms are modern and comfortable, and each of its 2 floors has an 24-hour butler. *(305 rooms)*

Novotel New York

★★★

226 West 52nd Street
Midtown West

PRICE CATEGORY

$$

Located on Broadway in the heart of the Theater District, this hotel has a unique seven-floor lobby. Rooms feature either king-size beds and a pull-out sofa or two double beds, all with modern furnishings and baths. *(474 rooms)*

Paramount

★★★

235 West 46th Street
Midtown West

PRICE CATEGORY

$$$

The Paramount is a chic, modern hotel often frequented by celebrities. A dramatic staircase is the centerpiece of Philippe Starck's stylish design. A coffee shop and trendy bar are located in the lobby. *(610 rooms)*

St. Moritz

★★

50 Central Park
Midtown West

PRICE CATEGORY

$

Ideally situated on Central Park South, the St. Moritz overlooks the park. This old-fashioned, affordable hotel has recently undergone a major renovation. It is located close to many of the midtown attractions. *(680 rooms)*

Salisbury

★★

123 West 57th Street
Midtown West

The Salisbury is situated across the street from Carnegie Hall and is a short walk from Fifth Avenue. Its central location and large rooms (many of which feature kitchenettes) make it perfect for families. *(320 rooms)*

Shoreham Hotel

★★★

33 West 55th Street
Midtown West

The Shoreham is located one block from the Museum of Modern Art and is close to all the midtown attractions. Guest rooms are spacious and modern with cedar closets, refrigerators, cable TV and CD players. *(84 rooms)*

The Warwick

★★★

65 West 54th Street
Midtown West

Built by publisher William Randolph Hearst in 1927, the Warwick is located in the Theater District, and a short walk from Central Park. Rooms include cable TV, two-line phones and marble bathrooms. *(425 rooms)*

 Crowne Plaza

★★★

1605 Broadway
Midtown West

Described by *Newsweek* as the "most gorgeous building in Manhattan", the Crowne Plaza has exceptional views, a full range of services and amenities, and Manhattan's largest indoor hotel pool. *(770 rooms)*

PRICE CATEGORY

$$$$

 Edison Hotel

★★

288 West 47th Street
Midtown West

Built in 1931, the Edison Hotel is one of the best values in Manhattan hotels. Situated in the heart of the Theater District, each guest room has individual temperature controls and a modern bath. *(1,000 rooms)*

PRICE CATEGORY

$

Royalton

★★★★

44 West 44th Street
Midtown West

A favorite with many celebrities, the Royalton features luxurious rooms with fireplaces, roomy baths and large beds. Philippe Starck designed the hallway, lobby and the nautical-style rooms. *(167 rooms)*

PRICE CATEGORY

$$$$

PRICE CATEGORY

$$$$

PRICE CATEGORY

$$$$

PRICE CATEGORY

$$$

New York Palace

★★★★

445 Madison Avenue
Midtown East

The New York Palace is annexed to the 1884 landmark Villard Houses. 55-stories high, this luxury hotel offers services which include business and fitness centers and several high quality restaurants. *(863 rooms)*

Omni Berkshire Place

★★★★

21 East 52nd Street
Midtown East

Have a complimentary copy of the *New York Times* delivered to your door each morning at this luxurious hotel on fashionable Madison Avenue. The health club features a sun-deck and massage service. *(396 rooms)*

Dumont Plaza

★★★

150 East 34th Street
Midtown East

Located in Murray Hill, the Dumont Plaza is a short walk from the Empire State Building and Macy's. The hotel features suite-style rooms with complete kitchen, cable TV and complimentary coffee and tea. *(247 suites)*

Doral Court

★★★

30 East 39th Street
Midtown East

The Doral Court is located in residential Murray Hill. This comfortable hotel has rooms that feature big-screen TVs, VCRs and walk-in closets. Guests are also welcome to use the Doral Fitness Center. *(199 rooms)*

Doral Inn

★★★

541 Lexington Avenue
Midtown East

Located near Grand Central Station, the Doral Inn has rooms designed and furnished to a high standard, but is moderately priced. Guests can use the health club, sauna and squash courts. *(655 rooms)*

Doral Park Avenue

★★★

70 Park Avenue
Midtown East

The bedrooms in this sophisticated and intimate Murray Hill hotel feature marble bathrooms and stocked minibars. Guests are also entitled to use the Doral Fitness Center. *(188 rooms)*

PRICE CATEGORY

$$$

PRICE CATEGORY

$$

PRICE CATEGORY

$$$

Eastgate Tower

★★

222 East 39th Stree
Midtown Eas

Located close to the midtown attractions, Eastgate Towe offers comfortable all-suite accommodation. Each sui has a complete kitchen with microwave, coffeemaker an full stove. *(188 suites)*

Hotel Intercontinental

★★★

111 East 48th Stree
Midtown Eas

Built in 1926, the Hotel Intercontinental has bee recently restored. Old-world in style, it has modern an comfortable guest rooms. Hotel services include a brand new, state-of-the-art business center. *(683 rooms)*

Jolly Madison Towers

★

22 East 38th Stree
Midtown Eas

Jolly Madison Tower is moderately priced and locate near Madison Avenue. The lobby is decorated with whi marble floors and a mirrored ceiling. The modern room feature rosewood furniture. *(246 rooms)*

Loews New York

★★★

569 Lexington Avenue
Midtown East

This moderately priced, high-quality hotel has recently received a multi-million dollar renovation. Guest rooms have modern furnishings including refrigerators, safes, TVs and two-line phones. *(688 rooms)*

Morgans

★★★

237 Madison Avenue
Midtown East

Morgans was built in 1929 to honor the early 19th-century banker J.P. Morgan. All rooms have modern amenities. Services include a baby-sitting service, fitness center and business facilities. *(113 rooms)*

New York Helmsley

★★★

212 East 42nd Street
Midtown East

The New York Helmsley is located near Grand Central Station. The hotel has 41 floors and services which include a multi-lingual staff and complimentary coffee and tea in the lobby. *(790 rooms)*

PRICE CATEGORY

$$$

PRICE CATEGORY

$$$

PRICE CATEGORY

$$$

Shelburne Murray Hotel

★★★

303 Lexington Avenue
Midtown East

The Shelburne Murray Hotel features spacious suites complete with full kitchen (including a microwave and refrigerator). Services include a multi-lingual staff, conference facilities and a fitness center. *(258 suites)*

The Tudor

★★★

304 East 42nd Street
Midtown East

This hotel is located near the midtown sights. Small and modern, the Tudor is best known for its high level of personal service. Rooms are contemporary and feature marble baths and in-room safes. *(300 rooms)*

Waldorf-Astoria

★★★★★

301 Park Avenue
Midtown East

Built in 1931, this world-famous hotel features a grand lobby decorated with painted murals, mahogany paneling and marble columns. The rooms contain beautiful French and English antiques. *(1,444 rooms)*

Radisson Empire

★★

4 West 63rd Street
pper West Side

cross from Lincoln Center, every room at the Radisson mpire has a large bath, TV, VCR and stereo with CD layer. The Tudor-style lobby is adorned with high eilings, wood paneling and oil paintings. *(376 rooms)*

Franklin

★

64 East 87th Street
pper East Side

ocated close to Museum Mile, the Franklin has an timate, charming atmosphere. Each room has a anopied bed, spacious closets and a comfortable bath. uests also receive complimentary breakfast. *(53 rooms)*

Hotel Wales

★

295 Madison Avenue
pper East Side

ocated in the Carnegie Hill historic district, near useum Mile, Hotel Wales has recently been restored its original turn-of-the-century glory. Breakfast and a are served in the Pied Piper Room. *(92 rooms)*

Regency

★★★★

540 Park Avenu
Upper East Sid

The exclusive Regency has nearly 400 elegant rooms.
full range of top-notch amenities includes 24-hour roor
service. Other hotel services include a fitness center an
a business center. *(362 rooms)*

PRICE CATEGORY

$$$$$

Barbizon

★★

140 East 63r
Upper East Sid

Once a safe haven for young ladies from wealthy familie
visiting the city, the Barbizon recently underwent a 4(
million dollar renovation. Rooms are modern and ar
reasonably priced for this expensive area. *(344 rooms)*

PRICE CATEGORY

$$$

Hotel Delmonico

★★★★

502 Park Avenu
Upper East Sid

Located close to Central Park, Hotel Delmonico house
the famous Christie's auction house. It offers suites
each with modern amenities including a fully equippe
kitchen, two color TVs and in-room safe. *(147 suites)*

PRICE CATEGORY

$$$$$

Lower Manhattan

Introduction . . .

INSIDER'S TIP

Walking tours provide an in-depth look at the architecture, history and sights of a neighborhood. Heritage Trails New York (page 223) enables you to explore historic Lower Manhattan, either with a guide or on your own, by following the colored trail markers on sidewalks and streets.

In addition to being the home of one of the world's most important financial centers, Lower Manhattan contains many of New York's top attractions and historic sights, including **South Street Seaport**, the **World Trade Center** and **Battery Park**, from where you can take the ferry to the **Statue of Liberty** and **Ellis Island** (pages 50-53). It is perhaps the best area to start a sightseeing tour of the city.

Statue of Liberty

Originally inhabited by the Iroquois and Algonquin Indians, Manhattan was named **New Amsterdam** by the Dutch who settled here in the 17th century. In 1653, a wall was built along the northern boundary of the settlement in order to keep its citizens safe from the wilderness and warring Indians beyond.

Bowling Green

Today, **Wall Street**, as it came to be known, is the heart of the Financial District. The winding streets of the old Dutch town can still be traced among the looming skyscrapers of the modern metropolis.

Under British rule, the landscape of Lower Manhattan came to resemble the parks and squares of London. Many of these, such as **Bowling Green** (page 63) still remain - though the surrounding fence, which still stands, is no longer topped with English royal crowns.

As the nation's first capital, post-Revolutionary New York was the seat of government and Lower Manhattan held its courts and government offices. General **George Washington**, the nation's first president, took his oath of office in a building on Wall Street which is now **Federal Hall**

Brooklyn Bridge and the East River

National Memorial (page 57). Nearby, **Fraunces Tavern Museum** (page 56) is the site of the farewell speech he made to his officers.

. . . Introduction

North of the Financial District, Manhattan's **Civic Center** comprises the courthouses and offices of local, state and federal government. Its focal point, City Hall (page 60), was built in 1812 and since that time has been the site of many political protests and demonstrations.

Also in City Hall Park is the infamous **Old New York County Courthouse**. Begun in 1862 and not finished until a decade later, it is better known as "Tweed Courthouse". Legend has it that Boss Tweed, leader of the political faction Tammany Hall, corruptly pocketed $10 million of the $14 million dollars allotted to pay for its construction.

Overlooking City Hall, the much larger **Municipal Building** houses government offices of all kinds, including the marriage bureau. At the foot of this imposing building lies the entrance to the Brooklyn Bridge and its pedestrian walkway (page 59).

Municipal Building

Further south, **Park Row**, which was once dubbed "Newspaper Row", was the hub of the early 19th-century daily newspaper business. It was also the home of **P.T. Barnum's American Museum** until it burned down in 1865.

South Street Seaport and Fulton Market

In the 19th century, **South Street Seaport** (page 54-55) was the heart of the maritime trade. After a period of decline, it has now been delightfully restored as a seaport village, complete with 19th- and early 20th-century buildings and tall ships moored in the harbor.

REFLECTIONS

'To Europe, she was America, to America she was the gateway of the earth. But to tell the story of New York would be to write a social history of the world.' – H.G. Wells

Nearby, **Hanover Square** (page 61) was once the home of English pirate William Kidd, better known as Captain Kidd.

North of Battery Park, at the North Cove Marina on the Hudson River, you can see yachts from all around the world docked in front of the **World Financial Center** (page 69). This steel and glass structure rises to spectacular heights, allowing sunlight to illuminate the palm trees, marble piazza and grand staircase of its interior, a shopping arcade known as the **Wintergarden Atrium**.

Lower Manhattan

Statue of Liberty . . .

ADDRESS

Liberty Island is located
off the tip of Manhattan.
Ferries depart from
Battery Park.
For ferry times and prices,
☎ 269-5755.
For information about
the Statue of Liberty,
☎ 363-3200.

HOURS

Mon-Sun: 9.15am-3.30pm
(later in summer).
Ferries depart every 30-45
minutes.

PRICES

There is no admission
charge at the
Statue of Liberty.

The Statue of Liberty was presented to the people of
the United States by the people of France in 1886, as
a symbol of friendship between the nations. Today, it
is recognized throughout the world as a symbol of
freedom.

Situated on **Liberty Island** in New York Harbor, the
Statue of Liberty rests on an 89-foot granite pedestal
and rises a total of 151 feet from base to torch. Lady
Liberty herself is more than 111 feet tall, and her
index finger alone is eight feet long. Her steel
framework and copper shell weigh a hefty 225 tons.

At the time of dedication, the statue was the tallest
structure in New York. Today, she is dwarfed by the
110-story World Trade Center which is clearly visible
from Liberty Island.

Although **the torch** is no
longer accessible to
visitors, you can go to
the crown by climbing
the 354 steps from the
bottom of the
monument.
Alternatively, there is an
elevator that takes you to
a panoramic observation
deck near the top of the
pedestal.

Inside the statue's base,
there is an exhibit which
chronicles her
extraordinary creation

Statue of Liberty

and history, including the unique fund-raising efforts
which make this monument a gift which is truly "from
the people".

The story of the Statue of Liberty began at a small
dinner party in 1865. The host was **Edouard Rene
Lefebvre de Laboulaye,** leader of the French "liberals"
– a political group established to promote a republican
government based on America's constitution.

Nearly a hundred years after the French had helped
America win its independence from Britain, French
and American dignitaries and guests reflected on the
relationship that had been forged between their
countries.

While discussing the approach of America's centennial
celebration, Laboulaye suggested that France should

. . . Statue of Liberty

give the U.S. a great monument as an everlasting symbol of their collective belief in human liberty and democracy.

Little could they anticipate what the Statue of Liberty would eventually mean to the millions of immigrants who were welcomed by the words of poet **Emma Lazarus**: "Give me your tired, your poor, your huddled masses, yearning to breathe free". Her poem, "The New Colossus", was written in 1883, but only gained fame after it was inscribed on a plaque and hung on a wall inside the pedestal, 20 years after it was written.

Under the direction of **Auguste Bartholdi**, a successful French sculptor, the copper sheets were shaped inside wooden molds, forming the "skin" of the statue. Famed engineer **Alexandre-Gustave Eiffel**, who later created the Eiffel Tower, joined the project by contributing the intricate "skeleton" support.

Since France's upper classes donated very little to the building of the statue, it became necessary to find a creative solution to spark public interest in the project. In the end, it was a lottery which proved successful in raising nearly all the necessary funds.

In the U.S., the appeal to the upper classes failed as miserably as it did in France. **Joseph Pulitzer**, a Hungarian immigrant, journalist and owner of the financial newspaper *The World*, saw a unique opportunity to use his paper as a way of raising funds while also boosting the circulation of his newspaper. He set a fund-raising goal of $100,000 and promised to publish in the newspaper the name of every individual contributor, no matter how small the amount. The goal was reached, then exceeded, and *The World*'s circulation dramatically increased.

With the French paying for the statue and the Americans paying for the pedestal and foundation, the Statue of Liberty was unveiled to the world on October 28, 1886. Over a million spectators filled the streets to watch a parade of more than 20,000 people. Wall Street businessmen, working on this public holiday, threw streams of message tape from their windows, creating the first of the renowned New York "ticker-tape" parades.

INSIDER'S TIP

During peak seasons the wait may be incredibly long, and the view from the enclosed crown is limited. A better option might be the elevator, which takes you to a panoramic observation deck near the top of the pedestal.

You can also avoid the long lines for the ferry ticket and save money by taking the New York Apple Tours' Statue of Liberty Express (page 219) which includes a double-decker sightseeing tour and a ferry ticket.

The Unveiling of the Statue of Liberty Enlightening the World by Edward Moran

ADDRESS

Ellis Island is located off the tip of Manhattan. For ferry times and prices, ☎ 269-5755.
For information about Ellis Island, ☎ 363-3200.

HOURS

Mon-Sun: 9.15am-3.30pm (later in summer).
Ferries depart every 30-45 minutes.

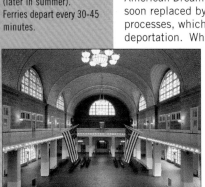

The Great Hall

Ellis Island . . .

Between 1892 and 1954, the immigration station at Ellis Island processed more than 17 million immigrants – the ancestors of over 40% of Americans today. Some of the more famous immigrants who arrived at Ellis Island include author and scientist **Isaac Asimov**, composer **Irving Berlin** and actors **Rudolph Valentino** and **Bella Lugosi**.

Ellis Island Immigration Museum

The majority of immigrants were underprivileged Europeans seeking economic and political freedom in the "New World". Upon entering New York Harbor, they were overwhelmed with excitement at the sight of the Statue of Liberty - the embodiment of the American Dream. For many, however, this moment was soon replaced by the reality of strict screening processes, which often meant detention or even deportation. What was called by some the "Island of Hope", became known by others as the "Island of Tears".

As the 20th century advanced, the number of immigrants arriving at Ellis Island sharply declined. When the immigration station closed in 1954, the site was abandoned and left to decay. During the early 1980s, **President Ronald Reagan** initiated a major renovation project to restore both the Statue of Liberty and Ellis Island as major national landmarks.

The **Statue of Liberty-Ellis Island Foundation** was formed as a private sector fund-raising effort to reach a $230 million goal. The largest restoration project of its kind in American history, it enabled Ellis Island to be reopened to the public on September 10, 1990.

Today, the focal point of a visit here is the **Ellis Island Immigration Museum**. Housed in the 100,000 square-foot main building, the museum is dedicated to providing a thorough history of the island's processing station and the significant role that immigration has played in America's development.

. . . Ellis Island

On the second floor, by the Great Hall, the statue of a young girl commemorates fifteen-year-old Annie Moore, from Ireland, who was the first immigrant to be processed at Ellis Island. She was welcomed amidst great festivity and celebration before she and her brothers were reunited with their parents, who had arrived a few years earlier.

The many exhibits utilize a variety of different media to convey the immigration experience. The photographic exhibit "**Through America's Gates**" chronicles the rigorous step-by-step process faced by would-be Americans.

On the third floor, there are a number of permanent exhibits such as "**Treasures from Home**" which

includes artifacts, personal belongings and clothing brought from the immigrants' home countries.

A library features taped reminiscences of immigrants and former employees of the station, sharing their

Baggage Room at the museum

own personal views and experiences of Ellis Island. An evocative half-hour documentary, "**Island of Hope/ Island of Tears**", was created by Oscar-winning filmmaker **Charles Guggenheim**. The film is shown daily, at no charge, and is presented twice every hour on a rotating schedule in two separate theaters.

A good way to make the most out of your visit to the Ellis Island Immigration Museum is to use the **audio tour**. Narrated by news anchorman **Tom Brokaw**, it guides you through the museum's highlights (it is also available in foreign languages). With *New York for less*, two people can take an audio tour for the price of one. You can pick them up the tour at the booth located to the left of the main entrance on the first floor of the building.

View of Manhattan from Ellis Island

On the grounds outside of the main building, the **American Immigrant Wall of Honor** was created to commemorate the immigrants, and was funded by their descendants. From the monument there are great views of the Manhattan skyline and the Statue of Liberty.

PRICES

There is no admission charge to the Ellis Island Immigration Museum.

DISCOUNT

2 audio tours for the price of 1 with voucher on page 271. Audio tours are also available in foreign languages.

South Street Seaport

Pace University
BROO
N ST
FULTON ST
SOUTH ST
HIGHWAY
19
South Stre
Seaport
Historic Dist
AL
PEARL ST
WATER ST
SOUTH ST
ST
E

ADDRESS

The South Street Historic District is centered around Fulton and South Streets.

Visitors' Center & Museum Shop: 12-14 Fulton Street
☎ 748-8600

For sailing reservations on the *Pioneer*, ☎ 748-8786.

DON'T MISS

An on-board look at the 1911 *Peking*, docked at Pier 16.

Although today the economic success of New York City is based on contributions from a wide range of industries, its initial fortune was largely the result of the success of its port.

Ideally placed both for European trans-Atlantic trade and, via the Hudson River and the Erie Canal, for commerce with the rest of America, New York Harbor quickly became the most important port in North America.

During the 19th century, the South Street Seaport area was the center of New York's maritime trade.

Piers at the South Street Seaport

South Street itself was known as the "street of ships".

After a long period of decline in the 20th century, it has now been fully restored to a seaport village, complete with refurbished 19th-century buildings, cobble-stoned streets and tall ships moored in the harbor.

This seaside village may seem somewhat out of place in such a busy city, but that is why New Yorkers flock here on their lunch breaks and after work to relax, shop or dine while enjoying great harbor views.

Schooner Pioneer against Lower Manhattan

Jutting over the East River, **Pier 17** (page 66) is a modern, enclosed pedestrian mall with three floors of shops and restaurants. Exterior stairways and outdoor wooden terraces offer spectacular views of Brooklyn, the Brooklyn Bridge, the historic ships in the harbor and the colossal skyscrapers of Lower Manhattan. You can also glimpse the second-longest suspension bridge in the world, the **Verrazano-Narrows Bridge** (page 237), which links Brooklyn and Staten Island.

Nearby, Seaport Liberty Cruises (page 220) and the Schooner Pioneer (page 55) depart from Pier 16.

At the **Fulton Fish Market** (page 62), eight million pounds of fish are sold every year, making it the largest fish market in the United States.

South Street Seaport Museum

Founded in 1967, the South Street Seaport Museum is comprised of exhibition galleries, historic art and archeological items and New York City's largest collection of restored early 19th-century buildings. Of these, the centerpiece redbrick Schermerhorn Row dates back to 1811-12. There are also historic ships, a maritime crafts center, museum stores, a library and a children's center – all contained within an 11-square-block landmark historic district.

South Street Seaport Museum

Exhibitions and public programs focus on the economic, social and cultural importance of New York's maritime heritage. Many of the exhibits offer a hands-on experience. At the re-created printing shop Bowne & Co. Stationers, for example, you can learn to use a 19th-century printing press.

On Pier 16, you can explore the cabins and decks of one of the world's largest fleets of historic ships. Built in 1911, the *Peking* is a 347-foot, four-masted steel vessel once used to carry cargo from the U.S. to South America. On board there is a 15-minute film, *Peking at Sea*, which allows you to see the ship in its oceanic environment.

The 1893 wooden fishing schooner, *Lettie G. Howard*, sponsors marine education programs. The *Wavertree*, an 1885 iron full-rigged ship, the *Ambrose*, a 1908 steel lightship and the *W.O. Decker*, a 1930 tugboat, are also located on Pier 16.

Built in 1885, the *Pioneer* is an iron cargo schooner which provides memorable cruises through New York Harbor. Daily sails are available from May through mid-September, and a 20% discount is offered to *New York for less* cardholders.

Admission tickets to the museum include entry to all galleries, historic ships, films, district tours and ship tours. Tickets can be purchased at the Museum Visitors' Center and the Pier 16 Ticketbooth. *New York for less* entitles you to two admissions for the price of one.

The Peking

HOURS

Apr-Sep: Mon-Wed and
Fri-Sun: 10am-6pm
Thu: 10am-8pm
Oct-Mar: Wed-Mon:
10am-5pm
Tue: closed

PRICES

Museum: Adult $6
Child free
Senior $5
Student $4

Pioneer: Adult $16
Child $6
Senior $13
Student $12

DISCOUNT

2 admissions to the museum for the price of 1 with voucher on page 271.

20% discount on any ticket for the schooner *Pioneer* with voucher on page 271.

10% discount in the museum shop with your *New York for less* card.

Fraunces Tavern Museum

In old New York, taverns were more than just drinking establishments – they were the center of social life.

During the Colonial and Revolutionary period, Samuel Fraunces owned and operated "The Queen's Head Tavern". In 1783, **George Washington**, who frequented the Queen's Head,

Fraunces Tavern Museum

delivered his heartfelt farewell speech to his army officers in its "Long Room". This room has been preserved in the style of an 18th-century tavern dining room and is open to visitors.

Located near Manhattan's financial district (on the only National Historic Landmark block below Wall Street), Fraunces Tavern Museum is housed in a restored 18th-century building and four adjacent 19th-century buildings.

From 1785-1787, this building housed the new nation's departments of Foreign Affairs (now called State), Treasury and War (currently Defense). Since then, it has been a mansion, post office, transportation hub, wax museum and even a dance studio.

Fraunces Tavern Museum

Fraunces Tavern Museum, founded in 1907, is committed to the study and interpretation of early American history and culture through a series of changing exhibitions, period rooms, tours, public programs and publications. There is also a constant schedule of programs for children, including special activities such as trying on costumes or learning to write with a quill pen.

Recent exhibitions and discussions have included "Myths of American History", an investigative look at history as portrayed in novels, films, on television and in history books, and "Much Depends on Dinner", a look at culinary customs in early New York.

The museum shop offers an interesting selection of early American gift items and books and gives a discount to *New York for less* cardholders.

ADDRESS

54 Pearl Street
☎ 425-1778

HOURS

Mon-Fri: 10am-4.45pm
Sat-Sun: 12noon-4pm

PRICES

Adult $2.50
Child $1
Senior $1
Student $1

DISCOUNT

2 admissions for the price of 1 with your *New York for less* card.

10% discount in the museum shop with your *New York for less* card.

Other Attractions . . .

The famed twin towers, which are known as Number One and Number Two, are certainly the best-known of the six buildings which comprise the **World Trade Center**. Built between 1966 and 1977, the complex is connected by an immense subterranean mall of shops and eateries (see page 69), as well as stations for the subway and PATH trains to New Jersey. For an incredible view of the city, ride the elevator to the observatory on the 107th floor of Number Two. Alternatively, you

The twin towers of the World Trade Center

can enjoy dinner or drinks at the recently re-opened Windows on the World restaurant at the top of Number One. *(Between Church Street and the West Side Highway, ☎ 435-4170. Observation deck: 9.30am-9.30pm or 11.30pm daily, depending on the season Adult $8, child $3, senior $3.50, student $8.)*

World Trade Center

Wall Street, 1922

The **New York Stock Exchange** started in the late 1700s with an agreement made by a small group of brokers who decided to trade only amongst themselves. Prior to this pact, trading occurred randomly on or near Wall Street. The NYSE has since grown into a formidable institution with a global effect on financial markets. Built in 1903, the present building's grand, neo-classical exterior is outstanding in the canyon of neighboring skyscrapers. Visitors can look out onto the action of the trading floor from a public viewing gallery. *(20 Broad Street, ☎ 656-5168. Mon-Fri: 9.15am-4pm. Sat-Sun: closed. Admission is free.)*

New York Stock Exchnage

"The Bull" on lower Broadway

The statue of George Washington on the front steps of **Federal Hall National Memorial** heralds the site where he took his oath of office as the first president of the United States in

. . . Other Attractions . . .

Federal Hall National Monument

1789. On the corner of Broad and Wall Streets, where Federal Hall stands, many of the most important events of 18th-century American history took place. It was here that the government of the newly formed United States began to function: Congress met for its first session in the original Federal Hall, the nation's first Capitol building. When the capital was moved to Philadelphia just a year later, the government of New York City moved into the building, using it as a City Hall. By the early 1800s, it became too small for the burgeoning bureaucracy of the largest city in the U.S. so the new City Hall (page 60) was built. The old Federal Hall was left to crumble and was eventually sold for scrap. The present building was built as the U.S. Customs House in 1842, in the Greek Revival style. It now houses an historical exhibit on the Constitution and is the place to pick up the Heritage Trails Walking Tours (page 225). *(26 Wall Street, ☎ 825-6870. Mon-Fri 9am-5pm. Sat-Sun: closed. Admission is free.)*

Trinity Church

Nearby, on Liberty Street, the imposing **Federal Reserve Bank** is the world's largest gold depository, and one of a dozen Federal Reserve banks nationwide. Currency printed here is identifiable by the letter B in the note's seal. Free guided tours are available four times a day, but reservations must be made 1-2 weeks in advance. *(33 Liberty Street, ☎ 720-6130. Tours: Mon-Fri: 10.30am, 11.30am, 1.30pm, 2.30pm. Sat-Sun: closed.)*

Federal Reserve Bank

Trinity Church

Trinity Church, which was the tallest structure in New York until the 1860s, is located at the western end of Wall Street. Its interior is an example of Gothic Revival architecture and its remarkable bronze doors, designed by Richard Morris Hunt, were modeled after Ghiberti's doors for the Florentine Baptistry in Italy. Captain Kidd is said to have loaned some equipment to help in the building of the church. This

...Other Attractions...

Episcopalian parish is one of the oldest in America, dating back to 1697. Classical concerts are often

given here and you can also attend services on Sundays at 11.15am. *(Broadway at Wall Street, ☎ 602-0872. Mon-Fri: 7am-6pm. Sat: 8am-4pm. Sun: 7am-4pm.)*

A few blocks north of Trinity Church on Broadway, **St. Paul's Chapel** is the oldest church building in Manhattan, surviving since 1766. Modeled after London's St.

St. Paul's Chapel

St. Paul's Chapel

Martin-in-the-Fields, it is perhaps most famous for being the site of George Washington's inaugural prayer service. The pew where he prayed has been preserved in his name. *(Broadway at Fulton Street, ☎ 602-0874. Mon-Fri and Sun: 10am-3pm. Sat: 10am-4pm.)*

St. Peter's Church

St. Peter's Church is the oldest Catholic parish in New York State, originating in 1785. The current church with its classical facade and Greek Revival style was constructed in 1838. *(16 Barclay at Church Street, ☎ 233-8355. Open for mass only.)*

Walking across the **Brooklyn Bridge** is a pleasure often overlooked by visitors to New York. Completed in 1883, the Brooklyn Bridge was the first to be made of steel. Its construction, which took 16 years, claimed the lives of at least 20 men, including chief architect John A. Roebling. The view of Manhattan, Brooklyn and the bridge itself, with its

Brooklyn Bridge, 1912

massive network of overhead cables, was described by poet Walt Whitman as the best medicine his soul had ever experienced. The walkway begins by City Hall Park and continues for about a mile before arriving in Brooklyn Heights (see page 228). The bridge originally linked what were then the separate cities of Manhattan and Brooklyn. Twin Gothic arches tower some 277 feet above the East River, anchoring what was once the world's largest suspension bridge. *(Chambers Street at City Hall Park. Open 24 hours.)*

Brooklyn Bridge

. . . Other Attractions . . .

City Hall

City Hall, built in 1812, is a charming example of early 19th-century American architecture. This Georgian-style structure was graced with marble on all sides except its north face because the architects underestimated the future growth of New York City and assumed that the city would never expand north of the building. You can visit City Hall during the hours listed below, or call for information about group tours. *(City Hall Park, below Chambers Street, ☎ 788-3071 (arts council), ☎ 788-7171 (group tours). Mon-Fri: 10am-4pm. Sat-Sun: closed. Admission is free.)*

City Hall

Constructed as headquarters for the thriving Woolworth 5 & 10 department stores, the 1913 **Woolworth Building** became New York's tallest structure, a position it held for 17 years. Nicknamed the Cathedral of Commerce, this $13.5 million dollar edifice still houses the headquarters of the Woolworth company. The lobby features caricatures of founder Frank W. Woolworth (who paid for the building in cash) and architect Cass Gilbert. The detail and design is spectacular and the lobby alone is worth a visit if you are nearby. *(233 Broadway. Open office hours.)*

Woolworth Building

The Shrine of Elizabeth Ann Seton is dedicated to the first American-born saint canonized by the Catholic Church. The house where she lived from 1801-1803 is a Federal-style building, curved to fit the shape of the road. Originally built in 1793, it is one of the few remaining examples of the early mansions of Lower Manhattan. *(7-8 State Street, ☎ 269-6865. Mon-Fri: 6:30am-4:30pm. Sun: 8am-6pm. Sat: closed. Masses are held daily.)*

Woolworth Building

Situated in Battery Park, **Castle Clinton National Monument** was built in the early 1800s as a defense against the recently expelled British. It never saw a battle, but over the years has instead been used as a

Shrine of Elizabeth Ann Seton

... Other Attractions ...

theater, an aquarium and, before the opening of Ellis Island, as an immigration center. In 1850, singer Jenny Lind, the "Swedish Nightingale", made her American debut here in front of an audience of over 5,000. Today, Castle Clinton features historical

displays and also acts as a visitors' center. It is also the place to buy tickets for the ferry to Liberty and Ellis Islands (pages 50-53). *(Battery Park, ☎ 344-7220. Mon-Sun: 8.30am-5pm.)*

Castle Clinton National Monument

Built in 1907, the **US Custom House** is a charming example of Beaux Arts architecture. Recently, the **Gustav Heye Center of the National Museum of the American Indian** has taken over three floors of the building. Part of the national Smithsonian Institute, the museum actively promotes the past and current cultures of the indigenous people of the Americas through fascinating exhibits and live performances. *(1 Bowling Green, ☎ 668-6624. Mon-Wed and Fri-Sun: 10am-5pm. Thu: 10am-8pm. Admission is free.)*

The **Staten Island Ferry** was started in 1810 by a young Staten Islander named Cornelius Vanderbilt. The ferry has carried commuters between the islands since and is a remarkably inexpensive way to get great views of New York Harbor and the Statue of Liberty. As for Vanderbilt, he went on to become one of the great 19th-century industrialists, making his immense fortune on the railroads. *(Whitehall Street, ☎ 806-5940. Mon-Sun: 24 hours a day. Ferries run every half hour. Round trip fare: 50¢.)*

In **Hanover Square**, a statue of Dutch mayor Abraham De Peyster stands near the house where he was born in 1657. At 1 Hanover Square, the brownstone **India House** was once the location of the New York Cotton Exchange, but is now home to Harry Cipriani's famous restaurant Harry's of Hanover Square (page 66). *Hanover Square at Pearl and Hanover Street.)*

The waterside **Vietnam Veterans' Plaza** pays tribute to veterans with a memorial wall of green glass.

Castle Clinton National Monument

Castle Clinton National Monument

National Museum of the American Indian

National Museum of the American Indian

Staten Island Ferry

. . . Other Attractions

Hanover Square

Designed by Maya Lin, it is etched with letters and writings from the veterans to their families. *(Water an South Streets.)*

Next to the Staten Island Ferry, the **Battery Maritime Building** once served as a terminal for ferries to Brooklyn, but is now used by the U.S. Coast Guard for service to Governor's Island. *(11 South Street. Closed to the public.)*

Statue of Dutch mayor Abraham de Peyster

Once the ticketing center for the Cunard passenger ship company, the magnificent **Cunard Building** is now a U.S. Post Office. The Great Hall has a colorful domed ceiling, with frescoes and detailed murals. *(25 Broadway, ☎ 363-9490. Mon-Fri: 8am-6pm. Sat-Sun: closed.)*

City Hall Park

Vietnam Veterans' Plaza

When **Fulton Fish Market** was established in the early 1800s, the fish arrived fresh every day from boats in the harbor. Today they arrive by land, but are still sold to many of the city's best restaurants. If you get up early enough (or stay up late enough), you can watch the traders in action any day of the week from midnight to about 8am. You can also take a guided tour of America's biggest fish market. *(South Street at Beekman Street, ☎ 748-8590 for tours.)*

Lower Manhattan street mural

Fulton Fish Market

Heritage Trails New York offers walking tours which tell the interesting history of Lower Manhattan and its sights. The map on the following pages shows exactly what sights are covered on the tours. On page 225 you will find more information about Heritage Trails New York and how to pick up the tours which originate at Federal Hall National Monument.

Open Spaces

Named after the battery of cannons which stood to protect the city, **Battery Park** is now the hub of downtown offshore activity. Ferries to the Statue of

Liberty and Ellis Island (pages 50-53) depart from here, and the Staten Island Ferry (page 61) is nearby.

Just north of Battery Park, the triangular **Bowling Green** was the city's first public park, established in 1733. It

Battery Park

Battery Park

has been used as a cattle market, a place for public bowling and today is once again a small green park. In 1776, after the signing of the Declaration of Independence, a demonstration took place here and rioters did some renovating of their own, removing the statue of Britain's King George III and the royal crowns that once topped the surviving fence.

One of the best recent redevelopment projects has been the major overhaul of the area along the Hudson River, including a paved path which has become a favorite place for joggers, rollerbladers and office workers out for a lunchtime stroll. Originating at Battery Park, the riverside esplanade provides views of the Statue of Liberty and Ellis Island and is lined with benches, trees and neatly landscaped borders.

Esplanade along the Hudson River

Continuing north, **Hudson River Park** is an open grassy expanse along the once seedy and run-down waterfront. Instead of decrepit piers and empty docks, there is now a large park which, on warm afternoons, is packed with New Yorkers sunbathing or playing ball – a secret Central Park for the downtown set.

Hudson River Park

Hudson River Park

By the Brooklyn Bridge, the early 19th-century **City Hall Park** was the place where the Declaration of Independence was read to Washington and his troops. The park contains multiple subway stations, a working fountain flanked by colorful flower gardens, and chess tables on which fierce competitions rage at lunch hour.

Heritage Trails New York . . .

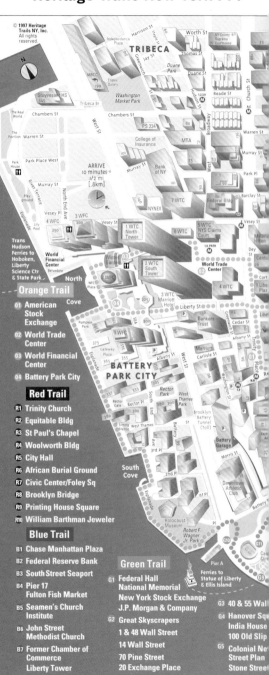

DON'T MISS

Heritage Trails New York (page 223) was created to enable visitors to discover the history and sites of Lower Manhattan. Either take one of the guided tours or explore the routes on your own by following the colored dots along the sidewalks and streets.

ADDRESS

Heritage Trails Visitor Center: Federal Hall National Memorial 26 Wall Street
☎ 269-1500

Orange Trail

O1 American Stock Exchange
O2 World Trade Center
O3 World Financial Center
O4 Battery Park City

Red Trail

R1 Trinity Church
R2 Equitable Bldg
R3 St Paul's Chapel
R4 Woolworth Bldg
R5 City Hall
R6 African Burial Ground
R7 Civic Center/Foley Sq
R8 Brooklyn Bridge
R9 Printing House Square
R10 William Barthman Jeweler

Blue Trail

B1 Chase Manhattan Plaza
B2 Federal Reserve Bank
B3 South Street Seaport
B4 Pier 17
Fulton Fish Market
B5 Seamen's Church Institute
B6 John Street Methodist Church
B7 Former Chamber of Commerce
Liberty Tower

Green Trail

G1 Federal Hall National Memorial
New York Stock Exchange
J.P. Morgan & Company
G2 Great Skyscrapers
1 & 48 Wall Street
14 Wall Street
70 Pine Street
20 Exchange Place
G3 40 & 55 Wall
G4 Hanover Sq
India House
100 Old Slip
G5 Colonial N
Street Plan
Stone Street

...Walking Tours Map

PRICES

Guided walking tours:
Adult $14
Child (7-12) $7,
under 6 free
Senior $10
Student $3

Self-guided tour book: $5

DISCOUNT

Guided walking tours:
Adult $3 off
Child $2 off when
accompanied by an adult

Self-guided tour book:
Special price of $2

Eating and Drinking

Eating in the **Financial District** generally means take-out and fast food. Many of the restaurants here are casual places serving basic "pub grub" alongside a vast selection of beers. After 5pm, Wall Streeters flock to the pubs, where they socialize and take advantage of the multitude of "happy hours" where drink specials are often served with complimentary snacks and bar food. One of the best-known after-work haunts is **John Street Bar and Grill** (page 68) where early evening drink specials draw a full house almost every night of the week.

Lower Manhattan Streets

INSIDER'S TIP

To avoid overpriced food at the Statue of Liberty, Ellis Island and on the ferry, stop by one of the delicatessens or pizzerias near Battery Park before boarding (see pages 67-68 for discounts).

Throughout the downtown area, there are also plenty of typical New York deli's which offer hot and cold buffets (selling food by the pound), sandwiches and just about anything else you might find in a grocery store. Pizzerias sell pizza by the slice (see page 68), hot breads and other quick and inexpensive items that provide sustenance during a busy day of sightseeing.

The food court on the third floor of **Pier 17** allows you to eat your meal in the large cafeteria-style dining room, or to sit outside on the deck overlooking Brooklyn and the Brooklyn Bridge with the seaport down below. For a treat, dine at **Liberty Cafe** (page 67), where you can enjoy both the food *and* the views.

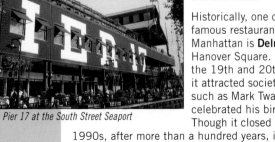

Pier 17 at the South Street Seaport

Historically, one of the most famous restaurants in Manhattan is **Delmonico's** in Hanover Square. Throughout the 19th and 20th centuries it attracted society figures such as Mark Twain, who celebrated his birthday here. Though it closed in the early 1990s, after more than a hundred years, it is expected to open again soon, freshly refurbished. Harry Cipriani, famous for his New York and Venetian restaurants, operates **Harry's of Hanover Square** in the old India House *(1 Hanover Square, 425-3412)*.

Liberty Cafe

Contemporary American

Pier 17, Third Floor
☎ 406-1111

Average meal: $20-25
for less discount: 25%
AM/MC/VS/DS

HOURS

Mon-Sun: 11.30am-
12midnight

Situated on the third floor of Pier 17 at the South Street
Seaport, Liberty Cafe has great views of the harbor, the
Statue of Liberty and the Manhattan skyline. Try seafood
specialties like Atlantic salmon or grilled calamari salad.

Mercantile Grill

American

126 Pearl Street
☎ 482-1221

Average meal: $10-15
for less discount: 25%
AM/VS/MC/DC

HOURS

Mon-Wed: 11am-10pm
Thu-Fri: 11am-12midnight
Sat: 11.30am-6pm
Sun: closed

This charming pub-style grill features exposed brick
walls and an oak bar. Wholesome Irish and American
dishes are served. The blackened chicken sandwich and
the *rigatoni á la vodka* are recommended.

The Beekman

International

15-17 Beekman Street
☎ 732-7333

Average meal: $10-15
for less discount: 25%
AM/MC/VS/DC/DS

HOURS

Mon-Fri: 10.30am-2am
Sat-Sun: closed

The Beekman is close to the Brooklyn Bridge, City Hall
and South Street Seaport. Classic cuisine is served in a
friendly, old-world pub atmosphere. Try favorites like
corned beef, *shrimp fra diablo* or *sole française*.

HOURS

Mon-Fri: 11am-9pm
Sat: 12noon-10pm
Sun: closed

HOURS

Mon-Sun: 11.30am-11pm

HOURS

Mon-Fri: 7.30am-7.30pm
Sat: 11am-5pm
Sun: closed

Bennie's Thai Cafe

Tha

88 Fulton Stree
☎ 587-893(

Average meal: $10-1!
for less discount: 25%
AM

Bennie's, located near the South Street Seaport, is a
casual restaurant where you can find authentic Thai and
vegetarian cuisine at excellent prices. Specialty dishes
include the *pad-Thai* and *tom-yum*.

John Street Bar and Grill

Americar

17 John Stree
☎ 349-3278

Average meal: $10-1!
for less discount: 25%
AM/MC/VS

This roomy restaurant and pub serves American fare in
a casual setting. Enjoy hearty dishes and pub fare like
buffalo wings, burgers and sandwiches. There is a wide
variety of international beers, both bottled and on tap.

Pranzo Pizzeria

Pizzeria

34 Water Stree
☎ 344-8068

Average meal: $5-1(
for less discount: 25%
AM/MC/VS

Situated near Battery Park, Pranzo is a good place for
traditional NYC pizza. Visit this pizzeria before boarding
the ferry for Liberty and Ellis Islands. Hot and cold
sandwiches, pastas and salads are also available.

Shopping

o New Yorkers, downtown shopping conjures up the
vord "bargain". Two of the best discount stores in
own are located here: **Syms** (*42 Trinity Place, ☎ 797-
199*), a warehouse discounter, and **Century
1** (*22 Cortlandt Street, ☎ 227-9092*), a
epartment store which carries everything
rom watches to perfume and designer
lothing – all at a discount. Extremely
opular with the Wall Street crowd, these
tores can be extremely crowded at lunch
me and after work.

lso scattered below Chambers Street, west
f Broadway, are a variety of discount stores
arrying excess stock and buy-outs at big
avings. These are not, however, the kind of
laces to shop if you are looking for
omething specific as they have limited
elections.

World Financial Center

or a more pleasant (and perhaps more
xpensive) shopping experience, visit the
tores around the **South Street Seaport** and
n **Pier 17**. Branches of familiar chains such as **J.
rew**, **Laura Ashley** and **The Sharper Image** can be
ound here, as well as interesting specialty and gift
hops. The **South Street Seaport's Museum Shop**
page 55), which offers a discount to *New York for less*
ardholders, has a selection of items that make good

C Cigars in the World Trade Center

souvenirs or gifts.

Another place to shop
downtown is at the **World
Financial Center** in
Battery Park City. Here
you will find major stores
like **Barneys New York** (*☎
945-1600*) and **Ann Taylor**,
as well as specialty shops

*Pier 17 and the South
Street Seaport*

ke **Godiva Chocolatier**, **Caswell-Massey** and **Gap Kids**.

he concourse shopping level underneath the **World
rade Center** also houses popular chain stores like the
he **Body Shop**, **The Gap** and **The Limited** together
rith many independent shops and eateries, in a giant
ubterranean shopping mall. One of the better
pecialty shops, **QC Cigars** (page 70), has an extensive
ange of cigars and accessories and offers a discount
o *New York for less* cardholders.

World Financial Center

or electronics, computers and music, **J&R Music
Vorld** (*23 Park Row, ☎ 732-8600*) is reliable, has a huge
election of merchandise and is competitively priced.

HOURS

Mon-Fri: 7am-8pm
Sat: 12noon-5pm
Sun: hours vary, call ahead

QC Cigars

Cigars & Accessories

**1 World Travel Center
Concourse shopping level
☎ 938-5834**

for less discount: 20%
AM/MC/VS

QC is located in the World Trade Center on the shopping
mall level. The store stocks a fine selection of traditional
favorites and new cigar brands. The humidors and other
cigar accessories make great souvenirs or gifts.

HOURS

Mon-Fri: 8am-5.30pm
Sat-Sun: closed

Ray's Jewelers

Jewelry

**3 Hanover Square
☎ 425-2250**

for less discount: 20% off
full price and sale items
AM/MC/VS/DC/DS

Ray's has been offering excellent value in jewelry for over
25 years. It sells 14-carat gold, watches, diamonds,
sterling silver and much more. Its location is close to
the downtown attractions and Wall Street.

HOURS

Mon-Wed: 7.30am-6.30pm
Thu-Fri: 7.30am-7pm
Sat: 11am-5pm
Sun: closed

Eclipse

Men's Clothing

**74 Broad Street
☎ 269-0521**

for less discount: 20%
AM/MC/VS/DS

Located in the Financial District, Eclipse caters to Wall
Street businessmen. The shop stocks a complete range
of men's clothing and suits. Jackets, coats, belts and
other accessories are also sold.

Soho, Chinatown and the Lower East Side

Introduction . . .

During the 19th century, **Soho**, the area <u>SO</u>uth of <u>HO</u>uston Street (pronounced "HOWston"), was an industrial district, filled with warehouses and factories. Today, it is overrun with chic galleries, boutiques, trendy bistros and bars (see pages 82 and 87).

Ethiopian Art from the Museum for African Art

The birthplace of industrial and pop art during the 1960s, Soho is still famous for its world-renowned art scene. **West Broadway**, the area's main thoroughfare, is home to some of the most important commercial galleries in New York City. Recently, however, a slow migration of some major galleries to Chelsea is threatening to split New York's art world into two separate spheres.

Soho also contains some well-known museums, the majority of which exhibit modern art. On Broadway, the **Guggenheim Museum Soho** (page 76) exhibits works with a focus on technology. Within a few blocks, you can also find the **New Museum of Contemporary Art** (page 78), the **Alternative Museum** (page 78) and the **Museum for African Art** (page 76) which displays a wide variety of African and African-American art, including sculpture and costumes.

DON'T MISS

Take a break from shopping in Soho to check out the cast-iron architecture that lines the streets, especially along Greene and Prince Streets.

Besides its famed art scene, Soho is also notable for having the world's largest collection of **cast-iron buildings**. Erected between 1860 and 1890 in the American-Industrial style, these iron buildings were shaped and painted with exquisite detail, mimicking Italianate, neo-Grecian and Victorian Gothic styles. At 84 Leonard Street, you can see a cast-iron building designed by **John Bogurdas**, inventor of this unique architecture.

Soho cast-iron buildings

In addition to spacious interiors and large windows, cast-iron architectural highlights include large iron

. . . Introduction . . .

ading bays and sidewalks covered with raised
rcular glass disks to let light into basement areas.

e original purpose of these structures was to house
e factories and sweatshops which were abundant in
is part of town. When these closed in the 1950s,
e area became what the City Club called in 1962,
he wasteland of New York".

e abandoned cast-iron buildings provided well-lit
ft spaces that became very desirable to artists.
any of the buildings were renovated, and a program
redevelopment was pioneered by residents and
evelopers who officially made the neighborhood an
storic area in 1973. Throughout the 1970s,
entrification continued to
ansform this former
dustrial slum into the
gh-priced, cosmopolitan
ot spot it is today.

*A realistic mural of a cast-iron building painted
on the side of a plain brick one*

particular architectural
terest, the **St. Nicholas
otel** *(521-523 Broadway)*
as built in the mid-1800s
a luxury hotel. Though
no longer exists, remains
its former glory can still
seen in its marble
terior.

ist south of Soho,
ibeca, the TRIangle
Elow CAnal is essentially
residential area favored by the likes of John F.
ennedy, Jr. and Robert DeNiro. In addition to his
ibeca Film Center *(325 Greenwich Street)*, DeNiro is
-owner of a collection of restaurants throughout the
eighborhood, many of which are frequented by
eople in the film industry.

odern Tribeca offers a glimpse of what Soho was like
ior to its current commercialization. When Soho's
al-estate prices skyrocketed during the late 1970s,
tists, photographers and other creative types
igrated to this previously undeveloped area, making
se of its large converted loft spaces to live and work.

ist west of Greenwich Street, numbers 37-41
arrison Street comprise a surviving row of early 18th-
entury Federal-style townhouses, beautifully restored
id slightly out-of-place amongst the industrial-style
uildings that surround it.

. . . Introduction . . .

Part of Tribeca's charm lies in its experimental galleries, small theaters and live music venues. To find out more about Tribeca's happenings and history, pick up the area's free monthly newspaper – the "**Tribeca Trib**".

Sidewalk dining in Little Italy

Despite Tribeca's recent revitalization, corporate America, with its coffeeshop, book and clothing store chains, has not yet invaded this territory. Instead, you will find an assortment of cozy coffee spots, "local" bars and some of the city's best restaurants (see page 82-83).

The areas east of Soho and Tribeca are ethnic enclaves that represent the lasting impact of immigration on New York. Population shifts have certainly changed the faces of these neighborhoods, but their original character remains.

Chinatown streets

Manhattan's **Chinatown** contains one of the largest Asian communities in the western world. The area centered around **Mott Street** is populated by more than 150,000 Chinese (mostly from Hong Kong), Taiwanese, Vietnamese, Thai and other Asian communities. All of these cultures are represented by a multitude of authentic restaurants (see page 82-83) offering some of the most delicious and inexpensive cuisine in town.

INSIDER'S TIP

For a bigger and more authentic Little Italy, visit the Belmont section of the Bronx (see page 231), a short walk from the Bronx Zoo and the Botanical Gardens (page 232).

Confucius Plaza, *(Bowery and Division Street)* is marked by a big stone statue of the ancient Chinese philosopher. Nearby, at Chatham Square, the **Kimlau War Memorial** is dedicated to the Chinese who were killed pursuing freedom and democracy in American wars.

Little Italy

Buddhist temples abound, including the **Eastern States Buddhist Temple of America** (page 79). Around the corner, on Bayard Street, the **Wall of Democracy** posts newspaper clippings and political writings about the political and social situation in China.

Observe the signs on the buildings and listen to the

. . . Introduction

conversations of the locals. You will realize that the area is completely self-sufficient, and that over half of its residents do not speak any English at all. The architecture also reflects the Chinese style – even the phone boxes are shaped to resemble Chinese pagodas.

In January and February, the streets swell with the festivities of **Chinese New Year**. Chinatown also becomes a focal point around the Fourth of July, when it supplies (illegal) fireworks to celebrants from all parts of the city and beyond.

Lower East Side, 1936.

Little Italy is slowly disappearing as

Tenement buildings

Chinatown expands into it, but **Mulberry Street** remains intact. The multitude of restaurants (see page 82-83) that run its length are the main reason to visit.

During the **San Gennaro Festival**, held each September, Mulberry Street is brought to life with food stalls, games and entertainment in a carnival-like atmosphere. If you can tolerate the crowds, you can sample Italian specialties such as fried dough or pastries.

DON'T MISS

A chance to catch a New York neighborhood in the process of gentrification – the Lower East Side (especially along Ludlow Street, below Howston) is a great place to shop and explore the streets before it is colonized by corporate America's stores and restaurants.

The character of the **Lower East Side** has been shaped by the millions of Russian and Eastern European Jews who settled the area in the late 19th and early 20th centuries. The **Lower East Side Tenement Museum** (see page 77) provides a fascinating history of these settlers and their subsequent impact on America, as well as a glimpse of what living conditions were like in the crowded tenement buildings, many of which still stand. Today, the area is only 10-15% Jewish, but many cultural institutions remain, including historic synagogues and distinct eating establishments (see page 83).

Artist Marco at work in his Lower East Side store

In recent years, a progressive, young community has formed on the Lower East Side and a number of lively shops, restaurants and bars have sprung up (see page 88).

Attractions . . .

Guggenheim Museum Soho

The Guggenheim Museum Soho is the downtown branch of the Solomon R. Guggenheim Museum. Opened to the public in 1992, it is located in a 19th-century landmark building in Soho's Cast-Iron Historic District. Designed by renowned architect Arata Isozaki, this unique gallery space features special exhibitions that complement those at the uptown Guggenheim.

Expanded and renovated in June 1996, the Guggenheim Museum Soho has a new focus on technology and the arts. With the support of German telecommunications carrier Deutsche Telekom A.G., four galleries on the main floor have been reconstructed and dedicated primarily to the presentation of multimedia art.

Additional exhibitions continue to present contemporary art, along with the Guggenheim's permanent collection.

Guggenheim Museum Soho

Private guided tours, available in English and other languages, focus on the museum's art, architecture and special exhibitions. *(575 Broadway, ☎ 423-3500. Wed-Fri and Sun: 11am-6pm. Sat: 11am-8pm. Mon-Tue: closed. Adult $8, child free, senior $5, student $5. 2 admissions for the price of 1 with voucher on page 271.)*

The Museum for African Art, founded in 1984, aims to increase the public's understanding and appreciation of the diversity and richness of African cultures. It educates through a variety of programs, including music and dance performances, storytelling series and film screenings.

Museum for African Art

The museum is one of the world's foremost publishers on the subject of African Art and publishes informative catalogues for its past and current exhibits.

The museum has one of the best displays of African art in the U.S. Exhibits change at least twice a year and feature decorative and ceremonial art, costumes, masks and other artistic representations of culture.

Museum for African Art

The museum's interior was designed by acclaimed

. . . Attractions

tist Maya Lin, who is perhaps most famous for her
eation of the Vietnam Veterans' Memorial
Washington, D.C.

the museum shop, you can find an
ssortment of books, textiles and crafts, all
which can be purchased at a discount with
ur *New York for less* card. *(593 Broadway,
966-1313. Tue-Fri: 10.30am-5.30pm. Sat-Sun:
2noon-6pm. Mon: closed. Adult $5, child
2.50, senior $2.50, student $2.50. 2 admissions
r the price of 1 and 10% discount at the
useum shop with your New York for less card.)*

*Shop at the Museum for
African Art*

The Lower East Side Tenement Museum
is located in an 1863 tenement
uilding, which has been designated a National
istoric Landmark.

stands as a powerful reminder of the challenges and
ardships faced by the millions of immigrants who
ame to America during the late 19th and early 20th
enturies. After passing through Ellis Island (pages
2-53), many of the new arrivals settled on the Lower
ast Side.

resently, two apartments have been restored in an
fort to chronicle the lives of their former tenants:
e Gumpertzes, a German-Jewish family from the
870s, and the Baldizzis, an Italian-Catholic family
om the 1930s.

*Lower East Side
Tenement Museum*

renovation in 1997 will lead to
e presentation of two new family
partments. The first is an Eastern
uropean Jewish family of 1918,
nd the second is a Sephardic
ewish family. The latter will host
e museum's first "hands-on"
partment in which visitors can see
hat it would have been like to be a
ember of an immigrant family.

*Preserved room at the Lower East Side
Tenement Museum*

uided tours, exhibits,
erformances and media
resentations recount and preserve the lives of the
eople who lived here between 1863 and 1935,
umbering close to 10,000 and coming from over 20
ations. *(90 Orchard Street, ☎ 431-0233. Gallery: Tue-Fri:
2noon-5pm. Sat-Sun: 11am-5pm. Mon: closed. Tours:
ue-Fri: 1pm, 2pm, 3pm. Sat-Sun: 11am-4:15pm, every 45
inutes. Gallery: free. Tours: adult $8, child $6, senior $6,
udent $6. 2 tours for the price of 1 and 10% discount at
e museum shop with voucher on page 271.)*

Other Attractions . . .

The New Museum of Contemporary Art is the younger version of the Museum of Modern Art, displaying the latest in the contemporary art scene. The museum houses no permanent collection but instead showcases the works of innovative contemporary artists. *(583 Broadway, ☎ 219-1222. Tue-Fri and Sun: 12noon-6pm. Mon: closed. Sat: 12noon-8pm. Adult $4, child free, senior $3, student $3, artist $3.)*

Immigrant family apartment at the Lower East Side Tenement Museum

Across the street, the **Alternative Museum** specializes in avant garde works of art. It emphasizes socio-political consciousness and vision in art. *(594 Broadway, 4th floor, ☎ 966-4444. Tue-Sat: 11am-6pm. Sun-Mon: closed. Suggested admission $3.)*

The New York City Fire Museum displays a fine collection of 18th- and 19th-century fire fighting memorabilia and equipment. Tours of the 1904 firehouse and its collection are given by New York City firefighters. *(278 Spring Street, ☎ 691-1303. Tue-Sat: 10am-4pm. Sun-Mon: closed. Suggested admission $4.)*

New Museum of Contemporary Art

The Clocktower Gallery, just north of City Hall Park in Tribeca, is home to the Institute for Contemporary Art. You can still climb inside the tower itself, catch a view of downtown Manhattan and watch the workings of the clock that casts its glow over Broadway at night. *(108 Leonard Street, ☎ 233-1096. Mon-Fri: 10am-6pm. Sat-Sun: closed. Admission is free.)*

New Museum of Contemporary Art

New York City Fire Museum

A.I.R. Gallery has been dedicated to showcasing women artists for over 20 years. *(40 Wooster Street, ☎ 966-0799. Tue-Sat: 11am-6pm. Sun-Mon: closed. Admission is free.)*

The prestigious **Gagosian Gallery** is run by Larry Gagosian, who has another eponymous gallery uptown (page 196) on Madison Avenue. Both have featured many contemporary and well-known works by artists

Clocktower Gallery

. . . Other Attractions . . .

such as Jasper Johns and Roy Lichtenstein. *(136 Wooster Street, ☎ 228-2828. Tue-Sat: 10am-6pm. Sun-Mon: closed. Admission is free.)*

420 West Broadway contains six separate galleries including some of Soho's best known names. One of these, **Leo Castelli**, was the headquarters for pop art during the 1960s and is now a haven for new artists. *(420 West Broadway, ☎ 431-5160. Tue-Sat: 10am-6pm. Sun-Mon: closed. Admission is free.)*

420 West Broadway

NY Earth Room is Walter de Maria's innovative 1977 gallery which features 140 tons of intricately sculpted soil. *(141 Wooster Street, ☎ 473-8072. Wed-Sat: 12noon-6pm. Sun-Tue: closed. Admission is free.)*

On Greene Street, between Canal and Grand Streets, from number 8 to number 34, is the longest stretch of cast-iron buildings in the world. Contained within the block at numbers 28-30 stands the so-called **Queen of Greene Street**. Her decorative features include columns, dormers, window arches and a tall mansard roof. Further up the block, at numbers 72-76, stands the **King of Greene Street** – five stories tall, replete with Corinthian-style columns. Both were created by a master of cast-iron design, Isaac Duckworth. *(8-34 and 72-76 Greene Street.)*

Alternative Museum

The recently refurbished **Haughwout Building**, known as the "Parthenon of cast iron", was constructed in 1857 for Edward Haughwout's fine china and glassware company. The exterior was inspired by a Venetian palazzo, while the interior boasted the world's first commercial passenger elevator, an invention which would later help make the skyscraper possible. *(488 Broadway.)*

New York Earth Room

The open doors of the **Eastern States Buddhist Temple of America** permit a glimpse of over 100 gold Buddhas glimmering amongst candles and incense. *(64b Mott Street, ☎ 966-6229. Mon-Sun: 9am-7pm.)*

Old St. Patrick's Cathedral, in Little Italy, was constructed in 1863 to replace the original building of 1809, which was destroyed by fire. In 1878, the archdiocese moved uptown to St. Patrick's Cathedral on Fifth Avenue (page 154). *(263 Mulberry Street, ☎ 226-8075. Open for mass only.)*

Queen of Greene Street

. . . Other Attractions

The **Police Building**, west of Mulberry on Center Street, is a gigantic structure that was built to house the police department in 1909. Today, underneath its impressive dome, some well-known celebrities and supermodels live in the building's luxury co-operative apartments. *(240 Center Street. Closed to the public.)*

Police Building

Originally founded in 1899 to make kosher wines for the Jewish immigrants who populated the area, **Schapiro's Winery** still ferments and bottles over 30 different varieties of wine. You can tour the last remaining operational winery in New York City and taste this thick, sweet wine described as "extra heavy" on the bottles' labels *(126 Rivington Street, ☎ 674-4404. Mon-Thu: 10am-5pm. Fri: 10am-2pm. Sun: 11am-4pm. Sat: closed. Free tours Sun: 11am-4pm.)*

When the **Eldridge Street Synagogue** first opened its doors in 1887 it was the pride of the neighborhood. Its interior was richly decorated and its stained glass windows were spectacular. A decreasing congregation cut the need for such a large synagogue and its doors were closed in the 1930s. A large-scale restoration project is now underway, and tours offer a glimpse of the ongoing renovation as well as a ten-minute film about the synagogue. *(12 Eldridge Street, ☎ 219-0888. Tours: Tue and Thu: 11.30am and 2.30pm. Sun: 11am-4pm, every hour. Mon, Wed and Fri-Sat: closed. Adult $4, child $2.50, senior $2.50, student $2.50.)*

Police Building

Eldridge Street Synagogue

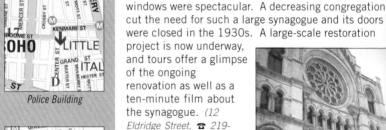

Eldridge Street Synagogue

Nearby, on Norfolk Street, the **Congregation Anshe Chesed** is New York's oldest synagogue building, though it is no longer used. Dating back to 1849, it was originally built to seat close to 1,500. *(172-176 Norfolk Street.)*

The **First Shearith Israel Graveyard** is the permanent home for a Jewish community dating back to the late 1600s. *(55-57 St. James Place.)*

Open Spaces

Washington Market Park *(Greenwich and Chambers Streets)*, in west Tribeca, is an ideal children's park – complete with a playground and sandbox. A great time to visit is during the evening concerts held on the bandstand during the summer. A large variety of farm-fresh foods can be found at the greenmarket, which takes place in front of the park on Greenwich Street several times a week.

Washington Market Park

Rollerblade, bike or simply stroll along the riverside on a paved path that continues from Battery Park (page 63) all the way to 14th Street in the West Village. Benches line the pathway and provide a cool respite from the hustle of the city. Street vendors park along the route, hoping to tempt the scores of rollerbladers with an ice cream or a lemonade.

Washington Market Park

Columbus Park

In the heart of Chinatown, **Columbus Park** is the only open space you will find amongst the narrow windy roads which surround it. Early in the morning, residents practice Tai Chi here and all day long there are games of Chinese Mah Jong and palm-readers giving advice to superstitious customers. It is difficult to imagine that this quiet park was once a dangerous slum. In the 1800s, even the police avoided the area, where levels of crime were so high that a murder a day was not uncommon.

Columbus Park

Sara D. Roosevelt Park is less a park than a strip of green running north-south between Chrystie and Forsyth Streets, from Canal to Houston Streets. This area can

Palm-readers in Columbus Park

become dangerous at night, but is a good place to take a break from daytime sightseeing and shopping in Chinatown and the Lower East Side.

Eating and Drinking

Both Soho and Tribeca have to their credit a number of excellent restaurants offering a wide range of international cuisine.

West Broadway, Soho's busiest street, is packed with lively cafés and restaurants. One of the best, **Caffe Novecento** (page 84), gives a discount to *New York for less* cardholders. Further south, in Tribeca, **Basset** (page 83) offers fresh coffee, desserts and homemade American cooking.

Once the center of New York's poultry and dairy trades, Tribeca is now the proud host of some of the finest restaurants in the world. New York diners recently mourned the loss of the city's top-ranked restaurant, **Bouley**, which closed after ten years. Nonetheless, this region retains its allure and association with fantastic dining experiences.

Chinatown Shopping

Mott Street

Chinatown offers a vast array of Asian cuisine at over 200 restaurants, including Szechuan, Hunan, Malaysian, Thai and Vietnamese. The main concentration of Chinese restaurants centers around **Mott Street**, while other Asian cuisines tend to be scattered along the surrounding streets.

Even the ice cream shops echo the neighborhood's ethnicity with flavors such as green tea, ginger and lychee making an appearance in cases normally stocked with vanilla and chocolate.

Chinatown markets draw residents from all over New York who come for the incredibly fresh seafood and vegetables, offered at remarkable prices.

Italian Pastries at Sambuca's Cafe in Little Italy

Vegetarians will need to tread carefully in these parts, however, since restaurants serve genuine regional dishes which may be unfamiliar. A "vegetable" dish may arrive bathed in a meat sauce, unless you clearly specify (in your best Cantonese, of course). To be on the safe side, there are a few strictly vegetarian restaurants, including **Tiengarden** (page 86).

Little Italy's **Mulberry Street** is crammed with cafés, restaurants and specialty shops. Some of the most

Eating and Drinking

authentic restaurants, like **Rocky's** (page 86), are often a little off the beaten path. Sidewalk cafés offer a variety of coffee, incredible Italian desserts and pastries. Some of them, like **Sambuca's Cafe** (page 86), make everything fresh on the premises.

On the Lower East Side, a number of trendy bistros have recently moved in beside long-established kosher delicatessens and restaurants. **Ratner's** *(138 Delancy Street, ☎ 677-5588)* was established in 1905 and remains one of the most famous kosher delis in New York.

There are also specialty stores which offer everything from wine and bialys to matzoh and knishes. Many of these have been around for decades.

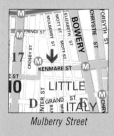

Mulberry Street

 Basset

American / Coffee & Tea Shop

123 West Broadway
☎ **349-1662**

Average meal: $10-15
for less discount: 25%
AM/MC/VS/DC/DS

At this country café in Tribeca, you can have fresh coffee and desserts, or enjoy homemade American fare with a southern flavor. The shrimp and sausage jambalaya and daily soups are highly recommended.

HOURS

Mon-Fri: 7.30am-9pm
Sat: 9am-6pm
Sun brunch: 9am-5pm

 **Barocco**

Italian

301 Church Street
☎ **431-1445**

Average meal: $20-25
for less discount: 25%
AM/MC/VS

Visit Barocco after sightseeing in bordering Soho, Chinatown or Tribeca. It serves modern Italian cuisine in a casually elegant atmosphere. Try the delicious *ravioli verdi* or the whole roast sea bass.

HOURS

Mon-Fri: 6pm-11pm
Sat: 6pm-10.30pm
Sun: closed

HOURS

Mon-Fri: 10am-2am
Sat: 10am-4am
Sun: closed

Caffe Novecento

Continental / Brazilian

343 West Broadway
☎ **925-4706**

Average meal: $15-20
for less discount: 25%
AM/MC/VS/DC

This chic, European-style restaurant is located in the heart of lively Soho. Enjoy dining and people-watching in this modern bi-level eatery. Chef's specialties include *empanadas* Novecento and *milanesa de carne*.

HOURS

Mon-Sun: 11am-11pm

Mao Mao

Chinese

143 Chambers Street
☎ **227-7399**

Average meal: $15-20
for less discount: 25%
AM/MC/VS/DC

Mao-Mao is located on Chambers Street in lower Tribeca, not far from the World Trade Center. It serves authentic Szechuan vegetarian and non-vegetarian dishes. The butterfly shrimp and triple delight are recommended.

HOURS

Mon-Fri: 11am-8pm
Sat-Sun: closed

Norma's

Continental

95 Duane Street
☎ **962-8350**

Average meal: $10-15
for less discount: 25%
AM/MC/VS

This Tribeca restaurant has been serving homemade American and continental cuisine for 18 years. The dining room features European scenes on hand-painted walls. The Spanish and Italian dishes are recommended.

5&10 No Exaggeration

Continental / Cabaret

77 Greene Street
☎ 925-7414

Average meal: $20-25
for less discount: 25%
AM/MC/VS/DC/DS

HOURS

Mon-Sun: 5pm-1am

5 & 10 No Exaggeration is a restaurant, bar, antique shop and performance studio. American and Continental cuisine is served, accompanied by live shows. Call ahead for schedule and reservations.

 # P.J. Charlton's

American / Continental

549 Greenwich Street
☎ 924-9532

Average meal: $15-20
for less discount: 25%
AM/DC

HOURS

Mon-Fri: 10am-10pm
Sat-Sun: closed

For 20 years, this Tribeca bistro has been serving a wide selection of pastas, steaks and seafood at reasonable prices. The daily specials are based on items fresh from the day's market.

 # El Pollo

Peruvian

482 Broome Street
☎ 431-5666

Average meal: $10-15
for less discount: 25%
AM/MC/VS/DC

HOURS

Mon-Fri: 11.30am-11pm
Sat-Sun: 12.30pm-
11.30pm

El Pollo specializes in mouth-watering marinated and rotisserie chicken. Inside, antique furniture, carvings and oil paintings abound. As a side dish, try the sweet plantains or curly fried potatoes.

Rocky's

Italian

45 Spring Street
☎ 274-9756

Average meal: $10-15
for less discount: 25%
AM/MC/VS/DC/DS

HOURS

Mon-Sun: 11am-11pm

Rocky's, a block from busy Mulberry Street, has been serving authentic, homecooked Italian cuisine for over 25 years. Try the tortellini with white prosciutto sauce and the delicious homemade cheesecake.

Sambuca's Cafe

Italian

105 Mulberry Street
☎ 431-0408

Average meal: $5-10
for less discount: 25%
AM/MC/VS

HOURS

Mon-Thu: 9.30am-2am
Fri-Sat: 9.30am-3am
Sun: 9.30am-2am

Sambuca's Cafe is located in the heart of Little Italy on Mulberry Street. It is perfect for Italian pastries, gourmet desserts and all types of coffee. The *tiramisu*, crafted by the owner himself, is made fresh every day.

Tiengarden

Vegetarian /Asian

170 Allen Street
☎ 388-1364

Average meal: $5-10
for less discount: 25%
Cash only

HOURS

Mon-Fri: 12noon-10pm
Sun: 12noon-10pm
Sat: closed

Tiengarden serves delicious vegetarian and vegan food near Chinatown. The vegetables are organically grown and all ingredients are natural. The "edible sculpture" *dim sum* has been featured in New York magazines.

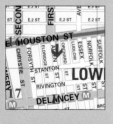

Shopping

Soho is a major New York City shopping district. From gourmet food markets to designer clothing, everything here exudes style. Although the majority of storefronts

Spring Street Market

display the chic and pricey contents you'll find inside, there are also a number of vintage clothing stores, specialty shops and street-side stands that sell reasonably priced goods. Many of the more

Antiques Fair and Collectibles Market

interesting Soho shops and boutiques offer a 20% discount to *New York for less* cardholders (pages 88-92).

For those fond of Flea Markets, visit the outdoor **Antiques Fair and Collectibles Market** *(Broadway and Grand Street, ☎ 682-2000. Sat-Sun: 9am-5pm)*. Also worth a look is the daily fair at the corner of Spring and Wooster Streets.

Another key commodity in the Soho shopping scene is art. **West Broadway**, in particular, is home to some of the world's best-known art galleries (see pages 78-79). Some of them have played a vital role in developing the careers of New York's best-known modern artists such as Andy Warhol and Roy Lichtenstein.

Shops in Soho

Canal Street, the dividing line between Soho and Tribeca, is a crowded shopping drag for inexpensive and imitation brand-name goods sprinkled amongst hardware and electrical supply stores. The eastern half of the street, which runs through Chinatown,

Orchard Street Shopping

contains mainly diamond and jewelry stores.

Both **Chinatown** and **Little Italy**, however, are best known for their authentic food markets. In Little Italy, you can still find shops which specialize in one particular type of item, such as breads, meats or pasta. There are also plenty of pastry shops where you can taste another Little Italy specialty (see page 82-83).

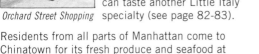
Spring Street Market

Residents from all parts of Manhattan come to Chinatown for its fresh produce and seafood at excellent prices. The best-known of the Chinese markets is **Kam Man Food Products** *(200 Canal Street,*

Bargain District

☎ 571-0330) where you will find any Asian grocery item you can imagine, and then some.

The **Lower East Side**, famous for its "**Bargain District**", which is centered around Orchard and Delancy Streets. On Sundays, **Orchard Street** is closed to traffic and becomes a bustling pedestrian mall. Before major discount stores moved into Manhattan, this area was the ultimate in bargain shopping. Today, prices are still competitive, though certainly not unrivaled. One advantage over discount chain shopping, however, is that there is sometimes room to "haggle" for a better price than that on the label.

A modern addition to the Lower East Side, **MarcoArt** (page 92) is an upbeat clothing boutique and art gallery north of the Bargain District, by Houston Street.

Enchanted Forest

Children & Gifts

85 Mercer Street
☎ **925-6677**

for less discount: 20%
AM/MC/VS/DC/DS

HOURS

Mon-Sat: 11am-7pm
Sun: 12noon-6pm

This magical store was chosen as "Best of New York" by *New York Magazine*. Classic, hand-crafted toys, puppets and stuffed animals can be found at this Soho shop, as well as a variety of books on fairy-tales and philosophy.

Alex Streeter

Original Jewelry

152 Prince Street
☎ **925-6496**

for less discount: 20%
AM

HOURS

Tue-Sat: 12noon-8pm
Sun: call for hours
Mon: closed

Alex Streeter has been selling art and designer jewelry for over 25 years. The artist designs each piece himself in a variety of unique styles and themes including archeological, science fiction and pop.

A Uno

Women's Clothing

98 Spring Street
☎ 343-2040

or less discount: 20%
AM/MC/VS

HOURS

Mon-Sun: 12noon-7pm

This European-style boutique offers clothing and accessories for women. Casual and sophisticated practical clothing is their specialty. Hats, scarves and jewelry are also available at reasonable prices.

 # Eastern Arts

Gifts & Crafts

07 Spring Street
☎ 966-4060

or less discount: 20%
AM/MC/VS

HOURS

Mon-Sat: 11am-7pm
Sun: 12noon-7pm

This exotic shop brings a touch of Asia to Soho with its hand-crafted arts. Its impressive display of Indonesian art includes carvings, masks and jewelry. You can find many interesting gifts in this colorful store.

 # What Comes Around Goes Around

Vintage Clothing

51 West Broadway
☎ 343-9303

or less discount: 20%
AM/MC/VS

HOURS

Mon-Fri: 11am-7pm
Sat: 11am-1am
Sun: 11am-8pm

This store carries collectibles and clothing from 1880-1980. Over 1,500 pairs of jeans makes it one of the largest collections of vintage denim in the country. Shoppers have included Bill Murray and Meg Ryan.

After the Rain

Crafts & Gifts

149 Mercer Street
☎ 431-1044

for less discount: 20%
AM/MC/VS/DC/DS

HOURS

Mon-Sat: 11am-7pm
Sun: 12noon-6pm

After the Rain is an excellent place to purchase a high quality gift. It sells an extensive collection of jewelry, handblown glass and unusual books. There is also an interesting selection of kaleidoscopes and optical toys.

Margo Manhattan

Original Jewelry

100 Thompson Street
☎ 925-0735

for less discount: 20%
AM/MC/VS

HOURS

Mon-Sun: 12noon-6pm

This modern boutique, which is owned by jewelry designer Margo Manhattan, features sterling silver and gold with semiprecious stones. A large, versatile collection of jewelry is available for both men and women.

Selima Optique

Optical Boutique

59 Wooster Street
☎ 343-9490

for less discount: 20%
AM/MC/VS

HOURS

Mon-Sat: 11am-7pm
Sun: 12noon-6pm

Selima Optique is a chic and trendy optical shop located on a cobble-stoned street in historic Soho. It specializes in high-end designer and vintage eyewear and also carries stylish hats, scarves and bags.

1909 Company

Vintage Clothing

53 Thompson Street
☎ 343-1658

or less discount: 20%
AM/VS/MC

This shop sells quality vintage clothing and accessories from 1900-1970. Designer brands sold include Gucci, Missoni and Hermés. Winona Ryder, Julia Roberts and Molly Ringwald have all shopped here.

Evolution

Natural History

120 Spring Street
☎ 343-1114

or less discount: 20%
AM/MC/VS/DS

Evolution makes natural history a part of your Soho shopping experience. It stocks all kinds of curious items and collectibles. Some of the more unique items are butterflies, skulls, skeletons and fossils.

Alpana Bawa

Clothing

41 Grand Street
☎ 965-0559

or less discount: 20%
AM/MC/VS

Variety in colors, patterns and textures is Alpana Bawa's trademark. The designer combines items from her native India with modern designs. Handmade dresses have been bought by the likes of Helena Christiansen.

MarcoArt

Clothing & Ar

186 Orchard Stree
☎ 253-107(

for less discount: 20%
AM/MC/VS

MarcoArt designs can be found on everything from
Swatch watches to clothing. This shop is a colorful, lively
boutique and art gallery. T-shirts, dresses and painting
are all designed by this well-known artist.

Danse Macabre

Crafts, Gifts & Collectible

263 1/2 Lafayette Stree
☎ 219-390

for less discount: 20%
AM/MC/VS

Resembling a Victorian parlor, this shop feature
macabre-themed articles. Masks, gargoyles, T-shirts and
jewelry are just some of the items available. Hand-carved
boxes, books, postcards and candles make popular gifts

Carrington & DaSilva

Crafts, Gifts & Accessorie

93 Reade Stree
☎ 571-351

for less discount: 20%
AM/MC/VS

Carrington and DaSilva is located in a spacious Tribec
cast-iron building. The shop is filled with uniqu
decorative gifts and crafts. Also sold are hats and othe
interesting accessories, many of which are handmade.

Greenwich Village

Introduction . . .

Greenwich Village refers to the entire area between Houston and 14th Streets, but is usually more clearly defined as the East and West Villages, divided by Broadway. Also known as "the Village", it is comprised of charming townhouses and quaint, tree-lined streets.

Greenwich Village

The **West Village**'s main thoroughfare, **Bleecker Street**, is brimming over with restaurants, shops and sidewalk cafés that tempt you to sit all day, watching the crowds until the coffee runs dry.

If you happen to be in New York City on Halloween, the **Village Halloween Parade** is the place to be. If you can stand the crowds, you will undoubtedly enjoy the outrageous costumes and festivities which make it one of the best celebrations of the year.

Sheridan Square *(Intersection of Seventh Avenue, West 4th and Barrow Streets),* was named after Civil War hero General Philip Sheridan whose statue stands in Christopher Park. In 1863, this was the site where a group of protesters, refusing to join the armed services, attempted to hang freed slaves, sparking the **Draft Riots**.

Since the 1960s, the West Village has become the center of the city's gay and lesbian community. A number of shops, bars and nightclubs in the area around Sheridan Square and along **Christopher Street** specifically cater to this market.

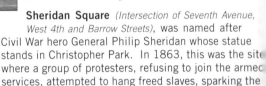

Halloween Parade

Washington Square Park (page 98), situated in the center of the Village, was a colonial cemetery and, during the Revolutionary War, a notorious hanging ground. When it was converted into a public park in the 1820s, however, the surrounding area became the center of New York's high society. Later, as the bohemian core of the city, many famous authors and artists lived and worked here – among them **Henry James**, **Edith Wharton**, **Mark Twain** and **Edna St. Vincent Millay**.

The imposing **Washington Memorial Arch** was built in 1889 to commemorate the 100th anniversary of the presidential inauguration of **George Washington**. Just above the arch, on the park's north side, is **The Row** – a series of distinctive Federal-style brick homes.

DON'T MISS

A stroll through the quiet tree-lined streets of the West Village. Just west of Seventh Avenue, streets such as Barrow, Bedford and Grove are good examples of West Village charm, and contain some of the oldest houses in the neighborhood.

. . . Introduction

New York University, the country's largest private university, is centered around Washington Square Park. The buildings on this urban campus are recognizable by the purple NYU flags that mark them.

New York University

Tucked away a block north of Washington Square Park, the cobble-stoned **Washington Mews** was originally built as stables for the homes facing the park. Converted into carriage houses around the turn of the century, they now serve as housing for New York University faculty.

Just east of Broadway, you can see the once fashionable homes known as **Colonnade Row** *(428-434 Lafayette Street)* built in 1833 by millionaires **John Jacob Astor** and **Cornelius Vanderbilt**. Nearby, the **Merchant's House Museum** (page 96) is the Village's only historic museum.

During the 1950s, artists migrated across Broadway to the inexpensive **East Village**. By the 1960s, beatnik philosophers **Jack Kerouac** and **Allen Ginsberg** were famous residents. Today, the tradition of the coffeehouse, with its music and poetry, is still an important part of the culture here, though new labels such as "spoken word" and "anti-folk" are used to categorize the evolution of these genres.

Unlike its western counterpart, the East Village is a little rough around the edges. Many of its residents consider it to be the last authentic bohemian neighborhood in the city, and it clings to its reputation as a haven for the creative and progressive.

INSIDER'S TIP

For a night out at one of the East Village's best dance clubs, Webster Hall (page 216) gives a discount on admission to *New York for less* cardholders, as well as priority entrance and a glass of champagne. See page 211-216 for more information on New York City nightlife.

St. Mark's in the East Village

The East Village has plenty of live music clubs and late-night bars. On **St. Mark's Place**, the East Village's main street, you will find a variety of cafés, bars, record stores and clothing boutiques. It is littered with live music flyers announcing the punk and rock shows which occur nightly. On the Bowery, legendary rock club **CBGB** *(315 Bowery, ☎ 982-4052)* has hosted famous bands like the Ramones and Talking Heads. Don't let the grubby exterior fool you, this place still books future stars. **Webster Hall** (page 216), one of the biggest nightclubs in New York, is a great place for dancing to the various types of music that are played on four different floors.

Merchant's House Museum

This landmark townhouse, built in 1832, is New York City's only family home preserved intact from the 19th century.

Located close to Washington Square Park, this was the home of a wealthy hardware merchant, **Seabury Tredwell**, and his family from 1835-1933. It became a museum in 1936 and is a fine example of the architecture which once dominated entire city blocks, as well as a fine representation of the lifestyle of an upper-middle-class 19th-century New York family.

Merchant's House Museum

When the house was built, it was equipped with all the modern-day conveniences and building technology available including pipes for gas lighting and a bell system for calling servants.

The exterior is constructed in a late Federal period architectural style. The most notable rooms of the Greek Revival-style interior are the elaborately crafted parlors, complete with free-standing Ionic columns and ornate fireplaces, doors and windows.

Parlor in the Merchant's House Museum

The ground floor is comprised of the original dining room and the kitchen. The dining room features an elegant black and gold marble mantle and a table set with porcelain from the Tredwell collection. The kitchen contains a beehive oven, a large fireplace and a soapstone sink into which water was pumped from a 4,000 gallon cistern in the garden.

On the main floor, the magnificent parlors are accompanied by two bedrooms and a study filled with the family's original furniture, clothing and memorabilia. These rooms provide a detailed look at life in the Tredwell household.

The top two floors were once servants' quarters and additional bedrooms for the eight Tredwell children.

ADDRESS

29 East 4th Street
☎ 777-1089

HOURS

Sun-Thu: 1pm-4pm
Fri-Sat: closed

PRICES

Adult $3
Child free
Senior $2
Student $2

DISCOUNT

2 admissions for the price of 1 with your *New York for less* card.

DON'T MISS

From cultural events and performances held in the parlors to parties and lunches in the garden, the museum's special programs offer additional opportunities to enjoy the house.

Other Attractions . . .

fferson Market Library was built in 1865 as a lunteer firehouse. When it later became a urthouse, it was named after president Thomas fferson. Now part of the New York Public Library stem, "Old Jeff", as it is affectionately known, atures Venetian Gothic-style spires, a watchtower d bell. In 1877, it was voted one of the ten most autiful buildings in the U.S. and is still considered architectural treasure. *(425 Sixth Avenue, ☎ 243-334. Mon and Thu: 10am-6pm. Tue and Fri: 12noon-6pm. ed: 12noon-8pm. Sat: 10am-5pm. Sun: closed. dmission is free.)*

Jefferson Market Library

st north of Washington Square ark, the **Salmagundi Club** was rmed in 1870 by prestigious literary gures like Edith Wharton, Henry mes and Herman Melville. Today, e club houses the American Artists' ofessional League, the American atercolor Society and the Greenwich llage Society for Historic eservation. *(47 Fifth Avenue, ☎ 255-740. Mon-Sun: 1pm-5pm. Admission is e.)*

Jefferson Market Library

rbes Magazine Gallery** contains the private llection of the late financial publisher Malcolm rbes. The gallery displays thousands of antique ys, an outstanding collection of objects by Russian weler Peter Carl Fabergé (including the famous abergé eggs) and an autographed copy of President braham Lincoln's *Gettysburg Address*. *(62 Fifth enue, ☎ 206-5548. Tue-Wed and Fri-Sat: 10am-4pm. n-Mon and Thu: closed. Admission is free.)*

Salmagundi Club

ie elegant **Grace Church** on Broadway was built by chitect James Renwick Jr., who also designed St. atrick's Cathedral (page 154). *(802 Broadway, ☎ 254-000. Mon-Tue and Thu-Fri: 10am-5.30pm. Wed: 11.30am-30pm. Sat: 12noon-4pm. Sun: masses at 9am, 11am, m.)*

ie old **Astor Library**, built in 1849, is a beautiful red ick brownstone building that was saved from estruction and restored by Joseph Papp in 1965. app, who founded the New York Shakespeare Festival 1954, later made the building home to the **Public heater**. It is well-respected for its new American oductions as well as the annual *Shakespeare in the ark* festival, which it stages every summer in Central ark (see page 206). *(425 Lafayette Street, ☎ 239-6200 r tickets.)*

Cooper Union

. . . Other Attractions

Founded by industrialist Peter Cooper in 1859, the **Cooper Union for the Advancement of Science and Ar**

was the city's first free, non-discriminatory college. The school still attracts talented young students and continues to produce notable contemporary artists. *(41 Cooper Square, ☎ 353-4100.)*

East Village street scene

Built in 1799, **St. Mark's-in-the-Bowery Church** is one of New York's oldest remaining churches. Situated on the former farm of Dutch colonial governor, Peter Stuyvesant, h and several generations of his descendants are buried here. *(131 East 10th Street, ☎ 674-6377. Mon-Sat: 10am-6pm. Sun: mass at 10.30am.)*

St. Mark's-in-the-Bowery

Anthology Film Archives (see nightlife, page 214) has two theaters which show new, classic and avant-garde films. There are also lectures and discussions on a variety of film-related topics. *(32 Second Avenue, ☎ 505-5181. Mon-Fri: 6pm-12midnight. Sat-Sun: 3pm-12midnight.)*

Open Spaces

On weekends, the former fountain in the middle of **Washington Square Park** (page 94) acts as a stage for

Tompkins Square Park

street performers (from musicians to comedians to sword-swallowers) who draw an audience of interested passers-by and bored teenagers. If there are still remnants of bohemian culture in the Village, this park is where you are most likely to find

Houses on Washington Square

them – amongst the acoustic guitars, African drums and amateur poetry.

Tompkins Square Park

Once a favorite haunt of New York's high society, Washington Square Park fell into decline during the 1970s and early 1980s, and became infested with drug dealers. In th mid-80s, however, a massive clean-up progran was initiated and the park is now a pleasant and lively place to visit.

In Alphabet City, just east of Avenue A, you will find **Tompkins Square Park**. Once a scene of social and political unrest, this park has recently become gentrified and is a good place to take a break after a shopping trip to the East Village.

Eating and Drinking

reenwich Village is packed with inexpensive
staurants and cafés serving all types of cuisine. In
e West Village, Bleecker Street is particularly busy
nd is home to **Talk of the Village** (page 100) and
tali West (page 102) which give discounts to
ew York for less cardholders.

Barocco to Go's fresh baked goods

earby, **Thomas Scott's** (see below) serves fine
merican cuisine on a charming West Village
reet. On the same block, **Chumley's** *(86 Bedford*
reet, ☎ *675-4449)* is a former speakeasy which,
uring Prohibition, was a watering hole for some of
ew York's greatest writers, including John Steinbeck.

Balducci's market

On Sixth Avenue,
Balducci's *(424 Sixth*
Avenue, ☎ *673-2600)* is an
old-world Italian food
market famous for the
quality and variety of its
products.

ome of the least expensive dining in Manhattan can
e found in the East Village, especially at some of the
hnic eateries. Sixth Street (between First and
econd Avenues) is known as **Little India**. This row of
dian restaurants occupies nearly every storefront on
e south side of the street. Around the corner, **Haveli**
age 103) is considered one of the best Indian
staurants in the city.

e East Village also has a number of trendy bistros
cluding the stylish **Tompkins 131** (page 104) which
verlooks Tompkins Square Park.

DON'T MISS

Outdoor dining in warm
weather — Angry Monk,
Roettele A.G., Cafe
Regionale, L'Oro di Napoli
and St. Dymphna's all
offer garden dining or
sidewalk tables.

Thomas Scott's on Bedford

ontemporary American

2 Bedford Street
627-4011

verage meal: $25-30
r less discount: 25%
C/VS/DC

HOURS

Mon-Thu: 6pm-11.30pm
Fri-Sat: 6pm-1am
Sun: 11.30am-11.30pm

n a quaint street in historic Greenwich Village, Thomas
cott's serves contemporary American cuisine in an
egant, romantic setting. A chef's specialty is the
elicious encrusted rack of lamb.

HOURS

Mon-Sat: 11am-7pm
Sun: 12noon-7pm

Barocco to Go

American / International

121 Greenwich Avenue
☎ 366-6110

Average meal: $10-15
for less discount: 25%
AM/MC/VS

Barocco to Go serves Tuscan-style fare in the West Village. Freshly made pizzas, salads, sandwiches and desserts are all prepared on the premises. This casual café is the perfect stop for a quick snack or a full meal.

HOURS

Mon-Thu and Sun: 12noon-4pm, 5.30pm-12midnight
Fri-Sat: 11am-4pm, 5.30pm-1am

Nadine's

International

99 Bank Street
☎ 924-3165

Average meal: $15-20
for less discount: 25%
AM/MC/VS

Chandeliers, candles and paintings create a romantic atmosphere at this West Village restaurant. An eclectic selection of dishes includes specialties like the cajun meatloaf or black bean pancakes.

HOURS

Mon-Thu: 5pm-1am
Fri-Sat: 5pm-4am
Sun: 5pm-12midnight

Talk of the Village

Continental

162 Bleecker Street
☎ 358-9385

Average meal: $10-15
for less discount: 25%
AM/MC/VS/DC/DS

Located on busy Bleeker Street in the West Village, Talk of the Village serves continental cuisine and a large selection of sandwiches and burgers. It is a great place to relax in a casual, bar-style atmosphere.

 La Belle Epoque

French / Creole

27 Broadway
254-6436

verage meal: $25-30
or less discount: 25%
M/MC/VS/DC/DS

et in an elegant turn-of-the-century Parisian-style
allroom, La Belle Epoque serves French and Creole
ontemporary and traditional cuisine like *salmon buerre
lanc*. The jazz brunch is recommended, reserve ahead.

Il Bocconcino

alian

68 Sullivan Street
982-0329

verage meal: $15-20
or less discount: 25%
M/MC/VS/DC

eally located between Soho and Greenwich Village, Il
occoncino serves hearty, Italian fare in a Romanesque
etting. Dine on chef's specialties such as the pasta, veal
lobster dishes.

L'Oro di Napoli

alian

06 Sullivan Street
598-4952

verage meal: $20-25
or less discount: 25%
M/MC/VS/DC/DS

Oro di Napoli is located in the West Village near
ashington Square Park. The décor is rustic and the
tmosphere is informal. Recommended dishes include
e seafood and pasta specials.

Au Bon Coin

French

85 MacDougal Stree
☎ 673-8184

Average meal: $15-20
for less discount: 25%
AM/MC/VS

This romantic French bistro serves fine food and wine
at very good prices. Enjoy chef's specialties such as
boeuf bourguignon and rack of lamb while you relax in a
cozy, softly-lit dining room.

Cucina Regionale

Italian

203 Thompson Stree
☎ 254-5187

Average meal: $20-25
for less discount: 25%
AM/MC/VS/DC

Cucina Regionale serves a full range of Italian specialties
at reasonable prices. Outdoor seating is available in
warm weather. After dinner, use your *New York for less*
card at Mondo Cane (page 216) blues club located upstairs.

Mitali West

Indian

296 Bleecker Stree
☎ 989-1367

Average meal: $15-20
for less discount: 25%
AM/MC/VS

This spacious West Village restaurant serves fine Indian
cuisine, offering an extensive choice of both vegetarian
and non-vegetarian dishes. Favorites include the *chicken
tikka* and vegetable curry.

Roettele A.G.

erman / Swiss

26 East 7th Street
674-4140

verage meal: $20-25
or less discount: 25%
M/MC/VS/DC

oettele A.G. serves German-Swiss cuisine with Italian
nd French accents. Inside, intimate rooms feature
ardwood floors and a fireplace. In warm weather, enjoy
pecials like cheese fondue in the outdoor garden.

HOURS

Mon-Thu: 12noon-3pm,
5.30pm-11pm
Fri-Sat: 12noon-3pm,
5.30pm-11.30pm
Sun: closed

Angry Monk

betan

6 Second Avenue
979-9202

verage meal: $15-20
or less discount: 25%
M/MC/VS/DC

his modern restaurant features delicious Tibetan
uisine. Specialty dishes include vegetable or meat
omo and the daily fish specials. You can dine outdoors
a spacious garden during the summer.

HOURS

Mon-Wed: 3pm-
12midnight
Thu-Sun: 4pm-
12midnight

Haveli

dian

00 Second Avenue
982-0533

verage meal: $15-20
r less discount: 25%
M/MC/VS/DC/DS

ound the corner from Indian Row, Haveli is considered
e of the city's best Indian restaurants. It successfully
mbines tradition with elegance. Try the *murgah tikka*
one of the flavorful vegetarian dishes.

HOURS

Mon-Sun: 12noon-
12midnight

HOURS

Mon-Thu: 5pm-11.30pm
Fri: 5pm-12.30am
Sat: 11am-12.30am
Sun: 11am-11pm

HOURS

Mon-Sun: 10am-
12midnight

HOURS

Mon-Fri: 6pm-2am
Sat-Sun: 11am-2am

Tompkins 131

Contemporary American

131 Avenue A
☎ 777-5642

Average meal: $20-25
for less discount: 25%
AM/MC/VS

This chic restaurant serves excellent contemporary American cuisine. The clientele is young and the atmosphere is sophisticated, yet fun. House specialities include tuna tartare with avocado and mango.

St. Dymphna's

Irish

18 St. Mark's Place
☎ 254-6636

Average meal: $10-15
for less discount: 25%
AM/MC/VS/DC

St. Dymphna's serves contemporary Irish cuisine and beers in a rustic atmosphere. Hearty country-style breads, soups and stews are recommended. Outdoor seating in the garden is available during the summer.

Nice Guy Eddie's

American

5 Avenue A
☎ 539-0902

Average meal: $10-15
for less discount: 25%
AM/MC/VS

American southwestern cuisine and tasty Cajun dishes are served here. A 1970s rock jukebox adds to the laid-back, fun atmosphere. Try the apple cider-soaked chicken breast with Creole ratatouille.

Shopping

he scenic, winding streets of the West Village offer an
eal shopping experience. You can stick to the main
oroughfares like **Bleecker Street**, where you will find
n assortment of stores selling everything from
osters to New York City T-shirts, or you can
xplore the side streets to discover hidden
easures.

he Village has plenty of specialty shops like
udson Street Papers (page 108), which has a
nique selection of greeting cards and gifts.
or something exotic, **Eastern Arts** (page 108)
nd **Truva** (page 106) import products from
round the world.

ambridge Camera Shop (page 107) is a
hotographic and electronic specialty shop
hich has been doing business for over 30
ars. If you came to New York without a
mera, this is a great place to rent or buy
hotographic equipment at a 20% discount
th your *New York for less* card.

Bleecker Street in the West Village

roadway is crammed with stores that are perfect for
urchasing basic items such as shoes and boots, jeans
nd casual clothing. **Authentic New York** (page 110)
arries a great selection of denim and leather goods.

ecause of the relatively low rents in the East Village,
any independent artists and designers have come
ere to set up galleries and shops. The result is a
eighborhood filled with an interesting collection of
outiques selling unusual and handmade items,
nerally at good prices. Shoppers can weave in and

out of dozens of stores, each
offering its own brand of unique
merchandise.

St. Mark's Place is the center of
the area's shopping activity, with
an abundance of vintage
clothing boutiques, record stores
and collectibles shops. You will
also find a number of places on

uva in the West Village

d around St. Mark's that offer a discount to *New
ork for less* cardholders. Tucked amongst vintage and
ecialty shops like **The "R" Store** (page 110) and
enue A Cards (page 110), **Swish** (page 111) is one
the best skateshops in New York, selling all the top
ateboard and streetwear brands. Around the corner
East 7th Street, **Howdy-Do** (page 112) has a
zzling display of American kitsch and collectibles.
is virtually a museum of vintage Americana.

DON'T MISS

The collection of vintage
lunch boxes at **Howdy-do**
(page 112): from Wonder
Woman to the Brady
Bunch, this store
stocks them all.

HOURS

Mon-Fri: 11am-6pm
Sat-Sun: closed

Tootsie's

Childre

554 Hudson Stre
☎ 242-018

for less discount: 20
AM/MC/VS/D

Tootsie's sells classic and contemporary children's bool
and toys. Everything from games and puzzles to puppe
can be found here, any of which would make a gre
children's gift or souvenir.

HOURS

Mon-Sat: 12.30pm-7pm
Sun: 1pm-6pm

Whiskey Dust

Vintage Clothing & Weste

526 Hudson Stre
☎ 691-557

for less discount: 20
AM/MC/VS/D

Colorful and fun, Whiskey Dust is stocked with weste
memorabilia and merchandise. High quality, new ar
vintage western apparel includes an extensive collectic
of jeans, cowboy hats and boots for men and women.

HOURS

Mon-Fri: 12noon-8pm
Sat: 11am-9pm
Sun: 12noon-8pm

Truva

Gifts & Craf

58 Greenwich Aven
☎ 462-404

for less discount: 20
AM/MC/VS/D

Truva is an authentic Turkish gift shop, selling tradition
goods like furniture and carpets. Picture frames, che
sets and copper items make great gifts. Ladies clothi
and accessories are sold in the adjacent boutique.

Cambridge Camera Shop

ameras & Electronics

5 Seventh Avenue
 675-8600

r less discount: 20%
M/MC/VS/DS

HOURS

Mon-Fri: 9am-6pm
Sun: 10am-3pm
Sat: closed

r 30 years, Cambridge Cameras has offered excellent
ices and helpful service. It carries a huge stock of new
id used photographic and electronic equipment.
ental, repair and film developing are also offered.

Post War Club

ntage Clothing

51 West 4th Street
 229-9027

r less discount: 20%
M/MC/VS/DS

HOURS

Mon-Sun: 12noon-10pm

ost War Club is located on busy West 4th Street in the
est Village. It is filled with vintage clothing and
teresting accessories at great prices. Choose from
andbags, shoes, shirts, dresses and jewelry.

Tah-Poozie

hildren, Toys & Novelties

) Greenwich Avenue
 647-0668

r less discount: 20%
M/MC/VS/DS

HOURS

Mon-Fri: 12noon-10pm
(longer hours in summer)
Sat: 11am-10pm
Sun: 12noon-9pm

h-Poozie features curiosities of interest to both
ildren and adults. It stocks a unique selection of toys,
nkets and novelties. You can also find postcards, world
usic CDs and New York mementos.

HOURS

Mon-Sun: 11am-8pm

HOURS

Mon-Sat: 11am-8pm
Sun: 12noon-6pm

Village Army Navy

Army Navy & Clothir

328 Bleecker Stre
☎ 242-666

for less discount: 20
AM/MC/V

Village Army Navy is located in the heart of the We
Village. It carries all the top brands and a wide selecti
of men's and women's clothing and accessories k
Timberland, Levi's, Calvin Klein, Polo and more.

Eastern Arts

Gifts & Craf

365 Bleecker Stre
☎ 929-746

for less discount: 25
AM/MC/VS/C

This exotic, Asian-themed crafts shop has an impressi
display of Indonesian art, including carvings, masks ar
jewelry. You can also obtain the discount at Eastern Art
Soho location (page 89).

Hudson Street Papers

Gif

357 Bleecker Stre
☎ 229-106

for less discount: 20
AM/MC/V

Hudson Street Papers carries an enormous selection
greeting cards, toys, jewelry and more. Decorative gif
such as candles and picture frames make great gifts ar
unusual souvenirs.

L'Uomo

Men's Clothing

383 Bleecker Street
☎ 206-1844

for less discount: 20%
AM/MC/VS

Mon-Sat:
12noon-7.30pm
Sun: 12noon-6pm

L'Uomo sells classic and contemporary men's clothing and accessories. It stocks a complete range of styles and sizes in both casual and business wear. Top designer brands such as Hugo Boss and Rene Lezard are available.

 # Village Chess Shop

Chess

230 Thompson Street
☎ 475-9580

for less discount: 20%
AM/MC/VS

HOURS

Mon-Sun: 12noon-
12midnight

This famous chess shop stocks chess sets, boards, books and software. Chess players are welcome and there are tables set up for playing. You can also find checkers, dominoes, backgammon and other games.

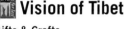 # Vision of Tibet

Gifts & Crafts

67 Thompson Street
☎ 995-9276

for less discount: 20%
AM/MC/VS

HOURS

Mon-Sun: 11am-7pm

Vision of Tibet stocks a multitude of Himalayan artifacts and crafts. Choose from exotic jewelry, clothing and other items. This is a great place to find an interesting, yet inexpensive, gift.

HOURS

Mon-Sat: 10am-8pm
Sun: 12noon-6pm

Authentic New York

Clothing

654 Broadway
☎ 253-1939

for less discount: 20%
MC/VS/DC/DS

Authentic New York carries everything from basic to trendy clothing, all at good prices. A huge stock of denim includes Calvin Klein, Guess and Levi's 501. Ralph Lauren clothing and Schott's leather are also available.

HOURS

Mon-Fri: 12noon-9pm
Sat-Sun: 12noon-11pm

The "R" Store

Vintage & Collectibles

111 St. Mark's Place
☎ 254-9668

for less discount: 20%
MC/VS

By Tompkins Square Park in the East Village, The "R" Store is a fun place to shop for American kitsch. Games, toys, dolls and other cultural collectibles are available at good prices.

HOURS

Mon-Fri: 11am-10pm
Sat: 11am-12midnight
Sun: 11am-9pm

Avenue A Cards

Posters, Gifts & Cards

121 St. Mark's Place
☎ 388-0923

for less discount: 20%
MC/VS

Located near Tompkins Square Park, this shop stays open late. An enormous selection of music, movie and art posters, cards and gifts is offered. Vintage European and American reprints are also available.

Swish

Skateshop & Clothing

15 St. Mark's Place
☎ 673-8629

or less discount: 20%
AM/MC/VS/DC

HOURS

Mon-Fri: 12noon-8.30pm
Sat: 12noon-9pm
Sun: 12noon-7.30pm

Established in 1993, Swish is NYC's original skateshop. It continues to carry the best skateboard brands and streetwear for men and women. Also stocked are watches, sunglasses and other accessories.

Norman's Sound & Vision

Music

7 Cooper Square
☎ 473-6599

or less discount: 20%
AM/MC/VS/DS

HOURS

Mon-Fri: 10am-11pm
Sat: 10am-12midnight
Sun: 10am-10pm

Located just off St. Mark's, Norman's sells both new and used CDs and videos. Their stock includes classical, country, rock, jazz, reggae and more. The Chelsea store (page 129) also carries an extensive selection of music.

Garage Sale

Vintage & Collectibles

6 First Avenue
☎ 260-2269

or less discount: 20%
AM/MC/VS

HOURS

Mon-Thu: 1pm-7pm
Fri-Sat: 1pm-8pm
Sun: 12noon-6pm

Garage Sale sells vintage clothing and accessories of every type. You can also find antiques and other collectibles such as handbags, jewelry and a unique collection of vintage lamps dating from the 1940s.

HOURS

Mon-Sat: 1pm-7pm
Sun: closed

HOURS

Tue-Thu: 12noon-10.30pm
Fri-Sat: 12noon-11.30pm
Sun: 2pm-10.30pm
Mon: 1pm-9.30pm

HOURS

Mon: closed
Tue-Thu: 3pm-11pm
Fri: 3pm-12midnight
Sat: 1pm-12midnight
Sun: 1pm-11pm

Howdy-Do

Vintage & Collectible

72 East 7th Stree
☎ 979-161

for less discount: 20%
AM/MC/V

A myriad of kitsch items represent decades of America
pop culture. Toy and television collectibles include dolls
lunch boxes and board games. Celebrities such as Bo
George, Bjork and Rosie O'Donnell shop here.

Back from Guatemala

Gifts & Craft

306 East 6th Stree
☎ 260-701

for less discount: 20%
AM/MC/V

Back from Guatemala has a unique collection c
clothing, jewelry and artifacts from over 30 countries
It sells musical instruments from cultures around th
world, and gifts such as picture frames and candles.

Unique Tableware

Housewares & Gift

340 East 6th Stree
☎ 533-825

for less discount: 20%
AM/MC/V

Unique Tableware sells china, crystal, ceramics an
glassware. You can also find candles and oil lamps in
variety of styles and colors. This eclectic store has plen
of interesting items that make great gifts.

Chelsea, Gramercy & the Flatiron District

Introduction . . .

During the 19th century, the construction of the elevated railroad helped transform **Chelsea** from farmland into a thriving commercial center. Carriages brought well-to-do women from around town to the stores which lined Broadway between Union Square and Madison Square, and it became known as "**Ladies' Mile**". As New York continued its expansion north, however, Chelsea was left behind as a warehouse district, while Herald Square and its new department store, **Macy's** (page 46), brought shoppers further uptown. Today, the retail industry has made a comeback in the area and you can now find national chains such as **Bed, Bath & Beyond** (620 Sixth Avenue, ☎ 255-3500), **Old Navy** (610 Sixth Avenue, ☎ 645-0663), **Filene's Basement** (620 Sixth Avenue, ☎ 620-3100) and **Barney's New York** department store (page 128).

Annex Antiques Fair and Flea Market

On weekends, one of the best things to do in Chelsea is to visit the **Annex Antiques Fair and Flea Market** (Sixth Avenue, between 24th and 25th Streets). This gigantic outdoor market has vintage clothing, antiques, furniture and more. Nearby, the **Chelsea Antiques Building** (110 West 25th Street) has 12 floors of antiques and collectibles. On the eighth floor, **Cafe Mozart** (page 126) is a good place for a light lunch after a day of antique and bargain hunting.

Recently, Chelsea has begun to acquire a reputation as an art center as more and more galleries are moving out of their longtime Soho homes and relocating into this less commercialized (and less expensive) area.

INSIDER'S TIP

The Empire State Building Observatory is one of the few attractions open late every evening and it makes a perfect place to visit after dinner when you can take in the illuminated Manhattan skyline from the 102nd floor.

The Manhattan waterfront has recently been the focus of major development plans. In Chelsea, the abandoned docks, warehouses and decrepit piers have given way to the **Chelsea Piers Sports and Entertainment Complex** (page 118) – a prime example of the potential for other waterfront development projects.

Aerial view of Chelsea Piers

. . . Introduction

The **Flatiron District** is also known as the "Photo District" because of the abundance of photography studios, labs and modeling agencies. This area has recently become popular for its cutting-edge restaurants (see page 128) and nightlife.

Rich in architectural detail, the triangular **Flatiron Building** was the tallest building in the world when it was finished in 1902. The best place to view it is from the traffic island a block north. From this angle, the building really does appear to be flat.

A short walk along Fifth Avenue will take you to the **Empire State Building** (page 116-117) where you can go up to the Observatory for some of the best views of the city. On the second floor of the building, you can try out the **New York Skyride** (page 117) and take a cinematic sightseeing tour of New York City.

Located in a slightly shabby area, **Madison Square Garden** (page 119), known by sports fans as "the Garden", is home to the New York Knicks basketball team.

Flatiron Building

Ivy-covered 19th-century townhouses remain on Irving Place and some of its neighboring streets. Of

particular charm and beauty are those surrounding the private **Gramercy Park** (page 122). This area is rich with the history of its literary and artistic past. Just south of the park, in Pete's Tavern on Irving Place, O. Henry wrote his ironic tale *The Gift of the Magi*. Edwin Booth's theatrical **Players Club** and the **National Arts**

Theodore Roosevelt's Birthplace **Club** (page 121) and are located in Gramercy Park townhouses. Not far from here, the **Little Church Around the Corner** (page 121) has been known as a spiritual refuge for actors since the 19th century.

You can visit one of the area's brownstone houses at **Theodore Roosevelt's Birthplace** (page 120), which not only offers a glimpse of the former president's early childhood home, but also a chance to examine the architecture of these charming buildings up-close.

 Empire State Building . . .

Dominating the skyline of midtown Manhattan, the Empire State Building rises to a height of 1,454 feet. Its fame began soon after talk of its construction, and it has since become a symbol of New York City which is recognized worldwide.

Lit with the colors of Independence Day

The building was completed on the site of the original Waldorf Astoria Hotel in 1931, in only one year and forty-five days – an amazing feat at the time. Although it came in under budget, it soon ran into financial trouble. In its early years, the effect of the 1929 stock market crash and the ensuing depression made tenants hard to find, and for a while it was nicknamed the "Empty State Building".

Upon its completion, the Empire State became the world's tallest building, a title it retained until the World Trade Center was built in the 1970s. In 1955, the American Society of Civil Engineers honored the structure as one of the seven modern wonders of the western hemisphere.

View from the Empire State Building's Observatory

The Empire State Building has appeared in more films than most Hollywood stars (over 100 in all) from *King Kong* to *Sleepless in Seattle* and *Independence Day*. In the 1960s, it was the subject of an Andy Warhol film which recorded the building for eight hours straight during which time the only thing that changed was the lighting.

The upper 30 floors of the building are illuminated nightly, from sunset to midnight, in a range of colors that reflect holidays and commemorate special events.

The Observatory offers panoramic views of Manhattan and beyond. High-speed elevators whisk passengers to the 86th floor where there are glass-enclosed viewing areas and outdoor promenades. There is also viewing from a second observatory on the 102nd Floor.

ADDRESS

350 Fifth Avenue
☎ 736-3100

HOURS

Mon-Sun: 9.30am-12midnight, last elevator at 11.30pm.

. . . Empire State Building

With the whole city laid out beneath you, you can see up to 80 miles on a clear day. Famous sights like the Chrysler Building, Yankee Stadium, Central Park, the World Trade Center and the Statue of Liberty are all visible. You can also see the surrounding boroughs and the bridges that link them to Manhattan.

Empire State Building at sunset

At night, the city lights offer an entirely different experience from daytime viewing. If you have the time, one of the best things to do is to go up to the Observatory just before sunset, when the lights from the buildings are first visible, then leave after the sky is completely dark. The skyline at sunset is breathtaking, and many of the sights, the bridges in particular, look best at this time.

The New York Skyride, located on the second floor of the Empire State Building, offers a state-of-the-art cinematic sightseeing tour of New York.

New York Skyride

Star Trek's James Doohan, better known as Scotty, and comedian Yakov Smirnoff are the pilots and guides on this 30-minute simulated flight through the city. The high-tech theater features a specially designed platform with hydraulic seats and wide screens which are syncronized to make you feel as if you are actually experiencing the ride.

This unusual tour of Manhattan includes simulated experiences such as a freefall off the top of the Empire State Building, a high speed ride between and over sights such as the Brooklyn Bridge, the World Trade Center and the Statue of Liberty and a chance to dodge traffic in Times Square – without leaving your seat. *(350 Fifth Avenue, Second Floor, ☎ 564-2224. Mon-Sun: 10am-10pm. Adult $10.50, child $8.50, senior $7, student $9. $2 off any admission with voucher on page 273.)*

New York Skyride's high-tech theater

PRICES

Adult $4.50
Child $2.25
Senior $2.25
Student $4.50

DISCOUNT

Adult 50¢ off, child free (when accompanied by an adult or senior), senior 25¢ off, student 50¢ off with voucher on page 271.

INSIDER'S TIP

New York Skyride is a good family activity and fits in well with a visit to the Observatory of the Empire State Building.

Chelsea Piers

Chelsea Piers Sports and Entertainment Complex is a 30-acre waterfront sports village encompassing a golf driving range, sports and fitness club, athletic facilities, ice and roller skating rinks and a marina. It is also the location of **Silver Screen Studios**, where popular television series such as *Law and Order* and major motion pictures such as *City Hall* with Al Pacino have been filmed here.

Driving stalls at the Golf Club

The Golf Club is Manhattan's only year-round, outdoor driving range. It has 52 covered and heated driving stalls which overlook the Hudson River. Every golf ball is mechanically retrieved and lifted on its tee – ready to be hit onto a 200-yard fairway.

Sky Rink

The Sports Center offers unparalleled opportunities in a variety of sports and has training facilities which include the world's longest indoor running track. You can take cross-training to new heights, literally, on the largest rock climbing wall in the northeastern U.S. An indoor arena contains facilities for basketball, soccer, baseball plus more unusual events like indoor sand volleyball. There is also a 6-lane swimming pool, a boxing ring and locker room facilities which include saunas, steam and massage rooms.

Sky Rink has the only year-round indoor ice skating facilities in Manhattan. Although it features two rinks, it is often unavailable for public skating in the evenings because of the many hockey leagues and professional organizations that practice here.

Roller rinks at Chelsea Piers

In warm weather, the massive outdoor sun-deck at the Sports Center is perfect for sunbathing and relaxing. From the Chelsea Piers promenade there are great views of the Hudson River.

ADDRESS

17th-23rd Streets at the Hudson River
☎ 336-6666

HOURS

Hours vary per activity. Discount applies Mon-Fri: opening time to 5pm.

PRICES

Golf: 14¢ per ball ($15 minimum), club rental $2 each / 3 for $5.

Ice Skating: Adult $9, Child $7 (plus rental $4)

Roller Skating: Adult $4, Child $3 (plus rental $7.50)

Sports Center: $25 per day

DISCOUNT

General admission (including golf, ice and roller skating, as well as day passes for the Sports Center) are offered at a 20% discount to *New York for less* cardholders (Mon-Fri: opening until 5pm). A 20% discount at the Chelsea Piers Store is also available. Both offers require the vouchers on page 273.

Other Attractions . . .

Well-known for its roster of literary and musical guests, the **Chelsea Hotel** was made notorious in the late 1970s by the highly publicized death of punk rock star Sid Vicious' girlfriend Nancy Spungeon. The brass plaques on the building's facade list the names of some of the hotel's more illustrious former guests including Dylan Thomas, Tennessee Williams and Mark Twain. Today, the hotel continues to cater to an off-

Chelsea Hotel

beat, artsy clientele. *(222 West 23rd Street, ☎ 243-3700.)*

Housed in a former Art Deco cinema, the **Joyce Theater** (see also page 213) is a well-respected center for dance.

Joyce Theater

Performances cover a tremendous range of styles from ballet to ballroom and everything in between. *(175 Eighth Avenue, ☎ 242-0800 for tickets.)*

Founded in 1817, the **General Theological Seminary** is a private facility for students preparing for the priesthood. Its beautiful grounds are a welcome oasis from the busy streets of Chelsea and guided tours are available during the summer. *(Ninth Avenue between 20th and 21st Streets, ☎ 243-5150. Mon-Fri: 12noon-3pm. Sat: 11am-3pm. Sun: closed.)*

General Theological Seminary

Built in 1854, the **Marble Collegiate Church** is the oldest Reformed Church in the city. It is probably best known, however, for its former pastor-turned-author Norman Vincent Peale who wrote *The Power of Positive Thinking.* *(1 West 29th Street, ☎ 686-2770. Mon-Sat: 9am-12noon, 2pm-4pm. Sun: 9am-2pm.)*

The **General Post Office** was created by the legendary New York architectural firm McKim, Mead and White in 1913. The colossal building is two city blocks long and is easily recognizable by its sweeping staircase and immense Corinthian columns. *(421 Eighth Avenue, ☎ 967-8585. Open 24 hours every day, including holidays.)*

General Post Office

Madison Square Garden is home to the New York Knicks basketball team and the New York Rangers hockey team. The 20,000-seat arena also hosts many other sporting and non-sporting events, including

. . . Other Attractions . . .

Madison Square Garden

major rock and pop concerts. Guided tours of the complex are available year round. *(4 Pennsylvania Plaza, ☎ 465-6741.)*

The Roman Catholic **St. John the Baptist Church** was founded in 1840 for German immigrants. The appearance of the exterior has become a little shabby, but the interior holds a variety of Gothic-style treasures, including marble arches and stained-glass windows. *(211 West 30th Street, ☎ 564-9070. Mon-Sun: 6am-6pm.)*

The busy **Appellate Division of the Supreme Court of the State of New York** hears appeals for civil and criminal cases from New York and the Bronx. Baseball great Babe Ruth, actor and dancer extraordinaire Fred Astaire and writer Edgar Allen Poe all participated in cases settled here. You can visit the building and see its elegant interior, but the court sessions are closed to the public. *(27 Madison Avenue, ☎ 340-0400. Mon-Fri: 9am-5pm. Sat-Sun: closed.)*

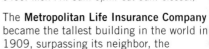

Parlor in Theodore Roosevelt's Birthplace

The **Metropolitan Life Insurance Company** became the tallest building in the world in 1909, surpassing its neighbor, the Flatiron Building. Its lighted 700-foot tower and four-faced clock are prominent features of the New York Skyline. *(1 Madison Avenue, ☎ 578-2211.)*

Theodore Roosevelt's Birthplace

Located in a Gramercy Park townhouse, **Theodore Roosevelt's Birthplace** has been reconstructed to represent the boyhood home of the 26th U.S. president. A national historic site, it includes period rooms, galleries and the largest selection of Teddy Roosevelt memorabilia anywhere. On Saturdays at 2pm, you can listen to chamber music concerts at no additional charge. *(28 East 20th Street, ☎ 260-1616. Adult $2, child (under 17) free, senior $2, student $2. Wed-Sun: 9am-5pm. Mon-Tue: closed.)*

Metropolitan Life Insurance Building

Police Academy Museum

The **Police Academy Museum** has an extensive collection of police memorabilia. On display are a variety of weapons and items such as police uniforms and daily registers describing a slew of

. . . Other Attractions

riminal and law enforcement activities, including
rohibition raids and bank robberies. *(235 East 20th
'treet, ☎ 477-9753. Mon-Fri: 9am-3pm. Sat-Sun: closed.
'ree admission.)*

National Arts Club

he **National Arts Club** was designed in the early
880s by one of the renowned architects of Central
'ark – Calvert Vaux. Members have included some of
.merica's finest 19th and 20th century artists, many
f whom contributed works that are still housed here.
lthough this is a private club, the collection is open
> the public for viewing at various times throughout
ne year. *(15 Gramercy Park South, ☎ 475-3424. Call
head for exhibition schedule.)*

Little Church Around the Corner

lext door, **The Players** is housed in the former home of
ctor Edwin Booth – famous not only for his
rofession, but also for his brother John Wilkes'
ssassination of President Lincoln. The theatrical
lub he began attracted the likes of Mark Twain and
Vinston Churchill as members. The only way to see
ne inside, however, is to arrange a group tour before
ou arrive. *(16 Gramercy Park South, ☎ 228-7610.
'rivate club.)*

he **Episcopal Church of the Transfiguration**,
etter known as the **Little Church Around the
orner**, has been known as a spiritual refuge for
ctors since the late 1800s. The name stuck when
n actor was refused burial at a nearby church
ecause of his profession, and the preacher
eferred his friend to the "little church around the
orner". Actress Sarah Bernhardt is said to have
ttended services here, and a window portrays actor
dwin Booth in his role as Hamlet. The church
naintains a special relationship with the thespian
ommunity. *(1 East 29th Street, ☎ 684-6770. Mon-
un: 8am-6pm.)*

The Flower District

ushman Row, in the heart of the Chelsea Historic
istrict, offers a glimpse of the mid-19th-century
illage that predated today's modern neighborhood.
uilt in the years 1839-1840 by banker Don Alonzo
ushman, these rowhouses are some of the best
urviving examples of New York City architecture in
ne Greek Revival style. Evidence of the
raftsmanship with which they were constructed is
isplayed in the intricate details of their facades.
406-18 West 20th Street.)*

he **Flower District** is Manhattan's main source for
lants and flowers – thousands of species are sold
ere. *(Sixth Avenue at 27-29th Streets.)*

Cushman Row

Open Spaces

Union Square Park

The enormous sun-deck at **Chelsea Piers Sports and Entertainment Complex** (page 118) is a great place to soak up the sun in warm weather. A stroll along the piers themselves are another good way to enjoy the Manhattan waterfront.

Union Square Greenmarket

Union Square Park is a busy, open space wedged between Broadway and Fourth Avenues, just above 14th Street. Most of its daytime visitors are local workers who come here to eat their deli-bought lunches on the park benches. On the streets around the park, there are a variety of good restaurants and outdoor cafés, including **Barocco Kitchen** (page 125).

Union Square is at its best, however, on Wednesdays and Saturdays when the **Union Square Greenmarket** brings regional farmers to the park to peddle their harvests.

Madison Square Park

Once a busy entertainment district and the site of **P.T. Barnum's Hippodrome**, **Madison Square** is now a tranquil park where, despite the nearby traffic, you can enjoy a little peace and quiet. A pleasant half hour can be spent examining the 19th-century statues and monuments situated throughout the grounds, and enjoying the view of the nearby Flatiron Building. Surrounding the park, other early 20th-century buildings, such as the **New York Life Insurance Company** and **Metropolitan Life Insurance Company** (page 120), add to the scenery. At night, the buildings are lit in a variety of colors which change with the seasons.

Madison Square Park

Gramercy Park

Organized baseball is said to have grown out of the famous **Knickerbocker Club**, formed in 1845, by a group of baseball enthusiasts who played regularly in the park.

Gramercy Park

Modeled after a London square, **Gramercy Park** is one of the quietest, most peaceful places in the city. The surrounding townhouses are stately and beautiful, but (to the dismay of everyone else) their residents are the only ones who possess keys to this private oasis.

Eating and Drinking

With the recent influx of stylish restaurants, the Flatiron District and the area around Union Square Park has become one of the city's prime eating and drinking destinations. Top restaurants like **Gramercy Tavern** *(42 East 20th Street, ☎ 477-0777)* and **Union Square Cafe** *(21 East 16th Street, ☎ 243-4020)* have set the pace for fresh newcomers seeking to please an audience of discriminating diners.

Several very good restaurants in this area offer discounts to *New York for less* cardholders. In the Photo District, you could try **F-stop** (see below), **Portfolio** (page 124) or **Caffe Bondi** (page 125), all of which provide top-notch food and service, at moderate prices.

Around Union Square, there are two excellent examples of the microbrew phenomenon that has recently hit New York City – **Zip City Brewing Company** (page 125) and **Heartland Brewery** (page 124). Both make their own beers on the premises, serve hearty food to complement the brews and are lively and fun.

Portfolio in the Flatiron District

When visiting the Empire State Building you could feast on an over-stuffed sandwich at **Mendy's East** (page 125), a kosher, delicatessen-style restaurant and steakhouse which is just a block away on 34th Street.

In the West 30s, roughly between Broadway and Sixth Avenue, **Little Korea** is the place to go for traditional dishes like Korean barbecue.

 # F-Stop

Contemporary American

8 West 20th Street
☎ 627-7867

Average meal: $25-30
for less discount: 25%
AM/MC/VS/DC

HOURS

Mon-Sun: 11.30am-11pm

This modern restaurant, gallery and lounge is located in the Photo District. It displays recent photographic works on a rotating basis. The herb barbecued chicken over nutty couscous is highly recommended.

HOURS

Mon-Thu: 11.30am-11pm
Fri: 11.30am-12midnight
Sat: 11am-12midnight
Sun: 11am-10pm

HOURS

Mon-Thu: 12noon-11pm
Fri-Sat: 12noon-
12midnight
Sun: 12noon-10pm

HOURS

Mon-Fri: 8am-8pm
Sat: 9am-5pm
Sun: closed

Portfolio

Italian

4 West 19th Street
☎ 691-3845

Average meal: $20-25
for less discount: 25%
AM/MC/VS/DC

This charming restaurant offers high quality food and service at great prices. The décor is chic and the limited edition artwork on the walls is for sale. Portfolio's homemade pasta dishes and daily specials are superb.

Heartland Brewery

American / Brewery

35 Union Square West
☎ 645-3400

Average meal: $15-20
for less discount: 25%
AM/MC/VS/DC

Heartland is located in an historic building with an on site brewhouse. The setting is a spacious loft with hand painted murals and wooden booths. An informal menu compliments the wide spectrum of beers available.

Barocco Kitchen

American / International

42 Union Square East
☎ 254-6777

Average meal: $10-15
for less discount: 25%
AM/MC/VS

On Union Square, Barocco Kitchen serves a variety of freshly made international dishes in a modern café setting. House specialties include vegetable and meat lasagna and fresh salads.

Cafe Bondi

Italian

7 West 20th Street
☎ 691-8136

Average meal: $25-30
or less discount: 25%
AM/MC/VS/DC

Sicilian cuisine is the specialty at this elegant, romantic restaurant. A cozy dining room and an airy garden enhance the dining experience. *Pasta con sarde* and *alamaretti alla griglia* are both excellent dishes.

HOURS

Mon-Thu: 11am-11pm
Fri-Sat: 11am-12midnight
Sun: 11am-9.30pm

Zip City Brewing Company

American / Brewery

3 West 18th Street
☎ 366-6333

Average meal: $15-20
or less discount: 25%
AM/MC/VS/DC

Located in the Flatiron District, this informal brewery has a lively, pub-style atmosphere. The menu is designed to suit the many varieties of beer which are brewed right on the premises. Try the Zip City beer crust pizza.

HOURS

Mon-Thu: 11.30am-
12midnight
Fri-Sat: 12noon-2am
Sun: 12noon-12midnight

Mendy's East

Delicatessen / Kosher

61 East 34th Street
☎ 576-1010

Average meal: $15-20
or less discount: 25%
AM/MC/VS/DC/DS

Mendy's East is located near the Empire State Building. It is an ideal place to enjoy lunch or dinner after visiting the attraction. This kosher restaurant serves a full range of tasty steaks and sandwiches and deli items.

HOURS

Mon-Thu: 11am-10pm
Fri: 11am-2.30pm
Sat: closed
Sun: 11am-10pm

Cafe Mozart

Café

110 West 25th Street
☎ 807-8763

Average meal: $5-10
for less discount: 25%
No credit cards

HOURS

Tue-Sun: 11am-6pm
Mon: closed

On the eighth floor of the Chelsea Antiques Center, Cafe Mozart serves a variety of coffees, teas and fresh-baked goods. The soups and sandwiches are great at lunchtime after browsing the many antique shops in the building.

Estoril Sol

Italian / Portuguese

382 Eighth Avenue
☎ 947-1043

Average meal: $20-25
for less discount: 25%
AM/MC/VS/DC/DS

HOURS

Mon-Fri: 12noon-10pm
Sat: 4pm-10pm
Sun: closed

For over 20 years, Estoril Sol has been serving Italian and Portuguese fare. Traditional décor and a fireplace complement the casual atmosphere. The *caldeirada* (fish stew) and the veal chops are highly recommended.

Tiziano

Italian / Mediterranean

165 Eighth Avenue
☎ 989-2330

Average meal: $15-20
for less discount: 25%
AM/MC/VS

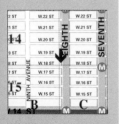

HOURS

Mon-Sun: 12noon-12midnight

This casual, romantic bistro serves Mediterranean dishes such as garlic and parmesan crusted tuna, which is highly recommended. Situated in Chelsea, Tiziano has an outdoor café and wood-burning brick oven.

Raj of India

Indian

336 Eighth Avenue
☎ 807-6678

Average meal: $10-15
or less discount: 25%
AM/MC/VS/DC/DS

HOURS

Mon-Sun: 12noon-11pm

Raj of India specializes in traditional cuisine from various regions in India. The atmosphere is comfortable and casual, and the décor is Indian. Try the *chicken tikka masala* or any of the combination platters.

 # Sahara Classic

Mediterranean / Turkish

92 Third Avenue
☎ 677-7106

Average meal: $15-20
or less discount: 25%
AM/MC/VS/DC/DS

HOURS

Mon-Sun: 11am-11pm

Sahara Classic serves traditional Mediterranean cuisine at reasonable prices. A friendly staff and comfortable dining room create a pleasant atmosphere in which to enjoy dishes like *baba ghanous* and chicken kebabs.

L'Oro di Napoli II

Italian

17 Second Avenue
☎ 213-1838

Average meal: $20-25
or less discount: 25%
AM/MC/VS/DC

HOURS

Mon-Sun: 12noon-12midnight

L'Oro di Napoli II has been serving flavorful Italian cuisine for 25 years. Enjoy house specialities, like homemade gnocchi or shrimp with linguini, in a pleasant setting, at either lunch or dinner.

Shopping

Barney's New York

Chelsea is well-known as a retail destination. The elegant department store **Barneys New York** *(106 Seventh Avenue,* ☎ *929-9000)* can be found here, as well as smaller clothing and gift boutiques like **Boombastik** (see below), which carries designer clothing and home furnishings. For sportswear and casual clothing, **Starting Line** (see below) and **Chelsea Army and Navy** (page 130) sell all the major brands.

Around the corner from **Emporio Armani** *(110 Fifth Avenue,* ☎ *727-3240)*, **Carapan** (page 130) is a quiet retreat which has a choice selection of bath, body and hair care products. A great place to buy an unusual gift is Gramercy Park's **Recherché** (page 129) – a favorite stop for young Hollywood actresses visiting New York City.

Starting Line

Clothing & Athletic Wear

180 Eighth Avenue
☎ 691-4729

for less discount: 20%
AM/MC/VS/DS

HOURS

Mon-Thu: 11am-9pm
Fri-Sat: 11am-10pm
Sun: 12noon-7pm

Starting Line offers stylish designer clothing for men and women, including a wide variety of jeans, jackets, shoes and bags. Popular brands like Adidas, French Connection and Puma are all stocked.

Boombastik

Clothing

204 Seventh Avenue
☎ 620-8180

for less discount: 20%
AM/MC/VS

HOURS

Mon-Fri: 9am-7pm
Sat: 10am-7pm
Sun: closed

This chic boutique carries trendy clothing and accessories. It features a large selection of men's and women's designer wear together with decorative home furnishings and gifts.

Recherché

Gifts

71 Third Avenue
☎ 979-1415

or less discount: 20%
AM/MC/VS

This elegant shop is the perfect place to find a unique gift. Items range from one-of-a-kind handmade objects to antique collectibles. Jewelry, pillows and specialty items are available, many made by local artisans.

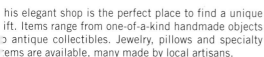
Decor Art Gallery

Art Gallery & Poster Shop

58 Seventh Avenue
☎ 604-9864

or less discount: 20%
M/MC/VS

This shop carries a large selection of posters and art covering many subjects. The *New York for less* discount also applies at the other Decor Art Galleries located at 53 Third Avenue and 333 Park Avenue.

Norman's Sound and Vision Too

Music

28 Seventh Avenue
☎ 255-0076

or less discount: 20%
M/MC/VS

Norman's sells both new and used CDs and videos. Their stock, which includes classical, rock, jazz and reggae is a good place to locate hard-to-find music. The discount also applies at Norman's in the East Village (page 111).

Chelsea Army and Navy

Army Navy & Clothing

111 Eighth Avenue
☎ 645-7420

for less discount: 20%
AM/MC/VS/DS

HOURS

Mon and Thu:
10am-7.45pm
Tue-Wed and Fri-Sat:
10am-6.30pm
Sun: 12noon-5.30pm

Chelsea Army and Navy offers sports apparel and army
navy gear, including a large range of jackets, shoes and
boots. A solid selection of well-known brands includes
clothing and accessories for both men and women.

Carapan

Gifts

5 West 16th Street
☎ 633-6220

for less discount: 20%
AM/MC/VS

HOURS

Mon-Sun: 10am-8pm

Carapan sells a fine selection of natural bath, body and
hair care products. Cards, candles, incense and oils are
also available. There are various Native American items
including "dreamcatchers" and decorations.

Galaxy Army & Navy

Army Navy & Clothing

859 Sixth Avenue
☎ 736-1166

for less discount: 20%
AM/MC/VS/DS

HOURS

Mon-Fri: 9am-5pm
Sun: 10am-7pm
Sat: closed

Galaxy Army and Navy stocks a full range of outdoor and
military gear. Apparel includes jeans, jackets, boots,
camping equipment and accessories. Brand names
include Lee, Levi's and Timberland.

Midtown West

Introduction . . .

Midtown West is the area which best exemplifies the busy streets of New York City seen on television and in the movies. The area is essentially commercial –

filled with tall office buildings and notorious for its "midtown traffic".

Entering the lower midtown from Chelsea, you will easily be able to identify your entrance into the **Garment District** (page 146) by the delivery trucks holding up traffic and the clothing trolleys delaying pedestrians along Seventh Avenue – known here as "**Fashion Avenue**".

Busy midtown streets

Before the late 19th century, **Herald Square**, named after the defunct Herald newspaper, was one of the seedier areas of New York. After the giant **Macy's** department store (page 146) was established in the late 1800s, however, it became a popular commercial and shopping district, a character that it retains to this day.

For visitors, Midtown West is best known for its **Theater District**. Although the majority of commercial theaters here are actually located on the side streets *off* Broadway, the term "Broadway" has come to collectively represent all the major theaters in the area.

Broadway at 34th Street, ca. 1910

This neighborhood has shown signs of becoming a center for New York theaters since the latter half of the 19th century. When the *New York Times* built their offices above what was known as Longacre Square, at the beginning of the 20th century, the newly named "**Times Square**" was connected to the subway system and quickly brought the hub of the Theater District to its present location.

Of the 40 or so active theaters, 22 of them have been designated historical landmarks. **The Lyceum** is the oldest and has operated continuously since it was built in 1903. The nearby **Shubert Theatre** welcomed an unknown Barbra Streisand in her 1962 Broadway debut.

Today, Times Square sees one-and-a-half million people pass through every day. It is famous for its

. . . Introduction

colossal neon signs, giant billboards and the neon apple that falls annually to ring in the New Year.

Recently, an aggressive make-over campaign has focused on shaking Times Square's grimy reputation. The closing of "adult" film theaters and shops along 42nd Street, coupled with major corporate openings like the **Virgin Megastore**, **All-Star Cafe** and **Disney Store** have literally changed the face of the area.

Times Square

Bryant Park (page 141), the only major park in Midtown Manhattan, was the site of the 1853 World's Fair. It had endured a long period of decay in the 20th century before being closed in 1989 for a complete make-over. Today, this tree-lined grassy expanse, with its neatly manicured lawns, is a great place to retreat from the hectic midtown sidewalks.

The nearby **International Center of Photography Midtown** (page 139) mounts some excellent photographic exhibits, often focusing on a particular genre or artist. Further north, you can experience three major New York City museums in just a few short blocks – the **Museum of Modern Art**, known as MoMA (page 134-135), the **American Craft Museum** (page 138) and **The Museum of Television and Radio** (page 136).

One of New York's most popular tourist attractions, **Rockefeller Center** (page 139) is great to visit all year round. The best time to come here, however, is during the holidays when the giant Christmas tree is lit in front of the GE Building and ice skaters fill the rink below.

Christmas Tree at Rockefeller Center

Around the corner, the legendary **Radio City Music Hall** is famous for its quality productions, and its *Christmas Spectacular*, which continues to draw the crowds year after year. The **Grand Tour** (page 137) provides a fascinating look behind-the-scenes at this landmark Art Deco building.

Along the Hudson River, you can visit the aircraft carrier *USS Intrepid* which is now the centerpiece of the **Intrepid Sea-Air-Space Museum** (page 138). Once a year, sailors from the U.S. Navy gather here for "Fleet Week". Although this is not an event that New Yorkers take part in, they are reminded of its existence when they suddenly notice packs of uniformed sailors filling the streets.

ADDRESS

*Museum and The MoMA
Book Store*:
11 West 53rd Street
☎ 708-9400

The MoMA Design Store:
44 West 53rd Street

HOURS

Museum:
Sat-Tue: 11am-6pm
Thu-Fri: 12noon-8:30pm
Wed: closed

The MoMA Book Store:
Sat-Wed: 11am-6.30pm
Thu-Fri: 11am-9pm

The MoMA Design Store:
Mon-Wed and Sat:
10am-6pm
Thu-Fri: 10am-8pm
Sun: 11am-6pm

 # The Museum of Modern Art . . .

The Museum of Modern Art holds the world's premier collection of modern art. Its unrivaled selection of 20th-century artists ranges from **Picasso** to **Warhol**, **Monet** to **Matisse**. Even if you're not very familiar with modern art, you will recognize many works here.

The Museum of Modern Art opened its first exhibition in 1929, displaying Post-Impressionist artists such as **Cézanne**, **Gauguin**, **Seurat** and Van Gogh who were hardly known in the United States at the time.

This new museum generated an immediate response from an appreciative public who were

Girl with Ball (1961) by Roy Lichtenstein

eager to learn more about the art of their day. In the first ten years of its life, the museum outgrew four temporary homes before moving into its current building.

Since its founding, the collection has grown to include approximately 100,000 paintings, sculptures, drawings, architectural models and plans, prints, photographs and design objects. The museum now receives over one-and-a-half million visitors each year.

Among the museum's finest (and most famous) paintings are Claude Monet's *Water Lilies*; Pablo Picasso's *Les Demoiselles d'Avignon*; Henri Matisse's *Dance*; **René Magritte**'s *The False Mirror*; Salvador Dali's *The Persistence of Memory* and Andy Warhol's *Gold Marilyn Monroe*. Perhaps the best known and most treasured painting is **Vincent Van Gogh**'s *The Starry Night*.

You will probably want to start your visit to the museum in the **Painting and Sculpture** galleries, situated on the second and third floors. There you will find major artists and movements from **Post-Impressionism** to **Pop Art**, including the majority of the museum's most famous works.

Sculpture Garden at MoMA

The second floor also houses the **Drawings** galleries, featuring works on paper by **Paul Klee**, Henri Matisse, **Georgia O'Keeffe** and **Robert Rauschenberg** as well as drawings that focus on a particular movement such as **Surrealism** and **Dada**.

. . . The Museum of Modern Art

he **Photography** galleries, on the second floor, span
ne entire history of the medium, including works by
artier-Bresson and **Stieglitz**.

n the third floor, the **Prints and Illustrated Books
ollection** covers artists from over 60 countries,
icluding an impressive selection of works by Picasso.
iverse and expansive, it features lithographs,
tchings, screenprints and woodcuts.

ne of the most unusual collections is that of
rchitecture and Design, located on the fourth floor.
rchitectural models and plans are featured alongside
esign objects which range from household appliances
nd furniture to high-tech equipment such as a
ell helicopter and a Formula One race car.

ne Museum of Modern Art was the first
iuseum to recognize the motion picture as an
t form. Since 1935, it has been collecting
nd preserving important films. It now
ossesses some ten thousand films as well as
our million film stills from all periods and
enres. Screenings are held daily in two
ieaters, and video exhibitions are scheduled on
regular basis.

addition to its permanent collection, MoMA
so mounts large temporary exhibitions.
ideed, of the 87,000 square feet of gallery
aace, 20,000 is reserved for temporary
xhibitions that display works and retrospective
udies of modern and contemporary artists.

ne museum's renowned publishing program has
roduced more than 500 books on the visual
ts including exhibition catalogues, books on modern
t, books that illustrate the museum's collections and
n annual journal called *Studies in Modern Art*. Many
these can be purchased at The MoMA Stores, which
fer a discount to *New York for less* cardholders.

ne Museum of Modern Art was the first New York City
useum to offer a random-access **digital audio guide**
r their permanent collection. It allows you to explore
e museum's painting and sculpture galleries at your
vn pace. You can select up to three hours of
ommentary by the museum's director and top
irators, who provide fresh insights and information
oout the works and the artists who created them.
ith your *New York for less* card you can obtain a
scount on admission and two audio tours for the
ice of one.

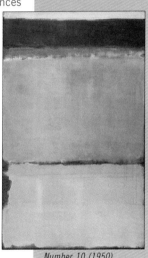

*Number 10 (1950)
by Mark Rothko*

ADDRESS

25 West 52nd Street
☎ 621-6800

HOURS

Mon: closed
Tue-Wed and Sat-Sun:
12noon-6pm
Thu: 12noon-8pm
Fri: 12noon-6pm, theater
open until 9pm

PRICES

Suggested admission:
Adult $6
Child $3
Senior $4
Student $4

DISCOUNT

20% discount at the
museum shop with your
New York for less card.

DON'T MISS

An individual screening of
your past favorite TV or
radio program or
advertisement.

🖼 The Museum of TV & Radio

Founded by **William S. Paley**, former head of the giant
CBS network, The Museum of Television & Radio is a
unique museum experience. It gives you the
opportunity to enjoy television and radio programs
spanning the entire history of the media.

Today, the museum possesses some 75,000 programs
from more than 75 years of television and radio
history. The programs include everything from news
and public affairs to
documentaries and
performing arts.
There are also
children's programs,
sports, comedy,
variety shows and
even commercial
advertising. You can
watch or listen to
everything from news
coverage of World
War II to **The Beatles**
playing on the **Ed
Sullivan Show**.

The Museum of TV and Radio

The entire collection
is catalogued in a
computerized library
database which
allows you to privately
screen or listen to a program of your choice. By
making a reservation at the front desk when you arrive
you can select up to six programs at a time. You then
go to an individual television and radio console where
you can watch or listen to your selections.

Exhibitions, a screening and listening series, seminars
and education classes are offered throughout the year
Every day, the museum presents programs in the two
main theaters and two screening rooms. Copies of the
daily schedule are available at the lobby front desk.

The seminars consist of in-person discussions with
prominent writers, producers, directors, actors and
others recognized for their work in programming.
There are also galleries with exhibits relating to
television and radio.

The museum's shop is located on the main floor and
offers T-shirts, posters, cassettes, postcards and other
gift items. There are also books on subjects related to
television and radio. With your *New York for less* card
you can receive a 20% discount off all goods.

Radio City Music Hall Grand Tour

adio City Music Hall, one of New York City's premier
ntertainment venues, is a landmark Art Deco building
ituated around the corner from Rockefeller Center.
pened in 1932, it escaped demolition in 1979 and

has since been
beautifully
restored.

Radio City is
probably most
famous for its
Rockettes – the
dance troupe that
draws over a
million spectators

Radio City Music Hall

its annual *Radio City Christmas Spectacular*, a 90-
inute holiday show in which Santa Claus makes a
ameo appearance. The *Radio City Spring
pectacular* is also very popular, especially with
hildren. The theater also hosts first-rate live music
cts and special events throughout the year.

rofessional guides lead you through the one-hour
rand Tour offering behind-the-scene views of the
eater's remarkable history and Art Deco
rchitectural splendor.

ou will meet one of the **Radio City Rockettes**, visit the
ostume shop and see 60 years worth of history-
aking fabrics, patterns and costume sketches. You
an also explore the celebrated Art Deco interior with
s block-long **Grand Foyer**, 24-carat gold leaf ceiling,
weeping staircase and pair of two-ton glass
handeliers.

ou see first-hand the incredible technology involved
creating these productions, including "curtains"
at create steam and rain, a
urlitzer organ that weighs 5 tons
nd has pipes ranging in size from a
w inches to 32 feet. You will learn
bout a stage elevator system so
ophisticated that its design was
orrowed by the U.S. Navy for
rcraft carriers during World War II.

ours depart approximately every
alf hour from Radio City Music
all's main lobby at the corner of
ixth Avenue and 50th Street. With
e *New York for less* voucher on

The Art Deco interior of Radio City Music Hall

age 275, you receive a free tour for every one that
ou purchase.

ADDRESS

1260 Avenue of the
Americas
☎ 632-4041

HOURS

Mon-Sat: 10am-5pm
Sun: 11am-5pm
Tours depart approximately
every half hour.

PRICES

Adult $13.75
Child $9
Senior $13.75
Student $13.75

DISCOUNT

2 tours for the price of 1
with voucher on page 275.

Intrepid Sea-Air-Space Museum

Other Attractions . . .

The Intrepid Sea-Air-Space Museum is housed aboard the aircraft carrier *USS Intrepid*. Docked on the Hudson River, a short distance from Midtown Manhattan, this World War II vessel has weathered bombs, kamikazes and torpedoes. It was designated a National Historic Landmark and, after 37 years of active duty, it is now the world's largest naval museum. It offers a complete history of naval aviation, space and undersea exploration.

In addition to the *Intrepid*, other painstakingly restored historic ships include the guided nuclear missile submarine *Growler* and the large fleet destroyer *Edson*. Also part of the flotilla are the Coast Guard cutter *Tamaroa*, which sits next to another World War II veteran, the destroyer escort *Slater* and the operational school ship *Elizabeth M. Fisher*. Touring these ships gives you a first-hand look at life at sea.

USS Intrepid

Exhibits focus on subjects such as World War II, the history of undersea and space exploration, aircraft and ship design and satellite communication. You can also see the world's fastest plane, a CIA spy plane, the *Lockheed A-12 Blackbird*, as well as a Russian *MIG 21*.

The SR-2 simulator takes visitors through a series of fast-moving maneuvers in less than seven minutes. This is a great place for children and, with *New York for less*, all admission prices are reduced 20%. *(Hudson River at 46th Street,* ☎ *245-2533. Mon-Sat: 10am-5pm. Sun: 10am-6pm (summer). Wed-Sun: 10am-5pm. Mon-Tue: closed (winter). Adult $10, child (12-17) $7.50, child (6-11) $5, senior and veteran $7.50, student $7.50. 20% off admission with voucher on page 275.)*

The interior of the American Craft Museum

The **American Craft Museum** recently celebrated its 40th year as America's most significant resource for 20th-century craft objects. Its mission is to collect, exhibit and preserve contemporary crafts and interpret their evolution over the course of the 20th century.

Since it opened in 1956, the museum has showcased the work of American craftspeople whose handmade objects are not only appreciated for their beauty, but

American Craft Museum

... Other Attractions ...

lso recognized for their spirit in a world of machine-
nade products.

American Craft Museum

he museum's extensive collection dates from
900 and contains an interesting and
nnovative mix of furniture and crafts.

)ver the years, there have been numerous
najor exhibitions ranging from the simple to
he unusual. Two examples of previous
xhibits are *The Ideal Home: 1900-1920* and
"Edible Drawings" by John Cage. The
nuseum also organizes exhibitions that tour the
ation.

rtists represented here have worked in a variety of
nedia including ceramics, glass, metal, wood and
lastic – often using the materials in unconventional

ICP Midtown

ways. You can see the
results of modern
techniques upon
traditional crafts such
as the updated art of
gold and
silversmithing.

Educational programs
strive to enhance
ublic awareness of contemporary crafts, while
vorkshops teach craftmaking techniques. *(40 West
3rd Street, ☎ 956-3535. Tue-Wed and Fri-Sun: 10am-6pm.
hu: 10am-8pm. Mon: closed. Adult $5, child free, senior
2.50, student $2.50. 2 admissions for the price of 1 with
oucher on page 275.)*

INSIDER'S TIP

On Tuesdays, from 6pm-
8pm, ICP Midtown has
a pay-what-you-wish
admission policy.

The International Center of Photography
Midtown is one of the few museums in the world
evoted solely to photography. The main ICP is
ocated on Museum Mile (see page 192). The
nidtown branch of this renowned photographic
nstitution is housed in a modern building a block
way from Bryant Park. Exhibits generally highlight a
articular genre or photographer. *(1133 Sixth Avenue,
☎ 768-4680. Tue: 11am-8pm. Wed-Sun: 11am-6pm. Mon:
losed. Adult $4, child $2, senior $2.50, student $2.50. 2
dmissions for the price of 1 with voucher on page 275.)*

*International Center of
Photography*

uilt between 1931 and 1940 by oil tycoon John D.
ockefeller, **Rockefeller Center** was originally
omprised of 14 buildings. Today, it occupies almost
hree city blocks. A total of 19 buildings are within
he complex, including Radio City Music Hall (page
37). The tallest building and centerpiece of the
omplex is the 70-story **GE Building** *(30 Rockefeller*

. . . Other Attractions . . .

Plaza), the headquarters of America's largest company, Rockefeller Center was declared a landmark in 1985 and is the largest privately owned business and entertainment center in the world. *(47th-50th Streets, between Fifth and Sixth Avenues.)*

Rockefeller Center

At Rockefeller Plaza, **NBC Studios** currently opens four shows to guests: *Saturday Night Live*, *The Rosie O'Donnell Show*, *In Person with Maureen O'Boyle* and *Late Night with Conan O'Brien*. For most shows, you must write for tickets months in advance, but for *Late Night with Conan O' Brien*, tickets are given out Tuesday through Friday, at 9am in NBC's main lobby, on the day of the show, call 664-3056 for more information or to make a reservation. *(30 Rockefeller Plaza, ☎ 664-3055. Hours vary.)*

30 Rockefeller Plaza

Ed Sullivan Theater

The **Late Show with David Letterman**, which was once based in the GE Building at Rockefeller Plaza, is now taped at the **Ed Sullivan Theater**. *(1697 Broadway, ☎ 975-1003 for ticket information.)*

The New York Public Library is New York City's main public research center. The interior is just as grand as the impressive facade where granite lions guard the entrance. The library hosts various exhibits and offers free one-hour tours Monday through Saturday at 11am and 2pm starting from the "friends desk" in Astor Hall. *(Fifth Avenue and 42nd Street, ☎ 661-7220. Mon and Thu-Sat: 10am-6pm. Tue-Wed: 11am-7.30pm. Sun: closed.)*

New York Public Library

New York Public Library

Jacob K. Javits Convention Center, which opened in 1986, is a 15-story glass building on the Hudson River which was designed for large-scale expositions and conventions. *(655 West 34th Street, ☎ 216-2000.)*

Shubert Alley, named after theater legend Sam S. Shubert, describes those theaters located west of Broadway on 44th and 45th Streets. The 1913 **Shubert Theater** is where *A Chorus Line* broke records as one of the longest running shows in Broadway history. Also of historical and architectural interest is **The Booth Theater**, built in the same year. *(Shubert Alley: West 44th-45th Streets. Shubert Theater:*

. . . Other Attractions

(21 West 45th Street. Booth Theater: 22 West 45th Street.)

Carnegie Hall

Built in 1924, the **City Center of Music and Drama** is magnificently detailed Moorish-style Masonic Shriners' Temple that later became home to the New York City Opera and Ballet. Today, no longer affiliated with the opera or ballet, the exquisitely restored City Center is still an important venue for dance performances. *(131 West 55th Street, ☎ 581-7909.)*

Carnegie Hall, New York's first and most prestigious concert hall, was financed by steel magnate Andrew Carnegie. Tchaikovsky conducted the opening performance in 1891. After being saved from destruction in the late 1950s, the building was declared a landmark. A refurbishment in 1986 restored the hall to its former glory. In 1991, Carnegie Hall opened an exhibit celebrating its first 100 years. Top American and international artists still perform here regularly. *(57th Street and Seventh Avenue, ☎ 247-7800.)*

Carnegie Hall at night

Open Spaces

Nestling behind the New York Public Library, **Bryant Park** seems like it would be more at home in Paris

Bryant Park

than in New York City. Its shady perimeter consists of a stone path where, in warm weather, folding chairs are set out for the hordes of office workers who descend upon the park at lunchtime.

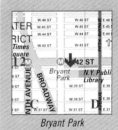
Bryant Park

A few years ago, it was chosen as the location for New York's **semi-annual fashion shows**. These shows attract huge crowds and have helped lend a more sophisticated image to what was, not long ago, a run-down and dangerous park.

Throughout the summer, the park holds a variety of free cultural events including concerts and outdoor movies shown on a giant screen at sunset.

Channel Gardens at Rockefeller Center is set between the British Empire Building and La Maison Française. It is a great place to relax after a busy day of sightseeing and shopping. The mermaid and dolphin fountains are surrounded by fresh flowers, making a great background for photo-taking.

Channel Gardens at Rockefeller Center

Eating and Drinking

Times Square is not only packed with traffic but also with over-priced, fast food restaurants that New Yorkers tend to avoid at all costs. Skip this area altogether and head to the side streets instead. Many of the restaurants on the following pages, all of which give a discount to *New York for less* cardholders, are in, or near, the Theater District.

Hardrock Cafe

At **Commonwealth Brewery** (see below) you can take a break from sightseeing to enjoy fine food and home-brewed beer at Rockefeller Center.

The "21" Club *(21 West 52nd Street, ☎ 582-7200)* started as a speakeasy. This brownstone landmark building (still flanked by its trademark jockey statues) retains the clublike atmosphere it had in bygone days, though a new chef promises a fresh perspective on its classic cuisine. More than 50,000 bottles make its wine cellar one of the world's largest.

Motown Cafe

Planet Hollywood *(140 West 57th Street, ☎ 333-7827)*, Hard Rock Cafe *(221 West 57th Street, ☎ 489-6565)* and Motown Cafe *(104 West 57th Street, ☎ 581-8030)* are just a few of the theme restaurants that line 57th Street. Despite the fact that jaded New Yorkers would never admit it, these places actually *can* be fun to visit and the food is of surprisingly good quality. Motown Cafe takes its theme a step further by also providing live entertainment.

Commonwealth Brewing Company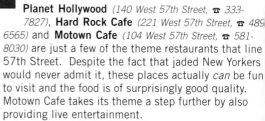

International / Brewer

35 West 48th Stree
☎ 977-226

Average meal: $20-2
for less discount: 25%
AM/MC/VS/DC/D

HOURS

Mon-Sat: 11.30am-11pm
Sun: 11.30am-9pm

At Rockefeller Center, this spacious brew-pub serve interesting international dishes and a variety of careful crafted beers in an upbeat atmosphere. Try the Bavaria butcher's skillet or the CBNY charbroiled angus burge

Avanti

Italian

700 Ninth Avenue
☎ 586-7410

Average meal: $20-25
or less discount: 25%
AM/MC/VS

HOURS

Mon-Thu: 12noon-3pm,
5pm-10.30pm
Fri-Sat: 12noon-2.30pm,
5pm-11pm
Sun: 12noon-3pm,
5pm-10.30pm

Avanti is romantic, yet casual, with separate bar and dining areas. It is a cozy restaurant featuring exposed brick walls and a fireplace. Enjoy modern Italian cuisine and favorites like homemade *gnocchi*.

 # Broadway Joe's Steakhouse

American / Steakhouse

315 West 46th Street
☎ 246-6513

Average meal: $20-25
or less discount: 25%
AM/MC/VS/DC/DS

HOURS

Mon-Sun: 11am-
12midnight

This landmark restaurant is a favorite with sports and theater celebrities. It has been serving the best in prime meats and seafood for 50 years. A "Wall of Fame" pictorial reflects the surrounding Broadway theaters.

 # The Playwright

Irish / American

202 West 49th Street
☎ 262-9263

Average meal: $10-15
or less discount: 25%
AM/MC/VS/DC

HOURS

Mon-Sun: 11.30am-
12midnight

Close to Times Square, the Playwright is a great stop for lunch or dinner. Enjoy Irish and American fare in a relaxed, informal pub atmosphere. Specialties include the authentic *"Baggot Street fish n' chips plate"*.

HOURS

Mon-Fri: 11.30am-
10.30pm
Sat: 4.30pm-10.30pm
Sun: closed

HOURS

Mon-Sat: 12noon-3pm,
5.30pm-11pm
Sun: 12noon-3pm,
5pm-10pm

HOURS

Mon-Sun:
11.30am-10.30pm

Maristella

Italian

69 West 55th Street
☎ 489-7655

Average meal: $15-20
for less discount: 25%
AM/MC/VS/DC/DS

Maristella serves Italian fare in a comfortable, modern
setting. The homemade ravioli and seafood dishes are
recommended. Open at 11.30am, Maristella is a good
choice for pre-theater lunch or dinner.

Bay Leaf

Indian

49 West 56th Street
☎ 957-1818

Average meal: $20-25
for less discount: 25%
AM/MC/VS/DC

Bay Leaf offers fine Indian cuisine in a modern setting.
It is a great place to come for a leisurely, high quality
lunch or dinner. Chef's specialties include *tandoori
shrimp haraginga.*

Il Brunello

Italian

56 West 56th Street
☎ 247-2779

Average meal: $15-20
for less discount: 25%
AM/MC/VS/DC

This friendly family-run restaurant offers good northern
Italian fare. Il Brunello is convenient to midtown
shopping and the Broadway theaters. Try any of the pasta
dishes or the veal and chicken combination.

Mike's American Bar and Grill

American

550 Tenth Avenue
☎ 246-4115

Average meal: $15-20
or less discount: 25%
AM/MC/VS

HOURS

Sun-Mon: 5.30pm-11pm
Tue-Sat: 5.30pm-
12midnight
Sat-Sun (brunch):
11am-4pm

Mike's is a casual, theme restaurant a short walk from the Theater District. Previous themes include musicals, TV shows and movies like *Star Wars*. You can enjoy hearty dishes like grilled pork chops and pastas.

MK Restaurant

Continental

440 Ninth Avenue
☎ 629-0744

Average meal: $15-20
or less discount: 25%
AM/MC/VS/DC/DS

HOURS

Mon-Fri: 11.30am-3pm,
5pm-9pm
Sat-Sun: closed

MK has been serving continental cuisine at reasonable prices for over 15 years. The décor is modern and the atmosphere is warm and friendly. Recommended dishes are breast of chicken Dijon and beef stroganoff.

Il Teatro

Italian

240 West 54th Street
☎ 245-8045

Average meal: $15-20
or less discount: 25%
AM/MC/VS/DC

HOURS

Mon-Fri: 11.30am-
10.30pm
Sat: 4.30pm-10.30pm
Sun: closed

Il Teatro is centrally located in the heart of New York's Theater District. The atmosphere is up-beat and piano entertainment is provided nightly. Choose from a broad selection of seafood, steaks and pastas.

Shopping

The Garment District *(Seventh Avenue between 34th and 42nd Streets)* is the heart of the fashion industry. Top designers and their expensive creations are tucked away in showrooms high above Seventh Avenue, which is known here as "**Fashion Avenue**".

Lord & Taylor

Times Square is a mecca for electronic and souvenir shops. **Taxi Stop** (page 147), is a great place to pick up New York City mementoes, while **Triton Gallery** (page 148), in the Theater District, specializes in Broadway-themed posters and prints. **Santino Photos** (page 148) carries souvenirs as well as photographic and electronic equipment.

Macy's

Diamond Row

On **Diamond Row** *(47th Street between Fifth and Sixth Avenues)* practically every shop window sparkles with diamonds and gold. The area became a center for the jewelry trade early in the century, when Jewish diamond merchants emigrated from Amsterdam.

Midtown West is home to many of New York's big department stores including **Macy's** *(Herald Square at 34th Street,* ☎ *695-4400)*, the world's largest. Its annual televised **Thanksgiving Day Parade** faithfully entertains the nation with gigantic character balloons, which float down Fifth Avenue. Across the street, **Manhattan Mall** *(Sixth Avenue and 33rd Street)* is a suburban shopping mall in the middle of Manhattan.

Lord & Taylor

On Fifth Avenue, **Lord & Taylor** *(424 Fifth Avenue,* ☎ *391-3344)* is best known for its classic American styles. During its winter sales, you can find timeless items like cashmere sweaters at substantial savings. **Bergdorf Goodman** *(754 Fifth Avenue,* ☎ *753-7300)* and **Henri Bendel** *(712 Fifth Avenue,* ☎ *247-1100)* tend to be quite expensive, though the quality of their merchandise is outstanding.

Macy's at Herald Square

Many designer boutiques line Fifth Avenue (see also Midtown East shopping, page 159) including famous (as in famously expensive) jeweler **Harry Winston** *(718 Fifth Avenue,* ☎ *245-2000)*. Even Hollywood stars who wear Winston's jewels to the Academy Awards *borrow* them. This is exactly what makes this museum-like store worth a peek.

MASH Army and Navy

Army Navy & Clothing

721 Eighth Avenue
☎ 765-1500

for less discount: 20%
AM/MC/VS/DS

HOURS

Mon-Thu: 10am-8pm
Fri: 10am-5pm
Sun: 10.30am-8pm
Sat: closed

MASH specializes in outdoor and casual items. Military surplus, camping gear, work shoes and boots are all available, as well as casual shirts, shoes, boots and jeans in a variety of name-brands.

 # Taxi Stop

Gifts & Souvenirs

724 Eighth Avenue
☎ 869-0344

for less discount: 20%
AM/MC/VS/DS

HOURS

Mon-Sun: 9am-11.30pm

Taxi Stop specializes in New York City T-shirts and souvenirs. It also carries posters, post cards and an assortment of trinkets. It is a great place to purchase novelty gifts, postcards or souvenirs.

 # Authentic New York

Clothing

433 Fifth Avenue
☎ 686-0778

for less discount: 20%
VS/MC/DC/DS

HOURS

Mon-Sat: 9am-8pm
Sun: 11am-7pm

A huge stock of denim includes Calvin Klein, Guess and Levi's 501. Ralph Lauren clothing and Schott's leather can also be found. Your *New York for less* discount also applies at the Greenwich Village location (page 110).

HOURS

Mon-Fri: 7.30am-6.30pm
Sat: 9.30am-4.30pm
Sun: hours vary,
call ahead

HOURS

Mon-Sat: 10am-6pm
Sun: closed

HOURS

Mon-Sun: 8am-8pm

Fromex 1 Hour Photo

Film Developing

1369 Sixth Avenue
☎ 307-1848

for less discount: 20% off
color film developing
AM/MC/VS/DS

One-hour photo developing allows you to see your vacation photos before you leave New York. With *New York for less*, you can save 20% when you have your color film developed at this and other Fromex locations.

Triton Gallery

Art Gallery & Posters

323 West 45th Street
☎ 765-2472

for less discount: 20%
AM/MC/VS/DC/DS

Triton carries a large selection of posters and art. Subjects range from classical art works and Broadway musicals to modern designs. You can also bring in your own poster to which they can custom fit a frame.

Santino Photos

Electronics & Souvenirs

1693 Broadway
☎ 397-6062

for less discount: 20%
AM/MC/VS

Santino Photos is stocked with a full range of high quality equipment. You can find laptop computers, video equipment, cameras and more. Top brands available include Sony, Canon, JVC and Panasonic.

Midtown East

Introduction . . .

Midtown East is synonymous with skyscapers, mega-corporations and Fifth Avenue. From outside Manhattan, you can see the mountainous peaks created by the enormous buildings located here, rising like steps to the Empire State Building (page 116-117) at 34th Street.

Grand Central Terminal

What distinguishes Midtown East from New York's other commercial districts is the architectural grandeur of many of its buildings. The 1920s construction boom led to the creation of skyscrapers such as the Empire State Building and the **Chrysler Building** (page 153). Both emerged as permanent fixtures of the Manhattan skyline and both bear the architectural details of the Art Deco era. With its stainless steel gargoyles and shiny hubcap decoration, the Chrysler Building is probably the quintessential example of the Art Deco style. The **Chanin Building** *(122 East 42nd Street)*, the area's first skyscraper, and the **News Building** (page 154) are also notable.

Waldorf-Astoria Hotel

More recently, corporate America's gleaming towers have adopted a simpler style, but have retained the ability to impress with a grandeur all their own. When **Lever House** *(390 Park Avenue)* was built in 1952, it was the first of its kind – sheer faces of glass and steel stood in stark contrast to the stone high-rises which surrounded it. Though Lever House set an architectural precedent, it now stands in the shadow of more modern (and much bigger) skyscrapers like the 1970s Citicorp Center, the IBM Building and the **Sony Building** *(550 Madison Avenue,* ☎ *833-8100)* whose ground floor is filled with interactive workstations, a retail store and hundreds of high-tech toys and games.

DON'T MISS

An architectural tour of Midtown East's famous skyscrapers – starting with the Municipal Art Society's free tour of Grand Central Terminal every Wednesday at 12.30pm (page 154).

Art Deco subway station

The **Met-Life Building** stands astride Park Avenue, dividing it in half, north to south. Cars must actually drive through and around the building in order to cross 42nd Street. Adjacent to it, **Grand Central Terminal** (page 153) is one of the most important transportation hubs in the city. From here, trains carry commuters to and from the nearby New York and Connecticut suburbs. A major renovation inside the main concourse will keep

. . . Introduction

most of the internal architectural details covered up for the next year or so.

Along Park Avenue, block-long residential buildings echo the grand scale of their commercial neighbors. One tribute to turn-of-the-century extravagance is the stunning **Villard Houses** (page 154).

The Plaza Hotel

On East 42nd Street, **Tudor City** was developed in the 1920s as a middle-class housing project constructed on an immense scale. Included within the 12 buildings are 3,000 apartments, a hotel, restaurants, shops and parks. The complex even has its own post office.

Murray Hill, situated in the East 30s, is named after the estate that once stood on the site. This residential neighborhood began as an enclave for turn-of-the-century New Yorkers wealthy enough to escape the crowded city downtown. Evidence of their lavish lifestyles can still be seen at the **Pierpont Morgan Library** (page 152), which was founded from J.P. Morgan's private collection. The area's brownstone homes and quiet streets continue to make it one of Manhattan's most desirable residential districts.

The former tradition of the "grand hotel" can still be seen at landmarks such as the **Waldorf-Astoria** (page 44 and 155) and **The Plaza** on Central Park South.

Fifth Avenue, the dividing line between Midtown East and Midtown West, is one of the most popular tourist destinations in town. With **Rockefeller Center** (page 139) on one side of the street, **St. Patrick's Cathedral** (page 154) and **Saks Fifth Avenue** (page 159) on the other, and just about every designer shop you could imagine in between, this is one of New York's best shopping and sightseeing areas.

On the East River, the **United Nations** building (page 153) is recognizable by the huge array of flags flying in front – one for each member nation. Interestingly, the area around the building is international territory and is not subject to United States law.

Flags at the United Nations

Pierpont Morgan Library

The Pierpont Morgan Library was founded In 1906 by legendary banker **J.P. Morgan** (1837-1913), who wanted to create an American institution for the arts and humanities to rival the great libraries of Europe.

The magnificent result, housed in a Renaissance-style palazzo, is a museum, research library and historic

landmark. It is now recognized as one of the world's premier artistic, literary and historical collections. The library's focus is the history, art and literature of Western civilization from the Middle Ages to the 20th century.

After purchasing the 9th-century *Lindau Gospels* in 1899, Morgan went on to acquire nearly 600 medieval and

Interior of the Pierpont Morgan Library

Renaissance manuscripts, many other rare books and bindings and a number of autographed manuscripts from English and American literary greats such as **Austen**, **Dickens**, **Thoreau** and **Twain**.

His collection also included more than 9,000 drawings and prints from the major French, German, Italian and Dutch schools as well as the country's largest and finest collection of **Rembrandt** etchings. There are also autographed music manuscripts (including Mozart's *Haffner Symphony*), a selection of Islamic manuscripts and roughly 1,200 Mesopotamian cylinder seals. Highlights of the collection are a rare vellum copy of the **Gutenberg Bible**, the medieval Dutch masterpiece *The Hours of Catherine Cleves*, Dürer's *Adam and Eve* and a letter from President George Washington to James Madison.

Following Morgan's death, his son, J.P. Morgan, Jr., increased the library's holdings and, in 1924, helped establish it as a public museum and research institution. Since this time, the collection has continued to grow.

There are tours of the library at 12noon from Tuesday to Friday. The adjacent shop, located in J.P. Morgan, Jr.'s former townhouse, offers items based on the museum's collection and grants a 10% discount to *New York for less* cardholders.

ADDRESS

29 East 36th Street
☎ 685-0610

HOURS

Tue-Fri: 10.30am-5pm
Sat: 10.30am-6pm
Sun: 12noon-6pm
Mon: closed
Bookshop closes 15 minutes before galleries.

PRICES

Suggested admission:
Adult $5
Child $3
Senior $3
Student $3

DISCOUNT

10% discount in the museum shop with your *New York for less* card.

DON'T MISS

The autographed manuscript of Charles Dickens' *A Christmas Carol*, the *Gutenberg Bible* and *The Hours of Catherine Cleves*.

Other Attractions . . .

ounded in 1945, the **United Nations** is an
rganization of nations that have banded together to
romote world peace. New York was chosen as its

United Nations

headquarters and an $8.5
million donation from John
D. Rockefeller, Jr. was used
to purchase the site. All of
the member nations are
represented in the General
Assembly, while additional
councils are represented by
selected delegates from
various member nations.
The Security Council is the
most powerful, and the one
most often spotlighted in
the media. It is the body

hat deals with international security and crises,
egotiating cease-fires, imposing economic sanctions
nd deploying military troops. Guided tours of the
ecurity Council Chamber and General Assembly Hall
re given daily, and are available in several foreign
anguages. In the lobby, you can see art and gifts
iven by various countries, including a chunk of moon
ock given by the U.S. and a model of *Sputnik 1* from
ne Soviet Union. *(First Avenue at 46th Street,* ☎ *963-
713. Mon-Sun: 9.15am-4.15pm (Mar-Dec). Mon-Fri:
.15am-4.15pm. Sat-Sun: closed (Jan-Feb).)*

United Nations

ompleted in 1930, the 77-story **Chrysler Building** is
ecognizable by its shining 7-story chrome top.
esigned for automobile pioneer Walter P. Chrysler,
ne building's brilliantly restored lobby
nce served as a car showroom and the
rt Deco tower was designed to look like a
ar's radiator grill. *(405 Lexington Avenue,*
• *682-3070. Mon-Fri: 7am-6pm. Sat-Sun:*
osed.)

Chrysler Building

rand Central Terminal**, built in 1913, is
renowned example of Beaux Arts
rchitecture. After years of steady
ecline, a major renovation in 1997 will
estore this landmark to its original
olendor. You can already see small
ections of the painted zodiac and
onstellation design on the turquoise blue
eiling, which has looked gray for years.
he four-faced clock above the
nformation booth is a well-known
endezvous spot in the middle of the enormous
oncourse. A food market, newsstands and the Oyster

Chrysler Building

. . . Other Attractions . . .

Grand Central Terminal

Bar seafood restaurant can also be found within the building. The Municipal Art Society, which was largely responsible for preserving Grand Central as a national landmark, provides free tours every Wednesday at 12.30pm (see page 224). *(East 42nd Street, at Park Avenue, ☎ 935-3960 for tours. Mon-Sun: 5am-1.30am.)*

Across the street, on the ground floor of the Philip Morris Building, there is a branch of the **Whitney Museum** (page 189). Viewing of the 20th-century art exhibits is enhanced by quiet tables and a coffee bar. *(120 Park Avenue, ☎ 878-2550. Mon-Wed and Fri: 11am-6pm. Thu: 11am-7.30pm. Sat-Sun: closed. Admission is free.)*

Grand Central Terminal

Built in 1931, the **News Building** is home to the *Daily News*, one of New York City's most popular papers, which was founded in 1919. Its lobby contains the largest interior globe in the world and is best known for its role as the home of the *Daily Planet* in the movie *Superman*. *(220 East 42nd Street. Mon-Fri: 8am-6pm. Sat-Sun: closed.)*

Directly across from Rockefeller Center, **St. Patrick's Cathedral** is the largest and most famous Catholic cathedral in the United States. Built to seat 2,500 people, it was completed in 1878, but its massive spires, which rise 330 feet into the air, were added seven years later. As impressive inside as out, some of the cathedral's best features include the tremendous Rose Window, the

St. Patrick's Cathedral

Great Organ and the enormous bronze doors at the entrance. The parish was moved to its grand Fifth Avenue site from the original downtown St. Patrick's (page 79) which remains in Little Italy. *(5th Avenue and 50th Street, ☎ 753-2261. Mon-Sun: 7.30am-8.30pm. Masses also held daily.)*

St. Patrick's Cathedral

Located behind St. Patrick's, the historic **Villard Houses** are a series of six townhouses designed by architects McKim, Mead & White during the late 19th century.

Villard Houses

. . . Other Attractions

ommissioned by Henry Villard, railroad industrialist
nd publisher of the *New York Evening Post*, the
alianate houses and elegant courtyard were intended

Waldorf-Astoria Hotel

to be residences but later
became part of the New York
Palace Hotel (page 40). *(457
Madison Avenue.)*

Built in 1931, the world-
famous **Waldorf-Astoria Hotel**
(page 44) is worth a look just
for its elegant lobby. This is
the hotel where kings,
queens, ambassadors and
U.S. presidents stay while
visiting New York City. *(301
Park Avenue, ☎ 355-3000.)*

Waldorf-Astoria Hotel

Created in 1907, the **Japan**
ociety has inhabited its present building since 1971.
sleek gallery hosts exhibitions spotlighting Japanese
t and culture. Its traditional Japanese garden is a
easant place to relax. *(333 East 47th Street, ☎ 832-*
55. Tue-Sun: 11am-5pm. Mon: closed. Suggested
mission $3.)

Tudor Park

Open Spaces

pened in 1991, the **Garden Court** at the Pierpont-
organ Library (page 152) is located beside
. Morgan, Jr.'s former townhouse. This
ree-story enclosed atrium, which is filled
th trees and plants, even has its own café.

ley Park, located on 53rd Street between
adison and Fifth Avenues, is known as the
est pocket park". This small grassy nook is
good place to bring a picnic lunch.
other small park, between Second and
ird Avenues at 51st Street, is **Greenacre**
rk.

43rd Street between First and Second
enues, **Tudor Park** is a quaint European-
le park featuring gravel paths and an
ricately decorated fence. After
scending a flight of stairs from Tudor Park,
u will arrive at the **Ralph J. Bunch Park** which is
uated directly in front of the United Nations.

Gardens at the United Nations

ere are several acres of park land and sculpture
rdens surrounding the **United Nations**. They provide
at views of the East River and nice places to relax
warm weather.

Eating and Drinking

Since restaurants in Midtown East compete for the lunch and dinner business of the nearby corporations their quality tends to be quite high.

Across the street from the exclusive auction house Christie's, **Akbar** (page 157) serves fine Indian cuisine in an elegant setting at reasonable prices. **Jimmy Sung's** (page 158) has been a New York favorite for 30 years. With its lavish interior, grand piano and private dining rooms, this restaurant surprises with a moderately priced menu.

There are some excellent Italian restaurants to be found in Midtown East, including **Il Gabbiano** (see below) and **Piccolo del Cetto** (page 157) which offer discounts to *New York for less* cardholders.

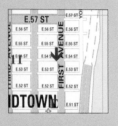

HOURS

Mon-Sun: 11.30am-11pm

Panda

Chinese

987 First Avenue
☎ 752-882

Average meal: $10-1
for less discount: 25%
AM/MC/VS/D

This modern restaurant offers a vast selection of traditional Chinese dishes. Enjoy the rice and nood specialties, or try the Peking duck. A friendly atmosphere complements the high quality food.

Il Gabbiano

Italia

232 East 58th Stree
☎ 754-103

Average meal: $20-2
for less discount: 25%
AM/MC/VS/DC/D

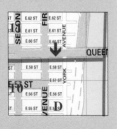

HOURS

Mon-Fri: 12noon-11pm
Sat-Sun: 4pm-11pm

Il Gabbiano provides a pleasant respite from the bus shopping area nearby. The menu features both northe and southern Italian cuisine. Specialties include grille medallions of venison loin with barolo sauce.

Akbar

Indian

475 Park Avenue
☎ 838-1717

Average meal: $20-25
or less discount: 25%
AM/MC/VS/DC/DS

On elegant Park Avenue, Akbar serves fine Indian cuisine in a palatial atmosphere at modest prices. Chef's specialties include lamb chops, chicken ginger and tandoori fish.

HOURS

Mon-Sat: 11am-3pm
5.30pm-11pm
Sun: 5.30pm-11pm

 # Ottomanelli's

Italian / American

951 First Avenue
☎ 758-3725

Average meal: $10-15
or less discount: 25%
AM/MC/VS/DC/DS

A great family restaurant, Ottomanelli's has a wide range of Italian and American favorites, like pastas, pizzas and burgers, at excellent prices. Checked tablecloths and hardwood floors add to the rustic atmosphere.

HOURS

Mon-Sun: 12noon-10pm

 # Piccolo del Cetto

Italian

146 East 44th Street
☎ 682-2565

Average meal: $20-25
or less discount: 25%
AM/MC/VS/DC

Piccolo del Cetto serves northern Italian cuisine in an elegant and romantic atmosphere. Enjoy fine Italian wine and dishes like homemade ravioli, veal chops or the highly recommended fish specials.

HOURS

Mon-Fri: 12noon-2.30pm,
5pm-10pm
Sat: 5pm-10pm
Sun: closed

Jimmy Sung's

Chinese

219 East 44th Street
☎ 682-5678

Average meal: $15-20
for less discount: 25%
AM/MC/VS/D

Jimmy Sung's offers authentic Hunan cuisine and regional Chinese dishes. A luxurious atmosphere and excellent prices make this a great overall experience. The house specialty, Peking duck, is recommended.

Cafe Soleil

Mediterranean

135 East 56th Street
☎ 832-0191

Average meal: $10-15
for less discount: 25%
No credit cards

This cozy Mediterranean café is a good place to enjoy flavorful, traditional dishes in a casual, café atmosphere. Specialties include Turkish meatballs, *shish-kababs* and an assortment of salads.

Sanwa Flower

Japanese

306 East 39th Street
☎ 681-0890

Average meal: $15-20
for less discount: 25%
AM/MC/VS/D

Close to the United Nations, Sanwa Flower serves both traditional and inventive Japanese cuisine. Try basics like *miso soup* or rice dishes, or feast on something more unique like the *enoki butter* or *gaindara kasuzuke*.

HOURS

Mon-Fri: 7am-8pm
Sat: 9am-6pm
Sun: closed

HOURS

Mon-Fri: 11.30am-3.30pm,
5.30pm-10.30pm
Sat- Sun: 12noon-3.30pm,
5.30pm-11pm

Shopping

From **Saks Fifth Avenue** (611 Fifth Avenue, ☎ 753-4000) department store to the scores of designer shops, Fifth Avenue is New York's best-known (and most expensive) shopping thoroughfare.

The exquisite jeweler **Cartier** (653 Fifth Avenue, ☎ 446-3400) is housed in one of the few remaining mansions which lined this street around the turn-of-the-century. Nearby, **Fortunoff** (681 Fifth Avenue, ☎ 758-6560) sells jewelry and fine housewares at less stratospheric prices.

Cartier

Gaze in the window of **Tiffany & Co.** (727 Fifth Avenue, ☎ 755-8000) as Audrey Hepburn did in the 1961 classic *Breakfast at Tiffany's* (no, you can't actually eat there). Better yet, go inside where you will find ten floors of practical and luxury items. Visitors are often surprised to find that, in Tiffany's,

not everything is incredibly expensive. Of course, very big stones have very big price tags, but there are many items which cost less than $50 and, no matter what you buy, you can still take home one of their famous "Tiffany blue" bags.

Tiffany & Co.

Next door, the ostentatious interior of **Trump Tower** (725 Fifth Avenue, ☎ 832-2000) has a 6-story atrium loaded with marble, brass, mirrors and a waterfall. Upstairs, the luxurious apartments are home to celebrities like Donald Trump himself.

Tiffany & Co.

F.A.O. Schwartz (767 Fifth Avenue, ☎ 644-9400) is a one-of-a-kind toy store made famous in the Tom Hanks film *Big*. Around the corner, on 57th street, you will find a strange mix of commercial superstores like the **Warner Bros. Studio Store** (1 East 57th Street, ☎ 754-0300) and **Niketown** (6 East 57th Street, ☎ 891-6453) alongside designer emporiums like **Chanel** (15 East 57th Street, ☎ 355-5050) and **Burberrys** (9 East 57th Street, ☎ 371-5010).

Saks Fifth Avenue

Further east, on Lexington Avenue, **Future Sports** (page 160) is a specialty store where you can find an entire range of sports collectibles and autographed memorabilia.

HOURS

Mon-Fri: 11am-10pm
Sat: 12noon-8pm
Sun: call for hours

Miracle Gifts

Gift

833A Second Avenu
☎ 922-136:

for less discount: 20%
AM/MC/V:

This charming gift shop sells traditional items importe
from Turkey. It also offers interesting crafts and work
by skilled artisans. You can find everything from textile
to furniture.

HOURS

Mon-Fri: 10am-8pm
Sat-Sun: 10am-6pm

Future Sports

Sports Collectible

659 Lexington Avenu
☎ 308-114

for less discount: 20%
AM/VS/MC/D

Future Sports is one of the largest sports memorabili
stores in the U.S. It sells autographed items fro
legends and present-day sports stars. Choose fro
photos, lithographs and sports equipment.

HOURS

Mon-Fri: 7.30am-7pm
Sat: 10am-6pm
Sun: 12noon-6pm

Fromex 1 Hour Photo

Film Developin

130 East 57th Stre
☎ 644-339

for less discount: 20% o
color film developir
AM/MC/VS/D

With your *New York for less* card, you can take you
pictures to Fromex for one-hour color film developir
and receive a 20% discount. The discount also applie
at Fromex's other Manhattan locations.

Upper West Side

Introduction . . .

The **Upper West Side** is bordered by **Central Park** to the east and **Riverside Park** and the Hudson River to the west. Like the Upper East Side, it has its share of opulence and wealth, but the Upper West Side possesses a very different character. The many actors

The Dakota

directors and artistic types who reside in its 19th-century apartment buildings and brownstone houses have helped to impart a creative, liberal character to this neighborhood that makes it quite distinct from its conservative east side counterpart.

The main avenues (Broadway, Columbus and Amsterdam) are a shoppers paradise by day (see page 179) and are crowded with revelers by night. Turn off the busy avenues, however, and you will find the quiet residential side streets for which the area is best known.

The Upper West Side first became a desirable residential neighborhood in the late 19th century. Uptown migration was partly due to the creation of Central Park and partly to the rising real estate prices in midtown Manhattan. The advent of elevated trains and eventually the subway, made commuting inexpensive and easy.

INSIDER'S TIP

At 72nd Street and Broadway, you can still catch a glimpse of the original subway buildings which once punctuated the train lines at street level.

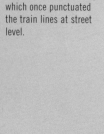

Broadway street scene and the 72nd Street subway station

In 1884, after four years of construction, New York City's first luxury residential apartment building, the **Dakota**, was completed. Nearly a hundred years later, one of the its most famous residents, John Lennon, was murdered in front of the building. Across the street, in Central Park, **Strawberry Fields** (page 210) has been created to honor his memory.

Other luxury apartment buildings followed the Dakota along Central Park West and charming brownstone buildings were erected on the cross streets during the 1890s. Completed in 1931, the landmark twin-towered **San Remo** is one of the most magnificent residences in th

. . . Introduction

city. Rising high above the trees, the San Remo is visible from much of Central Park and has been home to celebrities such as Marilyn Monroe, Paul Simon and Dustin Hoffman.

For visitors, the Upper West Side is best known for the performing arts. **Lincoln Center** (page 166) was built in the 1950s on the site of the slum area depicted in the musical *West Side Story*. Today, this single complex draws close to 5 million visitors a year and the surrounding streets are lined with shops, restaurants and expensive real estate.

On Central Park West, the enormous **American Museum of Natural History** (page 164-165) is one of New York City's most impressive museums and the only major museum on the Upper West Side. The recent addition of the dinosaur halls have proven to be extremely popular.

Lincoln Center

To the north-west of Central Park, **Morningside Heights** is home to **Columbia University** (page 169). Here, the streets reflect the needs of the students who frequent the many bookstores,

Brownstones on the Upper West Side

coffeeshops and inexpensive eateries that abound (see page 173).

A little further north, centered around 125th Street, Harlem has been pivotal to the development of African-American culture throughout this century. The 1920s "Harlem Renaissance" produced some of the best-known jazz musicians in the world. Artists such as Cab Calloway and Duke Ellington performed at venues like the **Apollo Theater** (page 171) and the **Cotton Club**.

Recently, Harlem has begun to show signs of another kind of renaissance. A new generation of residents, respectful of Harlem's past and tradition, are finding new ways to improve it for the future. Many young, successful African-Americans are returning to Harlem, refurbishing its beautiful brownstone houses and becoming new leaders in the community.

American Museum of Natural History . . .

Founded in 1869 by Albert S. Bickmore and supporters such as Theodore Roosevelt, Sr. and J.P. Morgan, the American Museum of Natural History has a long tradition of attracting and educating visitors from around the world.

The museum focuses upon a broad range of subjects, from insects to dinosaurs, from marine life to planetary science. Comprising 23 adjoining buildings, the American Museum of Natural History houses more than 30 million specimens and cultural artifacts.

Main entrance to the museum

ADDRESS

Central Park West at
79th Street
☎ 769-5100

HOURS

Sun-Thu: 10am-5.45pm
Fri-Sat: 10am-8.45pm
Mon: closed

There are 40 grand exhibition halls, numerous laboratories and teaching facilities and the largest natural history library in the western hemisphere. The scientific departments conduct research in anthropology, earth and planetary sciences, biology and paleontology.

Since 1887, the museum has also sponsored and supported thousands of scientific expeditions to every corner of the world. Two of the most noteworthy were the 1921-25 **Central Asiatic Expeditions to Mongolia**, which unearthed the first dinosaur eggs and a variety of new fossil mammals, and the 1897 **Jesup North Pacific Expedition**, led by Franz Boas, who later became famous for his theory that all cultures are intrinsically equal.

Allosaurus

PRICES

Suggested admission:
Adult $8
Child $4.50
Senior $6
Student $6
M1 admission: $12
(includes entrance to the museum plus either an audio tour or an IMAX feature).

DISCOUNT

2 M1 admissions for the price of 1 with voucher on page 275.

10% discount at the Garden Cafe with voucher on page 275.

Between 1994 and 1996, six new fossil halls were opened to display the museum's vast collection of dinosaurs and fossil vertebrates – recognized as the largest and most scientifically important in the world. The museum is now able to display more than 6,000 specimens, 85% of which are real fossils rather than the cast reproductions used at the majority of new museum exhibitions.

Dinosaurs in the Rotunda

Computer stations in these halls provide visitors with a hands-on account of the most current and innovative

. . . American Museum of Natural History 🏙️

cientific information. The **Miriam and Ira D. Wallach Orientation Center** provides an overview of the fossil alls and is a good place to start a tour f them.

he new dinosaur halls – the **Hall of aurischian Dinosaurs** and the **Hall of rnithischian Dinosaurs** – which pened in 1995, feature close to 100 ossil specimens. Included are two of he museum's best-known dinosaurs: *yrannosaurus Rex* and *Apotosaurus* formerly called *Brontosaurus*) both of hich have been remounted in light of ontemporary understanding of these animals.

A herd of African Elephants

he **Lila Acheson Wallace Wing of Mammals and Their xtinct Relatives**, which opened in 1994, contains the most significant selection of fossil mammals ever ssembled. The **Hall of Vertebrate Origins** examines he history of the physical development of vertebrates. ther museum highlights include the **Hall of Human Biology and Evolution**, the only permanent exhibit in the U.S. which documents the evolution of human life.

77th Street Facade

You can acquire a better understanding of how animals live within their environment at the **Hall f North American Mammals**, **Hall of African Mammals** and **Hall of North American Birds**, where pecimens are displayed in their natural surroundings.

he other permanent exhibition halls focus on a wide ange of subjects, including meteorites, gems, ocean fe, reptiles and amphibians. The cultural history of he people of various nations and continents is also ocumented.

Audio expeditions" are designed to help you better xplore the museum's enormous collections. Another ay to enhance your visit here is to take advantage of he **IMAX theater** which features thrilling and formative cinematic adventures.

resently, the **Hall of Life's Diversity** is under evelopment and is due to open in 1998. The ayden Planetarium is undergoing a major ansformation and will be reopened by the year 000.

DON'T MISS

The "touch fossils" which allow you to feel the actual fossilized remains of dinosaurs.

The amazing Star of India sapphire in the Hall of Gems.

INSIDER'S TIP

The museum is a great place to visit on Fridays and Saturdays when it's open late. You can view the exhibition halls, catch an IMAX film and have dinner at the Garden Cafe – all at a discount.

ADDRESS

Lincoln Center
Broadway from 62nd to
66th Streets
☎ 875-5350

HOURS

Classic Tour and *Piano Forte Tour*:
Mon-Sun: 10am-5pm

Art and Architecture Tour:
Mon-Sun: 2.30pm

PRICES

Classic Tour:
Adult $8.50
Child $4.50
Senior $7.25
Student $7.25

Piano Forte Tour:
Adult $15
Child $15
Senior $15
Student $15

Art and Architecture Tour:
Adult $10.50
Child $10.50
Senior $10.50
Student $10.50

DISCOUNT

20% discount on any tour
with voucher on page 277.

Lincoln Center

Lincoln Center is one of the world's leading performing arts centers. It is home to 12 resident companies dedicated to music, dance and theater including the **Metropolitan Opera**, **New York Philharmonic**, **New York City Ballet** and **New York City Opera** which gives a discount to *New York for less* cardholders (page 215).

Also on the campus is the distinguished **Juilliard School of Music**, **New York Public Library for the Performing Arts** and the **Vivian Beaumont Theater**, as

well as Lincoln Center's newest constituent – **Jazz at Lincoln Center**.

Every day, three different backstage tours are offered in order to provide a behind-the-

Metropolitan Opera House and Lincoln Center

scenes look at the history, artistry and architecture of this impressive arts center. Your *New York for less* card entitles you to a discount at any of the following Lincoln Center Tours.

On the one-hour **Classic Tour**, you can experience the main stages at Lincoln center – the **Metropolitan Opera House**, **Avery Fisher Hall** and the **New York State Theater**. You will hear stories about some of the artists who have appeared here and you may even catch a rehearsal in progress.

The **Piano Forte Tour** incorporates a visit to Klavierhaus into the Classic Tour. At this workshop, you will see how vintage musical instruments (some over a hundred years old) are refurbished by experts working in the European tradition. This rare opportunity is available by appointment only.

The new **Art and Architecture Tour** focuses on the magnificent structures which comprise Lincoln Center as well as the priceless works of art that fill them. Extensive research has been done in order to prepare a tour which illuminates its priceless treasures, many by famous artists like **Marc Chagall**, **Rodin** and **Robert Rauschenberg**.

All of the tours originate at the tour desk located on the concourse level of Lincoln Center, which you can access through the Metropolitan Opera House.

🎬 Sony IMAX Theatre

The Sony IMAX Theatre presents a truly unique film experience – combining 3D sight and sound technology with an 8-story screen in a plush, futuristic theater.

Sony IMAX Theatre

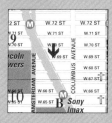

IMAX is the largest film format available. Each frame of film is ten times the size of 35 millimeter film, and is projected onto a silver screen 80 feet high and 100 feet wide - the largest in the world to present IMAX 3D.

High-tech headsets with liquid crystal lenses receive infra-red signals from the IMAX projector, creating the 3D visual effects. Built-in speakers "move" the sound from the front of the headset to the back so that the sound can come from behind you, or from anywhere in the room. The personal sound system overlaps with the speakers of the main system which are distributed

Rollercoaster ride from Across the Sea of Time

around the room. This theater is the first in the world to use this type of advanced sound technology.

There are currently several films being shown in 3D in addition to selected movies shown in the conventional format. *New York 3D: Across the Sea of Time* is the story of a young Russian boy who travels to New York on a quest for an ancestor who emigrated to America almost a hundred years ago. Filmed entirely on location in New York City, it mixes 3D black and white images of the early 20th-century with present-day New York.

You can "fly" over the Andes Mountains in *Wings of Courage*, a film which tells the true story of two aviation pioneers, starring **Val Kilmer** and **Tom Hulce**. Also playing, *Into the Deep*, takes theatergoers on an undersea exploration.

The most recent film to come to the IMAX is *L5: First City in Space*. It uses 3D computer-generated imagery, actual footage taken in space and data from NASA to simulate life on a floating station orbiting the earth.

L5: First City in Space

ADDRESS

1998 Broadway
☎ 336-5000

HOURS

Mon-Sun: 10am-12midnight

PRICES

Adult $9
Child $6
Senior $7.50
Student $6

DISCOUNT

2 admissions for the price of 1 for any IMAX feature with voucher on page 277.

Morris-Jumel Mansion

The Morris-Jumel Mansion is Manhattan's oldest remaining colonial residence. It is listed on the National Register of Historic Places and has been designated a New York City landmark.

This 1765 mansion was built in the Georgian style and its design was based on a similar one by 16th-century Italian architect **Andrea Palladio**. The restored exterior of the house, with its double-height portico, grand columns and triangular pediment, is an excellent example of colonial architecture.

Morris-Jumel Mansion

The mansion was originally built as a summer residence for British Colonel **Roger Morris** and his American wife Mary Philipse Morris. At the outbreak of the Revolutionary War in 1776, the Morrises fled to England, abandoning the house. During the war, General George Washington used the mansion as his headquarters during the **Battle of Harlem Heights**.

In 1810, **Stephen Jumel**, a wealthy French emigrant merchant, and his wife Eliza Bowen bought the house. A year after her husband died in 1832, Eliza Jumel married former Vice President **Aaron Burr** in the front parlor of the house. She divorced Burr only three years later. Considered one of the wealthiest women in New York, she remained in the mansion until her death in 1865.

In 1906, the **Washington Headquarters Association** undertook the responsibility to preserve and operate the mansion as a museum.

Morris-Jumel Mansion

Guided and self-guided tours illuminate specific people and events that have contributed to the history of the house. In terms of its age, architecture and historical importance, the Morris-Jumel Mansion is perhaps the greatest house in Manhattan.

ADDRESS

65 Jumel Terrace
☎ 923-8008

HOURS

Wed-Sun: 10am-4pm
Mon-Tue: closed

Morris-Jumel Mansion

PRICES

Adult $3
Child $2
Senior $2
Student $2

DISCOUNT

2 admissions for the price of 1 with your *New York for less* card.

Other Attractions . . .

Opened in 1989, the **Museum of American Folk Art** exhibits everything from Native American art and carvings to traditional American crafts like quilts and rugs. The museum hosts temporary exhibits in addition to its permanent display. It is small enough to visit in an hour or so. The museum also sponsors events for children and craft demonstrations. *(2 Lincoln Square, ☎ 595-9533. Tue-Sun: 11.30am-7.30pm. Mon: closed. Suggested admission $3.)*

Museum of American Folk Art

Founded in 1804, the **New York Historical Society** is the oldest museum in New York City. The society has a variety of paintings and furniture dating from the 17th century. *(2 West 77th Street, ☎ 873-3400. Library open Wed-Sun: 12noon-5pm. Mon-Tue: closed. Adult $5, child $2, senior $2, student $2.)*

New York Historical Society

The **Beacon Theater**, once a movie palace, is now a regular concert venue which hosts top performers. The opulent interior is a designated landmark. *(2214 Broadway at 74th Street, ☎ 496-7070.)*

Founded in 1973, the **Children's Museum of Manhattan** is dedicated to teaching and inspiring children with playful interactive programs and exhibits. The museum's activities include the newly installed SoundsFun – a 3,100 square foot playground with an emphasis on hearing. Children can touch, bang and jump on ear-themed props including an ear drum trampoline, all of which make various sounds. The Warner Media Center provides kids with the opportunity to interact with a camera, create special effects, then edit and watch the tape they have made. *(21 West 83rd Street, ☎ 721-1234. Mon and Wed-Thu: 1.30pm-5.30pm. Fri-Sun: 10am-5pm. Tue: closed. Adult $5, child $5 (under 1 year free), senior $2.50, student $5.)*

Columbia University's Low Library

Founded in 1754 in Lower Manhattan as King's College, **Columbia University** is New York City's contribution to the Ivy League. In the 1960s it was the site of numerous demonstrations and protests concerning the Vietnam War, racial and gender equality and other controversial issues. This urban campus has a series of architecturally impressive buildings including the Low Library, which was designed by architects McKim, Mead and White and is located in the university's central courtyard. Built in 1904, St. Paul's Chapel *(☎ 854-6625)* has a beautifully

Children's Museum of Manhattan

. . . Other Attractions . . .

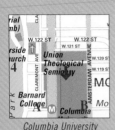

Columbia University

crafted brick interior and an impressive pipe organ. *(West 114th-120th Streets, between Broadway and Morningside Drive, ☎ 854-1754.)*

Grant's Tomb

In Morningside Heights, not far from Columbia University, **Grant's Tomb** contains the remains of Civil War commanding General Ulysses S. Grant and his wife. After winning the Civil War, General Grant went on to become the 18th president of the United States of America. In 1885, after Grant died, the American people honored him by raising over $600,000 to build this massive monument. The interior was inspired by the tomb of Napoleon. You can visit the two exhibit rooms which document the life and career of Ulysses S. Grant. *(West 122nd Street and Riverside Drive, ☎ 666-1640. Mon-Sun: 9am-5pm.)*

St. John the Divine

Begun in 1892, the Neo-Gothic-style **Cathedral of St. John the Divine** is the largest church in the United States and is intended to be the largest cathedral in the world when it is finally finished. Presently, only about two-thirds of the cathedral is complete, the rest is scheduled to be finished sometime late in the 21st century. Its towers, nave, buttresses and windows are exquisitely designed. The facade resembles Notre Dame in Paris, with a large bronze door in the center cast in Paris by M. Barbedienne, the same man who cast the Statue of Liberty. The cathedral hosts cultural events such as concerts, plays and exhibitions. *(Amsterdam Avenue at 112th Street, ☎ 316-2133.)*

Grant's Tomb

Hamilton Grange

The Cloisters, the medieval branch of the Metropolitan Museum of Art, is perched high atop a hill overlooking the Hudson River, from northern Manhattan's Fort Trynon Park. Housed in a reconstructed medieval-style monastery, the setting is perfectly suited for the outstanding collection it contains. Cloistered walkways, courtyards, exhibition halls and galleries complement medieval art, sculpture, tapestries, illuminated manuscripts and more. Even the gardens continue the medieval theme with plant

. . . Other Attractions

arieties typically grown at that time. *(Fort Trynon Park
t 190th Street, ☎ 923-3700. Mar-Oct: Tue-Sun: 9.30am-
.15pm. Mon: closed. Nov-Feb: Tue-Sun: 9.30am-4.45pm.
Mon: closed. Suggested admission: adult $7, child $3.50,
enior $7, student $3.50 includes same day
dmission to The Met (pages 184-185.)*

Hamilton Grange National Memorial is
he 1802 home of Alexander Hamilton,
o-author of the *Federalist Papers* and
he first Secretary of the U.S. Treasury.
Hamilton lived here with his family until
e was killed in a gun duel with Vice-
resident Aaron Burr in 1804. The
nterior is not open to the public.
*Convent Avenue at 141st Street, ☎ 283-
144.)*

*The Unicorn Tapestries (ca. 1500) at
The Cloisters*

The Apollo Theater was founded in
914 as an opera house for a strictly
hite audience. In 1934, it was opened to all races

and evolved into a premier
black entertainment venue.
Top Afican-American artists
such as Billie Holiday, Ella
Fitzgerald, Duke Ellington,
Michael Jackson and comedian
Sinbad have all performed
here. Wednesday night is
"Showtime at the Apollo", a
televised amateur night, where
fresh talents sing and dance in
the hope of being discovered.
*(253 West 125th Street, ☎ 864-
0372.)*

Apollo Theater in Harlem

*Cathedral of St. John the
Divine*

uilt in 1891, the **St. Nicholas Historic District** is
omprised of elegant townhouses designed by some of
he leading architects of the day. Harlem residents
ick-named the houses "Strivers' Row" because of the
uccessful African-Americans who resided in them.
*West 138th and West 139th Streets, between Seventh and
ghth Avenues.)*

pened in 1991, the **Schomburg Center for Research
nto Black Culture** is the nation's largest research,
ducational and cultural center for African-American
nd African culture and history. Its massive holdings
ere collected by the late curator and black
ntellectual, Arthur Schomburg and include rare
ooks, manuscripts and art. *(135th Street and Malcolm
Boulevard, ☎ 491-2200. Mon-Wed: 12noon-8pm. Thu-
at: 10am-6pm. Sun: closed.)*

Apollo Theater

Open Spaces

Created by Frederick Law Olmstead, who also designed Central Park, **Riverside Park** *(Hudson River, between 72nd and 145th Streets)* is a sliver of green space running alongside the river. It is an extremely popular spot with Upper West Siders who walk their dogs, jog and cycle along the banks of the Hudson while enjoying the spectacular views. Within the park, at 89th Street, the **Soldiers and Sailors Monument** commemorates those who fought and died in the Civil War.

Riverside Park

Established in the last century, **Claremont Riding Academy** *(175 West 89th Street, ☎ 724-5100)* is the only remaining stable in Manhattan. It offers horseback-riding lessons and rentals which allow you to ride indoors, or to enjoy Central Park on horseback.

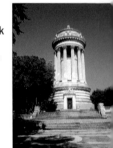

Set in the southeast corner of Lincoln Center, **Damrosch Park** is home to the annual Big Apple Circus. Throughout the summer, it also hosts free outdoor concerts and performances at the **Guggenheim Bandshell**. Across from Lincoln Center, **Dante Park** was designed in 1921 to honor the 600th anniversary of the author's death. This small, open area is marked by a bronze statue in his likeness.

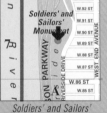

Soldiers' and Sailors' Monument

Soldiers' and Sailors' Monument

Next to the Cathederal of St. John the Divine (page 170), the **Children's Sculpture Garden** has an assortment of flowers and benches for resting as well as small plaques engraved with "words of wisdom". The garden also has a gigantic water-filled fountain with a winged hero battling with evil beasts. Surrounding the fountain, the *Ring of Freedom* features sculptures created by children.

Peace Garden at St. John the Divine

A pleasant spot to relax amidst an array of beautiful flowers is the **Lotus Garden** *(97th Street, between Broadway and West End Avenue, ☎ 580-4897)*.

Nearby, **Morningside Park** is a wooded area extending from 110th to 123rd Streets. Further north, the medieval gardens and courtyards at **The Cloisters** (page 170) provide a unique place to relax.

Eating and Drinking

The majority of restaurants on the Upper West Side are concentrated along Broadway, Amsterdam and Columbus Avenues. From Cuban-Chinese to wholesome American, you can find every type of cuisine imaginable.

Zabar's *(2245 Broadway, ☎ 787-2000)*, one of the best known gourmet markets in New York, stockpiles prepared foods, imported items, fresh-baked goods and even housewares – all of the best quality. It also has an adjacent café where you can relax with a cup of coffee and a fresh pastry.

Zabar's

For traditional Italian fare, you might try **Pappardella** (page 177) or **Farfalle** (page 178). **A.J. Gordon's Brewing Company** (page 176) has a cozy back room where you can relax by the fire and enjoy a freshly brewed beer with your meal. A good place to watch televised sports events and enjoy traditional American food is **Boomer's Sports Club** (page 175).

At one of the city's top comedy clubs, **Stand Up New York** (page 216), your *New York for less* card entitles you to a discount on admission to the club *and* on dinner. On Columbus Avenue, **Prohibition** (page 174) incorporates live jazz into the dining experience.

A.J. Gordon's Brewing Company on the Upper West Side

The Upper West Side is a good place to spend a night out "bar hopping" between the restaurants and bars crammed onto every block. Mainly attracting a college crowd, "happy hours" (with excellent deals on drinks) are the specialty here. Announced on giant chalk boards outside each establishment, a typical offer is two drinks for the price of one. Another favorite is "Ladies Night" where women drink for free for a few hours. For those with the patience and ability to balance their beverages while wedged between the bar and an enormous football player, these special evenings can be very economical and even fun.

In Morningside Heights, by Columbia University (page 169), there are a number of inexpensive eateries. **Fiesta Mexicana** (page 178) is revered by students for its hearty, low-priced Mexican fare.

In Harlem you can see a show at the famous Apollo Theater (page 171) before dining at **Sylvia's** *(☎ 966-0660)* which is, if not the best "soul food" in town, then at least the most famous.

Cafe Mozart

Viennese

154 West 70th Street
☎ 595-9797

Average meal: $10-15
for less discount: 25%
AM/MC/VS/DC/DS

HOURS

Mon-Thu: 8am-2am
Fri: 8am-3am
Sat: 10am-3am
Sun: 10am-2am

Cafe Mozart serves European cuisine in an Old Viennese-style atmosphere. Try the Viennese chicken *schnitzel* or one of the 50 varieties of dessert. Relax while listening to the live classical music which is performed nightly.

Prohibition

Contemporary American

503 Columbus Avenue
☎ 579-3100

Average meal: $20-25
for less discount: 25%
AM/MC/VS/DC

HOURS

Mon-Sun: 5:30pm-4am

This sophisticated restaurant serves tasty American cuisine. Live jazz is played every night and in warm weather you can sit outdoors. Chef's specialties include seared tuna and goat cheese ravioli.

Mendy's West

Delicatessen / Kosher

210 West 70th Street
☎ 877-6787

Average meal: $15-20
for less discount: 25%
AM/MC/VS/DC

HOURS

Mon-Thu: 5pm-12midnight
Sat: 6.30am-2am
Sun: 1pm-12midnight
Fri: closed

This friendly restaurant and sports bar serves great food at reasonable prices. Mendy's friendly staff will point out interesting sports memorabilia. The veal chops and pastrami sandwich are particularly recommended.

Vermouth

ontemporary American

55 Amsterdam Avenue
724-3600

verage meal: $15-20
or less discount: 25%
M/MC/VS/DC

HOURS

Mon-Fri: 5pm-4am
Sat-Sun: 12noon-4am

his lively café serves a variety of interesting American
shes. Try the gourmet pizzas and the steak, chicken,
rimp or vegetable skewers. Vermouth is a good place
enjoy a casual, yet chic, night out.

Mingala West

urmese

25 Amsterdam Avenue
873-0787

verage meal: $15-20
or less discount: 25%
M/MC/VS/DC/DS

HOURS

Mon-Thu: 12noon-11.30pm
Fri-Sat: 12noon-
12midnight
Sun: 12noon-11.30pm

ingala West offers traditional Burmese cuisine in an
otic setting. Specialties include red curry shrimp and
allops with string beans. A wide variety of salads and
oodle dishes is also available.

Boomer's Sports Club

merican

49 Amsterdam Avenue
362-5400

verage meal: $10-15
r less discount: 25%
M/MC/VS/DC

HOURS

Mon-Thu: 5pm-1am
Fri: 5pm-2am
Sat: 11.30am-2am
Sun: 11.30am-12midnight

is traditional American sports bar is fun, casual and
endly. It shows all kinds of sports games and events
25 televisions. Boomers is known for its delicious
icken wings.

A.J. Gordon's Brewing Co.

American / Brewe

212 West 79th Stre
☎ 579-977

Average meal: $10-1
for less discount: 25°
AM/MC/VS/D

A.J. Gordon's Brewing Company brews its own beer o
site, a wonderful accompaniment to the hearty America
fare, bar food and snacks that are served. A cozy bac
room features bookshelves and a fireplace.

Miss Elle's

America

226 West 79th Stre
☎ 595-435

Average meal: $15-2
for less discount: 25°
AM/MC/VS/DC/D

Miss Elle's is housed in a landmark brownstone buildir
with an enclosed garden atrium. The décor is romant
and the fare is American with an Italian influence. T
the hearty pot roast and mashed potatoes or the lasagn

Joe's Fish Shack

Seafo

520 Columbus Aven
☎ 873-034

Average meal: $15-2
for less discount: 25
AM/MC/VS/C

Joe's Fish Shack is an authentic seaside shanty ne
Central Park. Feast on an assortment of reasonab
priced seafood specialties. The seafood combo, oyste
and lobster are highly recommended.

Mughlai

Indian

320 Columbus Avenue
☎ 724-6363

Average meal: $15-20
for less discount: 25%
AM/MC/VS

HOURS

Mon-Fri: 5pm-11.30pm
Sat: 12noon-12midnight
Sun: 12noon-11pm

Mughlai serves savory northern Indian cuisine. A friendly staff and a comfortable dining room create a relaxed atmosphere in which to enjoy specialties such as tandoori dishes and freshly baked breads.

Pappardella

Italian

316 Columbus Avenue
☎ 595-7996

Average meal: $20-25
for less discount: 25%
AM/MC/VS/DC

HOURS

Mon-Sat: 12noon-
12midnight
Sun: 11am-12midnight

This modern trattoria offers excellent Italian food. The atmosphere is romantic and comfortable. Particularly recommended is the *ravioli fungi* with a mushroom cream sauce.

Firehouse

American

522 Columbus Avenue
☎ 787-3473

Average meal: $15-20
for less discount: 25%
AM/MC/VS/DC

HOURS

Mon-Sun: 12noon-
12midnight

This casual American restaurant serves inexpensive and tasty food. It is located in an antique firehouse filled with interesting memorabilia. Choose from ribs, chicken wings, gourmet pizzas, salads and more.

Farfalle

Italian

680 Columbus Avenue
☎ 666-2461

Average meal: $20-25
for less discount: 25%
AM/MC/VS/DC

Farfalle specializes in inventive Italian cooking. The décor is styled to resemble the Tuscan countryside and the food is delicious. Try *Farfalle gamberetti* with garlic cream sauce, shrimp and asparagus.

Fiesta Mexicana

Mexican

2823 Broadway
☎ 662-2535

Average meal: $10-15
for less discount: 25%
AM/MC/VS/DC

This cozy restaurant is decorated with a traditional Mexican theme. A full range of Mexican dishes is available at very reasonable prices. Chef's specialties include *quesadillas rancheras* and sizzling fajitas.

Hunan Balcony

Chinese

2596 Broadway
☎ 865-0400

Average meal: $10-15
for less discount: 25%
AM/MC/VS/DC

Hunan Balcony offers vegetarian and non-vegetarian Chinese dishes. Chef's specialties include the vegetarian paradise and pineapple chicken. Floor-to-ceiling windows offer great views of Upper Broadway.

Shopping

Although the Upper West Side is as filled with standard chain stores like **The Gap** and **Banana Republic**, there are also quite a few independent shops and boutiques which are worth investigating.

Creating your own pottery at Our Name is Mud

At **Our Name is Mud** (page 180) you can choose from a variety of objects which you can then design and paint to your liking. There are also items for sale which have been crafted either by local artists or on the premises.

INSIDER'S TIP

After a tiring day shopping, head to Barnes and Noble where you can relax in a comfortable armchair with a cup of coffee and a good book.

If you are looking for designer clothing, **Charivari** (257 Columbus Avenue, ☎ 496-8700) is an uptown staple for the best (and most expensive) of cutting-edge designer fashions. The funky designs at **Betsey Johnson** (248 Columbus Avenue, ☎ 362-3364) can be found nearby.

At the opposite end of the spectrum, **Alice Underground** (380 Columbus Avenue, ☎ 724-6682), on Columbus Avenue, is a well-stocked and trendy thrift shop. **Allan and Suzi** (416 Amsterdam, ☎ 724-7445) sells everything from platform shoes and feather boas to slightly worn designer wear.

Filene's Basement (2222 Broadway, ☎ 873-8000) is a discount superstore which carries brand-name clothing at good prices.

The book shop and café, **Barnes and Noble** (2289 Broadway, ☎ 362-8835) is gigantic, as are the music superstores **Tower Records** (2107 Broadway, ☎ 799-2500) and **HMV** (2081 Broadway, ☎ 721-5900), both of which are open late.

Zabar's food shop (page 173) has been a New York favorite for years, having evolved from its origins as a kosher deli in the 1930s. Its quality, selection and prices are among the best in the city.

The Columbus Avenue Street Fair (Columbus Avenue between 76th and 77th Streets) is held at P.S. (public school) 44 on Sundays. In addition to arts, crafts and antiques, there are goods imported from other countries, basic sportswear and even a small greenmarket.

Shopping on the Upper West Side

HOURS

Mon-Sat: 11.30am-8pm
Sun: 11.30am-6pm

Our Name is Mud

Crafts & Gift

506 Amsterdam Avenu
☎ 579-557

for less discount: 20%
AM/MC/V

Handmade crafts and gifts are available in this livel
shop and bright art studio. It sells pottery, scente
candles and other creations. Visitors can observe artist
at work or create their own art at the paint bar.

HOURS

Mon-Sat: 10am-8pm
Sun: 11am-6pm

Metro Art

Posters & Framin

2341 Broadwa
☎ 595-161

for less discount: 20%
AM/MC/V

Metro Art has a large collection of fine art prints c
famous artwork, landscapes and modern themes. Choos
from posters and lithographs (either with or withou
frames) or have a frame customized for you.

HOURS

Mon-Fri: 7:30am-9pm
Sat: 11am-6pm
Sun: 11am-5pm

Fromex 1 Hour Photo

Film Developin

2041 Broadwa
☎ 580-818

for less discount: 20% o
1 hour color film developin
AM/MC/VS/DC/D

Your *New York for less* card entitles you to receive 20%
off one-hour color film processing. The discount als
applies at the other Upper West Side Fromex locatio
(2151 Broadway, ☎ 496-2211).

Upper East Side

Introduction . . .

After the Civil War, the **Upper East Side** became a summer vacation spot for members of New York City's high society who had permanent residences downtown.

However, the building of elevated trains and the creation of Central Park in the 1870s led to the real development of the neighborhood. The wealthy built mansions on Fifth and Park Avenues near the salubrious setting of the park, while working class Europeans created ethnic enclaves on First, Second and Third Avenues.

Metropolitan Museum of Art

Along Fifth Avenue's former **Millionaire's Row**, some of the old mansions have been converted into museums and galleries, and the area is now referred to as the **Museum Mile**. The **Frick Collection** (page 188) and the **Cooper-Hewitt** (page 194) were once the homes of 19th-century entrepreneurs Henry Clay Frick and Andrew Carnegie, respectively. The Frick Collection maintains the feeling of a private residence while displaying works by artists such as Rembrandt and Renoir.

Guggenheim Museum (page 186-187) is an architectural anomaly on this row of classically-designed structures. Designed by Frank Lloyd Wright, the museum's modern exterior mirrors the works within it, including major pieces by Picasso and Matisse.

It would literally take weeks to view all of the treasures displayed in the imposing structures along this stretch of Fifth Avenue. Indeed, you could easily spend a couple of days at **The Metropolitan Museum of Art** (page 184-185), the largest museum in the western hemisphere, and only begin to scratch the surface.

INSIDER'S TIP

Many museums offer free or pay-what-you-wish admission one day a week, during special hours: Cooper-Hewitt (Tue; 5pm-9pm), The Jewish Museum (Tue: 5pm-8pm), Whitney (Thu: 6pm-8pm), Guggenheim (Fri: 6pm-8pm), National Academy of Design (Fri: 5pm-8pm)

Although it is unlikely that anyone would spend their entire time in Manhattan visiting museums, Museum Mile is a must-see, even if just for an afternoon.

The proximity of the museums to each other makes sampling a select

The Frick Collection

few in one day a viable possibility. On the following pages you will find information that will help you decide which ones best suit your interest. The majority of museums on Museum Mile offer a discount to *New York for less* cardholders.

. . . Introduction

Today, the Upper East Side, particularly the area close to Central Park and along Park Avenue, is still synonymous with old wealth. Posh apartment houses subject applicants to rigorous screening processes that have occasionally been a subject of controversy. Even wealthy celebrities have been known to be barred from living in some of these buildings.

On quiet streets in the East 60s, many of New York's exclusive clubs can be found (page 195-196). Catering to members only, many of these have survived almost unchanged from the end of the 19th century.

The **Whitney Museum of American Art** (page 189), on Madison Avenue, resembles an upside-down pyramid and exhibits modern works by prominent American artists such as Georgia O'Keeffe, Jasper Johns and Frank Stella.

Christie's on Park Avenue

Madison Avenue was once the name generically applied to the scores of advertising agencies that made their homes here. Since most of them have relocated, Madison Avenue and its exclusive shops (see page 202) have come to symbolize the wealth and extravagance of the Upper East Side. A short walk from here, you will find **Christie's** *(502 Park Avenue, ☎ 546-1000)* one of the best-known auction houses in the world.

At the northernmost point of the Museum Mile, the **Museo del Barrio** (page 194) has Latino culture as its focus, and its location marks the beginning of Spanish Harlem. This mainly Puerto Rican enclave is known to its residents as "El Barrio", meaning "the neighborhood". It has the largest Spanish-speaking population in New York City.

Roosevelt Island (page 196) is situated in the East River between Manhattan and Queens. Stretching the equivalent of more than 30 city blocks, it runs parallel to Manhattan from the United Nations (page 153) in Midtown East to **Carl Schurz Park** (page 197) on the Upper East Side. The island is a good place to view the river and the city, but the best part is getting there. Although the subway stops on Roosevelt Island, the aerial tram provides a unique mode of transportation which is much more fun.

Summer Days (1936) by Georgia O'Keeffe at the Whitney

ADDRESS

Fifth Avenue and 82nd
Street
☎ 879-5500

HOURS

Tue-Thu: 9.30am-5.15pm
Fri-Sat: 9.30am-8.45pm
Sun: 9.30am-5.15pm
Mon: closed

The Metropolitan Museum of Art . . .

Founded in 1870 by a group of American
businessmen, artists and scholars, the museum's
original collection consisted of 174 paintings from
three private European
collections. More than a
century later The
Metropolitan Museum of
Art, known simply as "The
Met", has grown to
include more than two
million works of art,
spanning 5,000 years of
culture, from prehistoric
times to modern day.

*Caroll and Milton Petrie
Sculpture Court*

From the first glimpse of
the museum's Fifth
Avenue entrance with its
Neo-Classical facade, you
know you are about to
embark upon an unforgettable journey in the world of
art. Inside, there are over two million square-feet of
space exhibiting one of the world's largest and most
impressive collections of paintings, sculptures,
photographs, decorative arts,
costumes, drawings, musical
instruments and much more.

*The American Wing of The
Metropolitan Museum of Art*

The Met has three enormous
floors and is ever-changing in
both size and configuration. The
Greek and Roman galleries have
recently been renovated with the
addition of the **Robert A. and
Renee E. Belfer Court**.

The galleries are arranged as 20
different collections which range
in content from Egyptian art to
20th-century art (including works by **Kandinsky,
Pollock** and **Warhol**). Some of the world's finest and
most recognizable pieces of French Impressionist,
Post-Impressionist, Romantic and Barbizon works can
be found in the **European Paintings Collection**,
located on the second floor.

PRICES

Suggested admission:
Adult: $8
Child: free when
accompanied by an adult
Senior: $4
Student: $4

The **Charles Engelhard Court**, a glass-enclosed garden
containing sculptures and paintings by American
artists, is one of the more popular attractions in the
museum. Located on all three floors, the **American
Wing** includes 25 furnished period rooms that are
accentuated by Chippendale furniture and Tiffany &

. . The Metropolitan Museum of Art

o. silver settings.

he Met has one of the most comprehensive ollections of Egyptian art and archaeological findings 1 the world. Of the nearly 35,000 pieces in the ollection, the most impressive are the **Tomb of erneb** and the **Temple of Dendur**, which are housed 1 a spectacular glass-enclosed gallery overlooking entral Park.

ther impressive collections are the **Arms and Armor** allery, the **Arts of Africa, Oceania and the Americas** alleries and the **Medieval Arts** gallery, all located on 1e first floor. The second floor houses a wide range of rt from Asia, including a Chinese art collection and a Jite of galleries displaying the arts of **South nd Southeast Asia**. Also situated on the econd floor is an exhibit focusing on the slamic-influenced art of Morocco, Central Asia nd India. The Islamic galleries are introduced y the **Nur ad-Din Room** from Syria. Complete ith a marble fountain, wood-panelled :ception area and stained-glass windows, the 10m is a representation of Ottoman wealth.

INSIDERS' TIP

The **Caroll and Milton Petrie European Sculpture Court**, located on the first floor, is a quiet and serene place to relax after a long day at the museum.

1e **Costume Institute** features everything from aditional folk costumes to 18th-century ball >wns and modern designs by the likes of alston and Balenciaga. Exhibition openings re gala events that draw New York's luminaries, ith the media in tow.

Temple of Dendur

eeing everything that The Met has to offer)uld literally take weeks. Therefore, the best thing to

Caroll and Milton Petrie European Sculpture Court

do is to visit one of the information desks located in the **Great Hall**, on the first floor. There you can pick up maps and brochures and sign up for one of the free multilingual tours provided by members of the staff. Museum policy stipulates that photographs can be taken for non-commercial use only (without a flash or tripod) and video cameras are prohibited.

DON'T MISS

The period rooms including a Frank Lloyd Wright living room in the American Wing.

Monet's *Garden at Sainte-Adresse* in the European Paintings gallery.

The wide variety of musical instruments which includes rare Asian and African instruments and priceless Stradivari violins.

> view more of the museum's medieval collection, sit **The Cloisters** (page 170-171) in northern anhattan.

🏙 Solomon R. Guggenheim Museum. . .

NEW YORK
TOP 10

Frank Lloyd Wright rotunda

Founded by the wealthy Solomon R. Guggenheim in 1937, his eponymous museum has now expanded far beyond his initial collection of European abstract art.

Dedicated to collecting, preserving and exhibiting modern and contemporary art. Some of the better known pieces in its permanent collection are by **Picasso, Kandinksy, Klee, Van Gogh** and **Cezanne**.

Unlike most of the world's museums, Solomon R. Guggenheim's vision of a "temple of non-objective painting" is perhaps as well-known for its physical structure as it is for the works of art that are housed within it.

Designed by Frank Lloyd Wright, the building was completed in 1959, after both his and Guggenheim's deaths. Its most notable feature is the six-story rotunda, which represents Wright's interpretation of ancient Mesopotamian ziggurats and provides the main gallery space.

Guggenheim was a wealthy industrialist who made his money in copper and silver mining. He began by collecting Old Masters more as an investment than a personal passion. However, after a 1929 meeting with artist **Vasily Kandinsky**, at which he purchased several of his paintings, Guggenheim began taking an interest in modern art that soon became a full-tim passion.

He gradually amassed a collection of works by other contemporary artists including **Marc Chagall, Jackson Pollock** and **Willem de Koonig** which grew to overwhelming proportions and led to the formation of

Guggenheim above Fifth Avenue

ADDRESS

1071 Fifth Avenue
☎ 423-3500

HOURS

Mon-Wed and
Sun: 10am-6pm
Fri-Sat: 10am-8pm
Sun: 10am-6pm
Thu: closed

PRICES

Adult $10
Child free
Senior $7
Student $7

. . . Solomon R. Guggenheim Museum

the Solomon R. Guggenheim Foundation.

After loaning his collection to various museums, Guggenheim commissioned Wright to build it a permanent home. The museum, which was Wright's only major New York commission, was to be named 'The Museum of Non-Objective Painting'. The resulting structure was initially criticized by commentators who seemed more interested in its design than the works within it. However, while it is true that the curves that make-up the rotunda's exterior do seem out of place beside an otherwise vertical Upper East Side, the Guggenheim has become one of New York's most photographed and best loved buildings. Indeed, in 1990 it became the youngest building ever to be designated a city landmark.

DISCOUNT

$2 off admission with voucher on page 277.

Wright's internal design deviates from the traditional gallery approach of housing works in a room-by-room format. Rather, Wright designed a spiralling walkway that constitutes the six-story rotunda. The walkway provides a quarter-mile of, what seems to be, endless works of art. The glass dome, which covers the museum's round top, provides natural light for the changing exhibits that line the walls.

Rotunda at the Guggenheim

Since the museum's opening, both its physical structure and its original collection of European abstract art have expanded. A major renovation that took place in the early 1990s left the exterior refurbished and the interior with much-needed additional space. More recently still, new Guggenheims have opened in Soho (page 76) and, as the first step of an international expansion program, in Spain.

From the original exhibition, which included two ramps devoted to Kandinsky's work, to more recent exhibitions including the works of Max Beckman, Robert Maplethorpe and an exhibit devoted to the art of Africa, the museum has proven that its interests reach beyond the limitations of more classical museums.

INSIDERS' TIP

The best way to see the exhibits in the rotunda is to ride the elevator to the top, then work your way down the spiraling ramp.

"Let every man practice the art he knows" was inscribed by Wright on the entrance floor to the museum. Perhaps no better words have been written to describe the structure or the art within.

The Frick Collection

Opened to the public in 1935, the Frick Collection is housed in the former residence of steel baron **Henry Clay Frick** (1849-1919). Designed by the architects **Carrère and Hastings**, architects of the New York Public Library on Fifth Avenue, this mansion was built in 1914.

The Frick Collection

ADDRESS

1 East 70th Street
☎ 288-0700

HOURS

Tue-Sat: 10am-6pm
Sun: 1pm-6pm
Mon: closed

One of its most delightful architectural features is the Garden Court located in the center of the museum. It provides a pleasant environment in which to relax and take in the magnificence of this former private home.

Frick stated in his will that the Frick Collection was founded "to encourage and develop the study of fine arts, and advance the knowledge of kindred subjects."

The breadth of his private collection is astounding, but nearly one-third of the paintings have been added since his death.

Courtyard at the Frick

The collection contains impressive works of Western art, dating from the early Renaissance to the late 19th century. Particularly notable are its Old Master paintings, Renaissance bronzes and French sculpture from the 18th century.

Masterpieces by artists such as **Rembrandt**, **Renoir**, **Vermeer**, **El Greco**, **Goya**, **Titian** and many more are on display here. Highlights include Rembrandt's *Self Portrait*, Vermeer's *Mistress and Maid*, Titian's *Man in a Red Cap*, **Holbein**'s *Sir Thomas More* and **Thomas Gainsborough**'s *Mall in St. James's Park*.

PRICES

Adult $5
Children under ten are not permitted in the galleries
Senior $3
Student $3

DISCOUNT

2 admissions for the price of 1 with voucher on page 277.

The museum is exceptional because the works are displayed in an untraditional, whimsical manner which combines historical periods in the intimate setting of a private home without typical museum features like ropes and descriptive placards. The furniture, decorative art works and porcelain are as remarkable as the paintings and sculptures.

Because of the unique nature of the museum, and the vulnerability of the objects on display, children under ten years of age are not permitted in the galleries.

Whitney Museum of American Art

Early 20th century sculptor and wealthy arts patron Gertrude Vanderbilt Whitney acquired a substantial studio collection during her lifetime. In 1930, after the Metropolitan Museum of Art rejected the

collection she had amassed, the Whitney Museum of American Art was founded.

The inverted pyramid, a minimalist building designed by Marcel Breuer (a member of the Bauhaus school), became the Whitney's current home in 1966. It is located on exclusive Madison Avenue.

The Whitney

The Whitney is dedicated to the gathering and exhibiting of 20th-century American art, with a particular emphasis on the work of living artists. The permanent collection includes 11,000 paintings, sculptures, prints, drawings and photographs representing over 1,700 artists. It is best known for its impressive showing of American artists like **Georgia O'Keeffe**, **Jasper Johns**, **Roy Lichtenstein** and the complete artistic estate of **Edward Hopper** - comprising approximately 2,000 pieces. Highlights include **Alexander Calder**'s *Calder's Circus*, Jasper John's *Three Flags*, Roy Lichtenstein's *Little Big Painting*, Edward Hoppers's *Early Sunday Morning*, Georgia O'Keeffe's *The White Calico Flower* and **Andy Warhol**'s *Green Coca Cola Bottles*.

Early Sunday Morning (1930) by Edward Hopper

In 1991 a photographic collection was assembled with important acquisitions including **Gerald Murphy**'s

Cocktail and **Agnes Martin**'s *The Islands*, a series of 12 photographs believed to be her most significant work.

Founded in 1970, the **New American Film and Video Series** shows the works of independent, non-

Poker Night (1948) by Thomas Hart Benton, 1948

commercial American filmmakers and video artists. Their innovative and provocative works are shown in the film and video gallery.

ADDRESS

945 Madison Avenue
☎ 570-3676

HOURS

Wed: 11am-6pm
Thu: 1pm-8pm
Fri-Sun: 11am-6pm
Mon-Tue: closed

PRICES

Adult $8
Child free
Senior $5
Student $6

DISCOUNT

2 admissions for the price of 1 with voucher on page 277.

🗽 Museum of the City of New York

America's first city museum was founded in 1923 as a place to assemble and permanently display material associated with the fascinating history of New York City and its people.

Its treasury contains more than 1.5 million paintings, prints, photographs, costumes, manuscripts, memorabilia and sculptures. Highlights include gowns worn at George Washington's Inaugural Ball, a massive silver collection dating from 1678, the city's earliest fire engines and Jacob Riis' photographs of urban poverty.

Museum of the City of New York

The museum possesses one of America's most renowned **photographic archives** with more than half a million images documenting New York City since the advent of photography itself.

An impressive display of period rooms taken from actual homes represents life in New York from the colonial period through the 20th century. A collection of **toys, dollhouses and miniatures** dating from 1769, meticulous in detail, provides its own commentary on New York social life.

The museum also has a fascinating exhibition of various artifacts relating to the history and culture of New York City. One of the most remarkable is a section of the B-25 bomber that crashed into the Empire State Building in 1945.

John D. Rockefeller's bedroom at the Museum of the City of New York

As part of its "Museum for a New Century" program, renovation and expansion will eventually allow the museum to more than double its exhibition galleries while continuing to serve as an outstanding educational resource and a major cultural attraction for New Yorkers and visitors alike.

The museum gift shop offers a 10% discount on all purchases. Present your *New York for less* discount card to obtain the discount.

ADDRESS

1220 Fifth Avenue
☎ 534-1672

HOURS

Tue: Group tours by appointment only
Wed-Sat: 10am-5pm
Sun: 1pm-5pm
Mon: closed

PRICES

Suggested admission:
Adult $5
Child $4
Senior $4
Student $4
Family $10

DON'T MISS

The display of period rooms, the collection of silver or the incredible photographic archives.

DISCOUNT

10% discount in museum shop with your *New York for less* card.

National Academy of Design

The National Academy of Design was founded by a group of successful artists in 1825 "to sustain an association of artists for the purpose of instruction and exhibition." The academy is located in a handsome 19th-century Beaux Arts townhouse on 5th Avenue, donated in 1940 by art patron Archer

Huntington and his wife, sculptor Anna Hyatt. As you enter the academy, notice Anna Hyatt Huntington's *Statue of Diana* which is located in the foyer at the bottom of the grand spiral staircase.

The National Academy of Design is an artist-run organization that consists of the museum, the **School of Fine Arts** and an honorary association

National Academy of Design

of artists. Many of America's finest architects, painters, sculptors and printmakers were among its founding members. These included Thomas Cole, Rembrandt Peale and the National Academy's first president Samuel F. B. Morse.

Each elected member was required to donate a self-portrait along with another piece of representative work. This practice resulted in the acquisition of an impressive collection of **19th- and 20th-century American art** that includes more than 8,000 paintings, drawings, architectural models, engravings and sculptures. Well-known artists and architects including **Winslow Homer**, **Frank Lloyd Wright** and **John Singer Sargent** are all represented.

Modeled after London's Royal Academy, the **National Academy of Design's School of Fine Arts**, which is the oldest art school in New York, offers courses specializing in painting, drawing, sculpture, anatomy, perspective and printmaking. It is dedicated to educating, training and exhibiting accomplished artists as well as young and unrecognized talents.

Exhibitions, tours, lectures and educational programs, which are held regularly, focus on American and European art. The Annual Exhibition displays new work from contemporary artists.

ADDRESS

1083 Fifth Avenue
☎ 369-4880

HOURS

Wed-Thu, Sat-Sun:
12noon-5pm
Fri: 12noon-8pm
Mon-Tue: closed

PRICES

Adult $5
Child $3.50
Senior $2
Student $3.50

DISCOUNT

2 admissions for the price of one with voucher on page 277.

INSIDER'S TIP

On Fridays from 5pm-8pm, admission to the museum is free.

International Center of Photography

Founded in 1974, the International Center of Photography (ICP) is the only museum in New York City (and one of the few museums world-wide) devoted solely to photography.

Housed in a landmark Federal-style mansion, its mission is to collect, preserve and present all aspects

International Center of Photography

of photography. ICP has a second exhibition gallery (ICP Midtown, page 139) which opened in 1989 and is located on Avenue of the Americas at 43rd Street.

Over 20 exhibitions are mounted at the ICP each year. Subjects include everything from photojournalism to experimental, cutting-edge photography. Many of the exhibitions feature film or video presentations which are shown in the ICP screening room.

Since its foundation, ICP has shown the work of over 2,000 photographers from around the world. Among the many outstanding photographers who have been featured are Harry Callahan, Man Ray, Ansel Adams and Annie Leibowitz.

ICP's Traveling Exhibitions program is the largest in the United States. It circulates photographic exhibits around museums, galleries and other art and educational institutions both in the U.S. and abroad.

The ICP library contains over 8,000 volumes on photography, 7,000 biographical files on photographers and 10,000 magazines and journals.

In addition, ICP maintains the largest full-time photography education program in the world. Courses, lectures and workshops are given by reputable photographers and cover a full range of photography-related topics. Interactive guided tours are avilable from Tuesday to Friday, 10am-2pm.

ADDRESS

1130 Fifth Avenue
☎ 860-1777

HOURS

Tue: 11am-8pm
Wed-Sun: 11am-6pm
Mon: closed

PRICES

Adult $4
Child $1
Senior $2.50
Student $2.50

DISCOUNT

2 admissions for the price of 1 with voucher on page 278.

The Jewish Museum

In 1904, Judge Mayer Sulzberger contributed his library and art collection to **The Jewish Theological Seminary of America** as an initial offering and foundation for a museum. In 1947, Mrs. Felix M. Warburg, a board member of the seminary, donated her 1908 chateau-style mansion on Fifth Avenue as the site for The Jewish Museum.

The scope and diversity of Jewish culture over the last 4,000 years is illustrated through a permanent collection of more than 27,000 paintings, sculptures, photographs, archeological artifacts and ceremonial items.

The focal point of the museum is the permanent exhibit *Culture and Continuity: The Jewish Journey*, which conveys Jewish ideas, values and culture as they have developed from ancient to modern times. Situated on two floors, this 11,000-square-foot exhibition contains 17 galleries with four main themes: *Forging an Identity*, *Interpreting a Tradition*, *Confronting Modernity* and *Realizing a Future*. Each section features a range of Jewish-related art and artifacts, including a space devoted to the Holocaust.

Goldfish Vendor (1928) by Reuven Rubin

The exhibit also features a replica of an ancient synagogue complete with original artifacts taken from various synagogues throughout the Mediterranean.

Perhaps the most impressive gallery examines **Sephardi**, **Ashkenazi** and **Eastern Jewish** culture. It contains ceremonial art including exquisitely crafted Torah arks and beautifully embroidered textiles.

The museum also holds temporary exhibitions covering topics ranging from historical events to individual interpretation of Jewish culture by prestigious contemporary artists. One recent exhibit featured the well-known Jewish artist **Marc Chagall**.

You can also visit the **Goodkind Resource Center** which offers books and periodicals as well as video and audio programming from the museum's vast archives.

ADDRESS

1109 Fifth Avenue
☎ 423-3200

HOURS

Mon: 11am-5.45pm
Tue: 11am-8pm
Wed-Thu and Sun:
11am-5.45pm
Fri-Sat: closed

PRICES

Adult $7
Child free
Senior $5
Student $5

DISCOUNT

2 admissions for the
price of 1 with voucher
on page 279.

The Jewish Museum

Other Attractions . . .

Museo del Barrio

The **Museo del Barrio**, founded in 1969, is the only museum in the United States showcasing Latin-American Art. The museum's permanent collection consists of over 200 wooden carvings of santos (saints) as well as Latin-related paintings, crafts, artifacts and sculpture. Temporary exhibits feature Latino artists and examine the Hispanic-American community. *(1230 Fifth Avenue, ☎ 831-7272. Wed-Sun: 11am-5pm. Mon-Tue: closed. Suggested admission: Adult $4, child free, senior $2, student $2.)*

Cooper-Hewitt Museum

The **Cooper Hewitt Museum** is located in a 64-room Georgian mansion, dating from 1901, which was once the home of industrialist Andrew Carnegie. More than 250,000 items make it one of the largest design collections in the world. Started in 1897 at the Cooper Union School for the Advancement of Science and Art, the collection was donated to the Smithsonian Institution in 1967 when it was moved to its current location. Its holdings include drawings, prints, textiles and ceramic art. *(2 East 91st Street, ☎ 860-6868. Tue: 10am-9pm. Wed-Sat: 10am-5pm. Sun: 12noon-5pm. Mon: closed. Adult $3, child free, senior $1.50, student $1.50.)*

Cooper-Hewitt Museum

Goethe House is located across the street from the Metropolitan Museum of Art. Lectures and films focus on German culture and current events. Goethe House also sponsors German films, complete with English subtitles, at various locations throughout the city. Call for ticket information and prices. *(1014 Fifth Avenue, ☎ 439-8700. Tue and Thu: 10am-7pm. Wed and Fri: 10am-5pm. Sat: 12noon-5pm. Sun: closed. Admission is free.)*

Henderson Place Historic District comprises a surviving row of more than 20 Queen Anne-style houses, built during the 1880s. Details such as gabled roofs, dormer windows and corner turrets enhance the brick and stone facades. The fine craftsmanship with which they were constructed is a vivid reminder of the architectural grandeur of the late 19th century. *(East End Avenue at 86th Street.)*

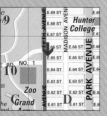

Temple Emanu-El

Built in 1929, **Temple Emanu-El** ("God is with us") is the largest synagogue in America, seating a congregation of over 2,500. The design of the temple

. . . Other Attractions . . .

s a mixture of Romanesque and Byzantine styles. *(1
East 65th Street, ☎ 744-1400. Sun-Fri: 10am-4.45pm. Sat:
service at 10.30am.)*

Gracie Mansion was built by
Archibald Gracie, an affluent
merchant, in 1799 and has
been the official home of New
York's mayor since 1942. The
mansion's Federal-style
architecture is one of the best-
preserved in the city. Guided
tours are available on
Wednesdays only and must be
reserved ahead. *(East End
Avenue at 88th Street, ☎ 570-4751. Wed: 10am-2pm (Apr-
Nov). Adult $4, child $4, senior $3, student $4.)*

Gracie Mansion

Founded in 1956 by John D. Rockefeller III, the **Asia
Society** was created to promote an understanding of
Asian culture. The society is housed in an eight-story
building and has maintained three galleries, one of
which displays Rockefeller's personal collection.
Events and activities include exhibitions, lectures,
films and music. *(725 Park Avenue, ☎ 288-6400. Tue-
Wed and Fri-Sat:
11am-6pm. Thu:
11am-8pm. Sun:
12noon-5pm. Adult
$3, child free, senior
$1, student $1.)*

Gracie Mansion

Asia Society

Built in 1880, the
**Seventh Regiment
Armory** was used in
every United States
war from the War of
1812 to the Second World War. Behind the imposing
exterior is an opulent setting filled with 19th-century
furnishings. Designed by Louis Comfort Tiffany, the
Veterans' Room and adjoining library are particularly
impressive. The Armory remains an active military
unit and also hosts cultural events. *(643 Park Avenue,
☎ 744-8180. Mon-Fri: open for tours by appointment only.
Sat-Sun: closed.)*

Asia Society

The Abigail Adams Smith Museum, built in 1799, was
named after the daughter of President John Adams.
This Federal-style building was once the carriage
house belonging to the Adams family, who resided in a
nearby estate. It was later converted to an inn. In
1924, it was purchased by the Colonial Dames of
America who restored it and made it into a museum.

Seventh Regiment Army

. . . Other Attractions

The nine-room house displays a collection which includes Federal furnishings and a letter from George Washington. *(421 East 61st Street, ☎ 838-6878. Mon-Fri: 12noon-4pm. (Jun-Jul also Tue: 11am-8pm). Sat-Sun: closed. Aug: closed. Adult $ 3, child free, senior $2, student $2.)*

Abigail Adams
Smith Museum

Built in 1917, the exclusive and sophisticated **Grolier Club** was where the wealthy men of the early 20th century once wheeled and dealed. The club is dedicated to the art of bookmaking, and houses a research library and an exhibition room. *(47 East 60th Street, ☎ 838-6690. Library and exhibition room open by appointment only.)*

The **Gagosian Gallery** has a collection of famous artists such as Andy Warhol, Willem de Kooning and Jackson Pollack. In Soho, there is also a downtown location of this gallery (see page 78). *(980 Madison Avenue, ☎ 744-2313. Tue-Sat: 10am-6pm. Sun-Mon: closed.)*

At the **Society of Illustrators**, you will find a unique collection of illustrations, ranging from advertisements and cartoons to war-time propaganda. *(128 East 63rd Street, ☎ 838-2560. Mon and Wed-Fri: 10am-5pm. Tue: 10am-8pm. Sun: 12noon-4pm. Sat: closed. Admission is free.)*

Tram to Roosevelt Island

Roosevelt Island is located in the East River between the Upper East Side of Manhattan and Queens. Originally inhabited by the Canarsie Indians, it was later sold to the Dutch. Known as Welfare Island, it was the site of a prison and a number of hospitals and asylums during the 19th century. In 1969 it was transformed into a residential community and, in 1986, its name was officially changed to Roosevelt Island in honor of President Franklin D. Roosevelt. Today, it is a prosperous suburb filled with beautiful parks and stunning views, only minutes from the busy streets of Manhattan. To get there, take either the Q or B subway trains or the Q102 bus. Better still, the Roosevelt Island tram car takes visitors on a scenic journey to and from the island. *(East River. Tram to Roosevelt Island: Second Avenue at 60th Street, ☎ 832-4540. Tram cars run every 15 minutes, Sun-Thu: 6am-2am. Fri-Sat: 6am-3.30am.)*

Roosevelt Island

Open Spaces

esigned in 1891, **Carl Schurz Park** *(East End Avenue nd the East River, between 84th and 90th Streets)* is amed after the German immigrant who became a ivil War general, U.S. Senator, editor f the *New York Evening Post* and *arper's Weekly* and, eventually, resident Rutherford B. Hayes' ecretary of the Interior from 1869- 875.

he highlight of this grassy park is a ng, wide sidewalk, named **John Finley alk**, after the former editor of the *ew York Times*, who was an avid hiker. he promenade provides great views of e East River and Queens, a path for llerbladers and joggers and a easant place to relax and watch the boats on the ver. Within the park, **Gracie Mansion** (page 195), e mayor's residence, dates back to 1799. The park so features a children's playground and fenced-in aygrounds for pets – one for big dogs, the other for

Carl Schurz Park on the East River

small.

Carl Schurz Park

Roosevelt Island's **Octagon Park** contains a promenade which provides magnificent views of the Manhattan skyline and the East River. The park also ntains recreational areas with tennis courts and cnic grounds. The island is encircled by a path hich makes an excellent route for walking, jogging or llerblading.

n the northern tip of Roosevelt Island, **Lighthouse ark** has open green spaces and views of the East ver.

Carl Schurz Park

side The **Metropolitan Museum of Art** (page 184), **stor Court** offers museum-goers an opportunity to lax in a tranquil Ming-style garden. It was designed a team of Chinese artisans in 1979. In addition, e rooftop **Sculpture Garden**, which is above the Oth-century wing of the museum, features a number outdoor sculptures and provides wonderful views of e city and Central Park.

Eating and Drinking

Madison Avenue is the pinnacle of New York art and fashion. It is *the* place for window shopping, bistro dining and people-watching. All along the avenue you will find gourmet food and specialty shops like **Caviarteria** (29 East 60th Street, ☎ 759-7410) and **Sherry-Lehmann** (679 Madison Avenue, ☎ 838-7500), one of the best-known wine stores in New York.

Gourmet food shop on the Upper East Side

Some of Manhattan's best restaurants are tucked away in the townhouses lining the shady streets of the Upper East Side. **Aureole** (34 East 61st Street, ☎ 319-1660) and **Daniel** (20 East 76th Street, ☎ 288-0033) are just two of the many top-ranked restaurants in the area.

In the exclusive Carlyle Hotel, **Café Carlyle** (35 East 76th Street ☎ 744-1600) is one of the more elegant places in town, perfect for after-dinner drinks and celebrity-watching, while being entertained by cabaret star **Bobby Short**.

Elaine's (1703 Second Avenue, ☎ 534-8103) has always been a favorite with theater and film celebrities, more for the social scene than the food. Another classic New York City haunt is the Oak Room (Fifth Avenue at 59th Street, ☎ 759-3000) at the Plaza Hotel.

Sharz Cafe (page 199) is a cozy Upper East Side bistro which has one of the best wines-by-the-glass selections in the city. For a moderately-priced meal in an elegant surroundings, **La Folie** (page 199) charms with its candle-lit dining room, grand piano and fireplace.

Across the street from Bloomingdale's department store, **Contrapunto** (page 200) and **Yellowfingers** (page 200) are two long-standing Italian eateries which are great places to unwind after a day of shopping and sightseeing.

East of Park Avenue, especially along Second and Third Avenues, the restaurants and shops tend to be less expensive. Some very good ones give discounts to *New York for less* cardholders (see pages 199-201). **Hunan Balcony Gourmet** (page 199) and **Chinatown East** (page 201) offer high quality, reasonably priced Chinese food. Nearby, **Doc Watson's** (page 201) is an amiable Irish pub which serves hearty meals at good prices.

REFLECTIONS

'The upper East Side of Manhattan...is the province of Let's Pretend.'
– Gail Sheehy,
Hustling (1971)

Sharz Cafe and Wine Bar

Italian / Mediterranean

177 East 90th Street
369-1010

Average meal: $20-25
or less discount: 25%
AM/MC/VS/DC

HOURS

Mon-Thu: 11.30am-11pm
Fri: 11.30am-12midnight
Sat: 11am-4pm,
5pm-12midnight
Sun: 11am-4pm

This cozy Mediterranean bistro has more than 40 wines by-the-glass. Entrées include more than 16 different pastas as well as various daily specials. Try the maple-glazed roast chicken or broiled rosemary lamb chops.

La Folie

French

422 Third Avenue
744-6327

Average meal: $20-25
or less discount: 25%
AM/MC/VS/DC

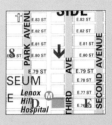

HOURS

Mon-Sun: 5pm-11pm

This elegant restaurant features a pleasant dining room with a fireplace and a grand piano. Candles and soft music enhance the atmosphere. Reasonable prices for a high quality dinner make this a great value.

Hunan Balcony Gourmet

Chinese

417 Second Avenue
517-2088

Average meal: $10-15
or less discount: 25%
AM/MC/VS/DC

HOURS

Mon-Fri and Sun:
12noon-12midnight
Sat: 12noon-1am

Hunan Balcony serves Chinese cuisine in a modern restaurant featuring a sunny atrium overlooking the avenue. Try the Hunan flower steak or the crispy shrimp and scallops with walnuts.

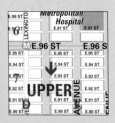

HOURS

Mon-Sat: 5pm-11pm
Sun: 11am-3pm,
5pm-11pm

Senza Nome

Italian

1675 Third Avenue
☎ 410-4900

Average meal: $20-25
for less discount: 25%
AM/MC/VS

Senza Nome applies innovative variations to classic
Italian favorites. Try the daily specials, which feature
the season's freshest ingredients. A glass-enclosed
terrace offers views of a lovely private sculpture garden.

HOURS

Mon-Thu: 12noon-11pm
Fri-Sat: 12noon-
12midnight
Sun: 2pm-10pm

Contrapunto

Italian

200 East 60th Street
☎ 751-8616

Average meal: $20-25
for less discount: 25%
AM/MC/VS/DC

Located across the street from Bloomingdales,
Contrapunto has been serving fine Italian cuisine for
more than ten years. Try the salmon with asparagus, wild
mushrooms and cauliflower mousse.

HOURS

Mon-Thu: 11.30am-1am
Fri-Sat: 11.30am-2am
Sun: 11.30am-12midnight

Yellowfingers

Italian / American

200 East 60th Street
☎ 751-8615

Average meal: $15-20
for less discount: 25%
AM/MC/VS/DC

For 30 years, this lively trattoria has been a neighborhood
favorite. Its second floor location offers you great views
of the streets below. Try the rosemary chicken salad or
grilled shrimp with tequila.

Chinatown East

Chinese

650 Third Avenue
987-3500

Average meal: $10-15
or less discount: 25%
AM/MC/VS

Chinatown East offers an extensive menu at very reasonable prices. The chef's specialties include sesame chicken and seafood delight. There is also a sushi bar where you can watch your food being prepared.

Doc Watson's

Irish / American

490 Second Avenue
988-5300

Average meal: $10-15
or less discount: 25%
AM/MC/VS/DS

HOURS

Mon-Fri: 12noon-
12midnight
Sat-Sun: 12noon-2pm

This friendly Irish-American restaurant serves good food at reasonable prices. The atmosphere is informal and a pleasant garden is open in the summer. Try one of the burgers or the Guinness stew.

The Barking Dog Luncheonette

American

678 Third Avenue
831-1800

Average meal: $10-15
or less discount: 25%
No credit cards accepted.

HOURS

Mon-Sun: 8am-11pm

The Barking Dog offers classic American food interpreted for the nineties. This comfortable spot is great for any meal, including Sunday brunch. In warm weather, sample the homemade dishes while dining outdoors.

Shopping

The ultra expensive shops and galleries on Madison Avenue give testament to the wealth of their patrons. Major designers such as **Calvin Klein** *(654 Madison Avenue, ☎ 292-9000)*, **Polo/Ralph Lauren** *(86? Madison Avenue, ☎ 606-2100)*, **Yves Saint Laurent** *(855 Madison Avenue, ☎ 472-5299)* and **Giorgio Armani** *(815 Madison Avenue, ☎ 988-9191)* have shops on this fashionable thoroughfare.

Bloomingdale's

Bloomingdale's *(1000 Third Avenue, ☎ 705-2000)* provides the quintessential Upper Eas Side shopping experience. Here you will find all of the major clothing brands under one roof. **Barney's New York** *(Madison Avenue at 61st Street, ☎ 945-1600)* sells top designer clothing with price tags to match. Both elegant and hip, Barney's is a favorite with New York's fashion cognoscenti.

The Upper East Side also offers high quality, less expensive shopping alternatives. On Lexington Avenue, **Carducci** (page 204) sells an assortment of fine leather goods.

Upper East Side boutiques

Sportswords (page 203) has an abundance of sports titles and is the only bookstore in New York City exclusively devoted to sports.

Most of the museums on **Museum Mile** have great shops offering unique gifts and souvenirs. Many of these offer a discount to *New York for less* cardholders.

Fromex 1 Hour Photo

Film Developin

182 East 86th Stree
☎ 369-482

for less discount: 20%
AM/MC/V

Fromex specializes in one-hour color film developing There is another location at 1058 Third Avenue at 63r Street (☎ 644-5678). Other locations are number 2041 and 2151 Broadway (Upper West Side).

Mud, Sweat and Tears

Crafts & Gifts

1566 Second Avenue
☎ 570-6868

for less discount: 20%
AM/MC/VS

HOURS

Mon-Sat: 11.30am-8pm
Sun: 11.30am-6pm

Handmade crafts and gifts are available in this lively
shop and art studio. It sells pottery, scented candles and
other creations. Visitors can observe artists at work or
create their own art at the paint bar.

Decor Art Gallery

Poster Shop & Framing

1156 Second Avenue
☎ 688-7078

for less discount: 20%
AM/MC/VS

HOURS

Mon-Sat: 10am-7.30pm
Sun: 11am-6pm

Decor Art carries a large selection of posters and art,
both with or without frames. Classic and modern art
from well-known artists can be purchased. This shop can
also fit a frame to any poster, photograph or artwork.

Sportswords

Bookshop

1475 Third Avenue
☎ 772-8729

for less discount: 20%
AM/MC/VS

HOURS

Mon-Wed: 11am-6pm
Thu: 11am-7pm
Sat: 11am-5pm
Sun: closed

Sportswords is the only bookstore in New York devoted
solely to sports. It stocks over 3,000 titles including
biographies, team histories and kids books. The discount
does not apply to out-of-print or autographed books.

Carducci Leather

Leather Goods

1324 Lexington Avenue
☎ 410-7799

for less discount: 20%
AM/MC/VS/DC/DS

Carducci Leather offers the finest in a variety of leather goods. Handbags, wallets and briefcases are just some of the items available. A wide range of colors, shapes and styles are offered.

Metropolitan Graphic Arts

Poster Shop & Framing

1457 Third Avenue
☎ 737-9703

for less discount: 20%
AM/MC/VS

Choose from a large collection of posters, lithographs, custom frames and fine art reproductions from well-known artists. There is another location on the Upper West Side at 2341 Broadway (☎ 595-1615).

Second Avenue Army Navy

Army Navy & Clothing

1589 Second Avenue
☎ 737-4661

for less discount: 20%
AM/MC/VS

Second Avenue Army Navy has a wide selection of men's and women's clothing and accessories. Top brands like Timberland, Levi's, Calvin Klein and Polo are all stocked. This store also carries all styles and sizes of jeans.

Central Park

Introduction . . .

The construction of Central Park was begun in 1858 by journalist and landscaper **Frederick Law Olmsted** and English architect **Calvert Vaux** on seemingly

The terrace at Belvedere Castle

undesirable swampland. Its creation, which took 20 years, involved moving millions of tons of soil and rocks, planting over five million trees and building ponds, lakes, a reservoir and roadways.

The result is an incredible wilderness in the heart of the busy metropolis. Its various areas incorporate many different types of natural landscape, which runs the gamut from open fields to thicketed forests.

Ball games, picnics and summertime outdoor concerts help make this 843-acre park a vibrant center of activity. At one famous open-air concert in 1981, more than half a million people came to the **Great Lawn** to watch Simon and Garfunke perform.

INSIDER'S TIP

To find out about special events and happenings, the Department of Parks and Recreation (☎ 360-3456) has a 24-hour recorded information line which provides information on activities in this and other city parks.

While Americans around the country spend their summers lounging by swimming pools and walking barefoot on their lawns, the closest

Rollerblading by the Bandshell

many New Yorkers get to the "great outdoors" is Central Park. This does not, however, stop them from putting on bathing suits, applying sunscreen and throwing their beach towels onto the sloping greens of the **Sheep Meadow** as if it were a sandy beach.

North of the Lake, **The Ramble** (*Between 72nd and 79th Streets,* ☎ *772-0210*) has over 30 acres of sylvan

Joggers in Central Park

wonderland filled with dirt paths and trickling brooks. Known as an excellent spot for bird-watching, excursions are held from Tuesday through Sunday from 11am-4pm. Binoculars and sketching materials are available free of charge.

Joseph Papp's **New York Shakespeare Festival** was founded in 1954, and its **Shakespeare-in-the-Park** productions are a favorite summertime event. Two different plays are staged throughout the summer at the outdoor **Delacorte Theater** (*West 81st Street,* ☎ *861-7277*). Tickets are free, but obtaining them is not so easy. New Yorkers

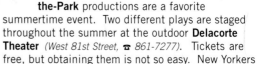

. . . Introduction

wait in shifts, staggering their lunch hours to be staggered with friends until the tickets are given out sometime after 1pm (arrive early). You can also get tickets at the Public Theater (page 97) on Lafayette Street – the same procedure applies. The tickets become more difficult to obtain towards the end of each production's run, when all the last-minute Shakespeare fans turn up in droves.

Summerstage is another free summer event that takes place at **Rumsey Playfield**. Whether the performances are reggae or opera, they always attract crowds who set up blankets and picnic anywhere within hearing distance.

Best known for its extremely popular walking and jogging route, the **Reservoir** (*Between 86th and 97th streets*) has recently been renamed to honor

Sledding in Central Park, 1898

Jacqueline Kennedy Onassis, who used to jog here regularly. Madonna is sometimes spotted jogging incognito with her bodyguards.

Take a stroll along the Mall – a grand tree-lined boulevard in the midst of the park. Little has changed since its days as a popular place to promenade during the late 19th century. **Horse-drawn carriages** are another popular way of seeing the park. You can check the rates and buy a ticket from a booth at **Grand Army Plaza** (*59th Street at Fifth Avenue*).

To step into another time zone altogether, visit the impromptu roller-skating rink just west of the Mall. Skaters here wear the four-wheeled rollerskates that seem so perfectly suited to the 1970s disco music that blasts from the fabricated D.J. booth in the center. Nearby, **Wollman Rink** (page 208) is one of the most popular outdoor attractions in the city and the main attraction in Central Park.

Although crime in the park is not commonplace, there have been a few very unpleasant and well-publicized incidents. Keep to the more populated areas if the park is unfamiliar to you and avoid roaming the park after dark. There are emergency phone boxes and telephones throughout the park as well as a 24-hour Park Line (☎ 570-4820).

Rollerbladers at Wollman Rink

Other Attractions . . .

Wollman Rink

Skating at **Wollman Rink** is a unique New York tradition. With its wide open space and fantastic views of the midtown skyline, it is perhaps one of the most spectacular outdoor skating rinks in the world.

Outdoor tables and a terrace overlook the rink, allowing you to watch the skaters below. Inside, there is a snack bar and a sports shop. The view of the skyscrapers bordering the park is especially beautiful at night, and the rink is open late most evenings.

All sessions are accompanied by music, you can stay for as long as you like and lessons are available. If you

Ice skating at Wollman Rink

don't have your own skates, you can rent them at the rink. In the winter, ice skaters fill the rink, but from April to October in-line skating becomes the main event.

The best way to reach Wollman Rink, located in the southeast corner of the park, is from the Grand Army Plaza entrance at 59th Street and 5th Avenue. *(Central Park at 63rd Street, ☎ 396-1010. Mon: 10am-4pm. Tue-Thu: 10am-8.30pm. Fri-Sat: 10am-11pm. Sun: 10am-9pm. Adult $7, child $3.50, senior $3.50, student $7, Skate rental $3.50. 2 admissions for the price of 1 with voucher on page 279.)*

Located in the southern portion of the park, the wooden, Gothic-style **Dairy** was built in 1870 and now serves as the main visitors' center. Inside, a short video about the history of the park as well as other park-related information is available. This is a good place to start a visit to the park, and to find out about any special events taking place. *(65th Street Transverse,*

Dairy

☎ 794-6565. Winter: Tue-Sun: 11am-4pm. Fri: 1pm-4pm. Summer: Tue-Sun: 11am-5pm. Fri: 1pm-5pm.)

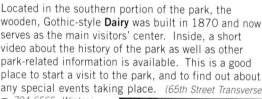

Carousel

The **Carousel**, which was imported from its old home at Coney Island (page 230), is a now a Central Park favorite with children. *(65th Street Transverse, ☎ 879-0244. Summer: Mon-Fri: 10.30am-8pm. Sat-Sun: 10.30am-6.30pm. Winter: Sat-Sun: 10.30am-5pm. 90¢.)*

The **Central Park Wildlife Conservation Center** has been creatively restored to maximize its small space. The 5½-acre zoo is home to more than 130 species and has three climate zones: the Tropics, the

. . . Other Attractions . . .

California coast and the Polar Circle. The Polar Circle exhibit contains a special tank that allows you to watch the polar bears on land and in the water. A

gallery, located outside the main entrance to the zoo, displays wildlife art. *(Fifth Avenue and 64th Street, ☎ 439-6500. Apr-Oct: Mon-Fri: 10am-5pm. Sat-Sun: 10.30am-5:30pm. Nov-Mar: Mon-Sun: 10am-*

Central Park Wildlife Conservation Center

:30pm. Adult $2.50, child 50¢ (under 3 free), senior $1.25, student $2.50.)

Central Park Wildlife Center

By the entrance to the Children's Zoo, the **Delacorte Musical Clock**, is also a favorite with children. Every half hour from 8am to 6pm the clock reveals animals that put on a musical performance. *(64th Street at Fifth Avenue, ☎ 861-6030.)*

Conservatory Water

Also known as the **Model Boat Pond**, the **Conservatory Water** is the site of model boat races every Saturday from March to November. On the north side of the pond is the Alice in Wonderland sculpture. Close by, a statue of Hans Christian Andersen is the site of summertime storytelling sessions. *(East 74th Street, ☎ 360-8133.)*

In the center of the park, the **Lake**, with its **Bow Bridge**, resembles a scene from a 19th-century painting thanks in part to the row boats that can be seen here on warm days. *(Between West 71st and 77th Streets.)*

Bethesda Terrace

Loeb Boathouse rents rowboats for $10 per hour, plus a $20 deposit. Private gondola tours are given for $30 per hour. You can also rent bicycles for $8-10 an hour. The boathouse has a restaurant and a café with outdoor seating available in warm weather. *(East 74th Street, ☎ 517-4723.)*

Bethesda Fountain and Terrace, the architectural centerpiece of the park, overlooks the Lake and offers one of the most scenic views in the park. *(72nd Street, ☎ 517-2233.)*

Loeb Boathouse

Beginning at 66th Street, **The Mall** is a tree-lined thoroughfare that leads up to an open area by the **Bandshell**, which has become a favorite impromptu

. . . Other Attractions

spot for in-line skaters. *(Between 66th and 72nd Streets.)*

Bethesda Fountain

Strawberry Fields is an international peace garden commemorating the life and death of John Lennon who lived nearby. There are 161 varieties of plant life on this three-acre preserve – a tribute to the 161 nations of the world. *(West 72nd Street.)*

Toy boats in the Conservatory Water

Belvedere Castle, the highest point in the park, is a fairy-tale structure with great views of the heavily forested Ramble to the south and the Great Lawn to the north. **The Discovery Chamber** is an educational center where children can learn about the park through fun-filled activities. Family workshops are available on Saturdays from 1pm to 2.30pm. The castle also serves as the headquarters for the Urban Park Rangers. *(West 79th Street, ☎ 772-0210.)*

Belvedere Castle

The **North Meadow Recreation Center** is located north of the Reservoir. The center has basketball courts and sponsors other recreational programs, including rock climbing courses. *(West 97th Street, ☎ 348-4867.)*

Showcasing the wrought-iron gates that once stood at Cornelius Vanderbilt's mansion is the **Conservatory Garden**. Thousands of plants, trees and shrubs adorn the three formal gardens. In the summer, free tours are given on Saturdays. *(West 104th Street, ☎ 860-1382. Mon-Sun: 8am-dusk.)*

Belvedere Castle

Just above the Conservatory Garden, is the recently refurbished **Harlem Meer**. The **Charles A. Dana Discovery Center** features ongoing educational exhibitions and programs relating to Central Park. In the summer, you can rent a fishing rod from the center and cast a line in the meer. *(110th Street and Fifth Avenue, ☎ 860-1370. Tue-Sat: 11am-5pm. Sun-Mon: closed.)*

Strawberry Fields

Conservatory Garden

New York
by Night

Introduction

More than any other city in the world, New York is known for its nightlife. "The city that never sleeps" offers endless nighttime opportunities well past

Manhattan skyline at night

midnight every night of the week. From quiet dining and classical performing arts to all-night clubbing and live music of every type, the city has something to offer everyone.

Among the best things to do in New York at night are: sightseeing from the top of the **Empire State Building** (page 116), which is open until midnight, and taking a **sightseeing cruise** (page 218) around the tip of Manhattan where you can enjoy magnificent views of the Statue of Liberty and the illuminated Manhattan skyline.

Throughout New York's neighborhoods, especially along the avenues, there are dense concentrations of **restaurants and bars**, while the majority of **clubs and live music venues** can be found downtown. Almost all bars are open late, some as late as 4am on weekends.

Midtown West is home to the world-renowned **Theater District** and its **Broadway** productions. In addition to commercial Broadway shows, there are many excellent secondary productions staged throughout the city. **Off-Broadway**, in particular, presents quality plays and musicals, often starring well-known film and television actors.

Webster Hall

Further downtown, **Greenwich Village** and **Soho** are late night hot spots for dining, bar hopping and clubbing. One of the best and biggest nightclubs is **Webster Hall** (page 216), which gives a discount to *New York for less* cardholders.

Free newspapers the *New York Press* and the *Village Voice*, available throughout the city, give up-to-date and detailed listings of events and venues, as do weekly magazines such as *New York* and *Time Out New York*.

The subway runs 24 hours every day and will accommodate any nightlife schedule, no matter how rigorous.

Nightlife

THEATERS

The **TKTS** booth *(West 47th Street and Broadway)* in Times Square sells tickets for Broadway shows at 50% off (plus a surcharge of $2.50). They must, however, be purchased on the day of performance only and no credit cards are accepted. Another drawback is that the lines can be daunting. As an alternative to TKTS, you can use your *New York for less* card to purchase tickets for Broadway shows in advance, while obtaining discounts of up to 50% (see page 215).

Les Misérables

DANCE

The **New York City Ballet** *(Lincoln Center, ☎ 870-5570)* performs at the New York State Theater, Lincoln Center. It is perhaps best-known for its production of *George Balanchine's The Nutcracker*, performed each holiday season. Leading dancers such as Mikhail Baryshnikov and Rudolf Nureyev have performed with the **American Ballet Theater** *(30 Lincoln Center Plaza, ☎ 362-6000)* whose productions are staged at the Metropolitan Opera House.

The **Joyce Theater** *(175 Eighth Avenue, ☎ 242-0800)* is the permanent home of Feld Ballets/NY and hosts performances in many different dance styles. Other venues for modern dance include **City Center** *(131 West 44th Street, ☎ 581-1212)*, **BAM** (page 215) and **the Merce Cunningham Studio** *(55 Bethune Street, ☎ 691-9751)*.

OPERA

The **Metropolitan Opera** has hosted legendary performers like Placido Domingo and Luciano Pavarotti. Performances are held from October to mid-April. *(Lincoln Center, ☎ 362-6000)*. Performing at Lincoln Center's New York State Theater, **New York City Opera** (page 215) offers a discount to *New York for less* cardholders. It has received critical acclaim for a varied repertoire of works from classics to world premieres. High-tech "supertitles" allow you to read English translations projected above the stage during the performance.

Evening in the Theater District

CONCERT HALLS

Carnegie Hall *(156 West 57th Street, ☎ 247-7800)* is the most historic concert hall in the city, dating back to 1891 (see page 141). **Avery Fisher Hall** is home to the prestigious New York Philharmonic. *(10 Lincoln Center, ☎ 874-2424)*.

Nightlife

FILM

For general information about movies playing around town, call **Moviephone** (☎ 777-3456). To see

independent, foreign and rare films, try the **Anthology Film Archives** (*32 Second Avenue*, ☎ 505-5181) or the **Angelica Film Center** (*18 West Houston Street*, ☎ 995-2000). You can also enjoy a unique cinematic experience at the **Sony IMAX Theatre** (page 167) where your *New York for less* card entitles you to two admissions for the price of one.

Times Square at night

COMEDY CLUBS

Stand-up New York (page 215), one of New York's top comedy clubs, offers a discount to *New York for less* cardholders. Other good venues for catching stand-up comedy are **Caroline's** (*1626 Broadway*, ☎ 757-4100) and **Dangerfield's** (*1118 First Avenue*, ☎ 593-1650), owned by comedian and actor Rodney Dangerfield.

REFLECTIONS

'I like New York because it engenders high expectations simply by its pace.' – Bill Bradley, *Life on the Run* (1976)

JAZZ CLUBS / LIVE MUSIC CLUBS

Much of New York's thriving jazz scene can be found in Greenwich Village, including blues club **Mondo Cane** (page 216). Jazz enthusiasts can also enjoy venues like the **Blue Note** (*131 West 3rd Street*, ☎ 475-8592), the **Village Vanguard** (*178 Seventh Avenue*, ☎ 255-4037) and Tribeca's **Knitting**

New York nightlife

Factory (*74 Leonard Street*, ☎ 219-3055). Popular rock clubs include the **Beacon Theater** (*2124 Broadway*, ☎ 496-7070) and **Roseland** (*239 West 52nd Street*, ☎ 249-8870) as well as many smaller clubs downtown, especially in the **East Village** (see page 95).

NIGHTCLUBS

New York's club scene changes rapidly with new clubs springing up constantly. A select few have managed to remain popular for a long period. Among these, try **Limelight** (*680 Sixth Avenue*, ☎ 807-7850), the **Palladium** (*126 East*

Dancing at Webster Hall

14th Street, ☎ 473-4141) and **Webster Hall** (page 216) which offers reduced admission, front-of-the-line status and a complimentary champagne toast to *New York for less* cardholders.

Broadway Theater Discounts

226 West 47th St., 3rd Flr
☎ **398-8383, ext. 30**
or (800) 223-7565, ext.
30

Save on orchestra or front
mezzanine tickets. Buy in
advance with a credit card or
at the above address ($10
service charge applies with
credit card). AM/MC/VS

With *New York for less*, you can obtain discounts of up
to 50% off tickets for top Broadway shows. Call in
advance to see which shows are available. Book by
credit card, or purchase tickets at the ticket office.

HOURS

Telephone reservations
are accepted
Mon-Fri: 10am-5pm

Brooklyn Academy of Music

30 Lafayette Ave., Brooklyn
☎ **(718) 636-4100 (info),**
(212) 307-4100 (tickets)
Fax: (718) 857-2021

With your for less card: 15%
off any BAM ticket. Buy
tickets by phone, fax or mail
(advance purchase possible).
MC/VS

Save 15% on tickets for any production at the oldest
performing arts center in America. If you are purchasing
your tickets by mail or fax, be sure to include alternate
dates and a phone number where you can be reached.

HOURS

Box office open:
Mon-Fri: 10am-6pm
Sat: 12noon-6pm
Sun (performance days
only): 12noon-4pm.

New York City Opera

New York State Theater,
Lincoln Center
☎ **870-5570 (info only)**

With your for less card:
$10 off all orchestra seats.
Buy tickets at box office
on day of performance.
AM/MC/VS

Enjoy an evening of opera at world-famous Lincoln
Center. New York City Opera's seasonal performances
include time-honored classics like La Bohème and
exciting new productions.

HOURS

Box office open:
Mon: 10am-7.15pm
Tue-Sat: 10am-8.15pm
Sun: 11.30am-7.15pm

HOURS

Thu-Sat: 10pm-4am

Webster Hall

Nightclub

125 East 11th Street
☎ 353-1600

$15 Thu, $20 Fri-Sat
$5 off admission
with your New York
for less card.
AM/MC/VS/DS

Webster Hall is New York City's premier nightclub. It encompasses over 40,000 square feet on 4 floors and has 4 DJs. With your *for less* card you get a discount, priority entrance *and* a free glass of champagne.

HOURS

Mon-Sun: 10am-3am

Mondo Cane

Live Music / Blues

205 Thompson Street
☎ 254-5166

$5 entrance
2 admissions for the
price of 1 with your
New York for less card
AM/MC/VS/DC

This live music club specializes in blues and jazz. It is situated on the second floor above Cucina Regionale (page 102) where you can dine before coming here for after-dinner drinks while listening to the performance.

HOURS

Mon-Fri: 6:30pm-1am
Sat: 6:30pm-12midnight

Stand Up New York

Comedy Club / Restaurant

236 West 78th Street
☎ 595-0850

Average meal: $15-20
2 admissions for the price of 1
and 25% discount on your
meal with your New York for
less card. AM/MC/VS/DC/D.

This well-established comedy club is also a high quality restaurant. Top comedians from all over the world perform nightly. American cuisine is served while you watch the show. The baked ziti is highly recommended.

Tours

ADDRESS

Pier 83, Hudson River at
West 42nd Street
☎ 563-3200

HOURS

*America's Favorite Boat
Ride*: Hours vary
depending on the season
from 9:15am-4:30pm.

Harbor Lights Cruise:
Sets sail at 5:30pm or
7pm depending on the
season.

PRICES

*America's Favorite Boat
Ride and Harbor Lights
Cruise*:
Adult $20
Child $10
Senior $16
Student $16

Circle Line Express:
Adult $17
Child $9
Senior $14
Student $14

Music Cruises: prices vary,
call 563-3200 for schedule
and fares.

DISCOUNT

20% off the regular price
of any Circle Line cruise
with voucher on page 279.

Circle Line Sightseeing Cruises

Circle Line Sightseeing cruises have been providing
guided tours of the New York waterways for more than
50 years.

The most
comprehensive
cruise is a three-
hour tour, which
makes a complete
circle around the
island of
Manhattan.
Known as

Circle Line Cruise

"**America's Favorite Boat Ride**", this tour covers 35
miles of coastline and travels past major sights and
attractions. The Statue of Liberty, **Ellis Island**, World
Trade Center, Empire State Building and Yankee
Stadium are just some of the highlights visible from
the boat, and are included in the lively commentary.
You will also sail underneath the Brooklyn and George
Washington Bridges. This cruise sails daily from early
March through late December and is also available in
an abbreviated two-hour version.

The **Harbor Lights Cruise** is a romantic two-hour
cruise that sets sail at dusk – providing both sunset
and nighttime views of Manhattan. It sails around the
tip of Manhattan and out to the Statue of Liberty as
the sun sets. It runs from
late March through
November.

In addition to sightseeing
tours, **live music cruises** are
also scheduled throughout
the summer (June through
September). On board these
2½-hour cruises you can
enjoy live jazz while taking in
skyline views. Reservations
are necessary on all music
cruises.

*Empire State Building
at sunset*

Other custom cruises sail
throughout the season
including two-hour **Family Cruises** and the **Circle Line
Captain's Club** – a series of cruises organized just for
seniors. The **Big Day Rate** promises a free cruise for
anyone celebrating their 50th Birthday.

With the voucher on page 279, you will receive a 20%
discount off the regular price of any Circle Line cruise

New York Apple Tours

Whether you have two days or two weeks to spend in New York, taking New York Apple Tours is the best way to maximize your time while visiting all the major sightseeing attractions in the city.

All tours are conducted on **double-decker buses** imported from London. Open and closed-top buses

allow you to tour New York City in any weather. As you see the sights of Manhattan, you are given a **live commentary** by an experienced on-board guide.

You can **hop off and on** as many

New York Apple double-decker bus

times as you like, allowing you to customize your sightseeing tour. With *New York for less*, you can obtain discounts on the two main tours.

The **Full City Tour** covers two consecutive days. The bus travels along major routes and by all the most popular sights including the Empire State Building, Times Square, Rockefeller Center and Lincoln Center. The bus travels the length of Manhattan, allowing you to visit neighborhoods from Chinatown to Soho to the

Upper East Side. Spend some time on Museum Mile or walking through Central Park, before re-boarding the bus and visiting South Street Seaport or Greenwich Village. There are also drop-off points for Liberty Helicopters (page 222) which also give discounts to *New York for less* cardholders.

Statue of Liberty

The **Statue of Liberty Express** includes the Full City Tour plus the ferry ticket to the **Statue of Liberty** and Ellis Island (page 50-53) and is a great way to avoid the inevitable lines for buying ferry tickets.

Purchase your tickets from a New York Apple Tours representative at the New York Apple Tours office or at one of the bus stops. Tickets may not be purchased at hotels or retail shops.

ADDRESS

Purchase tickets at Eighth Avenue and 50th Street or from uniformed ticket sellers on the bus or at one of the stops.
☎ 944-9200 (9am-6pm)

PRICES

Full City Tour:
Adult: $30
Child: $19

Statue of Liberty Express:
Adult: $40
Child $24

HOURS

Mon-Sun: 9am-6pm

DISCOUNT

$15 off adult and $8 off child prices for both the Statue of Liberty Express and the Full City Tour with voucher on page 281.

Seaport Liberty Cruises

Seaport Liberty Cruise by the Statue of Liberty

ADDRESS

Pier 16 at the South
Street Seaport.
☎ 630-8888

HOURS

Seaport Liberty Cruise:
Sails from 12noon-
7:30pm, hours vary
depending on the season.

Music Cruises:
Sets sail at 7pm, 9:30pm
and 10pm, depending on
the season.

PRICES

Seaport Liberty Cruises:
Adult $12
Child $6

Music Cruises:
Adult $15-$22

DISCOUNT

2 admissions for the
price of 1 with voucher
on page 279.

Seaport Liberty Cruises offer one-hour guided
sightseeing tours of Lower Manhattan and the Statue
of Liberty.

Highlights include attractions such as the Brooklyn
Bridge, Wall Street, Ellis Island and the World Trade
Center – all of which are visible from the ship. The
live commentary enriches your viewing of these
attractions and provides additional information about
the maritime history of South Street Seaport.

Seaport Liberty **one-hour cruises** sail on a regular
schedule from mid-March through late December.

From June to September you can also enjoy **live music
cruises** which present contemporary blues and jazz
artists against the backdrop of the Manhattan skyline.

Friday and Saturday nights, from May to October, two-
hour **DJ cruises** feature New York disc jockeys spinning
dance tunes on board.

Departing from Pier 16 at the South Street Seaport
(page 54), Seaport Liberty Cruises fits in well with a
visit to this historic district and is the official
sightseeing cruise of the South Street Seaport
Museum (page 54-55).

Snacks, sandwiches, beverages (including cocktails
and beer) and famous New York hot dogs are available
on board. You can also purchase T-shirts, hats and
other souvenirs.

The *New York for less* voucher on page 279 entitles
you to receive two tickets for the price of one on any of
the Seaport Liberty Cruises. Reservations are
necessary only for the music cruises.

World Yacht Dinner Cruises

here are quite a few restaurants in New York that fer great views of the city. None of them, however, an rival the ever-changing view of Manhattan offered a cruise which circumnavigates the island.

orld Yacht has combined an excellent meal with a xury cruise, for an unparalleled entertainment, ning and sightseeing experience. The fleet of ships

is comprised of five luxury dining yachts, all climate-controlled for year-round cruising. From the stately glass-enclosed dining areas, every table offers spectacular views of New York's famous skyline.

World Yacht

Departing from midtown on the Hudson River, the yacht sails past sights such as Ellis Island, the South

reet Seaport, United Nations and the illuminated ooklyn, Manhattan and Williamsburg Bridges before rning around to complete its three-hour tour. The ghlight of the trip is when the boat sweeps right der the Statue of Liberty, allowing you a close-up 2w of this flood-lit monument.

four-course dinner is served at a leisurely ce so that diners are free to explore the rious decks or head to the dance floor ere an orchestra plays.

ADDRESS

World Yacht Marina
Pier 81 at West 41st Street
and the Hudson River.
☎ 630-8100

HOURS

Mon-Sun: boards at 6pm,
sails 7pm-10pm.
Jun-Sep: additional cruise
every Friday boards at
7pm, sails 8pm-11pm.

meals are prepared fresh on board and e known for their quality. World Yacht is a ember of organizations such as The linary Institute of America, Commanderie s Cordons Bleus de France and the tional Restaurant Association.

Dining aboard World Yacht

me dishes from past menus include appetizers such *porcini ravioli*, shrimp cocktail and caviar, as well as trées like *filet mignon*, rack of lamb and the Fulton h Market selection of the day. There is also a wide nge of desserts, cakes and pastries.

servations are necessary for all cruises and proper ire is required. Jeans and sneakers are not rmitted and gentlemen must wear a jacket. *New rk for less* cardholders are entitled to a discount of 4 off the price of a dinner cruise Sunday through day evenings with the voucher on page 283.

PRICES

Per person: $62

DISCOUNT

$14 off the regular price
of dinner cruises Sun-Fri.

Liberty Helicopter Tours

You can experience spectacular views of Manhattan or any of Liberty Helicopters sightseeing tours. Each of the two heliport locations offer four pilot-narrated tours – all of which give a 20% discount to *New York for less* cardholders.

From the **Downtown Heliport** you can fly over New York Harbor past the Statue of Liberty and Lower Manhattan sites in only 4½ minutes on the **Statue Express**.

The **Torch of Freedom** adds to the Statue Express with a tour of the United Nations, Brooklyn,

A helicopter tour over New York Harbor

Manhattan and Williamsburg Bridges and the 110-story twin towers of the World Trade Center.

Manhattan's Grand Canyons allows you to soar through the canyons of Manhattan's skyscrapers and get close up views of sights such as the Empire State and Chrysler Buildings, Times Square and Central Park.

From the **West Side Heliport**, the **Liberty Sampler** takes you past the USS Intrepid, the Empire State and Chrysler Buildings, then up the Hudson River to Central Park. The **Torch of Freedom** and Manhattan's Grand Canyons are also available from the midtown location.

In addition, **The Big Picture** (offered at both locations) is the most comprehensive tour available. It provides nearly twenty minutes of sightseeing from the Statue of Liberty to the Bronx. You can get a bird's-eye view of all the attractions included in the other tours plus Yankee Stadium, the George Washington Bridge and the East and Harlem Rivers.

All tours are conducted in state-of-the-art jet helicopters, featuring climate-controlled cabins and unobstructed views from every seat – perfect for picture taking. Known for having high safety standards, Liberty Helicopters has continuously received the annual safety award from the Helicopter Association International.

Purchase tickets at the heliport only. In addition to a 20% discount on tours, *New York for less* cardholders are *not* charged the regular heliport surcharge.

ADDRESS

West Side Heliport:
West 30th Street and
12th Avenue

Downtown Heliport:
Pier 6 and the East River
☎ 487-4777 or
☎ (800) 542-9933 for
either location

HOURS

West Side Heliport:
Open daily (including
holidays): 9am-9pm.

Downtown Heliport:
Mon-Fri: 9am-6pm.

PRICES

*Liberty Sampler or Statue
Express*: $54
Torch of Freedom: $64
*Manhattan's Grand
Canyons*: $89
The Big Picture: $160

DISCOUNT

20% off the regular price
of any helicopter tour.

Heritage Trails New York

ower Manhattan is one of the best places to begin
ghtseeing in New York City. The concentration of
ajor sights and attractions offers a sweeping overview
the historical and modern metropolis.

s you walk along the streets of Lower Manhattan, you
ill notice a trail of brightly colored dots on the
dewalks. They map the "trails" of one of New York's

ost popular guided
alking tours –
eritage Trails New
ork.

New York Stock Exchange

bllowing in the
otsteps of Boston's
eedom Trail, New
ngland's most
opular tourist
traction, Heritage
ails is designed to
terest visitors by
ticing them with
e historical sites
d stories of one of
merica's oldest
odern cities.

ur different trails highlight more than fifty
ndmarks and historical sites, covering four-and-a-
lf miles.

e **Green Trail** is the most comprehensive and
cludes Federal Hall National Monument, the New
rk Stock Exchange, the Dutch City Hall Archeology
te, Castle Clinton National Monument and more.
e trails are always updated and new sites are added
gularly. Highlights of some of the other trails
clude the South Street Seaport, Brooklyn Bridge and
e World Trade Center.

map of the trails is included in this book on pages
-65. You can use it to choose a trail by deciding
ich attractions you would most like to see. Guided
urs begin at the **Heritage Trails Visitor Center**
cated at Federal Hall National Memorial (page 57-
).

th the voucher on page 283, all guided tours are $3
for adults and $2 off for children. If you prefer to
ke a tour at your own pace, you can purchase the
-page guidebook at a special price of $2. The
ide is in full-color and provides detailed information
out all the corresponding sights along the trails.

ADDRESS

Heritage Trails Visitor
Center: Federal Hall
National Memorial
26 Wall Street
☎ (888) 487-2457

HOURS

Mon-Sun: 9am-5pm.

PRICES

Guided walking tour:
Adult $14
Child (7-12) $7
(under 6 free)
Senior $10
Student $3

Self-guided tour book: $5

DISCOUNT

Guided walking tour:
Adult $3 off
Child $2 off
(when accompanied
by an adult)

Self-guided tour book:
Special price of $2

Discover New York Walking Tours

Discover New York is a tour series sponsored by the **Municipal Art Society**. These architectural and historical walking tours provide you with the seasoned expertise of the society while highlighting the best of New York City's cultural and geographical diversity.

Founded in 1893, The Municipal Art Society is a private, non-profit organization whose original aim was to beautify New York with public art.   It has adapted its goals to the times and today directs its efforts toward making New York a more habitable city (an enterprise welcomed by harried New Yorkers). It champions preservation in New York City by assisting

Colonnade Row on a walking tour of Greenwich Village

organizations that need guidance with planning, land use, zoning and development issues. The Municipal Art Society has been critical in the survival of many historical buildings.

The tours, which are led by architectural and urban historians, explore famous neighborhoods and districts such as Greenwich Village, the Flatiron District and Wall Street. Ethnic historians lead tours of Little Italy, Chinatown and the Lower East Side, pointing out New York City's rich multi-cultural communities.

They also explore themes that are both cultural and seasonal, such as the holiday tour "Best Dressed Landmarks of the Holidays", which takes a look at New York's most beautifully decorated buildings and plazas from Cartier and 19th-century Fifth Avenue mansions to Trump Tower.

Every Wednesday at 12:30pm the Municipal Art Society sponsors free tours of **Grand Central Terminal**.

Since tours and meeting times vary, it is best to call ahead to request a listing of the upcoming scheduled tours. Reservations are not required for weekday walking tours, but they are sometimes necessary for Saturday walking tours. Your *New York for less* card entitles you to a 20% discount on any Discover New York walking tour.

ADDRESS

457 Madison Avenue
☎ 439-1049 for tour schedule and meeting places. Call 935-3960 to make reservations.

PRICES

Guided walking tour:
Adult $10
Child $5
Student $8
Senior $8
(prices may vary per tour)

DISCOUNT

Guided walking tour:
20% discount off the regular price of any "Discover New York" tour with *New York for less* card.

Outer Boroughs

Introduction to Brooklyn . . .

In the early 1800s, Brooklyn was made up of a number of small independent communities isolated from Manhattan. This was changed forever by the advent of Robert Fulton's Manhattan steamship service in 1807.

View of Brooklyn from Manhattan

Speculators snatched up real estate hoping to lure Wall Street workers who could quickly and conveniently commute from Brooklyn to Manhattan's Financial District.

By the mid-19th century, the prosperous city of Brooklyn was the third largest in the country. The building of the **Brooklyn Bridge** (page 59) in 1883 linked the city to Manhattan and, in 1898, by a close vote, Brooklyn officially became part of New York City.

Today, the Brooklyn Bridge is as popular as it was when it was opened over 100 years ago. Nearly a mile across, it has a pedestrian pathway that offers unrivaled views of the Manhattan skyline and Brooklyn.

Brooklyn Promenade

Another great place to enjoy a wonderful view is the waterfront **Promenade** in **Brooklyn Heights**, where you can watch the sun set behind the Statue of Liberty. Officially declared New York's first historic district in 1965, Brooklyn Heights contains beautiful 19th-century brownstone buildings. Some of the best of these grand houses are those skirting the promenade, facing Manhattan. Plenty of restaurants can be found here as well, especially along Montague Street. At the top of Montague Street, **Borough Hall** is Brooklyn's oldest building. Built in 1851, in the Greek Revival style, it was originally used as Brooklyn's city hall.

Although Brooklyn Heights remains the borough's most visited and historic neighborhood, **Carroll Gardens**, **Park Slope** and **Cobble Hill** also contain blocks of beautifully preserved brownstones, quiet tree-lined streets and vibrant communities. Young, well-to-do Manhattanites are stretching their dollars as far as possible, moving deeper and deeper into the heart of Brooklyn, following inexpensive rents and leaving in

INSIDER'S TIP

Ride the subway to Brooklyn during the day to enjoy the museums, parks and restaurants. Stroll the promenade before making your way to the foot of the Brooklyn Bridge. Walk over the bridge to Mahattan at dusk to enjoy the sweeping views of the Manhattan skyline as the sun sets.

. . . Introduction to Brooklyn

heir wake a path of gentrification and escalating real
state prices. In addition to being a desirable
esidential area, **Park Slope** also has
istorical significance as the site of General
George Washington's 1776 retreat during the
Revolutionary War.

et another New York City park created by
Central Park planners Olmsted and Vaux,
Prospect Park (page 228), completed in
867, is considered to be their finest
chievement.

hey are also responsible for the design of
Grand Army Plaza which was constructed in
870 at the entrance to Prospect Park. In

*Mask from Zaire at the
Brooklyn Museum*

892, the **Soldiers' and Sailors' Memorial Arch** was
dded to commemorate those from Brooklyn who died
uring the Civil War. Every June, the plaza hosts the
Welcome Back to Brooklyn Festival, which honors all
ts native sons and daughters.

astern Parkway, originating at Grand Army Plaza
asses both the **Brooklyn Museum** (page 229) and the
Brooklyn Botanic Garden (page 229). When it opened
n 1897, the Brooklyn Museum was intended to be the
argest museum in the world. Although it never
eached this lofty ambition, it is nonetheless one of
ne great American cultural institutions. Close by, the
Brooklyn Children's Museum is the oldest museum of
ts kind in the United States.

he **Brooklyn Academy of Music** (page 215), world-
enowned for the quality of its productions, is
merica's oldest performing arts center in continuous
peration and gives a discount to *New York for less*
ardholders.

n southern Brooklyn, along the Atlantic coast, is
Brighton Beach. Dominated by the largest Russian
mmigrant community in the U.S., and known as
'Little Odessa", Brighton Beach is an ethnic
reasure and a great place to enjoy specialties like
odka and smoked sausages at authentic local
ateries.

Little Odessa, Brighton Beach

little further west, **Coney Island** was once a resort
or rich New Yorkers. In the early 1900s, it was
ransformed into a place for the general public when
ne subway made access cheap and easy for everyone.
oday, you can visit the beach, walk along the
oardwalk and see the 1927 Cyclone rollercoaster and
920 Wonder Wheel.

DON'T MISS

The New York Transit
Museum (page 228)
documents the history
of mass transit,
including New York City's
subway system, with
unique exhibits and
memorabilia.

Brooklyn Attractions . . .

The **New York Transit Museum** is housed in the old Court Street subway station in Brooklyn Heights. The museum contains 19 subway and elevated cars, an operating signal tower, antique turnstiles and a gift shop.

More than 100 years worth of artifacts and memorabilia include vintage trains with wicker seats and ceiling fans. The 1904 Brooklyn Union elevated car is one of the oldest in the museum's collection. This self-propelled train has a wooden body with a steel underframe powered from either an elevated trolley line or from the subway's third rail.

An art gallery features subway memorabilia once used to brighten riders' daily commutes plus custom-designed plaques, mosaics and other decorative elements.

1904 Brooklyn Union elevated car

The gift shop sells transit-themed items like token watches, strap-hanger ties and postcards. Other gift shops are located in Manhattan at Penn Station at 34th Street and Grand Central Terminal at 42nd Street and both offer discounts to *New York for less* card holders.

The museum also offers special transit-related exhibitions and programs. Tours include "Nostalgia Rides" which allow you to travel on vintage trains and buses via subway tunnels and New York City streets. *(Schermerhorn Street and Boerum Place, ☎ (718) 243-8601. Tue and Thu-Fri: 10am-4pm. Wed: 10am-6pm. Sat-Sun: 12noon-5pm. Mon: closed. Adult $3, child $1.50, senior $1.50, student $3. 2 admissions for the price of 1 with voucher on page 283 plus 10% discount in the gift shop with your New York for less card. Subway: 2,3,4,5 to Borough Hall.)*

Prospect Park, which opened in 1867, contains 526 acres of rich historical landscapes, including the 90-acre Long Meadow which is the largest open space in a U.S. urban park. At the top of Prospect Lake, Lookout Hill was notorious as a Revolutionary War burial ground. Another notable park sight is the Camperdown Elm, a large twisted tree dating from the 1870s. During the summer, the Music Grove bandstand holds open-air musical performances. Other park highlights include Lefferts Homestead *(☎ (718) 965-6505)*, the 1912 Coney Island carousel and the 1905 Italianate Boathouse which serves as the park's cafe and main information center. *(Flatbush Avenue at Grand Army Plaza, ☎ (718) 965-8951. Subway: 2,3 to Grand Army Plaza.)*

. . . Brooklyn Attractions . . .

The **Brooklyn Museum**, founded in 1823 as the Brookyln Apprentices' Library Association, is one of the oldest and largest art museums in the United States. Designed in the late 19th century by the prestigious architectural firm McKim, Mead and White, this Beaux Arts building measures 50,000 square feet.

Brooklyn Museum

The museum's permanent collection features more than 1.5 million objects, from ancient Egyptian masterpieces to contemporary art. The collection of Egyptian art is one of the best-regarded in the world. Highlights include statues, papyri, sarcophagi, mummy cases and the world-famous Brooklyn Black Head of the Ptolemaic Period.

The museum's collection of painting and sculpture includes American and European works dating from the 14th century to the present. The Brooklyn Museum was also the first museum to show African objects as art, and its display of works from central Africa is one of the most comprehensive and important in the world. Impressive art collections from the Pacific, Americas and Asia are also on display.

The Brooklyn Black Head, ca. 50 B.C.

The museum also has 28 period rooms ranging from a 17th-century Dutch-colonial farmhouse to a 19th-century Moorish Room, and from John D. Rockefeller's Manhattan mansion to a 20th-century Art Deco library. Two research libraries and an archive have extensive visual and textual materials on art, archeology and ethnology from ancient to modern times. *(200 Eastern Parkway, (718) 638-5000. Wed-Sun: 10am-5pm. Mon-Tue: closed. Suggested admission: adult $4, child free, senior $2, student $2. Subway: 2,3 to Eastern Parkway-Brooklyn Museum.)*

The **Brooklyn Botanic Garden**, next to the Brookyln Museum, has 52 acres of botanical treasures. The main attractions are the Japanese hill-and-pond garden and the new Steinhardt Conservatory Gallery, which houses one of the largest collections of bonsai

DON'T MISS

Visit the Brooklyn Museum's vast ancient Egyptian collection — the most extensive outside of Cairo and London. Some of the worlds finest pieces are on display here, including the Brooklyn Black Head which dates back to 50 B.C.

. . . Brooklyn Attractions

trees in the U.S. There is also an outdoor café and an immense rose garden. *(1000 Washington Avenue, ☎ (718) 622-4433. Tue-Fri: 8am-4.30pm. Sat-Sun: 10am-4.30pm. Mon: closed. Suggested admission $3. Subway: 2,3 to Eastern Parkway-Brooklyn Museum.)*

New York Aquarium

The Brooklyn Children's Museum, founded in 1899, was the first museum specifically designed for children. The museum offers a wide variety of hands-on exhibits and interactive educational programs. *(145 Brooklyn Avenue, ☎ (718) 735-4432. Wed-Fri: 2pm-5pm. Sat-Sun: 12noon-5pm. Mon-Tue: closed. Suggested admission $3. Subway: 3 to Kingston Avenue.)*

Located on Grand Army Plaza, the **Brooklyn Public Library** makes its home in an impressive 1941 Art Deco building. The library is appreciated nearly as much for its architectural splendor as its superb collection of books. On the second floor, art exhibits are presented on a rotating basis. *(Grand Army Plaza, Flatbush Avenue and Eastern Parkway, ☎ (718) 780-7700. Mon and Fri-Sat: 10am-6pm. Tue-Thu: 9am-8pm. Sun: 1pm-5pm. Subway: 2,3 to Eastern Parkway.)*

In the 1920s, **Coney Island** was calling itself the "World's Largest Playground". This seaside amusement park, complete with a boardwalk and pier filled with rides and games, once attracted more than one million visitors a day. Today, Coney Island is still a fun place to ride the amusements, visit the **New York Aquarium** and eat a famous Nathan's hot dog. *(Boardwalk and West 8th Street, ☎ (718) 265-3400. Subway: B,D,F,N to Stillwell Avenue-Coney Island.)*

Coney Island

The Brooklyn Academy of Music (page 215), also known as BAM,
is one of New York's pre-eminent entertainment venues. Hosting musical and theatrical performances of every kind, it is known for its avant garde productions. It is also home to the Brooklyn Philharmonic. *(30 Lafayette Avenue, ☎ (718) 636-4100. Subway: D,Q,2,3,4,5 to Atlantic Avenue.)*

DON'T MISS

In warm weather, visit Coney Island for a uniquely New York maritime experience. Spend an afternoon enjoying the beach, strolling along the boardwalk and enjoying rides like the Cyclone rollercoaster.

Introduction to the Bronx

the early 20th century, the Bronx was an affluent
suburb. Its main thoroughfare, the **Grand Concourse**,
was lined with expensive shops and apartment
buildings. Today, mention of the Bronx conjures up
images of the South Bronx, eroded by
economic hardship and urban decay. This
is not an accurate portrait of the entire
borough, however, and there are a number
of places worth visiting.

South Bronx

The North Bronx contains some charming
residential areas, ethnic communities and a
few major attractions. The Bronx Zoo, now
renamed the **Bronx International Wildlife
Conservation Park** (page 232),
encompasses 265 acres and is the largest urban zoo
in the country. Adjacent to the zoo, the **New York
Botanical Garden** (page 232) contains 12 outdoor
gardens, a conservatory and a series of walking trails,
many of which offer glimpses of the area's natural

New York Yankees

landscape. *New
York for less*
cardholders can
receive two
admissions to the
garden for the
price of one.

Facing the garden's
entrance, **Fordham
University** *(Southern
Boulevard, ☎ (718) 817-1000)*, founded in 1841, has a
pleasant campus consisting of Gothic-style stone
buildings and green open spaces. A short walk from
the zoo and botanical gardens, the **Belmont** section
boasts a **Little Italy** more authentic than its
Manhattan cousin. It is a great place to have lunch or
dinner after a visit to one of the North
Bronx attractions.

The South Bronx has one extremely
popular New York attraction – **Yankee
Stadium** (page 232). The stadium has its
own subway stop and can be reached safely
and easily from Manhattan.

Fordham University

On the northeast shore of Long Island
Sound, **Pelham Bay Park** is home to
Orchard Beach and the historic **Bartow Pell
Mansion** *(895 Shore Road, ☎ (718) 885-1461)*. Nearby,
City Island is a tiny maritime village complete with
seafood restaurants and marinas.

Bronx Attractions . . .

Founded in 1891, the **New York Botanical Garden** consists of over 250 acres of beautiful gardens and unspoiled forest, making it one of the oldest and largest gardens of its kind in the United States.

Visitors can enjoy a series of flower and rock gardens as well as walking trails. The Rose Garden contains close to 3,000 roses of various species.

In 1902, the Enid A. Haupt Conservatory was constructed. It contains 11 separate areas, each featuring a distinct botanical and geological focus.

Narrated tram tours accent the wide array of natural wonders contained within the various areas of the garden and have three convenient stops where you can get on and off as you wish. *(Southern Boulevard, ☎ (718) 817-8705. Nov-Mar: Tue-Sun: 10am-4pm. Mon: closed. Apr-Oct: Tue-Sun: 10am-6pm. Mon: closed. Adult $3, child (6-16) $1, senior $1, student $1. 2 admissions for the price of 1 with your New York for less card.)*

New York Botanical Garden

International Wildlife Conservation Park (formerly the Bronx Zoo) was founded in 1899 and is the largest city zoo in the United States. This immense preserve is home to over 4,000 animals. Among the exhibits are Jungle World, World of Darkness, Himalayan Highlands, World of Birds and the Children's Zoo. Wild Asia features a 25-minute narrated tour on a monorail train. For an excellent aerial overview of the park you can ride the Skyfari tramway. *(Fordham Road and the Bronx River Parkway, ☎ (718) 220-5100. Oct-Apr: Mon-Sun: 10am-4.30pm. May-Sep: Mon-Fri: 10am-5pm. Sat-Sun: 10am-5.30pm. Adult $3, child $1.50, senior $1.50, student $3. Free on Wednesdays. Subway: C,D to Fordham Road.)*

Llama ride at the International Wildlife Conservation Park

Yankee Stadium has been home to New York's beloved baseball team since 1923. Babe Ruth and Joe DiMaggio, two of baseball's greatest players, wore the

INSIDER'S TIP

Before going to the Botanical Garden, stop by Mike's Deli in Little Italy's Arthur Avenue Retail Market for a picnic lunch. (2344 Arthur Avenue, ☎ (718) 295-5033.)

. . . Bronx Attractions

famous blue and white pin stripes of the team. The ball park received a make-over in the 1970s and now seats up to 54,000 people. The stadium was particularly full during the 1996 season as the Yankees battled their way to win the World Series. *(East 161st Street at River Avenue, ☎ (718) 293-6000. Subway: 4,C,D to 161st Street.)*

The Van Cortlandt House Museum, originally the residence of wealthy New Yorker Frederick Van Cortlandt, is a preserved 1748 Georgian Colonial-style home. The interior contains American, English and Dutch period furnishings, and the dining room was used by General George Washington as a meeting place during the Revolutionary War. *(Van Cortlandt Park, ☎ (718) 543-3344. Tue-Fri: 10am-3pm. Sat-Sun: 11am-4pm. Mon: closed. Adult $2, child free, senior $1.50, student $1.50. Subway: 1,9 to 242 Street, Van Cortlandt Park.)*

Wave Hill is a landscaped estate featuring manicured lawns, gardens and greenhouses which overlook the Hudson River. Formerly the home and estate of financier George W. Perkins, the grounds at Wave Hill are now open to the public, and the Grand Hall is used regularly for concerts. *(West 249th Street and Independence Avenue, ☎ (718) 549-3200. Tue-Sun: 10am-4:30 pm (later in summer). Mon: closed. Adult $4, child (under 6) free, senior $2, student $2. Tue and Sat year round and everyday mid-Nov through mid-Mar: admission is free. Subway: 1,9 to 231st Street.)*

Aerial view of Yankee Stadium

Woodlawn Cemetery is the resting place for many of New York's most significant former residents. This burial ground is filled with impressively crafted mausoleums and tomb stones. Author Herman Melville, jazz great Duke Ellington and department store founder Richard H. Macy are all buried here. *(East 223rd Street and Webster Avenue, ☎ (718) 920-0500. Mon-Sun: 9am-4.30pm. Subway: 4 to Woodlawn Avenue.)*

North Wind Undersea Institute, located on City Island, is a small maritime museum featuring diving memorabilia and displays on the history of whaling. Interestingly, the museum has tanks containing seals that are trained to assist the police in underwater procedures. *(610 City Island Avenue, ☎ (718) 885-0701. Mon-Fri: 10am-5pm. Sat-Sun: closed. Adults $3, child $2, senior $3, student $3. Subway: 6 to Pelham Bay Park, then BX21 bus to City Island.)*

Introduction to Queens

Just north of Brooklyn, Queens is geographically New York's largest borough, comprising more than a third of the city and stretching over a hundred miles into Long Island. Originally named after **Queen Catherine**, the wife of Charles II of Great Britain, the borough was annexed by New York City in 1898, along with Brooklyn and Staten Island. It is now home to some 2 million residents.

American Museum of the Moving Image

Although it lacks a defined city center, it is home to a multitude of distinct ethnic enclaves including the mainly Greek area of **Astoria**, which is known as the Athens of New York. In fact, more than one-third of the population claims to have been born abroad.

Flushing Meadow-Corona Park

Two of the three main airports in the New York area are located in Queens – **John F. Kennedy** and **LaGuardia** (page 18). Both airports are easily accessible to Manhattan.

Near J.F.K. Airport, **Aqueduct Racetrack** *(110-00 Rockaway Boulevard, ☎ (718) 641-4700)* offers world-class horse racing. The former is the world's largest thoroughbred track and home of the Belmont Stakes, the third jewel in horse racing's triple crown.

Aquaduct Racetrack

The **Unisphere** globe, which stands in Flushing Meadow-Corona Park (page 235), marks the location of the 1939 and 1964 **World's Fairs**. The park also contains **Shea Stadium** (page 235) and the **USTA National Tennis Center** (page 235).

DON'T MISS

Both children and adults will be fascinated by the immense collection of movie memorabilia at the American Museum of the Moving Image (page 235).

Queens Museum (page 235) has a collection of memorabilia from both World's Fairs, including the Panorama, an 18,000-square-foot model of New York City. The **American Museum of the Moving Image** (page 235), housed in one of the Kaufmann-Astoria movie studios, provides a behind-the-scenes look at the art of the cinema. W.C. Fields and the Marx Brothers made films here.

Queens Attractions . . .

American Museum of the Moving Image holds the nation's largest public collection of film and video artifacts – more than 70,000 items. Housed in what was once Paramount Pictures film studio, the museum documents the production, promotion and exhibition of motion pictures and television through a series of unique temporary and permanent exhibits. "Behind the Screen" gathers highlights from the permanent collection with an emphasis on the making and marketing of media over the last 100 years.

You can learn about filmmaking techniques through hands-on exhibits like those which allow you to work with sound effects or read a scene from a movie and see how it was filmed.

There is also a variety of movie merchandise, costumes and memorabilia including the original Yoda from the *Empire Strikes Back* and a "gold-plated" chariot from the 1959 epic film *Ben Hur.*

American Museum of the Moving Image

(35th Avenue at 36th Street, Astoria, ☎ (718) 784-0077. Tue-Fri: 12noon-5pm. Sat-Sun: 11am-6pm. Mon: closed. Adult $7, child $4, senior $4, student $4. 2 admissions for the price of 1 plus 10% off in the museum shop with your New York for less card.)

Flushing Meadow-Corona Park, the site of the 1939 and 1964 World's Fairs, features a number of cultural and historical attractions. **Shea Stadium** *(☎ (718) 507-3499)* is home to the New York Mets, and the **US Tennis Center** *(☎ (718) 760-6200)* hosts the annual U.S. Open tennis championship every August. Also within the park, the **Unisphere**, a huge steel globe and remnant from the 1964 World's Fair, stands 12 stories high and weighs 350 tons. Aside from its attractions, the park is also an enjoyable place to simply relax. *(Flushing. Subway: 7 to Willets Point-Shea Stadium.)*

Queens Museum is also located inside Flushing Meadow-Corona Park and is housed in a building originally constructed for the 1939 World's Fair. The museum has an excellent collection of contemporary art including its prized possession – the Panorama. This model of New York City, designed for the 1964 World's Fair, was built to scale and contains every building in the city at the time. It takes up close to 20,000 square feet. *(Flushing Meadow-Corona Park, ☎ (718) 592-9700. Wed-Fri: 10am-5pm. Sat-Sun: 12noon-5pm. Mon-Tue: closed. Suggested Admission: Adult $3,*

. . . Queens Attractions

child $1.50, senior $1.50, student $1.50. Subway: 7 to Willets Point-Shea Stadium.)

The New York Hall of Science, also built for the 1964 World's Fair, is now an interactive museum for science and technology. This hands-on museum has over 160 exhibits with a wide range of topics including color, sound and light. *(111th Street and 48th Avenue, Flushing Meadow-Corona Park, ☎ (718) 699-0005.*

New York Hall of Science

Wed-Sun: 10am-5pm. Mon-Tue: closed. Adult $4.50, child $3, senior $3, student $4.50. Free admission Wed-Thu: 2pm-5pm. Subway: 7 to 111th Street.)

Bowne House, built in 1661, was originally a Quaker Friends' Meeting House and is the oldest religious site in the United States. Its owner, John Bowne, was banished here by Dutch governor Peter Stuyvesant for continuing to attend Quaker meetings after it had been outlawed. Tours of the colonial house are available, but you must call ahead to reserve. *(137-16 Northern Boulevard, between Main and Union Streets, ☎ (718) 358-9636. Subway: 7 to Main Street.)*

Kingsland House, within walking distance of Bowne House, now serves as the home of the Queens Historical Society. The society sponsors historical exhibitions and provides information about other borough attractions. Built in 1785, the farmhouse itself is a fine example of both English

View of Manhattan and the Queensboro Bridge from Queens

and Dutch architectural styles. *(Weeping Beach Park, 143-35 37th Avenue at Parson's Boulevard, ☎ (718) 939-0647. Tue and Sat-Sun: 2.30pm-4.30pm. Adult $2, child $1, senior $1, student $1. Subway: 7 to Main Street.)*

Jamaica Bay Wildlife Refuge is an ecological preserve managed by the National Parks Service. The site is home to a wide variety of plants and animals including over 300 species of birds. Park rangers give guided nature tours on the weekends. *(Cross Bay Boulevard at Broad Channel, ☎ (718) 318-4340. Mon-Sun: 8.30am-5pm. Admission is free. Subway: A to Broad Channel.)*

Introduction to Staten Island

Named Staaten Eylandt in 1609 by Dutch explorer **Henry Hudson**, Staten Island became a Dutch settlement in the early 1660s. Legend has it that the island was the grand prize is a boat race sponsored by England's **Duke of York** in 1687.

The first ferry service was introduced in 1713 to link Staten Island to Manhattan. Today the 50¢ round-trip ride on the **Staten Island Ferry** (page 61) is the main reason to go there. It provides stunning views of Lower Manhattan, the Statue of Liberty and New York Harbor.

After a successful stint as an oyster village, Staten Island was officially annexed to New York City in 1898. The island remains fairly rural – filled with expansive parks, rolling hills, residential neighborhoods and beautiful harbor views.

Staten Island has a number of historical sites and attractions of interest to visitors. The **Snug Harbor Cultural Center** (page 238) has a number of beautiful 19th-century buildings and serves as a center for cultural events, museums and gardens.

The **Richmondtown Historic Restoration** (page 238), containing buildings dating from the 17th to the 19th centuries, all painstakingly restored; and the **Alice Austen House** (page 238),

Verrazano Bridge

which overlooks New York Harbor and displays a vast collection of photographs of Staten Island and its residents taken in the late 19th and early 20th centuries.

In 1964 the imposing **Verrazano-Narrows Bridge** was built connecting the island to Brooklyn. Measuring 4,260 feet, it became the largest bridge in the United States, usurping the title from San Francisco's Golden Gate Bridge by only 60 feet. It also ranks as the world's second largest suspension bridge, falling short of England's Humber Bridge.

Recently, a campaign has been waged by Staten Island residents for secession from New York City. One sentiment is that tax dollars are being applied to inner city problems rather than their own. Another red-hot residential issue is the unwanted Fresh Kills; the largest landfill in the world, which is currently being used to dispose of all of New York City's garbage.

Staten Island Attractions

Founded in 1801 as a retirement home for sailors, the **Snug Harbor Cultural Center** now has 28 beautiful 19th-century buildings and serves as a center for cultural institutions and events. The Main House contains the Newhouse Center for Contemporary Art (☎ *(718) 448-2500)* and the Staten Island Children's Museum (☎ *(718) 273-2060)*. The Veterans' Memorial Hall is now a performance space for musicians. The 28-acre Staten Island Botanical Garden (☎ *(718) 273-8200)* features plants, flowers and a butterfly house. *(1000 Richmond Terrace. Grounds to the cultural center are always open and without admission charge. Staten Island Ferry, change to S40 bus or Snug Harbor trolley.)*

Historic Richmond Town on Staten Island

The **Richmondtown Historic Restoration** encompasses 103 acres and contains over 25 buildings dating from the 17th to the 19th centuries, meticulously restored to their original splendor. This authentic village and museum complex features a general store, courthouse, tavern and houses, and is devoted to documenting three centuries of Staten Island life, culture and history. *(441 Clarke Avenue, ☎ (718) 351-1611. Jan-Mar: Wed-Fri: 1pm-5pm. Sat-Tue: closed. Apr-Jun and Sep-Dec: Wed-Sun: 1pm-5pm. Mon-Tue: closed. Jul-Aug: Wed-Fri: 10am-5pm. Sat-Sun: 1pm-5pm. Mon-Tue: closed. Adult $4, child $2.50 (under 6 free), senior $2.50, student $4. Staten Island Ferry, change to S74.)*

DON'T MISS

Tours of Richmondtown Historic Restoration begin every half hour, originating at the Historic Museum. Highlights include the Voorlezer's House, which is the oldest elementary school house in the U.S.

The **Alice Austen House**, built in 1710, overlooks New York Harbor. The house has a collection of approximately 8,000 of Austen's photographs of Staten Island and its residents taken from 1880 to 1930. *(2 Hylan Boulevard, ☎ (718) 816-4506. Thu-Sun: 12noon-5pm. Mon-Wed: closed. Suggested admission $3. Staten Island Ferry, change to S51 bus to Hylan Park.)*

Staten Island Ferry

Built in 1947, the **Jacques Marchais Center of Tibetan Art** houses one of the largest collections of Tibetan art outside of Tibet. In 1991, it was visited by the Dalai Lama. *(338 Lighthouse Avenue, ☎ (718) 987-3500. Apr-Nov: Wed-Fri: 1pm-5pm, by appointment only. Adult $3, child $1, senior $2.50, student $2.25. Staten Island Ferry, change to S74 bus.)*

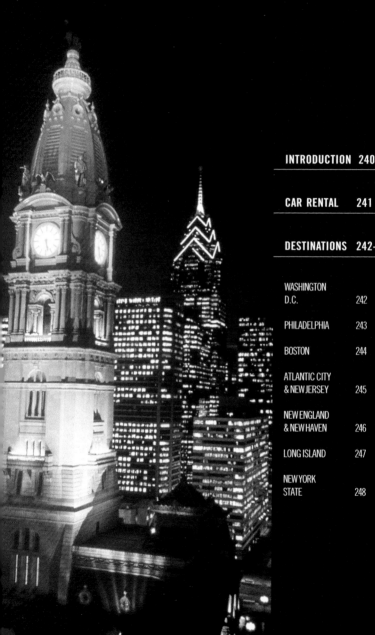

Beyond New York

Grand Central Terminal

Introduction

There are a large number of exciting destinations within few hours of New York. Cities such as Boston, New Haven, Philadelphia, Atlantic City and Washington D.C. all offer a unique perspective on the history and culture of the United States. This chapter gives a brief description of some of the best places to visit, how to get there and what to do and see when you arrive. Listed below are some suggestions on the various modes of transportation for excursions from Manhattan.

TRAINS

New York has two train stations – **Grand Central Terminal** and **Pennsylvania Station** (referred to as Penn Station). **Amtrak** (☎ 582-6875), departing from Penn Station, operates long-distance trains to national

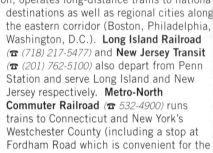

destinations as well as regional cities along the eastern corridor (Boston, Philadelphia, Washington, D.C.). **Long Island Railroad** (☎ (718) 217-5477) and **New Jersey Transit** (☎ (201) 762-5100) also depart from Penn Station and serve Long Island and New Jersey respectively. **Metro-North Commuter Railroad** (☎ 532-4900) runs trains to Connecticut and New York's Westchester County (including a stop at Fordham Road which is convenient for the

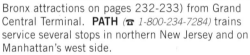

Atlantic City beaches

Bronx attractions on pages 232-233) from Grand Central Terminal. **PATH** (☎ 1-800-234-7284) trains service several stops in northern New Jersey and on Manhattan's west side.

BUSES

Long-distance and commuter bus lines depart from **Port Authority Bus Terminal** (☎ 564-8484). **Greyhound** (☎ 1-800-231-2222) services the entire nation. **Adirondack Pine Hill Trailways** (☎ 1-800-225-6815) service upstate New York; **Peter Pan Bus Lines** (☎ 1-800-343-9999) and **Bonanza Bus Lines** (☎ 1-800-556-3815) service New England; and **New Jersey Transit** services New Jersey (☎ (201) 762-5100).

Penn Station

PLANES

New York is a major hub for national and international air travel. Prices for regional flights are often comparable to those for the train and are much faster (especially from New York to Boston or Washington, D.C.). Major national carriers include **American Airlines** (☎ 1-800-433-7300), **Continental** (☎ 1-800-231-0856), **Delta** (☎ 1-800-241-4141) and **United Airlines** (☎ 1-800-241-6522).

Port Authority

🚗 Car Rental

For visitors planning a trip out of town, renting a car is often the most convenient way to travel. From New York City, you can access every major roadway that runs along the east coast to the destinations mentioned on the following pages. Renting a car can also be more economical than regional transportation, especially when traveling with a family.

Oldsmobile 88

Avis has been setting the standard in car rentals for more than 50 years. With your *New York for less* card, you can receive a **20% discount off Avis' SuperValue rates**. If there is a lower rate available at the time you make your reservation, your *New York for less* card entitles you to a **5% discount off the special rate** (whatever that happens to be). This discount is valid at all participating Avis locations in the U.S.

In addition to a special rate on rentals, you can also receive a **free upgrade** at any participating New York City location. Reserve any Avis Intermediate through Full Size 4-door car, then present the coupon (voucher) on page 285 at participating locations in Manhattan or at New York City airports. You will then be upgraded one car group at no extra charge. The upgrade applies to weekend, weekly and daily rates (minimum of 2 days rental required) and is subject to the terms and conditions listed on the coupon.

Obtaining these discounts is easy. Simply dial the toll-free reservations line at 1-800-831-8000.

Buick Skylark

Inform the reservations agent of the Avis Worldwide Discount (AWD) number **#K194100**. This code will access the *New York for less* discount mentioned above.

If you would like to take advantage of the free upgrade, you must inform the reservations agent of this as well. When you pick up your car, you should turn in the upgrade voucher on page 285.

Renters must meet Avis age, driver and credit requirements. The minimum age is 25, but may vary by location.

RESERVATIONS

For reservations and information, call 1-800-831-8000.

Manhattan locations:
345 South End Avenue
68 East 11th Street
217 East 43rd Street
240 East 54th Street
310 East 64th Street
420 East 90th Street
460 West 42nd Street
216 West 76th Street
153 West 54th Street

There are also Avis counters by the baggage claim areas at J.F.K., LaGuardia and Newark Airports.

Washington, D.C.

Founded in 1791, specifically as the capital of the United States, Washington, D.C. is not part of any state, but is a unique "Federal district".

Jefferson Memorial

Famous historical attractions, monuments and memorials include the Library of Congress, National Archives, Vietnam Veterans' Memorial, Arlington National Cemetery and, of course, the home of the president – the White House (☎ *(202) 208-1631)*. You can also visit the Supreme Court (☎ *(202) 479-3211)*, the Federal Bureau of Investigation (FBI) and the U.S. Capitol, the home of Congress (☎ *(202) 285-6827)*. Many of these attractions are free to the public and open seven days a week.

1997 will see the opening of several new monuments and attractions, such as the F.D.R. Memorial, the Civil War Memorial and the Women's Memorial commemorating servicewomen from all eras and services. The "Newseum" will incorporate state-of-the-art multimedia exhibits into an educational facility dedicated solely to the news.

The White House

Although federal government plays a critical role in the economy and industry of Washington, there is also a wealth of cultural attractions, galleries, stores, restaurants and performing arts which attract some 20 million annual visitors to the city. The National Gallery of Art (☎ *(202) 737-4215)*, National Air and Space Museum (☎ *(202) 357-1552)* and the Smithsonian Institution (☎ *(202) 357-2700)* (which celebrated its 150th anniversary in 1996) are known throughout the world for their amazing collections.

Throughout the year, there are festivals and special events such as the Cherry Blossom Festival held in early April and Independence Day Celebrations each July 4th. Solemn ceremonies take place on Veterans' Day, November 11, and Pearl Harbor Day, December 7th.

Vietnam Veterans' Memorial

FOR VISITOR INFORMATION

Tourist Information
1212 New York Avenue
Suite 600,
NW, Washington, D.C.
20005
☎ (202) 789-7000

GETTING THERE

From Penn Station, take Amtrak national railway (☎ 1-800-872-7245). Trains depart frequently throughout the day and the trip takes 3-4 hours.

Philadelphia

In 1682, Quaker William Penn founded Philadelphia, the "City of Brotherly Love", as a haven for religious freedom in the New World.

Philadelphia's role in the Revolutionary War and the birth of the new nation was critical. On Market Street, visitors can see two of the nation's most recognizable and important historical monuments, the Liberty Bell and Independence Hall (☎ (215) 597-8974).

The Liberty Bell

The Liberty Bell, perhaps best known for its famous crack, was once used to announce each victory won by the patriots during the Revolutionary War. Independence Hall was the place where the Declaration of Independence was adopted on July 4, 1776 and where the Constitution of the United States was drafted in 1787. It was also home to Congress from 1790-1800, during the ten years that Philadelphia was capital of the new nation.

The city has a number of historical areas including Society Hill and Olde City. These neighborhoods,

Independence Hall

once frequented by George Washington, Thomas Jefferson and Benjamin Franklin, feature picturesque cobblestone streets and Federal-style townhouses. The Betsy Ross House (☎ (215) 627-5343) claims to be the place where the famous seamstress designed the first American flag.

The Philadelphia Museum of Art (☎ (215) 763-8100) houses over 2,000 years of art and artifacts from around the world. Nearby, the Rodin Museum (☎ (215) 684-7788) features a fine collection of the artist's sculptures. The Franklin Institute Science Museum (☎ (215) 448-1208) has a multitude of interactive exhibits plus one of the world's premier dinosaur exhibits.

Fairmount Park (☎ (215) 685-0000) is the largest landscaped urban park in the world. It features historic mansions, the nation's first zoo, a Japanese house and garden and the Victorian Boat House Row, where crew races are held throughout the year on the Schuykill River.

FOR VISITOR INFORMATION

Philadelphia Convention
& Visitors Bureau
1515 Market Street
Suite 2020,
Philadelphia, PA 19102
☎ 1-800-537-7676

GETTING THERE

From Penn Station, take Amtrak national railway (☎ 1-800-872-7245). Trains depart frequently throughout the day and the trip takes approximately 2 hours.

Philadelphia Museum of Art

Boston

Rich in American history, Boston played an instrumental role in the nation's struggle for independence. Until the mid-18th century, its status as a prestigious port town made it the largest and most important city in America.

Boston at night

Today, Boston remains one of the nation's top cultural, historical and financial cities. It combines historic charm with modern sophistication and innovation. Unlike many other major U.S. cities, most of Boston's best sites can be seen on foot.

Visitors can walk the Freedom Trail, marked by a red line on the ground, which covers 16 historic sites.

Boston Skyline

The tour begins at the Visitor Information Center at Boston Common (☎ *(617) 536-4100)*. Follow the line past government buildings, churches and burial grounds, including the Old State House, which was built in 1712 and made history on July 18, 1776 when the Declaration of Independence was read there.

The city of Boston is also home to an array of museums including the Museum of Fine Arts (☎ *(617) 267-9300)* and the Children's Museum (☎ *(617) 426-6500)*. The Boston Tea Party Museum (☎ *(617) 338-1773)* commemorates the colonists' 1773 dumping of a ship load of British tea into the harbor to protest unfair taxes.

Boston Harbor

The Faneuil Hall Marketplace, formerly a place for political debate, is now a restored market filled with shops and eateries. In Beacon Hill, the Bull and Finch pub *(84 Beacon Street,* ☎ *(617) 226-1492)* was the motivation for the long-running hit TV show *Cheers*.

Across the Charles River lies Cambridge, home of Harvard University (☎ *(617) 495-1000)*. Call ahead for tours of its campus which highlight the architecture and history of America's most famous university.

FOR VISITOR INFORMATION

Greater Boston Convention and Visitors' Bureau
P.O. Box 490
Prudential Tower
Suite 400
Boston, MA 02199
☎ 1-800-888-5515

GETTING THERE

From Penn Station, Amtrak (☎ 1-800-872-7245) operates frequent service to Boston. Trip takes 4-6 hours.

Atlantic City & New Jersey

Across the Hudson River from Manhattan is Liberty
State Park. Take the weekend ferry service
(☎ 1-800-533-3779) to the park for great views of the
Statue of Liberty, a picnic lunch and a visit to the
Liberty Science Center (☎ (201) 451-0006). The
biggest science museum in the New York area, Liberty

Science Center is a
favorite with children
who enjoy the hands-
on exhibits and
modern displays.

Atlantic City is one of
the most popular
vacation destinations
in the country with

Atlantic City casino

over 37 million annual visitors. The city is known for
its 24-hour casinos, entertainment and luxurious
accommodation. The boardwalk, built in 1870, has
4½ miles of attractions, amusements, shops
and food vendors where you can try local
specialties such as saltwater taffy and frozen
custard.

Nearby, historic Cape May is a charming
town that has a number of Victorian-style
mansions, pleasant shopping areas and
quality seafood restaurants. Other similar
South Jersey shorefront resort towns are
Ocean City, Sea Isle City, Stone Harbor and
Wildwood.

Princeton is best known as the home of New
Jersey's only Ivy League institution,
Princeton University (☎ (609) 258-3000).

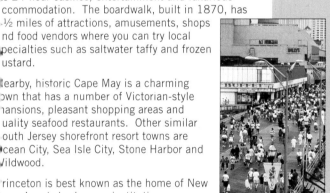

Atlantic City Boardwalk

Chartered in 1746 as the
College of New Jersey, Princeton
University is one of the oldest
and finest schools in the U.S.
Princeton Battlefield State Park
commemorates General George
Washington's victory at the
Battle of Princeton in 1777.

Six Flags Great Adventure
(☎ (908) 928-1821) is the largest
theme park in the state and has
the largest drive-through safari
outside Africa. Vernon Valley/

Princeton University

Great Gorge Action Park (☎ (201) 827-2000) has over 50
trails for winter skiing and a large theme park with
water sports and other activities.

FOR VISITOR INFORMATION

New Jersey Division
of Tourism
CN 826
Trenton, NJ 08625
☎ 1-800-537-7397

Atlantic City Convention
& Visitors Authority
2314 Pacific Avenue
Atlantic City, NJ 08401
☎ (609) 449- 7130
☎ 1-888-228-4748

GETTING THERE

From the Port Authority
Bus Terminal, New
Jersey Transit
(☎ (201) 762-5100)
operates bus service
between New York
and many destinations
in New Jersey

New England & New Haven

The colony of New Haven was established in 1638 by a group of Puritans. It evolved as an important seaport and, eventually, as an industrial center.

Davenport College, Yale University

Yale College was founded in 1701 when the "Collegiate School", which was based in several Connecticut towns, was moved to New Haven. Today you can take guided tour of the ivy-covered campus for a glimpse of the institution which counts amongst its graduates four U.S. presidents, including George Bush and President Clinton.

Yale's Peabody Museum of Natural History (☎ *(203) 432-5050)*, built in 1866, is one of the oldest natural history museums in the U.S. Beinecke Rare Book and Manuscript Library (☎ *(203) 432-2977)* possesses one o the finest collections of its kind in the world (including a Gutenberg Bible), housed in an architecturally unique building that uses translucent pieces of marble in lieu of windows. Yale University Art Gallery (☎ *(203) 432-0600)* is the oldest university art museum in the country. Founded in 1832, it contain over 100,000 objects and works of art starting from Egyptian times, and includes paintings by Van Gogh, Monet and Picasso.

Beinecke Rare Book and Manuscript Library, Yale

Long Wharf Theater (☎ *(203)787-4282)* is known for its excellent theatrical productions which sometimes sta famous actors like Al Pacino, Kathleen Turner and Joanne Woodward. Yale Repertory (☎ *(203) 432-1234)* and the Shubert Performing Arts Center (☎ *(800) 228-6622)* also host quality productions from the classics t new works.

Further along the Connecticut coastline Mystic Seaport (☎ *(203) 572-5315)*, recreates the area's maritime history. Highlights include restored houses, shops and tall ships.

New Haven Symphony Orchestra

One of the newest attractions in Connecticut is the Foxwoods Resort Casino (☎ *(860)885-3000)*, New England's answer to Atlantic City.

FOR VISITOR INFORMATION

The Greater New Haven Convention and Visitors Bureau
1 Long Wharf Drive
New Haven, CT 06511
☎ (203) 777-8550
☎ 1-800-332-STAY

Yale University Visitor Center
149 Elm Street
New Haven, CT 06520
☎ (203) 432-2300

GETTING THERE

From Grand Central Terminal, take Metro-North commuter rail (☎ 532-4900) or, from Penn Station, Amtrak (☎ 1-800-872-7245) runs express. Service from either station is frequent and the trip lasts less than 2 hours.

Long Island

ong Island is the largest island connected to the
ontinental U.S. It is separated from the state of
Connecticut on the north by the Long Island Sound
nd surrounded by the Atlantic Ocean to the south
nd east.

ong Island has quaint towns, pretty villages, historic
useums and numerous sights. The island is also
ecoming well-known for its wines, which come from
more than 15
vineyards.

Long Island beaches

The main reason
New Yorkers visit
Long Island,
however, is for the
beach. There are
more than 150
public beaches on
the island, many

f which encourage recreational activities like fishing,
iking and picnicking. The largest of the Long Island
eaches (six miles long), Jones Beach (☎ *(516)
85-1600)*, is a 240-acre park which is also known for
ie outdoor concerts held in its marine theater.

he Hamptons are *the* place for Manhattanites with
ash and time to spare. Magnificent beach-side
ansions strewn along the coast are the summer
omes of many celebrities and rich businessmen. As
tribute to excess and luxury, there is even a "beauty
us" which offers patrons beauty services *en route* to
ieir weekend retreats.

re Island is a unique, 26-mile strip of land
cated off the coast of the south shore.
uch of the island is part of a national park.
helter Island is very peaceful, but can only
e reached by ferry.

ong Island Railroad makes frequent stops
cross the island which are convenient to
ong Island's beaches and attractions.

ess than an hour from Manhattan, Nassau
ounty has a multitude of historical, cultural
d recreational opportunities. There are 114
useums and historical societies ranging in focus and
ettings from the Cold Spring Harbor Whaling
useum (☎ *(516) 367-3418)* to the Sagamore Hill
ational Historic Site (☎ *(516) 922-4470)* to the
anderbilt Museum, Mansion, Marine Museum,
anetarium and Park (☎ *(516) 854-5555).*

Westbury House, Old Westbury Gardens

FOR VISITOR INFORMATION

Long Island Convention
& Visitors Bureau
350 Vanderbilt Motor Pkwy
Hauppauge, NY 11788
☎ (516) 951-3440

GETTING THERE

From Grand Central
Terminal, Long Island
Railroad (☎ (718) 217-
5477) services many
destinations on
Long Island.

New York State

To most people, New York means New York City and its immediate surrounds. Beyond the densely populated metropolitan area, however, New York State offers visitors a variety of recreational activities, cultural events and historic sites.

Niagara Falls

New York State is best seen by car (see page 241). It is an ideal way to enjoy the scenic countryside, which is most impressive in autumn when the leaves turn various shades of red and gold. The Finger Lake Vineyards (☎ (800) 548-4386) are a good destination at this time of year. In the winter, "upstate" is popular with New Yorkers who like to ski at the state's mountain areas (☎ (800) 342-5826).

The Adirondacks (☎ (800) 487-6867) are one of the most popular mountain ranges for skiing and summertime recreation. Lake

Aerial view of the Thousand Islands

George (☎ (518) 668-5044) is a 32-mile lake that was carved into the Adirondack Mountains by retreating Ice Age glaciers. The village of Lake Placid (☎ (800) 447-5224) and its Olympic Mountain was the site of the 1932 and 1980 Winter Olympics and is still a popular resort for winter sports.

Baseball fans will probably not want to miss Cooperstown, home of the National Baseball Hall of Fame (☎ (607) 547-7200). For horse racing, head to Saratoga and the Saratoga Racetrack (☎ (518) 584-6200), which is the oldest in the country.

The state's most popular natural attraction is Niagara Falls (☎ (800) 338-7890). Tourists line-up at Prospect Point (☎ (716) 278-1770) or board the Maid of the Mist (☎ (716) 284-8897), which heads into the base of the falls, to witness the 40-million gallons of water that rush over the falls every minute.

Saratoga Racetrack

The Thousand Islands (☎ (800) 847-5623) and Seaway Trail (☎ (800) 732-9298) comprise a 454-mile-long region sprinkled with islands in both the St. Lawrence River and Lake Ontario. Some islands are so small that they can barely hold a tent, others are large enough to be occupied by small cabins. Camping, fishing, boating and Boldt Castle (☎ (315) 482-9724) make the Thousand Islands area a summertime getaway option.

FOR VISITOR INFORMATION

Division of Tourism
One Commerce Plaza,
Albany, NY 12245
☎ 1-800-225-5697

GETTING THERE

From Penn Station, Amtrak (☎ 1-800-872-7245) travels to many locations in Upstate New York. From Port Authority Bus Terminal, take Greyhound (☎ 1-800-231-2222).

Visitor Information

Calendar of Events

January

Chinese New Year celebrations. *(First full moon after Jan 19. Chinatown.)*

February

Black History Month, celebrating African-American culture and history nation-wide.

March

St. Patrick's Day Parade *(Mar 17. Fifth Avenue.)*

April

Easter Parade *(Sun Mar 30, 1997. Sun Apr 12, 1998. Fifth Avenue.)*

May

Martin Luther King Jr., Memorial Parade *(Sun May 18, 1997. Sun May 17, 1998. Fifth Avenue.)*

June

Museum Mile Festival *(Tue Jun 10, 1997. Tue Jun 9, 1998. Fifth Avenue, between 82nd and 105th Streets, ☎ 535-7710.)*

July

Summerstage free outdoor concerts and performances. *(Jun-Aug. Rumsey Playfield, Central Park, ☎ 360-2777.)*

August

Shakespeare in the Park presents free Shakespeare plays performed in an open-air theater. *(Jun-Sep. Delacorte Theater, ☎ 598-7100.)*

Mostly Mozart classical music performances at Lincoln Center. *(Jul-Aug. Avery Fisher Hall, ☎ 875-5030.)*

September

Washington Square Music Festival *(Late Jul-Sep. Washington Square Park, ☎ 431-1088.)*

Feast of San Gennaro, Little Italy's famous street fair. *(Third week of Sep. Mulberry Street, ☎ 226-9546.)*

October

Columbus Day Parade *(Mon Oct 13, 1997. Mon Oct 12, 1998. Fifth Avenue, between 44th and 86th Streets.)*

Big Apple Circus *(Oct-Jan. Lincoln Center, ☎ 875-5400.)*

Greenwich Village Halloween Parade *(Oct 31. Sixth Avenue, between Spring and 23rd Streets.)*

New York City Marathon *(Last Sun in Oct or first Sun in Nov. ☎ 860-4455.)*

November

Macy's Thanksgiving Day Parade *(Thu Nov 27, 1997. Thu Nov 26, 1998. Central Park West and Broadway to Herald Square, ☎ 494-4495.)*

December

Lighting of the Christmas Tree *(Early Dec. Rockefeller Center.)*

Christmas Spectacular *(Dec. Radio City Music Hall, ☎ 632-4000.)*

New Year's Eve celebrations throughout the city, from the dropping of the ball in Times Square to fireworks at the South Street Seaport.

Children's New York

New York has many **attractions** that will keep children entertained throughout their visit to the city. Of these, some of the best offer special discounts on children's admission with the *New York for less* card.

The Empire State Building (page 116), for example, admits children free when accompanied by an adult. The New York Skyride (page 117), Sony IMAX Theatre (page 167), American Museum of Natural History (page 164), Wollman Rink (page 208), Intrepid Sea-Air-Space Museum (page 138), Chelsea Piers Sports and Entertainment Complex (page 118), South Street Seaport Museum (page 55), the schooner Pioneer (page 55) and the Museum of the Moving Image (page 235) are other children's favorites that offer substantial discounts to *New York for less* cardholders.

Other places of interest for children include the New York Hall of Science (page 236), New York Aquarium (page 230), the Central Park Wildlife Conservation Center (page 208) and the Bronx International Wildlife Center (page 232).

Carousel at Central Park

Children's museums are custom designed for the young set. The Children's Museum of Manhattan (page 169), Brooklyn Children's Museum (page 230), Children's Museum of the Arts *(72 Spring Street, ☎ 941-9198)* and the Staten Island Children's Museum *(1000 Richmond Terrace, ☎ (718) 273-2060)* are sure to please.

Throughout the year, **special events and festivals** such as the Big Apple Circus *(Oct-Jan. Lincoln Center, ☎ 875-5400)* and Barnum and Bailey Circus *(Mar-May. Madison Square Garden, ☎ 465-6741)* are among the most anticipated.

Kids will think they have gone to heaven when they visit New York's most famous **toy store**, F.A.O. Schwarz (page 159). Other kids favorites include Warner Bros. Studio Store (page 159) and Toy Park *(112 East 86th Street, ☎ 427-6611)*. Also popular are the magical Enchanted Forest (page 88) and Tootsies (page 106) which give a 20% discount to *New York for less* cardholders. These shops carry an imaginative selection of children's books, games and stuffed animals.

Theme restaurants such as Planet Hollywood (page 142), Hard Rock Cafe (page 142) and Motown Cafe (page 142) have good choices of food and interesting memorabilia for children to enjoy.

INSIDER'S TIP

A beautiful day at the park is something to be enjoyed by parents and children alike. Many of New York's parks have children's playground areas. Central Park (pages 205), Hudson River Park (page 63) and Carl Schurz Park (page 197) are perhaps the best.

Visitor Information

CLIMATE

See "When to Go" page 16.

CUSTOMS

See "Visas and Entry Requirements" page 17.

ELECTRIC CURRENT

The U.S. uses 110V (60 hz) and most appliances from overseas will require a transformer. Check with your hotel regarding sockets for electrical devices.

EMBASSIES / CONSULATES

Australia (☎ 408-8400); Canada (☎ 596-1700); France (☎ 606-3688); Germany (☎ 308-8700); Great Britain (☎ 745-0200); Ireland (☎ 319-2555); Israel (☎ 499-5300); Italy (☎ 737-9100); Japan (☎ 371-8222); Netherlands (☎ 246-1429); South Africa (☎ 213-4880); Spain (☎ 355-4080); Sweden (☎ 751-5900); Switzerland (☎ 758-2560).

EMERGENCIES

For ambulance, fire or police, dial 911 from any telephone (free call, open 24 hours).

Hospitals (with 24 hour emergency rooms) - Bellvue Hospital *(First Avenue and East 29th Street, ☎ 562-4141)*; Cabrini Medical Center *(227 East 19th Street, ☎ 995-6120)*; Mount Sinai Hospital *(Fifth Avenue and 101st Street, ☎ 241-6500)*; New York Hospital *(East 70th Street at York Avenue, ☎ 746-5454)*; Roosevelt Hospital *(428 West 59th Street, ☎ 523-4000)*; St. Vincent's Hospital *(Seventh Avenue at 11th Street, ☎ 604-7000)*.

Health care and emergency treatment in New York can be very expensive. You will be required to pay for any medical treatment you receive, so it is advisable to take out a comprehensive travel and health insurance policy before arriving in New York.

ETIQUETTE

By law, smoking in New York is not allowed in public places, including the subway, buses, museums, theaters and in many restaurants' dining areas. Be sure to inquire at each restaurant if, and where, there are special areas for smoking.

Although New Yorkers are often portrayed in the movies as being rude, most simply have very busy schedules and tend to keep to themselves. However, in general people will be friendly and helpful, particularly to foreigners and will be happy to help you with directions.

Mt. Sinai Hospital

St. Vincent's Hospital

. . . Visitor Information . . .

HEALTH AND SAFETY

Doctors - In the Yellow Pages, look under "Physicians and Surgeons" to find doctors.

Drugstores / Pharmacies (open 24 hours) - Kaufman's *(557 Lexington Avenue, ☎ 755-2266)* and Plaza Pharmacy *(251 East 86th Street, ☎ 427-6940)*.

Safety - In contrast to its TV image, recent years have been a dramatic fall in New York City's crime levels. However, as in any other large city, you should protect your valuables and watch out for pickpockets in crowded areas, particularly in and around Times Square. Areas to avoid after dark are Central Park, Alphabet City (the area east of Avenue B) and desolate areas along the rivers and piers.

See also Emergencies on page opposite.

LOST PROPERTY

For lost property on subways or buses, phone the MTA *☎ (718) 625-6200)*; for taxis, phone the Taxi and Limousine Commission *(☎ 302-8294)*. For property lost more than 48 hours, call the Police Property Clerk *☎ 374-5084)*.

BAGGAGE STORAGE

Due to security reasons, there are no longer any public lockers for storing personal belongings in the main transportation centers. You can, however, check baggage at Grand Central Station, Penn Station and Port Authority for approximately $2 per day.

MARKETS

There are a variety of interesting antique markets, fairs and greenmarkets.

Annex Antiques Fair

The **Annex Antiques Fair and Flea Market** is a huge flea market where you can find antiques, furniture, clothing and jewelry. *(Sixth Avenue at 26th Street, ☎ 243-5343. Sat-Sun: 9am-5pm.)*

Around the corner, the **Chelsea Antiques Building** contains 12 floors of antiques and collectibles. *(110 West 25th Street, ☎ 929-0909. Mon-Sun: 10am-6pm.)*

Greenwich Village Flea Market is small, but is known for having good bargains. *(P.S. 41, Greenwich Street at Charles Street, ☎ 752-8475. Sat: 12noon-7pm.)*

Chelsea's Annex Antiques Fair and Flea Market

. . . Visitor Information . . .

The **Soho Antique Fair and Collectibles Market** sells inexpensive clothing plus odds and ends. *(Broadway a Grand Street, ☎ 688-0000. Mon-Sat: 9am-5pm.)*

Union Square Greenmarket

At the popular **Union Square Greenmarket**, regional farmers converge to sell a plethora of freshly harvested goods. *(Union Square at 14th Street and Broadway, ☎ 477-3220. Mon, Wed and Fri-Sat: 8am-6pm.)*

Antiques, collectibles and clothing can be found at the **P.S. 44 Flea Market**. *(Columbus Avenue, between West 76th and West 77th Street, ☎ 316-1088. Sun: 10am-6pm.)*

MAIL / POST

Post offices - Generally open Mon-Fri: 9am-6pm, Sat: 9am-12.30pm, the main post office at Eighth Avenue and 33rd Street is open 24 hours a day, 365 days a year.

U.S. Mailbox

Mail boxes - Letters and cards can be mailed at post offices or mail boxes (painted blue), found throughout the city.

Stamps, packages & shipping costs - You can purchase stamps from post offices or from many shops. The cost of shipping packages depends on the size of the package, the destination and the speed of service. Mail weighing less than an ounce, sent within the U.S., is 32 cents. Sending a postcard overseas costs 50 cents and a letter (less than an ounce) is 60 cents

MEDIA

Listings - A great way to find out what's happening in New York is to pick up one of its weekly magazines or papers. *New York* magazine and *Time Out New York* are two of the more comprehensive. The weekly *Village Voice* and *New York Press* are packed with things to see and do and are free. A contain full listings and information about the best in New York eating and drinking, cinemas, theaters, nightclubs and many other forms of entertainment.

New York newsstand

Newspapers - New York City has several daily newspapers. The most popular is the *New York Times* The *Daily News*, *New York Post* and *New York Newsda* also have large readerships. In addition, the city has multitude of weekly, monthly, foreign language and special interest papers.

Radio - New York has a multitude of radio stations tha

... Visitor Information ...

ir every form of radio entertainment. The main ones
re on the FM dial: 92.3 WXRK for rock music and
hock-jock Howard Stern in the morning; 92.7 WDRE
or modern and alternative rock; 93.9 for classical;
7.1 for hip-hop; 101.9 for contemporary jazz; 103.5
or country; and 104.3 for hard rock.

elevision - The main national stations are 2 (CBS), 4
NBC), 5 (Fox), 7 (ABC), 9 & 11 (independent) and
3 (PBS). Most hotels have cable TV which allows you
watch over 50 stations.

IONEY

urrency - The American currency is the dollar ($),
onsisting of 100 cents (¢). There are four commonly
sed American coins: penny (1 cent), nickel (5
ents), dime (10 cents), quarter (25 cents). Notes,
hich are also known as bills, come in $1, $2 (rare
ut in circulation), $5, $10, $20, $50 and $100
enominations.

loney changing - You can change money at banks or
t bureaux de change. Although bureaux de change
:ay open longer, they sometimes charge high
ommissions (transaction fees).

lutual of Omaha / Travelex - With the *New York for
?ss* voucher on page 283, you can exchange currency
" traveler's checks commission-free at any of the
lutual of Omaha / Travelex locations listed on the right.

redit cards - Major credit cards are accepted just
bout everywhere in
ew York. Check
dividual restaurant
nd shop entries for
redit cards accepted.
lso see page 16.

Santa at Lord & Taylor

ATIONAL HOLIDAYS

any attractions and
lops are likely to be closed on the following days:

ew Year's Day	*Jan 1*
artin Luther King Day	*Jan 20 (1997) / Jan 19 (1998)*
esident's Day	*Feb 17 (1997) / Feb 16 (1998)*
emorial Day	*May 26 (1997) / May 25 (1998)*
dependence Day	*Jul 4*
ıbor Day	*Sep 1*
olumbus Day	*Oct 13 (1997) / Oct 19 (1998)*
eteran's Day	*Nov 11*
nanksgiving Day	*Nov 27 (1997) / Nov 26 (1998)*
ıristmas Day	*Dec 25*

MUTUAL OF OMAHA / TRAVELEX NEW YORK LOCATIONS

Manhattan location:
Travelex America
530 Fifth Avenue
(within British Airways
ticketing office)

JFK terminals:
British Airways (arrivals
and departures), TWA
domestic (departures),
TWA international
(arrivals and ground floor
departures), American
Airlines (arrivals and
departures), Delta
(concourse departures and
customs arrivals) and in
the International Arrivals
Building (West Wing
departures and East Wing
arrivals and departures).

LaGuardia:
US Air Terminal
(departures) and Main
Terminal (departures).

Newark:
Terminals A (departures),
B (arrivals and
departures) and C
(departures).

Mutual of Omaha /
Travelex also has locations
in other U.S. and
international airports.

. . . Visitor Information . . .

OPENING HOURS

Banks - Generally, banks are open Mon-Fri: 9.30am-3pm or 3.30pm. Some branches are open later and some are also open on Saturday mornings. Most banks have 24-hour cash machines from which you can withdraw money.

Bars / Restaurants - Restaurants and bars in New York City tend to be open quite late, often serving food past 11pm, with most bars closing around 2am. All of the restaurants in this guide have their hours stated.

Shops - In general, shops are open from Mon-Sat: 10am-7pm. In Greenwich Village and Soho, many shops stay open later, especially on weekends. The hours of each shop in this guide are listed.

Sundays - Typically, New York's streets are less crowded on Sundays, making them ideal for sightseeing. In addition, many shops, markets and attractions are open, though their hours are usually more restricted.

Cathedral of St. John the Divine

RESTROOMS / TOILETS

There are very few public restrooms, and none at subway stations. Museums, hotels, department stores and restaurants are your best bet when sightseeing.

RELIGIOUS SERVICES

Listed below are the addresses and phone numbers of various religious denominations and places of worship. To find a religious service close to you, contact the following:

St. Patrick's Cathedral

Buddist *(New York Buddist Temple, 331 Riverside Drive,* ☎ *678-0305)*; Episcopalian *(Cathedral of St. John the Divine, Amsterdam Avenue at 112th Street,* ☎ *316-7400, or, Trinity Church, Broadway and Wall Street,* ☎ *602-0800)*; Jewish *(Central Synagogue, 652 Lexington Avenue,* ☎ *838-5122)*; Muslim *(Mosque of Islamic Brotherhood, 130 West 113th Street,* ☎ *662-4100)*; Roman Catholic *(St. Patrick's Cathedral, Fifth Avenue at 50th Street,* ☎ *753-2261)*; Unitarian *(All Souls Unitarian, 1157 Lexington Avenue,* ☎ *535-5530)*.

SPECIAL TRAVELERS

Disabled - Many of New York's hotels, attractions and restaurants have facilities for the disabled. The

. . . Visitor Information . . .

ayor's Office for People with Disabilities (☎ 788-2830) rovides information and the free publication *Access uide for People with Disabilities*.

enior citizens - Seniors (generally defined as 65 or der) usually receive reduced admission at tractions. This is in addition to the discount they an obtain with *New York for less*.

tudents - The International Student Identity Card is ecessary for students to obtain concessions. It can e purchased from the International Educational xchange *(205 East 42nd Street, ☎ 661-1414)* or the New rk Student Center *(895 Amsterdam Avenue, 666-3619)*. Proof of your student status is required obtain the card.

ay and lesbian - The Gay and Lesbian Switchboard *Mon-Sun: 10am-12midnight, ☎ 777-1800)* provides formation and assistance on gay activities and ents happening in New York City.

INSIDER'S TIP

Boomer's Sports Club (page 175) is filled with sports memorabilia and has more than 25 televisions on which to watch sporting events. *New York for less* cardholders receive a 25% discount.

ORTS

ew Yorkers take their sports very seriously, pecially football, basketball and baseball. ew York Yankees fans were especially pleased hen their beloved "Bronx bombers" were ctorious in the 1996 World Series. Tickets r all major sporting events can be ordered by lling Ticketmaster *(☎ 307-7171)*.

New York Yankees

ootball - The season runs from Sep-Jan and played at the Meadowlands in New Jersey. ew York's two home teams are the Giants and the ts.

asketball - The Knicks play their season from Oct-Jun Madison Square Garden.

aseball - From Apr-Oct, you can catch a game of seball played by the Yankees or the Mets.

e hockey - Hockey season runs from Oct-Apr. The angers and the Islanders are New York's home teams.

orking out - Many hotels have fitness facilities. At e Chelsea Piers (page 118), *New York for less* rdholders are entitled to a discount on one-day sses and various athletic activities.

XES

e U.S. does not have an export tax program or a lue added tax (VAT). Instead, all shoppers are quired to pay state sales tax (8½%) in addition to e marked price. Unfortunately, this tax cannot be claimed when a foreigner leaves the country.

Chelsea Piers

. . . Visitor Information . . .

TELEPHONES

When dialing within Manhattan you do not need to dial the 212 area code, but only the seven-digit telephone number. Any phone number in this book listed with an area code means that it is outside the 212 dialing area, and you must dial 1+area code+phone number (e.g. 1-718-555-1234). A call within the five boroughs of New York City (area codes 212 and 718) costs 25 cents from a public phone. For discounts on long-distance calls see page 8.

New York Convention & Visitors Bureau

TIPPING

Tipping is customary in New York, even for the most basic services. Although tipping may seem strange or unnecessary to some overseas visitors, keep in mind that a service charge is rarely included in the bill and that employers are not required by law to pay tipped employees the minimum wage, because it is assumed that the majority of their earnings will be in tips.

Restaurants - A 15-20% tip on the total bill is standard. So that the service is not reduced by the discount, when using the *New York for less* card it is recommended that you tip on the total amount of the bill, before the discount is applied.

Taxis / Bartenders / Hairdressers - The standard tip is 15-20%.

Porters / Bellhops - The normal tip is $1 per bag, depending on the number of bags, the distance carried and the overall service.

TOURIST INFORMATION

New York Convention & Visitors Bureau is the main source for tourist information in the city. Multi-lingual operators are available as is a wide range of brochures and helpful information. *(2 Columbus Circle, ☎ 1-800-692-8474. Mon-Fri 9am-6pm. Sat-Sun: 10am-3pm.)*

Grand Central Terminal, **Penn Station** and **Port Authority Bus Terminal** also supply visitor information.

TRAVELING IN NEW YORK

Subway - The subway is the fastest and easiest way to get around New York City. Each one-way fare costs $1.50 and can be paid with a MetroCard or a token bought at a station. Subways run frequently, 24 hours a day, seven days a week. The last of the famous graffiti-covered subway trains was taken out of service in 1989.

INSIDER'S TIP

For more information about getting around in New York see page 19.

A subway train in Manhattan

. . . Visitor Information

Buses - Public buses also run 24 hours a day, seven days a week. The fare is $1.50 and can be paid with a MetroCard or a token. If you need to change buses ask for a free transfer, *when you board.*

Taxis - Yellow cabs are available when the center light is on, but not when the "Off Duty" side lights are on as well. Fares are $2 for the first eighth of a mile, 30¢ for each additional fifth of a mile. There is also a 50¢ surcharge added to the fare in the evening.

Car - The cost and aggravation of city driving and parking make cars practically useless within New York City. Renting a car can, however, be very practical for out-of-town trips (see page 241).

TRAVELING OUTSIDE NEW YORK

There is a vast transportation network linking New York to other U.S. cities (see page 240).

USEFUL TELEPHONE NUMBERS

Airports - J.F.K. (☎ *(718) 244-4444*); LaGuardia (☎ *(718) 476-5000*); Newark (☎ *(201) 961-6000*).

Credit cards - American Express (☎ *1-800-528-4800*); Visa (☎ *1-800-336-8472*); Mastercard (☎ *1-800-307-7309*); Diners Club (☎ *1-800-234-6377*); Discover (☎ *1-800-347-2683*).

Emergencies - Dial ☎ 911 for police, fire and ambulance assistance. For dental emergencies, Emergency Dental Associates (☎ *972-9299*).

Helpline - The Samaritans (☎ *673-3000*), 24 hours.

Subway / bus information - MTA (☎ *(718) 330-1234*).

Train information - Metro-North (☎ *532-4900*) at Grand Central Terminal; Amtrak (☎ *582-6875*), New Jersey Transit (☎ *(201) 762-5100*) and Long Island Railroad (☎ *217-5477*) at Penn Station.

Visitor information - New York Convention & Visitors Bureau (☎ *1-800-692-8474 or* ☎ *397-8222*).

WEIGHTS, MEASUREMENTS & CLOTHING SIZES

In the U.S., the imperial, not the metric system is used.

Clothing sizes - To convert American women's clothing sizes to British, add 2 (e.g. an American size 8 is a British 10), for shoes, subtract 2 (e.g. an American 8 is a British 6). Men's suit and shirt sizes are the same in Britain and America, but shoes are ½ size bigger in America (e.g. an American 10 is a British 9½).

Taxis and a horse-drawn Hansom Cab

Index of Discounters . . .

ATTRACTIONS AND MUSEUMS

TOURS

NIGHTLIFE

KEY TO ABBREVIATIONS

LM=Lower Manhattan
SO=Soho, Chinatown & the Lower East Side
GV=Greenwich Village
CH=Chelsea, Gramercy & the Flatiron District
ME=Midtown East
MW=Midtown West

UW=Upper West Side & Harlem
UE=Upper East Side
CP=Central Park
OB=Outer Boroughs
★= Hotel rating (see page 32)

. . . Index of Discounters . . .

TELS

TO CREDITS

ublishers would like to thank the following people and organizations for permission to reproduce their photographs over they retain copyright. Any omission from this list is unintentional and every effort will be made to include these in the dition of this publication.

Sweeney (principal photography); Bob Strong (cover photo); The Museum of the City of New York: Edward Moran. The ing of the Statue of Liberty Enlightening the World. Oil on canvas. 39½ x 49½", The J. Clarence Davies Collection. John nann. Central Park-Summer, Looking South, New York, 1865. Colored lithograph, 11 3/4 x 17 5/8", The J. Clarence s Collection. DeWit View, 1672. Line engraving on copper, Gift of Mrs. William Sloane. Looking West on Wall Street, 1922, ron Collection. Sledding, Central Park, 1898, The Byron Collection. Immigrants on Battery Park, 1901, The Byron tion. Broadway North from 34th Street, c.1910, The Byron Collection. Lewis Hine, Empire State Building Construction, c. Permanent Deposit of the Empire State Building. Berenice Abbott, Pike and Henry Streets, 1936. Purchase Mrs. Elon r Acquisition Fund. T.H. McAllister Co., Flatiron Building, 1909. Lantern Slide. Greeley Square, 1898, The Byron tion. West 59th Street and 5th Avenue, 1905, The Byron Collection. Brooklyn Bridge, 1912, Photographer unknown. ay Construction Workers in Tunnel. New York Skyline, c. 1932, The Wurts Collection. Gilbert Stuart, Portrait of George ngton, 1796, Gift of John Hill Morgan. Dance on the Battery in the Presence of Peter Stuyvesant, A. Durand, 1838. City ark from the NW Corner of Broadway and Chambers St. Purchase of Manhattan from the Indians, 1626, Peter Minuit oor Lo, The Clarence J. Davies Collection. Pulling down the statue of George III at the Bowling Green, City of New York, 776. 19th Century steel engraving. New York Convention & Visitors Bureau; Bridget O'Neil; Joseph O'Neil; Virgin Atlantic s; Soho Grand Hotel; Southgate Towers; Rihga Royal; Best Western Woodward; Doubletree Guest Suites; Hotel Gorham; ield; Michelangelo; Millennium Broadway; Gayle Gleason, New York Renaissance; Novotel New York; Morgans; ount; Tom Vack; St. Moritz; Salisbury; Shoreham Hotel; The Warwick; Crowne Plaza; Edison Hotel; New York Palace; Omni hire Palace; Dumont Plaza; Lou Hammond & Associates, Inc.; Doral Court; Doral Inn; Doral Park Avenue; Eastgate Tower; ntercontinental; Jolly Madison Towers; Loews New York; Morgans; Todd Eberle; New York Hemsley; Shelburne Murray Hotel; dor; Waldorf-Astoria; Radisson Empire; Franklin; Hotel Wales; Regency; Barbizon; Hotel Delmonico; National Park Service s; Brain Feeney; Charley Van Pelt; South Street Seaport Museum; Frank Lusk; Fraunces Tavern Museum; The Museum for n Art; Lower East Side Tenement Museum; Steve Brosnahan; 5 & 10 No Exaggeration; Stan Ries; Deborah Jaffe; ann; Skyline Multimedia Entertainment, Inc.; Fred George; Roberto Johnson; John Ortner; Frank DeSisto; Eva Heyd; Dan h; Chun Y. Lai; Todd Eberle; American Museum of Natural History; Scott Frances/Esto; Lincoln Center; Sony IMAX es; Morris-Jumel Mansion, Inc.; Eastern National; The Metropolitan Museum of Art; David Heald; The Frick Collection, ork; Whitney Museum of American Art; National Academy of Design; The Jewish Museum; Peter Aaron/Esto; John Parnell; rchive; New York City Opera; Gerardo Samoza; Webster Hall; New York Cruise Lines, Inc.; Julian Olivas; Heritage Trails ork; New York Transit Museum; Kristin Holcomb; Patricia Lauman Bazelon; Peter Howard Photographer Inc.; New York cal Garden; Scott Bowron; Sarah Wells; Bart Barlow; Avis Car Rental Company; Photos courtesy of Washington, D.C. ntion & Visitors Association; Courtesy of Philadelphia Convention and Visitors Bureau; R. Andrew Lepley; Jim McWilliams; . Widmaier Jr.; Kevin Reilly; Courtesy of Greater Boston Convention and Visitors Bureau; Courtesy of Atlantic City ntion and Visitors Authority; Robert P. Matthews; Courtesy of Greater New Haven Convention & Visitors Bureau; Stuart Yale University; Michael Marsland; Courtesy of Long Island Convention & Visitors Bureau; Photos by Robert Lipper, -Metro Publications; NYS Department of Economic Development; Darren McGee; Tony Stone Images.

... Index of Discounters ...

Shops

. . . Index of Discounters . . .

. . . Index of Discounters . . .

Restaurants

American	The Barking Dog Luncheonette	201	UE
American	Boomer's Sports Club	175	UW
American	Firehouse	177	UW
American	John Street Bar and Grill	68	LM
American	Mercantile Grill	67	LM
American	Mike's American Bar & Grill	145	MW
American	Miss Elle's	176	UW
American	Nice Guy Eddie's	104	GV
American (Contemporary)	F-Stop	123	CH
American (Contemporary)	Liberty Cafe	67	LM
American (Contemporary)	Prohibition	174	UW
American (Contemporary)	Thomas Scott's on Bedford	99	GV
American (Contemporary)	Tompkins 131	104	GV
American (Contemporary)	Vermouth	175	UW
American / Brewery	A. J. Gordon's Brewing Co.	176	UW
American / Brewery	Heartland Brewery	124	CH
American / Brewery	Zip City Brewing Company	125	CH
American / Coffee & Tea Shop	Basset	83	SO
American / Continental	P. J. Charlton's	85	SO
American / International	Barocco Kitchen	124	CH
American / International	Barocco to Go	100	GV
American / Irish	Doc Watson's	201	UE
American / Irish	The Playwright	143	MW
American / Italian	Ottomanelli's	157	ME
American / Italian	Yellowfingers	200	UE
American / Steakhouse	Broadway Joe's Steakhouse	143	MW
Argentinian / Continental	Caffe Novecento	84	SO
Asian / Vegetarian	Tiengarden	86	SO
Brazilian / Continental	Caffe Novecento	84	SO
Brewery / American	A. J. Gordon's Brewing Co.	176	UW
Brewery / American	Heartland Brewery	124	CH
Brewery / American	Zip City Brewing Company	125	CH
Brewery / International	Commonwealth Brewing Co. NY	142	MW
Burmese	Mingala West	175	UW
Cabaret / Continental	5 & 10 No Exaggeration	85	SO
Café	Café Mozart	126	CH
Chinese	Chinatown East	201	UE
Chinese	Hunan Balcony	178	UW
Chinese	Hunan Balcony Gourmet	199	UE
Chinese	Jimmy Sung's	158	ME
Chinese	Mao Mao	84	SO
Chinese	Panda	156	ME
Coffee & Tea Shop / American	Basset	83	SO
Continental	MK Restaurant	145	MW
Continental	Norma's	84	SO
Continental	Talk of the Village	100	GV
Continental / American	P. J. Charlton's	85	SO
Continental / Brazilian	Caffe Novecento	84	SO
Continental / Cabaret	5 & 10 No Exaggeration	85	SO
Creole / French	La Belle Epoque	101	GV
Delicatessen / Kosher	Mendy's East	125	CH
Delicatessen / Kosher	Mendy's West	174	UW
French	Au Bon Coin	102	GV
French	La Folie	199	UW
French / Creole	La Belle Epoque	101	GV
German / Swiss	Roettele A.G.	103	GV
Indian	Akbar	157	ME

... Index of Discounters ...

estaurants

Ellis Island Immigration Museum (page 52)

No. of paid audio tours: 1 or 2 (please circle)

Voucher valid for up to 4 people:
maximum 2 free audio tours

South Street Seaport Museum (page 55)

No. of paid admissions: 1 or 2 (please circle)

Voucher valid for up to 4 people:
maximum 2 free admissions

Schooner Pioneer (page 55)

No. of adults	1	2	3	4	Circle as appropriate: voucher valid for up to 4 people
No. of children	1	2	3	4	
No. of seniors	1	2	3	4	
No. of students	1	2	3	4	

Guggenheim Museum Soho (page 76)

No. of paid admissions: 1 or 2 (please circle)

Voucher valid for up to 4 people:
maximum 2 free admissions
[code: PRLONDON]

Lower East Side Tenement Museum (page 77)

No. of paid tours: 1 or 2 (please circle)

Voucher valid for up to 4 people:
maximum 2 free tours

Empire State Building Observatory (page 116)

No. of adults	1	2	3	4	Circle as appropriate: voucher valid for up to 4 people
No. of children	1	2	3	4	
No. of seniors	1	2	3	4	
No. of students	1	2	3	4	

This voucher entitles the holder of a valid *New York for less* card to the following discount at the **Ellis Island Immigration Museum** (page 52):

2-for-1 Audio tours: one free audio tour with each audio tour of equal or greater value purchased (maximum 2 free audio tours)

Cannot be combined with any other promotional offer.
Voucher expires on December 31st, 1998.

This voucher entitles the holder of a valid *New York for less* card to the following discount at the **South Street Seaport Museum** (page 55):

2-for-1 Admission: one free admission with each admission of equal or greater value purchased (maximum 2 free admissions)

Cannot be combined with any other promotional offer.
Voucher expires on December 31st, 1998.

This voucher entitles the holder of a valid *New York for less* card to the following discounts at **Schooner Pioneer** (page 55):

Adult	20% discount	Senior	20% discount
Child	20% discount	Student	20% discount

Cannot be combined with any other promotional offer.
Voucher expires on December 31st, 1998.

This voucher entitles the holder of a valid *New York for less* card to the following discount at the **Guggenheim Museum Soh** (page 76):

2-for-1 Admission: one free admission with each admission o equal or greater value purchased (maximum 2 free admissions

Cannot be combined with any other promotional offer.
Voucher expires on December 31st, 1998.

This voucher entitles the holder of a valid *New York for less* card to the following discount at the **Lower East Side Tenement Museum** (page 77):

2-for-1 Tours: one free tour with each tour of equal or greater value purchased (maximum 2 free tours)

Cannot be combined with any other promotional offer.
Voucher expires on December 31st, 1998.

This voucher entitles the holder of a valid *New York for less* card to the following discounts at the **Empire State Building Observatory** (page 116):

Adult	50¢ off	Senior	25¢ off
Child	Free (with adult)	Student	50¢ off

Cannot be combined with any other promotional offer.
Voucher expires on December 31st, 1998.

New York Skyride (page 117)

No. of adults	1 2 3 4	Circle as
No. of children	1 2 3 4	appropriate: voucher valid
No. of seniors	1 2 3 4	for up to
No. of students	1 2 3 4	4 people

Chelsea Piers (page 118)

No. of adults	1 2 3 4	Circle as
No. of children	1 2 3 4	appropriate: voucher valid
No. of seniors	1 2 3 4	for up to
No. of students	1 2 3 4	4 people

Chelsea Piers (page 118)

No. of adults	1 2 3 4	Circle as
No. of children	1 2 3 4	appropriate: voucher valid
No. of seniors	1 2 3 4	for up to
No. of students	1 2 3 4	4 people

Chelsea Piers Store (page 118)

Save 20% on goods purchased at the
Chelsea Piers Store

The Museum of Modern Art (page 134)

No. of adults	1 2 3 4	Circle as
No. of children	1 2 3 4	appropriate: voucher valid
No. of seniors	1 2 3 4	for up to
No. of students	1 2 3 4	4 people

MoMA Audio Guides (page 134)

No. of paid audio guides: 1 or 2 (please circle)

Voucher valid for up to 4 people:
maximum 2 free audio guides

This voucher entitles the holder of a valid *New York for less* card to the following discounts at the **New York Skyride** (page 117):

Adult	$2 off	Senior	$2 off
Child	$2 off	Student	$2 off

Cannot be combined with any other promotional offer.
Voucher expires on December 31st, 1998.

This voucher entitles the holder of a valid *New York for less* card to the following discounts on general admission to the **Chelsea Piers Sports and Entertainment Complex** (page 118):

Adult	20% discount	Senior	20% discount
Child	20% discount	Student	20% discount

This offer applies Mon-Fri from opening time to 5pm only.
Voucher expires on December 31st, 1998.

This voucher entitles the holder of a valid *New York for less* card to the following discounts on general admission to the **Chelsea Piers Sports and Entertainment Complex** (page 118):

Adult	20% discount	Senior	20% discount
Child	20% discount	Student	20% discount

This offer applies Mon-Fri from opening time to 5pm only.
Voucher expires on December 31st, 1998.

This voucher entitles the holder of a valid *New York for less* card to the following discounts at **Chelsea Piers Store** (page 118):

Save 20% on goods purchased
in the Chelsea Piers Store

Cannot be combined with any other promotional offer.
Voucher expires on December 31st, 1998.

This voucher entitles the holder of a valid *New York for less* card to the following discounts at **The Museum of Modern Art** (page 134):

Adult	$1 off	Senior	$1 off
Child	$1 off	Student	$1 off

Cannot be combined with any other promotional offer.
Voucher expires on December 31st, 1998.

This voucher entitles the holder of a valid *New York for less* card to the following discount at **The Museum of Modern Art** (page 134):

2-for-1 Audio guides: one free audio guide with each audio guide of equal or greater value purchased (max. 2 free guides)

Cannot be combined with any other promotional offer.
Voucher expires on December 31st, 1998.

Radio City Music Hall Grand Tour (page 137)

No. of paid tours: 1 or 2 (please circle)

Voucher valid for up to 4 people:
maximum 2 free tours

Intrepid Sea-Air-Space Museum (page 138)

No. of adults	1	2	3	4	Circle as
No. of children	1	2	3	4	appropriate: voucher valid
No. of seniors	1	2	3	4	for up to
No. of students	1	2	3	4	4 people

American Craft Museum (page 138)

No. of paid admissions: 1 or 2 (please circle)

Voucher valid for up to 4 people:
maximum 2 free admissions

ICP Midtown (page 139)

No. of paid admissions: 1 or 2 (please circle)

Voucher valid for up to 4 people:
maximum 2 free admissions

American Museum of Natural History (page 164)

No. of paid M1 admissions: 1 or 2 (please circle)

Voucher valid for up to 4 people:
maximum 2 free M1 admissions

Garden Cafe (page 164)

Save 10% at the American Museum of Natural History's
Garden Cafe

This voucher entitles the holder of a valid *New York for less* card to the following discount at **Radio City Music Hall** (page 137):

2-for-1 Grand Tours: one free Grand Tour with each Grand Tour of equal or greater value purchased (maximum 2 free tours)

Cannot be combined with any other promotional offer.
Voucher expires on December 31st, 1998.

This voucher entitles the holder of a valid *New York for less* card to the following discounts at the **Intrepid Sea-Air-Space Museum** (page 138):

Adult	20% discount	Senior	20% discount
Child	20% discount	Student	20% discount

Cannot be combined with any other promotional offer.
Voucher expires on December 31st, 1998.

This voucher entitles the holder of a valid *New York for less* card to the following discount at the **American Craft Museum** (page 138):

2-for-1 Admission: one free admission with each admission of equal or greater value purchased (maximum 2 free admissions)

Cannot be combined with any other promotional offer.
Voucher expires on December 31st, 1998.

This voucher entitles the holder of a valid *New York for less* card to the following discount at the **International Center of Photography Midtown** (page 139):

2-for-1 Admission: one free admission with each admission of equal or greater value purchased (maximum 2 free admissions)

Cannot be combined with any other promotional offer.
Voucher expires on December 31st, 1998.

This voucher entitles the holder of a valid *New York for less* card to the following discount at the **American Museum of Natural History** (page 164): one free M1 admission (includes an IMAX feature film or an audio tour) with each M1 admission of equal or greater value purchased (maximum 2 free M1 admissions)

Cannot be combined with any other promotional offer.
Voucher expires on December 31st, 1998.

This voucher entitles the holder of a valid *New York for less* card to the following discount at the **American Museum of Natural History** (page 164):

10% discount at the Garden Cafe

Cannot be combined with any other promotional offer.
Voucher expires on December 31st, 1998.

Guggenheim Museum (page 186)

No. of adults	1	2	3	4	Circle as
No. of children	1	2	3	4	appropriate: voucher valid
No. of seniors	1	2	3	4	for up to
No. of students	1	2	3	4	4 people

The Frick Collection (page 188)

No. of paid admissions: 1 or 2 (please circle)

Voucher valid for up to 4 people:
maximum 2 free admissions

Whitney Museum (page 189)

No. of paid admissions: 1 or 2 (please circle)

Voucher valid for up to 4 people:
maximum 2 free admissions

National Academy of Design (page 191)

No. of paid admissions: 1 or 2 (please circle)

Voucher valid for up to 4 people:
maximum 2 free admissions

This voucher entitles the holder of a valid *New York for less* card to the following discounts at the **Solomon R. Guggenheim Museum** (page 186):

Adult	$2 off	Senior	$2 off
Child	$2 off	Student	$2 off

Cannot be combined with any other promotional offer.
Voucher expires on December 31st, 1998.

This voucher entitles the holder of a valid *New York for less* card to the following discount at the **Frick Collection** (page 188):

2-for-1 Admission: one free admission with each admission of equal or greater value purchased (maximum 2 free admissions)

Cannot be combined with any other promotional offer.
Voucher expires on December 31st, 1998.

This voucher entitles the holder of a valid *New York for less* card to the following discount at the **Whitney Museum** (page 189):

2-for-1 Admission: one free admission with each admission of equal or greater value purchased (maximum 2 free admissions)

Cannot be combined with any other promotional offer.
Voucher expires on December 31st, 1998.

This voucher entitles the holder of a valid *New York for less* card to the following discount at the **National Academy of Design** (page 191):

2-for-1 Admission: one free admission with each admission of equal or greater value purchased (maximum 2 free admissions)

Cannot be combined with any other promotional offer.
Voucher expires on December 31st, 1998.